# The European Championship
## A Complete History
(Part I: 1960-1976)

Richard Keir

First published 2018
by Rowanvale Books Ltd
The Gate
Keppoch Street
Roath
Cardiff
CF24 3JW
www.rowanvalebooks.com

A CIP catalogue record for this book is available from the British Library.
ISBN: 978-1-911569-67-1

Thanks to UEFA, plus the football associations of the following countries: Azerbaijan, Belarus, Cyprus, Georgia, Greece, Netherlands, Portugal, Russia and Ukraine.

# Contents

# INTRODUCTION

The idea of a pan-European competition for national teams was first mooted in 1927 by the then General Secretary of the French Football Federation, Henri Delaunay. There had been various regional competitions, dating back to 1884 with the inaugural Home International (British) Championship, and the first continental championship had been staged in South America as early as 1916, but it wasn't until 1957 that Delaunay would have his vision realised.

Unfortunately, he had passed away in 1955 – but his son, Pierre, who succeeded him as UEFA General Secretary, was instrumental in getting the tournament off the ground. From an initial field of seventeen nations for the first edition, in the sixty years since, the competition has grown to include all fifty-four UEFA members (Gibraltar being the latest country to compete), with the Final Tournament expanding from four teams in 1960 to twenty-four teams in 2016.

This is the first in a series of books charting the history of the competition, leading up to the 2020 Finals, when the tournament will celebrate its sixtieth anniversary.

# 1958-1960

## QUALIFICATION

For the first ever pan-European continental competition, UEFA set a deadline of 4th June 1958 for entries. By the appointed date, only seventeen nations had confirmed their participation. Notable absentees included West Germany, Italy, the Netherlands and Sweden, who would be runners-up in their own World Cup later that summer. The Republic of Ireland were the only participants from the British Isles. The tournament was organised as a knockout format over two legs, home and away, up to the semi-finals, where one country would host matches from that stage onwards.

### PRELIMINARY ROUND

With an odd number of entries, a preliminary round was necessary to eliminate one team, leaving a field of sixteen nations to contest the remainder of the tournament. The Republic of Ireland and Czechoslovakia drew the short straw. Strangely, it was played fully six months after the first ever game, and after a few of the first round ties had taken place. In the first leg in Dublin, the Irish led 2-0 at half-time, thanks to goals from 'Liam' Tuohy and a Noel Cantwell penalty, but they couldn't add to it in the second half. Their advantage was halved within three minutes of the return game in Bratislava, when Czechoslovak keeper Imrich

Stacho dispatched a penalty; then second half goals from Titus Buberník, Ladislav Pavlovič and Milan Dolinský put Czechoslovakia comfortably through to the first round proper.

## FIRST ROUND

The very first match took place on 28th September 1958 in front of just over 100,000 spectators in Moscow's Lenin Central Stadium between the Soviet Union and Hungary, where Anatoliy Ilyin wrote himself into the history books with the first ever goal in the fourth minute. Further goals from Slava Metreveli and Valentin Ivanov put the Soviets in a commanding position, before a late counter from János Göröcs gave the Hungarians a glimmer of hope for the return leg in Budapest; but a solitary goal from Yuriy Voynov in the fifty-eighth minute was enough to take the Soviets through.

In Paris, the French cantered to a 7-1 victory over Greece, which included doubles for Just Fontaine (top scorer at the 1958 World Cup with thirteen goals), Thadée Cisowski and Jean Vincent. They also took the lead in the return in Athens through Stéphane Bruey, but were denied another win when their captain, Roger Marche, put through his own goal near the end.

Romania struggled to break down a stubborn Turkish defence in the first half of their tie in Bucharest, but second half goals from Nicolae Oaidă, Gheorghe Constantin and Constantin Dinulescu appeared to put the tie out of sight. In the return leg in Istanbul, two goals from Lefter Küçükandonyadis brought the Turks back into it, but the Romanians held out in the final half-hour to squeeze through.

In Oslo, the part-time Norwegians did well to restrict Austria to a single goal win, thanks to Erich Hof's first half strike, but in the return leg in Vienna, the Austrians romped to a 5-2 success, with Hof adding another couple of goals, as well as Horst Nemec.

An all-Eastern-European clash saw Yugoslavia ease to a 2-0 victory over Bulgaria in Belgrade with Milan Galić's opener coming inside sixty seconds, Lazar Tasić adding a second three minutes from time. In the second leg in Sofia, Todor Diev gave the Bulgarians hope with an early second-half strike, but the Yugoslavs snuffed that out almost immediately when Muhamed Mujić equalised. Nine minutes from the end, Nikola Kovachev and Dragoslav Šekularac had a *contretemps*, and both became the first dismissals in the competition.

Portugal travelled behind the Iron Curtain and came away from East Germany with a 2-0 lead through goals from 'Matateu' and Mário Coluna. The East Germans put up a better performance in the return in Oporto but still went down 3-2, with Coluna contributing another couple of goals.

Spain (including three players from Real Madrid, who'd recently won a fourth consecutive European Cup) travelled to Chorzów and, despite conceding the first goal, eased to a 4-2 victory over Poland, with both Alfredo Di Stéfano and Luis Suárez netting twice. The second leg in Madrid was a formality once Di Stefano had opened the scoring after half an hour, and they netted twice more in the second half, to coast to a 3-0 win.

The final first round tie pitted the Czechoslovaks against the amateurs of Denmark. The first leg in Copenhagen produced a 2-2 draw, with all the goals coming in a terrific first half. Two goals in as many minutes by Poul Pedersen and Bent Hansen had the Danes in command early on, but strikes from Ladislav Kačáni and Milan Dolinský brought Czechoslovakia level by the interval. In the return match in Brno, the Danes struck first through John Kramer, but Titus Buberník quickly levelled; in the second half, the Czechoslovaks' superior fitness told as they notched up four unanswered goals, with Buberník netting again and Adolf Scherer also grabbing a brace.

## QUARTER-FINALS

The quarter-final ties produced an incredible twenty-seven goals in six matches, and also the first political intervention, when the Spanish nationalist government prevented the national team from travelling to the Soviet Union, therefore allowing their opponents a free pass to the Final Tournament. At Colombes, France and Austria treated the fans to a goal fest. The French raced into a 3-0 lead through a brace from Just Fontaine and a Jean Vincent strike, then Walter Horak pulled one back just before the break. Rudolf Pichler netted a second for the Austrians midway through the second half, but Fontaine netted his third of the game soon afterwards to stifle Austrian hopes of a remarkable comeback, and Vincent added a fifth for good measure near the end. In the return match in Vienna, Horst Nemec gave Austria a first-half lead, but by the hour mark the French were 2-1 ahead through Jean-Jacques Marcel and Bernard Rahis. Although Erich Probst swiftly equalised, two late goals from François Heutte and a penalty from Raymond Kopa gave *Les Bleus* another comprehensive victory.

In Oeiras, on the outskirts of Lisbon, Portugal looked to be coasting after goals from Joaquim Santana and 'Matateu' put them 2-0 up against Yugoslavia; but a late goal from Borivoje Kostić gave the Yugoslavs some hope for the return. By half-time in Belgrade, they had levelled the tie on aggregate. Domiciano Cavém's counter for the Portuguese was sandwiched between strikes from Dragoslav Šekularac and Zvezdan Čebinac. The second half, however, was one-way traffic as Yugoslavia cut loose with three unanswered goals, two of them falling to the prolific Kostić.

Another all-Eastern-European tie pitted Romania against Czechoslovakia. In the first leg in Bucharest, the home side's chances were dashed when first-half goals from Josef Masopust and Vlastimil Bubník gave the Czechoslovaks an advantage they were never likely to concede, and in Bratislava they cantered to an easy 3-0 win, with all of the goals coming inside the first twenty minutes, including a double from Buberník.

# MATCH DETAILS

## PRELIMINARY ROUND

5 April 1959     Ref: Lucien VAN NUFFEL (Belgium)
Dalymount Park, DUBLIN (Att. 37,500)

REPUBLIC OF IRELAND  -  CZECHOSLOVAKIA
2:0 (2:0)

1:0 Tuohy (22'), 2:0 Cantwell (42' pen.)

EIR: (Coach: Selection Committee)
James O'NEILL, Brendan McNALLY, Noel
CANTWELL, Michael McGRATH, Charles HURLEY,
Patrick SAWARD, Thomas HAMILTON, Christopher
DOYLE, George CUMMINS, William TUOHY, Alfred
RINGSTEAD

CZE: (Coach: Rudolf VYTLACIL)
Imrich STACHO, Jiří TICHÝ, Ján POPLUHÁR, Gustáv
MRÁZ (Jiří HILDEBRAND 23'), Svatopluk PLUSKAL,
Titus BUBERNÍK, Jan BRUMOVSKÝ, Anton
MORAVČÍK, Ladislav KAČÁNI, Pavol MOLNÁR,
Tadeáš KRAUS

10 May 1959     Ref: Joseph BARBÉRAN (France)
Tehelné pole, BRATISLAVA (Att. 41,691)

CZECHOSLOVAKIA  -  REPUBLIC OF IRELAND
4:0 (1:0)

1:0 Stacho (3' pen.), 2:0 Buberník (57'), 3:0 Pavlovič
(67'), 4:0 Dolinský (75')

CZE: (Coach: Rudolf VYTLACIL)
Imrich STACHO, Jiří TICHÝ, Ján POPLUHÁR, Ladislav NOVÁK, Štefan MATLÁK, Titus BUBERNÍK, Ladislav PAVLOVIČ, Adolf SCHERER, Vlastimil BUBNÍK, Ladislav KAČÁNI, Milan DOLINSKÝ

EIR: (Coach: Selection Committee)
James O'NEILL, Richard WHITTAKER, Noel CANTWELL, Francis O'FARRELL, Charles HURLEY, Michael McGRATH, Alfred RINGSTEAD, Thomas HAMILTON, Arthur FITZSIMONS, George CUMMINS, William TUOHY

CZECHOSLOVAKIA won 4-2 on agg.


## FIRST ROUND

28 September 1958        Ref: Alfred GRILL (Austria)
Tsentralniy Stadion V.I. Lenina, MOSCOW (Att. 100,572)

### USSR - HUNGARY
### 3:1 (3:0)

1:0 Ilyin (4'), 2:0 Metreveli (20'), 3:0 Ivanov (32'), 3:1 Göröcs (84')

URS: (Coach: Gavriil KACHALIN)
Vladimir BELYAEV, Vladimir KESAREV, Anatoliy MASLYONKIN, Boris KUZNETSOV, Yuriy VOYNOV, Viktor TSARYOV, Slava METREVELI, Valentin IVANOV, Nikita SIMONYAN, Alekper MAMEDOV, Anatoliy ILYIN

HUN: (Coach: Lajos BARÓTI)
Béla BAKÓ, Béla KÁRPÁTI, Ferenc SIPOS, László SÁROSI, Dezső BUNDZSÁK, Pál BERENDI, László BUDAI, János GÖRÖCS, Lajos CSORDÁS, Lajos TICHY, József BENCSICS

27 September 1959     Ref: Józef KOWAL (Poland)
Népstadion, BUDAPEST (Att. 78,481)

## HUNGARY - USSR
### 0:1 (0:0)

0:1 Voynov (58')


HUN: (Coach: Lajos BARÓTI)
Gyula GROSICS, Sándor MÁTRAI, Ferenc SIPOS, László SÁROSI, József BOZSIK, Károly SÁNDOR, János GÖRÖCS, Flórián ALBERT, Lajos TICHY, Máté FENYVESI, Antal KOTÁSZ

URS: (Coach: Mikhail YAKUSHIN)
Lev YASHIN, Vladimir KESAREV, Anatoliy MASLYONKIN, Boris KUZNETSOV, Yuriy VOYNOV, Igor NETTO, Slava METREVELI, Anatoliy ISAEV, Valentin IVANOV, Valentin BUBUKIN, Mikhail MESKHI

USSR won 4-1 on agg.


1 October 1958     Ref: Gottfried DIENST (Switzerland)
Parc des Princes, PARIS (Att. 37,590)

## FRANCE - GREECE
### 7:1 (3:0)

1:0 Kopa (23'), 2:0 Fontaine (25'), 3:0 Cisowski (29'), 3:1 Yfantis (48'), 4:1 Vincent (61'), 5:1 Cisowski (68'), 6:1 Fontaine (85'), 7:1 Vincent (87')

FRA: (Coach: Albert BATTEUX)
Dominique COLONNA, Raymond KAELBEL, André LEROND, Armand PENVERNE, Maurice LAFONT, Jean-Jacques MARCEL, Yvon DOUIS, Raymond KOPA, Just FONTAINE, Thadée CISOWSKI, Jean VINCENT

GRE: (Coach: Vittorio MARTINI)
Savvas THEODORIDIS, Panagiotis PAPOULIDIS, Konstantinos LINOXILAKIS, Dimitris STEFANAKOS, Neotakis LOUKANIDIS, Konstantinos POLIHRONIOU, Pavlos EMMANOUILIDIS, Dimitris THEOFANIS, Ilias YFANTIS, Konstantinos NESTORIDIS, Ioannis HOLEVAS

3 December 1958    Ref: Vincenzo ORLANDINI (Italy)
Stádio Leoforos, ATHENS (Att. 18,833)

### GREECE - FRANCE
### 1:1 (0:0)

0:1 Bruey (71'), 1:1 Marche (85' og)

GRE: (Coach: Antonis MIGIAKIS)
Savvas THEODORIDIS, Panagiotis PAPOULIDIS, Konstantinos LINOXILAKIS, Sotiris ANGELOPOULOS, Konstantinos POLIHRONIOU, Giannis NEMBIDIS, Giorgos SIDERIS, Andreas PAPAEMMANOUIL, Ilias YFANTIS, Konstantinos NESTORIDIS, Stilianos PSYHOS

FRA: (Coach: Albert BATTEUX)
Claude ABBES, Raymond KAELBEL, Roger MARCHE, René FERRIER, Bruno BOLLINI, André LEROND, Maryan WISNIESKI, Roland GUILLAS, Stéphane BRUEY, Stanislas DOMBECK, Léon DELADERIERE

FRANCE won 8-2 on agg.

2 November 1958        Ref: Gottfried DIENST
(Switzerland)
Stadionul 23 August, BUCHAREST (Att. 67,200)

### ROMANIA - TURKEY
### 3:0 (0:0)

1:0 Oaidă (62'), 2:0 Constantin (77'), 3:0 Dinulescu (81')

ROM: (Coach: Augustin BOTESCU)
Constantin TOMA, Corneliu POPA, Alexandru
KARIKAS, Dumitru MACRI, Vasile ALEXANDRU,
Ion NUNWEILLER, Nicolae OAIDĂ, Gheorghe
CONSTANTIN, Constantin DINULESCU, Haralambie
EFTIMIE, Nicolae TĂTARU

TUR: (Coach: Leandro REMONDINI)
TURGAY Şeren, İSMAIL Kurt, BASRI Dirimlili,
MUSTAFA Ertan, NAÇI Erdem, AHMET Berman,
HILMI Kiremitçi, CAN Bartu, METIN Oktay, KADRI
Aytaç, LEFTER Küçükandonyadis

Note: Turgay went off injured in the seventy-seventh
minute


26 April 1959          Ref: Borče NEDELKOVSKI
                                    (Yugoslavia)
Mithatpaşa Stadi, ISTANBUL (Att. 23,567)
                TURKEY - ROMANIA
                      2:0 (1:0)

        1:0 Lefter (13' pen.), 2:0 Lefter (54')

TUR: (Coach: Leandro REMONDINI)
ÖZCAN Arkoç, İSMAIL Kurt, BASRI Dirimlili, MUSTAFA
Ertan, NAÇI Erdem, AHMET Berman, HILMI Kiremitçi,
CAN Bartu, SUAT Mamat, LEFTER Küçükandonyadis,
KADRI Aytaç

ROM: (Coach: Augustin BOTESCU)
Constantin TOMA, Corneliu POPA, Alexandru KARIKAS,
Valeriu SOARE, Emeric JENEI, Ion NUNWEILLER,
Nicolae OAIDĂ, Vasile ALEXANDRU, Ion
ALEXANDRESCU, Francisc ZAVODA, Vasile ANGHEL

ROMANIA won 3-2 on agg.


20 May 1959                    Ref: Werner BERGMANN
                                        (East Germany)
Ullevaal Stadion, OSLO (Att. 27,566)

NORWAY - AUSTRIA
0:1 (0:1)

0:1 Hof (32')


NOR: (Coach: Kristian HENRIKSEN)
Asbjørn HANSEN, Arne NATLAND, Hans Jacob
MATHISEN,    Roar    JOHANSEN,    Thorbjørn
SVENSSEN, Tore HALVORSEN, Bjørn BORGEN,
Per KRISTOFFERSEN, Harald HENNUM, Kjell
KRISTIANSEN, Rolf Birger PEDERSEN

AUT: (Coach: Karl DECKER)
Kurt SCHMIED, Heinrich BÜLLWATSCH, Erich
HASENKOPF, Gerhard HANAPPI, Karl STOTZ, Karl
KOLLER, Walter HORAK, Adolf KNOLL, Erich HOF,
Josef HAMERL, Karl SKERLAN


23 September 1959    Ref: Dimosthemis STATHATOS
                                          (Greece)
Praterstadion, VIENNA (Att. 34,989)

AUSTRIA - NORWAY
5:2 (3:2)

1:0 Hof (2'), 1:1 Ødegaard (19'), 2:1 Nemec (21'), 3:1
Hof (25' pen.), 3:2 Ødegaard (35'), 4:2 Skerlan (60'),
5:2 Nemec (73')

AUT: (Coach: Karl DECKER)
Kurt    SCHMIED,    Rudolf    OSLANSKY,    Erich
HASENKOPF, Gerhard HANAPPI, Karl STOTZ, Karl

KOLLER, Paul HALLA, Erich HOF, Horst NEMEC, Wilhelm HUBERTS, Karl SKERLAN

NOR: (Coach: Kristian HENRIKSEN)
Sverre ANDERSEN, Arne BAKKER, Åge SPYDEVOLD, Arne NATLAND, Thorbjørn SVENSSEN, Arnold JOHANNESSEN, Rolf Bjørn BACKE, Åge SØRENSEN, Harald HENNUM, Ove ØDEGAARD, Finn GUNDERSEN

AUSTRIA won 6-2 on agg.

31 May 1959          Ref: Mihai POPA (Romania)
Stadion J.N.A., BELGRADE (Att. 23,418)

YUGOSLAVIA - BULGARIA
2:0 (1:0)

1:0 Galić (1'), 2:0 Tasić (87')

YUG: (Coach: Ljubomir LOVRIĆ/Dragomir NIKOLIĆ/ Aleksandar TIRNANIĆ)
Vladimir BEARA, Bruno BELIN, Tomislav CRNKOVIĆ, Dobrosav KRSTIĆ, Vasilije ŠIJAKOVIĆ, Lazar TASIĆ, Dragoslav ŠEKULARAC, Aleksandar PETAKOVIĆ, Branko ZEBEC, Milan GALIĆ, Branislav MIHAJLOVIĆ

BUL: (Coach: Stoyan ORMANDZHIEV/Krum MILEV)
Georgi NAYDENOV I, Ilia KIRCHEV, Kiril RAKAROV, Ivan DIMITROV, Hristo LAZAROV, Stoyan KITOV, Stefan ABADZHIEV, Ivan KOLEV, Panayot PANAYOTOV, Bozhidar MITKOV, Akeksandar VASILEV

25 October 1959          Ref: Kurt TSCHENSCHER
                                        (West Germany)
Stadion Vasil Levski, SOFIA (Att. 27,560)

BULGARIA - YUGOSLAVIA
1:1 (0:0)

1:0 Diev (55'), 1:1 Mujić (57')


BUL: (Coach: Stoyan ORMANDZHIEV/Krum MILEV)
Georgi NAYDENOV I, Kiril RAKAROV, Manol
MANOLOV, Ivan DIMITROV, Dimitar LARGOV, Nikola
KOVACHEV, Todor DIEV, Georgi SOKOLOV, Panayot
PANAYOTOV, Dimitar YAKIMOV, Ivan KOLEV

YUG: (Coach: Ljubomir LOVRIĆ/Dragomir NIKOLIĆ/
Aleksandar TIRNANIĆ)
Blagoje VIDINIĆ, Vladimir DURKOVIĆ, Fahrudin
JUSUFI, Stevan BENA, Tomislav CRNKOVIĆ, Lazar
TASIĆ, Luka LIPOŠINOVIĆ, Dragoslav ŠEKULARAC,
Muhamed MUJIĆ, Borivoje KOSTIĆ, Branislav
MIHAJLOVIĆ

Red cards: Kovachev (81'), Šekularac (81')

YUGOSLAVIA won 3-1 on agg.


21 June 1959                Ref: Alois OBTULOVIČ
                                (Czechoslovakia)
Walter-Ulbricht-Stadion, EAST BERLIN (Att. 25,000)

EAST GERMANY - PORTUGAL
0:2 (0:1)

0:1 'Matateu' (12'), 0:2 Coluna (67')


EGR: (Coach: Friedrich GÖDICKE)
Karl-Heinz SPICKENAGEL, Bringfried MÜLLER,
Werner HEINE, Konrad WAGNER, Waldemar
MÜHLBACHER, Manfred KAISER, Horst ASSMY,
Günter SCHRÖTER, Gerhard VOGT, Lothar MEYER,
Günther WIRTH

POR: (Coach: José Maria ANTUNES)
ACÚRCIO Alves Carrelo, VIRGÍLIO Marques Mendes, ÂNGELO Gaspar Martins, Fernando Mamede MENDES, Raúl António Leandro de FIGUEIREDO, VICENTE Da Fonseca Lucas, Carlos Domingos DUARTE, António Dias TEIXEIRA, Sebastião Lucas da Fonseca 'MATATEU', Mário Esteves COLUNA, Domiciano Barrocal Gomes CAVÉM

28 June 1959          Ref: Juan GARAY Gardeazábal
(Spain)

Estádio das Antas, OPORTO (Att. 19,124)

PORTUGAL - EAST GERMANY
3:2 (1:0)

1:0 Coluna (45'), 1:1 Vogt (47'), 2:1 Coluna (62'), 3:1 Cavém (68'), 3:2 Kohle (72')

POR: (Coach: José Maria ANTUNES)
ACÚRCIO Alves Carrelo, VIRGÍLIO Marques Mendes, ÂNGELO Gaspar Martins, Fernando Mamede MENDES, Raúl António Leandro de FIGUEIREDO, ALFREDO Saúl Abrantes de Abreu, Carlos Domingos DUARTE, António Dias TEIXEIRA, Sebastião Lucas da Fonseca 'MATATEU', Mário Esteves COLUNA, Domiciano Barrocal Gomes CAVÉM

EGR: (Coach: Friedrich GÖDICKE)
Klaus THIELE, Bringfried MÜLLER, Werner HEINE, Konrad WAGNER, Werner UNGER, Siegfried WOLF, Roland DUCKE, Günter SCHRÖTER, Gerhard VOGT, Dieter ERLER, Horst KOHLE

PORTUGAL won 5-2 on agg.

28 June 1959          Ref: Arthur ELLIS (England)
Stadion Śląski, CHORZÓW (Att. 71,469)

### POLAND - SPAIN
### 2:4 (1:2)

1:0 Pol (34'), 1:1 Suárez (40'), 1:2 Di Stéfano (41'), 1:3
Suárez (52'), 1:4 Di Stéfano (56'), 2:4 Brychczy (62')

POL: (Coach: Czeslaw KRUG/Jean PROUFF)
Tomasz STEFANISZYN, Henryk SZCZEPAŃSKI,
Roman KORYNT, Jerzy WÓZNIAK, Marceli
STRZYKALSKI, Edmund ZIENTARA, Ernest POL,
Lucjan BRYCHCZY, Stanisław HACHOREK, Jan
LIBERDA, Krzysztof BASZKIEWICZ

SPA: (Coach: Selection Committee)
Antonio RAMALLETS Símon, Ferran OLIVELLA
i Pons, Jesús GARAY Vecino, Sigfrido GRACIA
Royo, Joan SEGARRA Iracheta, Enrique GENSANA
Merola, Justo TEJADA Martínez, Enrique MATEOS
Mancebo, Alfredo DI STÉFANO Laulhé, Luis SUÁREZ
Miramontes, Francisco GENTO López


14 October 1959      Ref: Károly BALLA (Hungary)
Estadio Santiago Bernabéu, MADRID (Att. 62,070)

### SPAIN - POLAND
### 3:0 (1:0)

1:0 Di Stéfano (30'), 2:0 Gensana (69'), 3:0 Gento (85')

SPA: (Coach: Selection Committee)
Antonio RAMALLETS Símon, Ferran OLIVELLA
i Pons, Jesús GARAY Vecino, Sigfrido GRACIA
Royo, Joan SEGARRA Iracheta, Enrique GENSANA
Merola, Justo TEJADA Martínez, Ladislao KUBALA
Stécz, Alfredo DI STÉFANO Laulhé, Luis SUÁREZ
Miramontes, Francisco GENTO López

POL: (Coach: Czeslaw KRUG/Jean PROUFF)
Tomasz STEFANISZYN, Henryk SZCZEPAŃSKI, Roman KORYNT, Fryderyk MONICA, Witold MAJEWSKI, Henryk GRZYBOWSKI, Krzysztof BASZKIEWICZ, Ernest POL, Stanisław HACHOREK, Edmund ZIENTARA, Zbigniew SZARZYŃSKI

SPAIN won 7-2 on agg.


23 September 1959          Ref: Johan BRONKHORST
                                        (Netherlands)
Idrætsparken, COPENHAGEN (Att. 32,000)

DENMARK - CZECHOSLOVAKIA
2:2 (2:2)

1:0 Pedersen (17'), 2:0 Hansen (19'), 2:1 Kačáni (29'),
2:2 Dolinský (42')

DEN: (Coach: Arne SØRENSEN)
Per Funch JENSEN, Erling Linde LARSEN, Poul JENSEN, Bent HANSEN, Hans Christian NIELSEN, Erik Pondal JENSEN, John DANIELSEN, Henning ENOKSEN, Jørn SØRENSEN, Poul PEDERSEN, Harald NIELSEN

CZE: (Coach: Rudolf VYTLACIL)
Imrich STACHO, Jiří TICHÝ, Ján POPLUHÁR, Ladislav NOVÁK, Štefan MATLÁK, Titus BUBERNÍK, Ladislav PAVLOVIČ, Adolf SCHERER, Vlastimil BUBNÍK, Ladislav KAČÁNI, Milan DOLINSKÝ


18 October 1959             Ref: Helmut KÖHLER
                                      (West Germany)
Stadion Za Lužánkami, BRNO (Att. 31,217)

CZECHOSLOVAKIA - DENMARK
5:1(1:1)

0:1 Kramer (33'), 1:1 Buberník (39'), 2:1 Scherer (47'),
3:1 Buberník (56'), 4:1 Dolinský (63'), 5:1 Scherer (86')

CZE: (Coach: Rudolf VYTLACIL)
Viliam SCHROJF, Jiří TICHÝ, Ján POPLUHÁR,
Ladislav NOVÁK, Svatopluk PLUSKAL, Titus
BUBERNÍK, Ladislav PAVLOVIČ, Anton MORAVČÍK,
Pavol MOLNÁR, Adolf SCHERER, Milan DOLINSKÝ

DEN: (Coach: Arne SØRENSEN)
Erling SØRENSEN, Richard Møller NIELSEN, Poul
JENSEN, Bent HANSEN, Hans Christian NIELSEN,
Flemming NIELSEN I, Poul PEDERSEN, John
KRAMER, Henning ENOKSEN, John DANIELSEN,
Jørn SØRENSEN

CZECHOSLOVAKIA won 7-3 on agg.


## QUARTER-FINALS

13 December 1959      Ref: Manuel ASENSI Martín
(Spain)
Stade Olympique Yves-du-Manoir, COLOMBES
(Att. 43,775)

### FRANCE - AUSTRIA
### 5:2 (3:1)

1:0 Fontaine (6'), 2:0 Fontaine (18'), 3:0 Vincent (38'),
3:1 Horak (40'), 3:2 Pichler (65'), 4:2 Fontaine (70'),
5:2 Vincent (82')

FRA: (Coach: Albert BATTEUX)
Georges LAMIA, Jean WENDLING, Roger MARCHE,
Armand PENVERNE, Robert JONQUET, René
FERRIER, François HEUTTE, Raymond KOPA, Just
FONTAINE, Lucien MULLER, Jean VINCENT

AUT: (Coach: Karl DECKER)
Kurt SCHMIED, Paul HALLA, Karl NICKERL, Gerhard HANAPPI, Karl STOTZ, Karl KOLLER, Walter HORAK, Helmut SENEKOWITSCH, Horst NEMEC, Rudolf PICHLER, Karl HÖFER

27 March 1960          Ref: Leo HELGE (Denmark)
Praterstadion, VIENNA (Att. 39,229)

### AUSTRIA - FRANCE
### 2:4 (1:0)

1:0 Nemec (26'), 1:1 Marcel (46'), 1:2 Rahis (59'), 2:2 Probst (64'), 2:3 Heutte (77'), 2:4 Kopa (83' pen.)

AUT: (Coach: Karl DECKER)
Rudolf SZANWALD, Johann WINDISCH, Erich HASENKOPF, Gerhard HANAPPI, Giuseppe KOSCHIER, Karl KOLLER, Walter HORAK, Paul KOZLICEK, Horst NEMEC, Wilhelm HUBERTS, Erich PROBST

FRA: (Coach: Albert BATTEUX)
Georges LAMIA, Jean WENDLING, Raymond KAELBEL, Bruno RODZIK, René FERRIER, Jean-Jacques MARCEL, Pierre GRILLET, Lucien MULLER, Raymond KOPA, Bernard RAHIS, François HEUTTE

FRANCE won 9-4 on agg.

8 May 1960          Ref: Joseph BARBÉRAN (France)
Estádio Nacional, OEIRAS (Att. 39,978)

### PORTUGAL - YUGOSLAVIA
### 2:1 (1:0)

1:0 Santana (30'), 2:0 'Matateu' (70'), 2:1 Kostić (81')

POR: (Coach: José Maria ANTUNES)
ACÚRCIO Alves Carrelo, VIRGÍLIO Marques
Mendes, ÂNGELO Gaspar Martins, Fernando
Mamede MENDES, GERMANO de Figueiredo, David
Abraão JÚLIO, HERNÂNI Ferreira da Silva, Joaquim
SANTANA da Silva Guimarães, Sebastião Lucas
da Fonseca 'MATATEU', Mário Esteves COLUNA,
Domiciano Barrocal Gomes CAVÉM

YUG: (Coach: Ljubomir LOVRIĆ/Dragomir NIKOLIĆ/
Aleksandar TIRNANIĆ)
Milutin ŠOŠKIĆ, Vladimir DURKOVIĆ, Fahrudin
JUSUFI, Ante ŽANETIĆ, Tomislav CRNKOVIĆ,
Željko PERUŠIĆ, Dragoslav ŠEKULARAC, Muhamed
MUJIĆ, Branko ZEBEC, Milan GALIĆ, Borivoje
KOSTIĆ

22 May 1960          Ref: Josef STOLL (Austria)
Stadion J.N.A., BELGRADE (Att. 43,000)

YUGOSLAVIA - PORTUGAL
5:1 (2:1)

1:0 Šekularac (8'), 1:1 Cavém (29'), 2:1 Čebinac (45'),
   3:1 Kostić (50'), 4:1 Galić (79'), 5:1 Kostić (88')

YUG: (Coach: Ljubomir LOVRIĆ/Dragomir NIKOLIĆ/
Aleksandar TIRNANIĆ)
Milutin ŠOŠKIĆ, Vladimir DURKOVIĆ, Fahrudin
JUSUFI, Ante ŽANETIĆ, Žarko NIKOLIĆ, Željko
PERUŠIĆ, Zvezdan ČEBINAC, Tomislav KNEZ,
Dragoslav ŠEKULARAC, Milan GALIĆ, Borivoje
KOSTIĆ

POR: (Coach: José Maria ANTUNES)
ACÚRCIO Alves Carrelo, VIRGÍLIO Marques
Mendes, Mário JOÃO, Fernando Mamede MENDES,
GERMANO de Figueiredo, David Abraão JÚLIO,

HERNÂNI Ferreira da Silva, Joaquim SANTANA da Silva Guimarães, Sebastião Lucas da Fonseca 'MATATEU', Mário Esteves COLUNA, Domiciano Barrocal Gomes CAVÉM

YUGOSLAVIA won 6-3 on agg.


22 May 1960          Ref: Andor DOROGI (Hungary)
Stadionul 23 August, BUCHAREST (Att. 61,306)

ROMANIA - CZECHOSLOVAKIA
0:2 (0:2)

0:1 Masopust (8'), 0:2 Bubník (45')

ROM: (Coach: Augustin BOTESCU)
Petre MÎNDRU, Corneliu POPA, Alexandru APOLZAN, Valeriu SOARE, Emeric JENEI, Ion NUNWEILLER, Emanoil HAŞOTI, Gavril RAKSI, Viorel MATEIANU, Haralambie EFTIMIE, Nicolae TĂTARU

CZE: (Coach: Rudolf VYTLACIL)
Imrich STACHO, Jozef BOMBA, Ján POPLUHÁR, Ladislav NOVÁK, Titus BUBERNÍK, Josef MASOPUST, Ladislav PAVLOVIČ, Josef VOJTA, Andrej KVAŠŇÁK, Vlastimil BUBNÍK, Milan DOLINSKÝ


29 May 1960          Ref: Leif GULLIKSEN (Norway)
Tehelné pole, BRATISLAVA (Att. 31,057)

CZECHOSLOVAKIA - ROMANIA
3:0 (3:0)

1:0 Buberník (1'), 2:0 Buberník (15'), 3:0 Bubník (18')

CZE: (Coach: Rudolf VYTLACIL)
Viliam SCHROJF, Jozef BOMBA, Ján POPLUHÁR, Ladislav NOVÁK, Titus BUBERNÍK, Josef MASOPUST,

Ladislav PAVLOVIČ, Josef VOJTA, Vlastimil BUBNÍK, Milan DOLINSKÝ, Andrej KVAŠŇÁK

ROM: (Coach: Augustin BOTESCU)
Petre MÎNDRU, Corneliu POPA, Alexandru FRONEA, Valeriu SOARE, Vasile ALEXANDRU, Ion NUNWEILLER, Gheorghe CACOVEANU, Gheorghe CONSTANTIN, Constantin DINULESCU, Viorel MATEIANU, Nicolae TĂTARU

CZECHOSLOVAKIA won 5-0 on agg.


SPAIN withdrew. USSR was given a walkover to the final tournament.

# GOALSCORERS

## 5 GOALS

Titus BUBERNÍK (Czechoslovakia), Just FONTAINE (France)

## 4 GOALS

Jean VINCENT (France)

## 3 GOALS

Erich HOF, Horst NEMEC (both Austria), Milan DOLINSKÝ (Czechoslovakia), Mário Esteves COLUNA (Portugal), Alfredo DI STÉFANO Laulhé (Spain), Borivoje KOSTIĆ (Yugoslavia)

## 2 GOALS

Vlastimil BUBNÍK, Adolf SCHERER (both Czechoslovakia), Thadée CISOWSKI, Raymond KOPA (both France), Ove ØDEGAARD (Norway), Domiciano Barrocal Gomes CAVÉM, Sebastião Lucas da Fonseca 'MATATEU' (both Portugal), Luis SUÁREZ Miramontes (Spain), LEFTER Küçükandonyadis (Turkey), Milan GALIĆ (Yugoslavia)

## 1 GOAL

Walter HORAK, Rudolf PICHLER, Erich PROBST, Karl SKERLAN (all Austria), Todor DIEV (Bulgaria), Ladislav KAČÁNI, Josef MASOPUST, Ladislav PAVLOVIČ, Imrich STACHO (all Czechoslovakia), Bent HANSEN, John KRAMER, Poul PEDERSEN (all

Denmark), Gerhard VOGT, Horst KOHLE (both East
Germany), Stéphane BRUEY, François HEUTTE,
Jean-Jacques MARCEL, Bernard RAHIS (all France),
Ilias YFANTIS (Greece), János GÖRÖCS (Hungary),
Lucjan BRYCHCZY, Ernest POL (both Poland),
Joaquim SANTANA Silva Guimarães (Portugal),
Gheorghe CONSTANTIN, Constantin DINULESCU,
Nicolae OAIDĂ (all Romania), Noel CANTWELL,
William TUOHY (both Republic of Ireland), Enrique
GENSANA Merola, Francisco GENTO López
(both Spain), Anatoliy ILYIN, Valentin IVANOV,
Slava METREVELI, Yuriy VOINOV (all USSR),
Zvezdan ČEBINAC, Muhamed MUJIĆ, Dragoslav
ŠEKULARAC, Lazar TASIĆ (all Yugoslavia)


OWN-GOALS

Roger MARCHE (France) vs Greece

# FINAL TOURNAMENT
# (FRANCE - 6-10 JULY 1960)

## VENUES (Stadia)

MARSEILLES (Stade Vélodrome), PARIS (Parc des Princes)

---

## SEMI-FINALS & THIRD PLACE MATCH

### FRANCE vs YUGOSLAVIA

In the opening semi-final in Paris, the hosts and Yugoslavia produced a dramatic encounter which would see one of the greatest comebacks in the competition's history. The game started frantically, with Milan Galić opening the scoring in the eleventh minute. It was a cracking shot from twenty-five yards that flew past Georges Lamia, but Jean Vincent levelled things up within a minute when his swerving cross eluded everyone to sneak in at the far post. It stayed that way until François Heutte thrashed home from just inside the box to put the hosts in front, just before the interval.

Within ten minutes of the restart, both sides had netted again. Maryan Wisnieski slotted in from close range, then Ante Žanetić replied for Yugoslavia from a tight angle. Just after the hour mark, Heutte grabbed his second from a suspiciously offside position to put France 4-2 up. With fifteen minutes left, it looked like France were in the Final – but the Yugoslavs sensationally scored three goals within four minutes to win the match. Firstly, Tomislav Knez skillfully volleyed in Dragoslav Šekularac's long cross; then Lamia's dreadful throw-out was intercepted; from the cut-back, Dražen Jerković stabbed home the equaliser, and in their next attack Lamia failed to hold Knez's shot. Jerković was on hand to knock in the rebound, leaving the French completely shellshocked.

## USSR vs CZECHOSLOVAKIA

The other semi-final in Marseilles was a more straightforward affair, as the Soviet Union strolled to an easy victory over Czechoslovakia. The Czechoslovaks began well, and Lev Yashin had to be at his best to push away an angled shot from Vlastimil Bubník, but then Valentin Ivanov opened the scoring for the Soviets in the thirty-fourth minute from six yards, following a neat pass from Viktor Ponedelnik. Eleven minutes after the break, Ivanov extended the lead with a fabulous dribble through the Czechoslovak defence, before exchanging passes with Ponedelnik and smashing the ball high into the net. Ten minutes later, Ponedelnik netted from a rebound after Valentin Bubukin's shot came back off a defender. Within a minute, Czechoslovakia's misery was compounded when they were awarded a penalty but Josef Vojta shot woefully past the post.

## FRANCE vs CZECHOSLOVAKIA

There was some consolation for the Czechoslovaks in the third-place match, as they defeated the hosts 2-0 in Marseilles. After an even first half, Czechoslovakia stepped it up after the break. Vlastimil Bubník opened the scoring just before the hour mark when he latched onto Ladislav Novák's long pass, then Ladislav Pavlovič dispossessed Michel Stievenard and ran on to score from a tight angle between Jean Taillandier and the near post a couple of minutes from the end.

## FINAL

### USSR vs YUGOSLAVIA

The first ever Final of the European Nations Cup took place on Sunday 10th July at the Parc des Princes, Paris, in front of almost 18,000 spectators. This was only the fourth meeting between the sides. Of the previous three, all in the last two Olympic Games, each side had won once and drawn once. The Soviet Union were unchanged from their semi-final line-up, whereas the Yugoslavs had made three changes: Blagoje Vidinić replacing Milutin Šoškić in goal, Željko Matuš for Knez out wide, and skipper Branko Zebec surprisingly omitted, with Jovan Miladinović coming in. Borivoje Kostić had taken over the captaincy.

The Yugoslavs had the better of the early exchanges. Šekularac just failed to get his head to Galić's teasing cross, then Kostić sent a speculative drive from the left side of the box, just over the bar. Midway through the half, the Soviets spurned a great chance when Ivanov found a way through the Yugoslav defence, but he shot straight at Vidinić, who parried with his legs to safety. Vidinić's huge kick upfield was misjudged by the Soviet defence, but Galić failed to connect properly and sliced his effort well wide. The centre-forward made up for that miss, though, in the forty-third minute, when he stooped in front of Igor Netto to head home Jerković's inviting cross from the right.

Early in the second half, Galić wasted another opportunity when put through on the right, but he dragged his shot beyond the far post. It was a costly miss, as a minute later the Soviets equalised. Bubukin broke forward from midfield and blasted a shot from fully thirty yards, which Vidinić spilled and Slava Metreveli was quickest to the rebound to slot home from six yards out. The Soviet Union now dominated, and they created several chances, the best of which was Bubukin's header, which flew just wide after some lovely skill from Metreveli. Yugoslavia almost retook the lead when Šekularac caught Yashin off his line with a speculative free-kick, but the keeper got back just in time to palm the ball over. Then, just before the end, Ivanov missed an absolute sitter when he sliced Givi Chokheli's low cross well wide from six yards out. After ninety pulsating minutes, an extra thirty minutes were required for either team to find a winning goal.

The Soviets had the first opportunity when Mikhail Meskhi latched onto Ivanov's cross, but Vidinić pushed his shot away. Then the Yugoslavs were inches away after Yashin completely missed Kostić's corner and Jerković headed just past the post. In the second period Anatoliy Krutikov tried his luck from long range, which Vidinić tipped over, and at the other end Galić somehow failed to connect with Matuš' cross right in front of the goal. In the 113th minute came the decisive moment. Ivanov lofted a cross from the left, and Ponedelnik rose unmarked to head high into the net. In the final moments Bubukin was played in, but Vidinić raced off his line to clear. Seconds later, English referee Arthur Ellis blew the final whistle, and the Soviet Union became the first winners of the 'Coupe Henri Delaunay'.

# MATCH DETAILS

## SEMI-FINALS

6 July 1960 (20.00)          Ref: Gaston GRANDAIN
(Belgium)

Parc des Princes, PARIS (Att. 26,370)

### FRANCE - YUGOSLAVIA
### 4:5 (2:1)

0:1 Galić (11'), 1:1 Vincent (12'), 2:1 Heutte (43'), 3:1 Wisnieski (53'), 3:2 Žanetić (55'), 4:2 Heutte (62'), 4:3 Knez (75'), 4:4 Jerković (78'), 4:5 Jerković (79')

FRA: (Coach: Albert BATTEUX)
Georges LAMIA, Jean WENDLING, Bruno RODZIK, Jean-Jacques MARCEL, Robert HERBIN, René FERRIER, François HEUTTE, Lucien MULLER, Maryan WISNIESKI, Michel STIEVENARD, Jean VINCENT (Capt.)

YUG: (Coach: Ljubomir LOVRIĆ/Dragomir NIKOLIĆ/ Aleksandar TIRNANIĆ)
Milutin ŠOŠKIĆ, Vladimir DURKOVIĆ, Fahrudin JUSUFI, Ante ŽANETIĆ, Branko ZEBEC (Capt.), Željko PERUŠIĆ, Tomislav KNEZ, Dražen JERKOVIĆ, Dragoslav ŠEKULARAC, Milan GALIĆ, Borivoje KOSTIĆ

6 July 1960 (20.30)          Ref: Cesare JONNI (Italy)
Stade Vélodrome, MARSEILLES (Att. 25,184)

### USSR - CZECHOSLOVAKIA
### 3:0 (1:0)

1:0 Ivanov (34'), 2:0 Ivanov (56'), 3:0 Ponedelnik (66')

URS: (Coach: Gavriil KACHALIN)
Lev YASHIN, Givi CHOKHELI, Anatoliy MASLYONKIN, Anatoliy KRUTIKOV, Yuriy VOYNOV, Igor NETTO (Capt.), Slava METREVELI, Valentin IVANOV, Viktor PONEDELNIK, Valentin BUBUKIN, Mikhail MESKHI

CZE: (Coach: Rudolf VYTLACIL)
Viliam SCHROJF, František ŠAFRÁNEK, Ján POPLUHÁR, Ladislav NOVÁK (Capt.), Titus BUBERNÍK, Josef MASOPUST, Josef VOJTA, Vlastimil BUBNÍK, Andrej KVAŠŇÁK, Anton MORAVČÍK, Milan DOLINSKÝ

## THIRD PLACE MATCH

9 July 1960 (18.00)        Ref: Cesare JONNI (Italy)
Stade Vélodrome, MARSEILLES (Att. 9,438)

### FRANCE - CZECHOSLOVAKIA
### 0:2 (0:0)

0:1 Bubník (58'), 0:2 Pavlovič (88')

FRA: (Coach: Albert BATTEUX)
Jean TAILLANDIER, Bruno RODZIK, André CHORDA, Jean-Jacques MARCEL, Robert JONQUET (Capt.), Robert SIATKA, François HEUTTE, Yvon DOUIS, Maryan WISNIESKI, Michel STIEVENARD, Jean VINCENT

CZE: (Coach: Rudolf VYTLACIL)
Viliam SCHROJF, František ŠAFRÁNEK, Ján POPLUHÁR, Ladislav NOVÁK (Capt.), Josef MASOPUST, Titus BUBERNÍK, Ladislav PAVLOVIČ, Josef VOJTA, Pavol MOLNÁR, Vlastimil BUBNÍK, Milan DOLINSKÝ

# FINAL

10 July 1960 (21.30)     Ref: Arthur ELLIS (England)
Parc des Princes, PARIS (Att. 17,966)

### USSR - YUGOSLAVIA
### 2:1 AET (0:1/1:1)

0:1 Galić (43'), 1:1 Metreveli (49'), 2:1 Ponedelnik (113')

URS: (Coach: Gavriil KACHALIN)
Lev YASHIN, Givi CHOKHELI, Anatoliy MASLYONKIN, Anatoliy KRUTIKOV, Yuriy VOYNOV, Igor NETTO (Capt.), Slava METREVELI, Valentin IVANOV, Viktor PONEDELNIK, Valentin BUBUKIN, Mikhail MESKHI

YUG: (Coach: Ljubomir LOVRIĆ/Dragomir NIKOLIĆ/ Aleksandar TIRNANIĆ)
Blagoje VIDINIĆ, Vladimir DURKOVIĆ, Fahrudin JUSUFI, Ante ŽANETIĆ, Dražen JERKOVIĆ, Dragoslav ŠEKULARAC, Jovan MILADINOVIĆ, Željko PERUŠIĆ, Željko MATUŠ, Milan GALIĆ, Borivoje KOSTIĆ (Capt.)

# GOALSCORERS

## 2 GOALS

François HEUTTE (France), Milan GALIĆ, Dražen JERKOVIĆ (both Yugoslavia), Valentin IVANOV, Viktor PONEDELNIK (both USSR)

## 1 GOAL

Vlastimil BUBNÍK, Ladislav PAVLOVIČ (both Czechoslovakia), Jean VINCENT, Maryan WISNIESKI (both France), Slava METREVELI (USSR), Tomislav KNEZ, Ante ŽANETIĆ (both Yugoslavia)

# SQUADS

## CZECHOSLOVAKIA

## GOALKEEPERS

Justin JAVOREK (23.08.1932/TJ Červená Hvežda Bratislava), Viliam SCHROJF (02.08.1931/TJ Slovan Bratislava)

## DEFENDERS

Ladislav NOVÁK (05.12.1931/VTJ Dukla Praha), Ján POPLUHÁR (12.08.1935/TJ Slovan Bratislava), František ŠAFRÁNEK (02.01.1931/VTJ Dukla Praha), Jiří TICHÝ (06.12.1933/TJ Červená Hvežda Bratislava)

## MIDFIELDERS

Titus BUBERNÍK (12.10.1933/TJ Červená Hvežda Bratislava), Josef MASOPUST (09.02.1931/VTJ Dukla Praha), Anton MORAVČÍK (03.06.1931/TJ Slovan Bratislava), Svatopluk PLUSKAL (28.10.1930/ VTJ Dukla Praha)

## FORWARDS

Vlastimil BUBNÍK (18.03.1931/TJ Rudá Hvežda Brno), Milan DOLINSKÝ (14.07.1935/TJ Červená Hvežda Bratislava), Andrej KVAŠŇÁK (19.05.1936/TJ Spartak Sokolovo Praha), Pavol MOLNÁR (13.02.1936/TJ Červená Hvežda Bratislava), Ladislav PAVLOVIČ (08.04.1926/TJ Tatran Prešov), Josef VACENOVSKÝ (09.07.1937/VTJ Dukla Praha), Josef VOJTA (19.04.1935/TJ Spartak Sokolovo Praha)

# FRANCE

## GOALKEEPERS

Georges LAMIA (14.03.1933/OGC de Nice), Jean TAILLANDIER (22.01.1938/Racing Club de France (Paris))

## DEFENDERS

André CHORDA (20.02.1938/OGC de Nice), Robert HERBIN (30.03.1939/AS Saint-Étienne), Robert JONQUET (03.05.1925/Stade de Reims), Bruno RODZIK (29.05.1935/Stade de Reims), Robert SIATKA (20.06.1934/Stade de Reims), Jean WENDLING (29.04.1934/Stade de Reims)

## MIDFIELDERS

René FERRIER (07.12.1936/AS Saint-Étienne), Jean-Jacques MARCEL (13.06.1931/Racing Club de France (Paris)), Lucien MULLER (03.09.1934/Stade de Reims)

## FORWARDS

Yvon DOUIS (16.05.1935/Le Havre AC), François HEUTTE (21.02.1938/Racing Club de France (Paris)), Paul SAUVAGE (17.03.1939/Stade de Reims), Michel STIEVENARD (21.09.1937/Racing Club de Lens), Jean VINCENT (29.11.1930/Stade de Reims), Maryan WISNIESKI (01.02.1937/Racing Club de Lens)

# USSR

## GOALKEEPERS

Vladimir MASLACHENKO (05.03.1936/FK Lokomotiv

Moskva), Lev YASHIN (22.10.1929/FK Dinamo Moskva)

## DEFENDERS

Givi CHOKHELI (27.06.1937/FC Dinamo Tbilisi), Vladimir KESAREV (26.02.1930/FK Dinamo Moskva), Anatoliy KRUTIKOV (21.09.1933/FK Spartak Moskva), Anatoliy MASLYONKIN (29.06.1930/FK Spartak Moskva), Viktor TSARYOV (02.06.1931/FK Dinamo Moskva)

## MIDFIELDERS

Igor NETTO (09.01.1930/FK Spartak Moskva), Yuriy VOINOV (29.11.1931/FK Dinamo Kiev)

## FORWARDS

German APUKHTIN (12.06.1936/TSKA Moskva), Valentin BUBUKIN (23.04.1933/FK Lokomotiv Moskva), Valentin IVANOV (19.11.1934/FK Torpedo Moskva), Zaur KALOYEV (24.03.1931/FC Dinamo Tbilisi), Yuriy KOVALYOV (06.02.1934/FK Dinamo Kiev), Mikhail MESKHI (12.01.1937/FC Dinamo Tbilisi), Slava METREVELI (30.05.1936/FK Torpedo Moskva), Viktor PONEDELNIK (22.05.1937/SKA Rostov-na-Donu)

## YUGOSLAVIA

## GOALKEEPERS

Milutin ŠOŠKIĆ (31.12.1937/FK Partizan Beograd), Blagoje VIDINIĆ (11.06.1934/FK Radnički Beograd)

## DEFENDERS

Tomislav CRNKOVIĆ (17.06.1929/NK Dinamo Zagreb), Vladimir DURKOVIĆ (06.11.1937/FK Crvena Zvezda Beograd), Fahrudin JUSUFI (08.12.1939/FK Partizan Beograd), Žarko NIKOLIĆ (16.10.1938/FK Vojvodina Novi Sad)

## MIDFIELDERS

Jovan MILADINOVIĆ (30.01.1939/FK Partizan Beograd), Željko PERUSIĆ (23.03.1936/NK Dinamo Zagreb), Ante ŽANETIĆ (18.11.1936/NK Hajduk Split), Branko ZEBEC (17.05.1929/FK Crvena Zvezda Beograd)

## FORWARDS

Milan GALIĆ (08.03.1938/FK Partizan Beograd), Dražen JERKOVIĆ (06.08.1936/NK Dinamo Zagreb), Tomislav KNEZ (09.06.1938/FK Borac Banja Luka), Borivoje KOSTIĆ (14.06.1930/FK Crvena Zvezda Beograd), Željko MATUŠ (09.08.1935/NK Dinamo Zagreb), Muhamed MUJIĆ (25.04.1932/FK Velež Mostar), Dragoslav ŠEKULARAC (08.11.1937/FK Crvena Zvezda Beograd)

# 1962-1964

## QUALIFICATION

After the success of the inaugural tournament, twelve additional countries confirmed their entry for the second edition, bringing the total to twenty-nine participants. The format, once again, was a two-legged knockout system up to the semi-finals. There would be thirteen first-round ties, with the winners being joined by the Soviet Union (the holders), Austria and Luxembourg, who were all given a bye to the next round. Some of the stronger nations, such as Italy and England, took part this time, but West Germany and Scotland were again among the absentees.

## PRELIMINARY ROUND

Scandinavian neighbours Norway and Sweden got the tournament underway when they met in Oslo. Two goals from Örjan Martinsson gave the away side a first-leg advantage, and they added to that when Leif Eriksson netted early in the second half of the return leg. John Krogh soon equalised for the Norwegians, but they never looked like adding to it, and Sweden eased through.

Minnows Malta were totally outclassed in Copenhagen as the Danes cruised to a 6-1 victory, which included a hat-trick from Ole Madsen I. He also notched the opening goal in the second leg, and although the Maltese equalised, two further goals gave Denmark another comfortable win.

In Dublin, debutants Iceland gave the Republic of Ireland a scare in the first leg. Ríkharður Jónsson brought them level following 'Liam' Tuohy's early strike, but Ambrose Fogarty restored the Irish lead just before the interval, and then two second-half goals from Noel Cantwell put them in a commanding position. Jónsson netted a second for the Icelanders near the end, but any hopes of an Icelandic comeback in the second leg were scuppered when Tuohy netted eight minutes from the break. Iceland did manage to equalise through Gardar Árnason in the second period, but the Irish comfortably held out for the remainder of the match to progress.

England, making their tournament bow, entertained 1960 host nation France in Sheffield, and it was the guests who came flying out the blocks when Yvon Goujon netted in the eighth minute. It took a penalty from 'Ron' Flowers early in the second half to give the English a share of the spoils. By the time of the return leg, England had a new manager, 'Alf' Ramsey, who would lead them to World Cup glory in 1966, but he suffered a nightmare debut in Paris, as the French ran riot to lead 3-0 at the break through goals from Maryan Wisnieski, Yvon Douis and Lucien Cossou. England rallied in the second half, and goals from 'Bobby' Smith and 'Bobby' Tambling brought them back into the game, but Wisnieski made it 4-2 soon afterwards. Cossou netted his second strike in the eighty-second minute to restore the hosts' three-goal cushion.

Northern Ireland produced arguably the best away performance of the round after goals from Derek Dougan and William Humphries gave them a 2-0 victory in Poland, and they repeated that scoreline in the return game in Belfast, with 'Johnny' Crossan and 'Billy' Bingham netting this time.

In Madrid, Spain blew Romania away in a blistering opening spell during which they netted four goals inside twenty minutes and eventually won 6-0, with Vicente Guillot grabbing three of them. Romania salvaged some pride in the second leg when they led 3-0 by the hour mark, but José Veloso soon pulled a goal back to stifle Romanian hopes of a sensational comeback.

Yugoslavia and Belgium served up a cracking game in the first leg of their tie in Belgrade, where the Yugoslavs were thrice in the lead, with the eventual winning goal coming in the eighty-eighth minute through Velibor Vasović. The return in Brussels was tame in comparison, with Milan Galić's strike midway through the first half sufficient to see Yugoslavia through.

Wales travelled to Budapest to take on a strong Hungarian side, and although 'Terry' Medwin levelled Flórián Albert's early strike, the Hungarians eventually prevailed 3-1 with further goals from Lajos Tichy and Károly Sándor. In the return in Cardiff, the Welsh reduced the arrears midway through the first period when 'Cliff' Jones converted a penalty, but the Hungarians defended stoutly and thirteen minutes from time they drew level, also from the penalty spot, through Lajos Tichy.

In Sofia, Bulgaria took on Portugal, including seven players from Benfica who'd won a thrilling European Cup Final against Real Madrid earlier in the year. After a tepid first half, the game burst into life early in the second period when Eusébio netted for Portugal, but the home side fought back to win with a three goal salvo inside twelve minutes, two of them from star forward Georgi Asparuhov. In the second leg, two first-half goals from Hernâni levelled the tie, and it looked like the Portuguese would ease through when

Mário Coluna added a third soon after the interval; but a goal from Hristo Iliev six minutes from time saved the Bulgarians, which meant that the first ever play-off match was necessary to decide who went through. On neutral ground in Rome, it was Bulgaria who prevailed, with Asparuhov the hero scoring the only goal in the eighty-sixth minute.

Two debutants met in Amsterdam, and in an even first period, 'Tonny' Van der Linden struck first for the Dutch, before Charles Hertig equalised shortly before the break for the Swiss. For most of the second half it looked like 1-1 would be the outcome, but in the final quarter of an hour, the Dutch netted twice within a minute through 'Sjaak' Swart and 'Henk' Groot to take a lead into the second leg. They increased their advantage in Berne when Pieter Kruiver slotted home after just seven minutes, and although Switzerland managed to level the match through Anton Allemann in the seventy-second minute, Holland rode out the remainder of the match to progress.

The shock result of the round was provided by East Germany. They were given little chance against Czechoslovakia, who only five months earlier had been runners-up to Brazil at the 1962 World Cup in Chile, but in East Berlin two second-half goals from Dieter Erler and a Kurt Liebrecht penalty put the home side in dreamland, though a last-minute consolation from Rudolf Kučera gave the Czechoslovaks hope for the return leg. In Prague, the East Germans frustrated the home team, but eventually Václav Mašek broke the deadlock midway through the second half, and it looked like they would earn a play-off at worst. Sensationally, with five minutes to go, Peter Ducke popped up to level the match and send the Czechoslovakians spinning out.

Italy, making their debut, dished out a six goal thrashing to Turkey in a one-sided affair in Bologna, with four of them falling to Alberto Orlando, and 'Gianni' Rivera grabbing the other two. With the return a formality, the Italians settled for a single goal victory, courtesy of an eighty-sixth minute strike from Angelo Sormani.

For the second tournament in a row, politics intervened when Albania were drawn to meet Greece; with both countries having no diplomatic relations, the Greeks blinked first and refused to play the tie, so the Albanians were given a walkover to the next round.

## FIRST ROUND

The opening game of the round produced another surprise result when Northern Ireland travelled to Bilbao and came away with a 1-1 draw. They had defended stoutly for almost an hour before Amancio put the Spaniards in the lead – but, with fourteen minutes remaining, William Irvine popped up to equalise. In the return leg at a packed Windsor Park, the Irish again for the most part held their own, but midway through the second half, 'Paco' Gento scored and that was enough to see Spain through.

In Belgrade, Yugoslavia and Sweden played out a drab, goalless match, the first in the competition's history, but in contrast the second leg was a cracker, with the game swinging one way then the other. Slaven Zambata put the Yugoslavs ahead midway through the first period, but two goals from Örjan Persson either side of the interval gave Sweden the lead, which only lasted three minutes as Milan Galić levelled. Finally, in the seventy-second minute, Harry Bild had the last word to win it for the Swedes.

Denmark continued their goal fest, scoring twice in each half as they thumped Albania 4-0 in Copenhagen, but the Albanians had the consolation of winning the return in Tirana, thanks to an early strike from their main star Panajot Pano. When the Netherlands were paired with Luxembourg, a resounding Dutch victory was expected – but what followed would go down as one of the Championship's all-time biggest shocks. The first leg in Amsterdam started well enough for the Dutch, as Klaas Nuninga scored after only five minutes, but Paul May equalised before half-time and that was how it finished. Luxembourg had given up hosting rights for the return leg, which was played in Rotterdam, and again the score was 1-1 at the interval. Camille Dimmer had netted first for Luxembourg, with Kruiver levelling for the Dutch; then, midway through the second half, Dimmer scored again, but the Dutch couldn't find a second equaliser and, sensationally, the minnows were through to the quarter-finals.

The Republic of Ireland travelled to Vienna and defended magnificently to obtain a goalless draw against the fancied Austrians. The return in Dublin produced a classic encounter, and it was the Austrians who struck first through Walter Koleznik in the thirty-eighth minute, with Cantwell levelling right on half-time. Midway through the second period, Fogarty edged the Irish in front, only for 'Rudi' Flögel to equalise seven minutes from time. A play-off now looked likely, but in a frantic finish, the Irish were awarded a penalty in the final minute, which Cantwell converted to win the tie.

France must have had a feeling of *déjà vu* when they were drawn to meet Bulgaria, who had eliminated them in the qualifiers for the previous World Cup; in the first leg in Sofia, a twenty-fourth minute strike from Todor Diev was enough to give the Bulgarians victory. In the opening period of the return, the French struggled to break down a determined defence, but just before the interval, Goujon broke the deadlock to level the tie. More of the same ensued in the second half; then, with fifteen minutes remaining, Dimitar Yakimov slotted an equaliser. However, on this occasion, the French didn't let their heads go down, and within six minutes they'd buried the memory of that World Cup elimination by netting twice through 'Roby' Herbin and Goujon again to win the tie.

The tie of the round saw the holders drawn against Italy, but in reality it was a bit of a damp squib, as the Soviets easily won the first leg in Moscow through first-half goals from Viktor Ponedelnik and Igor Chislenko. Any faint Italian hopes of retrieving the tie were extinguished when Gennadiy Gusarov put the Soviets further ahead in the thirty-third minute of the return leg, then 'Sandro' Mazzola's weak penalty was easily saved by Lev Yashin, and all the Italians could muster was a last-minute consolation from Rivera.

The last match of the round saw East Germany paired with Hungary, and, after accounting for Czechoslovakia in the previous round, the East Germans were hoping to surprise another Eastern European neighbour. However, the Hungarians proved too strong in the first game, although it took them until the eighty-eighth minute to find a winner through Gyula Rákosi after Jürgen Nöldner had cancelled out Ferenc Bene's earlier strike. The return leg in Budapest was a thriller, as the home team were thrice ahead, only to be pegged back each time, with Dieter Erler getting the final goal in the eighty-first minute. The East Germans never gave up, but they couldn't find the extra goal that would have earned them a play-off.

# QUARTER-FINALS

Following their opponents' exploits in the previous round, the Danes couldn't afford to underestimate Luxembourg after they were drawn together, and so it proved, as it took a play-off to finally see off the minnows after two hard-fought matches. In the first game, Luxembourg came flying out the traps and Louis Pilot netted within sixty seconds, but in the tenth minute, Ole Madsen equalised. Midway through the half, Henri Klein restored the lead, only for Madsen to equalise again before half-time. The second period started like the first – only this time it was the Danes who got the quickfire goal, with Madsen completing his treble. Within five minutes, Klein netted his second and that was the end of the scoring. Denmark were favourites to complete the job in Copenhagen, but they were stunned in the thirteenth minute when Johny Leonard put Luxembourg ahead. Madsen equalised within three minutes and it stayed that way until the seventieth minute, when Madsen continued his one-man goalscoring exploits by putting the Danes in front, only for 'Ady' Schmit to level with six minutes remaining. A play-off in neutral Amsterdam was therefore required to decide who would go through to the Finals, and it was that man Madsen, with his eleventh goal of the qualifiers, who made all the difference, with the only goal, just before the interval.

After the Northern Irish had run Spain close in the previous round, it was the turn of the Republic of Ireland to travel to the Iberian Peninsula with hopes of causing an upset – but in the heat of Seville they simply wilted. In a blistering first half, Spain scored four times, with Amancio getting a brace. 'Andy' McEvoy did grab a goal for the Irish in between, but that was their only crumb of comfort. The Spaniards eased off in the second period, and only added one further goal through Marcelino near the end. In a low-key second leg, the Spaniards cruised to a 2-0 victory, with the game a personal triumph for Pedro Zaballa who – in his only appearance for *La Roja* – scored both goals.

France had high hopes of making it through to their second consecutive Final Tournament when drawn against Hungary, but by the sixteenth minute of the first leg, they had a mountain to climb, after the Hungarians had scored twice in a minute through Flórián Albert and Lajos Tichy. Midway through the second half, Tichy added his second, and although Lucien Cossou pulled one goal back, the French were well beaten on their own patch. In the return in Budapest, Nestor Combin gave the French hope with a goal after only two minutes, but once Ferenc Sipos had equalised midway through the half, that spelled the end of France's chances. Ferenc Bene applied the *coup de grâce* in the second half to win the game for Hungary.

In the last quarter-final tie, the holders travelled to Sweden for the first leg. For the first hour, this was a cagey affair; then Valentin Ivanov put the Soviet Union in front, before 'Kurre' Hamrin gave the home fans something to cheer by equalising three minutes from time. The second leg in Moscow started quite slowly, but after half an hour, 1960 hero Ponedelnik broke the deadlock, then added a second early in the second half. Hamrin pulled a goal back with twelve minutes left to leave the Soviets sweating, but only briefly, as Valeriy Voronin restored the home side's two-goal cushion in the eighty-third minute, and the Soviet Union were through to the Final Tournament to defend their title.

# MATCH DETAILS

## PRELIMINARY ROUND

21 June 1962     Ref: Gilbert BOWMAN (Scotland)
Ullevaal Stadion, OSLO (Att. 28,249)

### NORWAY - SWEDEN
### 0:2 (0:2)

0:1 Martinsson (9'), 0:2 Martinsson (40')

NOR: (Coach: Wilhelm KMENT)
Sverre ANDERSEN, Anders SVELA, Ragnar LARSEN, Roar JOHANSEN, Trygve ANDERSEN, Olav NILSEN, Roald JENSEN, Arne PEDERSEN, John KROGH, Erik JOHANSEN, Håkon Olav BLENGSLI

SWE: (Coach: Lennart NYMAN)
Bengt NYHOLM, Orvar BERGMARK, Lennart WING, Gösta LUNDELL, Åke JOHANSSON, Prawitz ÖBERG, Bengt BERNDTSSON, Owe OHLSSON, Örjan MARTINSSON, Harry BILD, Lennart BACKMAN


4 November 1962          Ref: Werner BERGMANN
                                      (East Germany)
Malmö Stadion, MALMÖ (Att. 8,726)

### SWEDEN - NORWAY
### 1:1 (0:0)

1:0 Eriksson (49'), 1:1 Krogh (60')

SWE: (Coach: Lennart NYMAN)
Arne ARVIDSSON, Hans MILD, Lennart WING, Yngve BRODD, Åke JOHANSSON, Prawitz ÖBERG, Leif

ERIKSSON, Owe OHLSSON, Örjan MARTINSSON, Leif SKIÖLD, Örjan PERSSON

NOR: (Coach: Ragnar LARSEN)
Sverre ANDERSEN, Ragnar LARSEN, Edgar STAKSETH, Roar JOHANSEN, Finn THORSEN, TrygveANDERSEN, RoaldJENSEN,ArnePEDERSEN, John KROGH, Olav NILSEN, Oddvar RICHARDSEN

SWEDEN won 3-1 on agg.

28 June 1962      Ref: Pieter ROOMER (Netherlands)
Idrætsparken, COPENHAGEN (Att. 10,622)

DENMARK - MALTA
6:1 (3:0)

1:0 O. Madsen I (9'), 2:0 O. Madsen I (14'), 3:0 Clausen (22'), 4:0 O. Madsen I (49'), 4:1 Theobald (57'), 5:1 Enoksen (70'), 6:1 Bertelsen (80')

DEN: (Coach: Poul PETERSEN)
Erik GAARDHØJE, Kaj JOHANSEN, Poul JENSEN, Bent HANSEN, John MADSEN, Jørgen OLESEN, Carl BERTELSEN, Helge JØRGENSEN, Ole MADSEN I, Henning ENOKSEN, Eyvind CLAUSEN

MAL: (Coach: Carm BORG)
Alfred MIZZI, John PRIVITERA, Emmanuel DEBATTISTA, Frank ZAMMIT, Joseph CILIA, Vincent FALZON, Edward THEOBALD, Joseph URPANI, Tony CAUCHI, Emmanuel BORG, Publius DEMANUELLE

8 December 1962      Ref: Raoul RIGHI (Italy)
Imperu Istadium, GZIRA (Att. 6,987)

MALTA - DENMARK
1:3 (1:2)

0:1 O. Madsen I (13'), 1:1 Urpani (37'), 1:2 Christiansen (42'), 1:3 Bertelsen (48')

MAL: (Coach: Carm BORG)
Alfred MIZZI, John PRIVITERA, Joseph CILIA, Emmanuel ATTARD, Louis THEOBALD, Emmanuel BORG, Edward THEOBALD, Joseph URPANI, Frank ZAMMIT, Samuel NICHOLL, Joseph CINI

DEN: (Coach: Poul PETERSEN)
Erik GAARDHØJE, Kaj JOHANSEN, Preben JENSEN, Egon JENSEN, John MADSEN, Jens PETERSEN, Carl BERTELSEN, Carl Emil CHRISTIANSEN, Ole MADSEN I, Tommy TRŒLSEN, Eyvind CLAUSEN

DENMARK won 9-2 on agg.

12 August 1962          Ref: Robert SMITH (Wales)
Dalymount Park, DUBLIN (Att. 19,848)

REPUBLIC OF IRELAND - ICELAND
4:2 (2:1)

1:0 Tuohy (11'), 1:1 R. Jónsson (37'), 2:1 Fogarty (40'), 3:1 Cantwell (65'), 4:1 Cantwell (76'), 4:2 R. Jónsson (87')

EIR: (Coach: Selection Committee)
Alan KELLY, Anthony DUNNE, Thomas TRAYNOR, Patrick SAWARD, Charles HURLEY, Michael MEAGAN, Alfred HALE, John GILES, Noel CANTWELL, Ambrose FOGARTY, William TUOHY

ICE: (Coach: Rikharður JÓNSSON)
Helgi DANÍELSSON, Arni NJÁLSSON, Bjarni FELIXSON, Garðar ÁRNASON, Hörður FELIXSON, Sveinn JÓNSSON, Skúli AGÚSTSSON, Þórólfur BECK, Rikharður JÓNSSON, Ellert SCHRAM, Þórður JÓNSSON

2 September 1962     Ref: Arnold NILSEN (Norway)
Laugardalsvöllur, REYKJAVÍK (Att. 9,014)

### ICELAND - REPUBLIC OF IRELAND
### 1:1 (0:1)

0:1 Tuohy (37'), 1:1 Árnason (59')

ICE: (Coach: Rikharður JÓNSSON)
Helgi DANÍELSSON, Arni NJÁLSSON, Bjarni
FELIXSON, Garðar ÁRNASON, Jón STEFÁNSSON,
Sveinn JÓNSSON, Skúli AGÚSTSSON, Þórólfur
BECK, Rikharður JÓNSSON, Ellert SCHRAM,
Sigurþór JAKOBSSON

EIR: (Coach: Selection Committee)
Alan KELLY, Brendan McNALLY, Thomas TRAYNOR,
Ronald NOLAN, Charles HURLEY, Patrick SAWARD,
Dermot CURTIS, Ambrose FOGARTY, Noel
CANTWELL, Noel PEYTON, William TUOHY

REPUBLIC OF IRELAND won 5-3 on agg.

3 October 1962     Ref: Frede HANSEN (Denmark)
Hillsborough Stadium, SHEFFIELD (Att. 35,380)

### ENGLAND - FRANCE
### 1:1 (0:1)

0:1 Goujon (8'), 1:1 Flowers (57' pen.)

ENG: (Coach: Walter WINTERBOTTOM)
Ronald SPRINGETT, James ARMFIELD, Ramon
WILSON, Robert MOORE, Maurice NORMAN, Ronald
FLOWERS, Michael HELLAWELL, Christopher CROWE,
Raymond CHARNLEY, James GREAVES, Alan HINTON

FRA: (Coach: Henri GUÉRIN)
Pierre BERNARD, Jean WENDLING, MARYAN

Synakowski, André LEROND, André CHORDA, Joseph BONNEL, Yvon GOUJON, René FERRIER, Laurent ROBUSCHI, Raymond KOPA, Paul SAUVAGE

27 February 1963          Ref: Josef KANDLBINDER
(West Germany)
Parc des Princes, PARIS (Att. 23,986)

### FRANCE - ENGLAND
### 5:2 (3:0)

1:0 Wisnieski (3'), 2:0 Douis (32'), 3:0 Cossou (43'), 3:1 Smith (57'), 3:2 Tambling (74'), 4:2 Wisnieski (75'), 5:2 Cossou (82')

FRA: (Coach: Henri GUÉRIN)
Pierre BERNARD, Jean WENDLING, MARYAN Synakowski, André LEROND, Bruno RODZIK, Joseph BONNEL, Yvon GOUJON, Robert HERBIN, Maryan WISNIESKI, Yvon DOUIS, Lucien COSSOU

ENG: (Coach: Alfred RAMSEY)
Ronald SPRINGETT, James ARMFIELD, Ronald HENRY, Robert MOORE, Brian LABONE, Ronald FLOWERS, John CONNELLY, Robert TAMBLING, Robert SMITH, James GREAVES, Robert CHARLTON

FRANCE won 6-3 on agg.


10 October 1962          Ref: Bertil LÖÖW (Sweden)
Stadion Śląski, CHORZÓW (Att. 31,500)

### POLAND - NORTHERN IRELAND
### 0:2 (0:1)

0:1 Dougan (19'), 0:2 Humphries (54')

POL: (Coach: Ryszard KONCEWICZ)

Edward SZYMKOWIAK, Henryk SZCZEPAŃSKI, Władysław KAWULA, Stanisław OŚLIZŁO, Ryszard BUDKA, Bernard BLAUT, Lucjan BRYCHCZY, Eugeniusz FABER, Jan LIBERDA, Norbert GAJDA, Roman LENTNER

NIR: (Coach: Robert PEACOCK)
Robert IRVINE, James MAGILL, Samuel HATTON, Alexander ELDER, Robert BLANCHFLOWER, James NICHOLSON, William HUMPHRIES, Hubert BARR, Derek DOUGAN, James McILROY, William BINGHAM

28 November 1962          Ref: Dittmar HUBER
(Switzerland)
Windsor Park, BELFAST (Att. 28,833)

NORTHERN IRELAND - POLAND
2:0 (1:0)

1:0 Crossan (9'), 2:0 Bingham (64')

NIR: (Coach: Robert PEACOCK)
Robert IRVINE, James MAGILL, Terence NEILL, Alexander ELDER, Robert BLANCHFLOWER, James NICHOLSON, William BINGHAM, John CROSSAN, Derek DOUGAN, James McILROY, Robert BRAITHWAITE

POL: (Coach: Ryszard KONCEWICZ)
Edward SZYMKOWIAK, Henryk SZCZEPAŃSKI, Stanisław OŚLIZŁO, Włodzimierz ŚPIEWAK, Antoni NIEROBA, Ryszard GRZEGORCZYK, Józef GAŁECZKA, Lucjan BRYCHCZY, Erwin WILCZEK, Roman LENTNER, Eugeniusz FABER

NORTHERN IRELAND won 4-0 on agg.

1 November 1962    Ref: Kevin HOWLEY (England)
Estadio Santiago Bernabéu, MADRID (Att. 45,000)

## SPAIN - ROMANIA
### 6:0 (4:0)

1:0 Guillot (7'), 2:0 Veloso (9'), 3:0 Collar (17'), 4:0
Guillot (20'), 5:0 Guillot (70'), 6:0 Macri (81' og)

SPA: (Coach: José VILLALONGA Llorente)
José VICENTE Train, Enrique Pérez Díaz 'PACHÍN',
Francisco Rodríguez García 'RODRI', Isacio CALLEJA
García, Francisco García Gómez 'PAQUITO', Jesús
GLARÍA Jordán, Enrique COLLAR Monterrubio,
ADELARDO Rodríguez Sánchez, José Luis Fidalgo
VELOSO, Vicente GUILLOT Fabián, Francisco
GENTO López

ROM: (Coach: Constantin TEASCĂ)
Vasile SFETCU, Mircea GEORGESCU, Ion
NUNWEILLER, Dumitru MACRI, Emil PETRU,
Constantin KOSZKA, Zoltan IVANSUC, Titus OZON,
Marin VOINEA, Dumitru POPESCU, Vasile GERGELY


25 November 1962    Ref: Georgios PELOMIS
(Greece)
Stadionul 23 August, BUCHAREST (Att. 72,762)

## ROMANIA - SPAIN
### 3:1 (2:0)

1:0 Tătaru (2'), 2:0 Manolache (8'), 3:0 Constantin
(61'), 3:1 Veloso (65')

ROM: (Coach: Gheorghe POPESCU)
Ion VOINESCU, Corneliu POPA, Ion NUNWEILLER,
Dumitru IVAN, Emil PETRU, Constantin KOSZKA,
Ion PIRCĂLAB, Gheorghe CONSTANTIN, Cicerone
MANOLACHE, Vasile GERGELY, Nicolae TĂTARU

SPA: (Coach: José VILLALONGA Llorente)
José VICENTE Train, Feliciano Muñoz RIVILLA,
Isacio CALLEJA García, Francisco García Gómez
'PAQUITO', Jesús GLARÍA Jordán, Enrique COLLAR
Monterrubio, AMANCIO Amaro Varela, José Luis
Fidalgo VELOSO, Vicente GUILLOT Fabián, Francisco
GENTO López, Francisco Rodríguez García 'RODRI'

SPAIN won 7-3 on agg.


4 November 1962            Ref: Alois OBTULOVIČ
                                (Czechoslovakia)
Stadion J.N.A., BELGRADE (Att. 25,430)

YUGOSLAVIA - BELGIUM
3:2 (2:1)

1:0 Skoblar (12'), 1:1 Stockman (26'), 2:1 Skoblar (32'
pen.), 2:2 Jurion (58'),3:2 Vasović (88')

YUG:   (Coach:   Ljubomir   LOVRIĆ,   Prvoslav
MIHAJLOVIĆ, Hugo RUŠEVLJANIN)
Milutin ŠOŠKIĆ, Slavko SVINJAREVIĆ, Fahrudin
JUSUFI, Petar RADAKOVIĆ, Velibor VASOVIĆ, Željko
PERUŠIĆ, Spasoje SAMARDŽIĆ, Vojislav MELIĆ,
Slaven ZAMBATA, Milan GALIĆ, Josip SKOBLAR

BEL: (Coach: Arthur CEULEERS, Constant VANDEN
STOCK)
Jean NICOLAY, Yves BARÉ, Georges HEYLENS,
Pierre HANON, Lucien SPRONCK, Laurent VERBIEST,
Joseph JURION, Paul VAN HIMST, Jacques
STOCKMAN, Paul VAN DEN BERG, Wilfried PUIS


31 March 1963         Ref: Vicente José CABALLERO
                            Camacho (Spain)
Stade du Heysel, BRUSSELS (Att. 24,583)

## BELGIUM - YUGOSLAVIA
## 0:1 (0:1)

### 0:1 Galić (21')

BEL: (Coach: Arthur CEULEERS, Constant VANDEN STOCK)
Jean NICOLAY, Georges HEYLENS, Jean CORNELIS, Pierre HANON, Laurent VERBIEST, Martin LIPPENS, Jacques STOCKMAN, Paul VAN DEN BERG, Paul VAN HIMST, Joseph JURION, Wilfried PUIS

YUG: (Coach: Ljubomir LOVRIĆ, Prvoslav MIHAJLOVIĆ, Hugo RUŠEVLJANIN)
Milutin ŠOŠKIĆ, Novak TOMIĆ, Mirsad FAZLAGIĆ, Velibor VASOVIĆ, Željko PERUŠIĆ, Spasoje SAMARDŽIĆ, Đorđe PAVLIĆ, Milan GALIĆ, Vojislav MELIĆ, Josip SKOBLAR, Vladimir POPOVIĆ

YUGOSLAVIA won 4-2 on agg.

7 November 1962          Ref: Józef KOWAL (Poland)
Népstadion, BUDAPEST (Att. 40,000)

### HUNGARY - WALES
### 3:1 (2:1)

1:0 Albert (6'), 1:1 Medwin (18'), 2:1 Tichy (35'), 3:1 Sándor (48')

HUN: (Coach: Lajos BARÓTI)
Antal SZENTMIHÁLYI, Sándor MÁTRAI, Kálmán MÉSZÖLY, Kálmán SÓVÁRI, Ernő SOLYMOSI, Ferenc SIPOS, Károly SÁNDOR, János GÖRÖCS, Flórián ALBERT, Lajos TICHY, Máté FENYVESI

WAL: (Coach: Selection Committee)
Anthony MILLINGTON, Stuart WILLIAMS, Melvyn HOPKINS, Terrence HENNESSEY, Melvyn NURSE,

Victor CROWE, Terence MEDWIN, Ivor ALLCHURCH,
Melfyn CHARLES, Royston VERNON, Barrie JONES

20 March 1963                 Ref: Samuel SPILLANE
                              (Republic of Ireland)
Ninian Park, CARDIFF (Att. 30,413)

### WALES - HUNGARY
### 1:1 (1:0)

1:0 C. Jones (23' pen.), 1:1 Tichy (77' pen.)

WAL: (Coach: Selection Committee)
David HOLLINS, Stuart WILLIAMS, Graham
WILLIAMS, Terrence HENNESSEY, Michael
ENGLAND, Alwyn BURTON, Barrie JONES, Phillip
WOOSNAM, Graham MOORE, Ivor ALLCHURCH,
Clifford JONES

HUN: (Coach: Lajos BARÓTI)
Antal SZENTMIHÁLYI, Sándor MÁTRAI, Kálmán
MÉSZÖLY, László SÁROSI, Ernő SOLYMOSI, Ferenc
SIPOS, Károly SÁNDOR, János GÖRÖCS, Flórián
ALBERT, Lajos TICHY, Máté FENYVESI

HUNGARY won 4-2 on agg.

7 November 1962     Ref: SEMIH Zoroğlu (Turkey)
Stadion Vasil Levski, SOFIA (Att. 31,318)

### BULGARIA - PORTUGAL
### 3:1 (0:0)

0:1 Eusébio (49'), 1:1 Asparuhov (65'), 2:1 Asparuhov
(72'), 3:1 Diev (77')

BUL: (Coach: Georgi PACHEDZHIEV)
Georgi NAYDENOV I, Vasil METODIEV, Ivan

DIMITROV, Dobromir ZHECHEV, Dimo DIMOV, Nikola KOVACHEV, Todor DIEV, Dimitar YAKIMOV, Georgi ASPARUHOV, Hristo ILIEV, Ivan KOLEV

POR: (Coach: José Maria ANTUNES)
Alberto da COSTA PEREIRA, ÂNGELO Gaspar Martins, Fernando da Conceição CRUZ, Domiciano Barrocal Gomes CAVÉM, Raúl Martins MACHADO, José CARLOS da Silva, António José SIMÕES da Costa, EUSÉBIO da Silva Ferreira, HERNÂNI Ferreira da Silva, Mário Esteves COLUNA, Manuel SERAFIM Monteiro Pereira


16 December 1962          Ref: Henri FAUCHEUX
                                              (France)
Estádio do Restelo, LISBON (Att. 25,836)

PORTUGAL - BULGARIA
3:1 (2:0)

1:0 Hernâni (4'), 2:0 Hernâni (27'), 3:0 Coluna (54'),
3:1 Iliev (84')

POR: (Coach: José Maria ANTUNES)
Alberto da COSTA PEREIRA, ÂNGELO Gaspar Martins, Fernando da Conceição CRUZ, Mário Esteves COLUNA, Raúl Martins MACHADO, José CARLOS da Silva, JOSÉ AUGUSTO Pinto de Almeida, EUSÉBIO da Silva Ferreira, Augusto Francisco ROCHA, HERNÂNI Ferreira da Silva, António José SIMÕES da Costa

BUL: (Coach: Georgi PACHEDZHIEV)
Georgi NAYDENOV I, Vasil METODIEV, Ivan DIMITROV, Hristo ILIEV, Ivan VUTSOV, Dimo DIMOV, Todor DIEV, Stefan ABADZHIEV, Georgi ASPARUHOV, Ivan KOLEV, Nikola KOVACHEV

4-4 on agg.

## PLAY-OFF

23 January 1963          Ref: Giuseppe ADAMI (Italy)
Stadio Olimpico, ROME (ITALY) (Att. 2,336)

### BULGARIA - PORTUGAL
1:0 (0:0)

1:0 Asparuhov (86')

BUL: (Coach: Georgi PACHEDZHIEV, Béla VOLENTIK)
Yordan YOSIFOV, Vasil METODIEV, Ivan DIMITROV, Ivan VUTSOV, Petar VELICHKOV, Nikola KOVACHEV, Todor DIEV, Stefan ABADZHIEV, Georgi ASPARUHOV, Hristo ILIEV, Spiro DEBARSKI

POR: (Coach: José Maria ANTUNES)
Alberto da COSTA PEREIRA, Alberto Augusto Antunes FESTA, Fernando da Conceição CRUZ, Mário Esteves COLUNA, Raúl Martins MACHADO, António Manuel Louro PAULA, António José SIMÕES da Costa, Joaquim SANTANA da Silva Guimarães, José Augusto da Costa Sénica TORRES, Augusto Francisco ROCHA, Manuel SERAFIM Monteiro Pereira

11 November 1962     Ref: Joaquim Fernandes dos CAMPOS (Portugal)
Olympisch Stadion, AMSTERDAM (Att. 64,350)

### NETHERLANDS - SWITZERLAND
3:1 (1:1)

1:0 Van der Linden (11'), 1:1 Hertig (43'), 2:1 Swart (75'), 3:1 Groot (76')

NET: (Coach: Alexandru SCHWARTZ)
Petrus VAN DER MERWE, Augustinus HAAK, Anton PRONK, Pieter OUDERLAND, Gerardus

VAN WISSEN, Bernardus MULLER, Jesaia SWART,
Hendrik GROOT, Anthonie VAN DER LINDEN,
Jacobus PRINS, Mathijs CLAVAN

SWI: (Coach: Karl RAPPAN)
Felix ANSERMET, Heinz SCHNEITER, Ely
TACCHELLA, André GROBÉTY, Jakob KUHN, Paul
STEHRENBERGER, Charles HERTIG, Norbert
ESCHMANN, Roger VONLANTHEN, Philippe
POTTIER, Anton ALLEMANN

31 March 1963       Ref: Josef KANDLBINDER
(West Germany)
Wankdorf Stadion, BERNE (Att. 31,794)

SWITZERLAND - NETHERLANDS
1:1 (0:1)

0:1 Kruiver (7'), 1:1 Allemann (72')

SWI: (Coach: Karl RAPPAN)
Karl ELSENER, Heinz SCHNEITER, Werner
LEIMGRUBER, André GROBÉTY, Hans WEBER, Ely
TACCHELLA, Bruno BRIZZI, Rolf WÜTHRICH, Jakob
KUHN, Walter HEURI, Anton ALLEMANN

NET: (Coach: Alexandru SCHWARTZ)
Eduard PIETERS GRAAFLAND, Augustinus HAAK,
Anton PRONK, Pieter OUDERLAND, Gerardus VAN
WISSEN, Jean KLAASSENS, Jesaia SWART, Hendrik
GROOT, Pieter KRUIVER, Marinus BENNAARS,
Coenraad MOULIJN

NETHERLANDS won 4-2 on agg.

21 November 1962     Ref: Sergeiy ALIMOV (USSR)
Walter-Ulbricht-Stadion, EAST BERLIN (Att. 22,077)

## EAST GERMANY - CZECHOSLOVAKIA
## 2:1 (0:0)

1:0 Erler (60'), 2:0 Liebrecht (80' pen.), 2:1 Kučera (90')

EGR: (Coach: Károly SÓS)
Horst WEIGANG, Klaus URBANCZYK, Werner
HEINE, Hans-Dieter KRAMPE, Manfred KAISER,
Kurt LIEBRECHT, Henning FRENZEL, Dieter ERLER,
Peter DUCKE, Günter SCHRÖTER, Roland DUCKE

CZE: (Coach: Rudolf VYTLACIL)
Viliam SCHROJF, Jan LÁLA, Svatopluk PLUSKAL,
Jiří TICHÝ, Ladislav NOVÁK, Andrej KVAŠŇÁK, Josef
MASOPUST, Tomáš POSPÍCHAL, Josef KADRABA,
Rudolf KUČERA, František VALOŠEK

31 March 1963          Ref: Károly BALLA (Hungary)
Strahov Stadion, PRAGUE (Att. 19,504)

## CZECHOSLOVAKIA - EAST GERMANY
## 1:1 (0:0)

1:0 Mašek (66'), 1:1 P.Ducke (85')

CZE: (Coach: Rudolf VYTLACIL)
Vladimír MOKROHAJSKÝ, Jan LÁLA, Svatopluk
PLUSKAL, Ján POPLUHÁR, Ladislav NOVÁK, Andrej
KVAŠŇÁK, Josef MASOPUST, Tomáš POSPÍCHAL,
Adolf SCHERER, Rudolf KUČERA, Václav MAŠEK

EGR: (Coach: Károly SÓS)
Harald FRITZSCHE, Klaus URBANCZYK, Werner
HEINE, Hans-Dieter KRAMPE, Manfred KAISER,
Kurt LIEBRECHT, Henning FRENZEL, Dieter ERLER,
Peter DUCKE, Jürgen NÖLDNER, Roland DUCKE

EAST GERMANY won 3-2 on agg.

2 December 1962          Ref: Lucien VAN NUFFEL
(Belgium)
Stadio Comunale, BOLOGNA (Att. 26,553)

## ITALY - TURKEY
## 6:0 (4:0)

1:0 Rivera (15'), 2:0 Orlando (22'), 3:0 Orlando (29'),
4:0 Orlando (35'), 5:0 Rivera (47'), 6:0 Orlando (85')

ITA: (Coach: Edmondo FABBRI)
William NEGRI, Cesare MALDINI, Vincenzo
ROBOTTI, Paride TUMBURUS, Francesco JANICH,
Romano FOGLI, Alberto ORLANDO, Giacomo
BULGARELLI, Angelo SORMANI, Giovanni RIVERA,
Ezio PASCUTTI

TUR: (Coach: Ljubomir SPAJIĆ)
ÖZCAN Arkoç, CANDEMIR Berkman, AHMET
Berman, SUAT Mamat, NAÇI Erdem, MUSTAFA
Yürür, TARIK Kutver, ŞEREF Has, ŞENOL Birol,
METIN Oktay, KADRI Aytaç

27 March 1963          Ref: Dimitar RUMENCHEV
(Bulgaria)
Mithatpaşa Stadi, ISTANBUL (Att. 27,290)

## TURKEY - ITALY
## 0:1 (0:0)
## 0:1 Sormani (86')

TUR: (Coach: BÜLENT Eken)
TURGAY Şeren, MUZAFFER Sipahi, SÜREYYA
Özkefe, ÖZER Kanra, GÜNGÖR Tetik, ISMET Yurtsu,
OGÜN Altiparmak, ŞEREF Has, NEDIM Doğan, SUAT
Mamat, UĞUR Köken

ITA: (Coach: Edmondo FABBRI)
Lido VIERI, Cesare MALDINI, Giacinto FACCHETTI,

Paride TUMBURUS, Alessandro SALVADORE, Giovanni TRAPATTONI, Alberto ORLANDO, Giorgio PUIA, Angelo SORMANI, Mario CORSO, Giampaolo MENICHELLI

ITALY won 7-0 on agg.

GREECE withdrew. ALBANIA was given a walkover to the next round.

BYES: AUSTRIA, LUXEMBOURG, USSR

## FIRST ROUND

30 May 1963          Ref: Cesare JONNI (Italy)
Estadio San Mamés, BILBAO (Att. 27,960)
### SPAIN - NORTHERN IRELAND
1:1 (0:0)

1:0 Amancio (58'), 1:1 W. Irvine (76')

SPA: (Coach: José VILLALONGA Llorente)
José VICENTE Train, Feliciano Muñoz RIVILLA, Luis María ETXEBERRIA Igartua, Severino REIJA Vázquez, Francisco García Gómez 'PAQUITO', Enrique Pérez Díaz 'PACHÍN', AMANCIO Amaro Varela, FÉLIX RUIZ Gabarri, Emilio MOROLLÓN Estébanez, ADELARDO Rodríguez Sánchez, Enrique COLLAR Monterrubio

NIR: (Coach: Robert PEACOCK)
Robert IRVINE, James MAGILL, Martin HARVEY, Terence NEILL, Alexander ELDER, William McCULLOUGH, William BINGHAM, John CROSSAN, William IRVINE, William HUMPHRIES, Robert BRAITHWAITE

30 October 1963          Ref: Andries VAN LEEUWEN
(Netherlands)
Windsor Park, BELFAST (Att. 45,809)

NORTHERN IRELAND - SPAIN
0:1 (0:0)

0:1 Gento (66')

NIR: (Coach: Robert PEACOCK)
Victor HUNTER, James MAGILL, John PARKE, Martin
HARVEY, Terence NEILL, William McCULLOUGH,
William BINGHAM, William HUMPHRIES, Samuel
WILSON, John CROSSAN, James HILL

SPA: (Coach: José VILLALONGA Llorente)
José Casas Gris 'PEPÍN', Feliciano Muñoz RIVILLA,
Ferran OLIVELLA i Pons, Severino REIJA Vázquez,
Ignacio ZOCO Esparza, FÉLIX RUIZ Gabarri, Jesús
PEREDA Ruiz de Temiño, Luis DEL SOL Cascajares,
José Antonio ZALDÚA Urdanavia, Luis SUÁREZ
Miramontes, Francisco GENTO López

SPAIN won 2-1 on agg.


19 June 1963          Ref: Karl KAINER (Austria)
Stadion J.N.A., BELGRADE (Att. 45,098)

YUGOSLAVIA - SWEDEN
0:0

YUG: (Coach: Ljubomir LOVRIĆ, Prvoslav
MIHAJLOVIĆ, Hugo RUŠEVLJANIN)
Milutin ŠOŠKIĆ, Novak TOMIĆ, Fahrudin JUSUFI,
Vladimir POPOVIĆ, Velibor VASOVIĆ, Željko
PERUŠIĆ, Spasoje SAMARDŽIĆ, Drago SMAJLOVIĆ,
Vladimir KOVAČEVIĆ, Milan GALIĆ, Josip SKOBLAR

SWE: (Coach: Lennart NYMAN)

Bengt NYHOLM, Orvar BERGMARK, Lennart WING, Bengt GUSTAVSSON, Åke JOHANSSON, Hans MILD, Kurt HAMRIN, Torbjörn JONSSON, Prawitz ÖBERG, Lennart BACKMAN, Örjan PERSSON


18 September 1963      Ref: John TAYLOR (England)
Malmö Stadion, MALMÖ (Att. 20,774)

### SWEDEN - YUGOSLAVIA
### 3:2 (1:1)

0:1 Zambata (23'), 1:1 Persson (31'), 2:1 Persson (60'), 2:2 Galić (64'), 3:2 Bild (72')

SWE: (Coach: Lennart NYMAN)
Bengt NYHOLM, Hans ROSANDER, Lennart WING, Orvar BERGMARK, Åke JOHANSSON, Hans MILD, Lennart BACKMAN, Prawitz ÖBERG, Agne SIMONSSON, Harry BILD, Örjan PERSSON

YUG: (Coach: Ljubomir LOVRIĆ, Prvoslav MIHAJLOVIĆ, Hugo RUŠEVLJANIN)
Milutin ŠOŠKIĆ, Mirko BRAUN, Fahrudin JUSUFI, Vladimir POPOVIĆ, Velibor VASOVIĆ, Željko PERUŠIĆ, Spasoje SAMARDŽIĆ, Vojislav MELIĆ, Slaven ZAMBATA, Milan GALIĆ, Josip SKOBLAR


SWEDEN won 3-2 on agg.


29 June 1963     Ref: Johan BOSTRÖM (Sweden)
Idrætsparken, COPENHAGEN (Att. 26,640)

### DENMARK - ALBANIA
### 4:0 (3:0)

1:0 Petersen (20' pen.), 2:0 Madsen I (31'), 3:0 Clausen (40'), 4:0 Enoksen (49')

DEN: (Coach: Poul PETERSEN)
Erik Lykke SØRENSEN, Kaj JOHANSEN, Jens Jørgen HANSEN, Bent HANSEN, Birger LARSEN, Jens PETERSEN, Eyvind CLAUSEN, Ole SØRENSEN, Ole MADSEN I, Palle BRUUN, Henning ENOKSEN

ALB: (Coach: Loro BORIÇI)
Sulejman MALIQATI, Fatbardh DELIALLISI, Skënder HALILI, Fatmir FRASHËRI, Gëzim KASMI, Lin SHLLAKU, Lorenç VORFI, Mehdi BUSHATI, Pavllo BUKOVIKU, Panajot PANO, Fiqiri DURO


30 October 1963          Ref: Joseph NAUDI (Malta)
Stadiumi Qemal Stafa, TIRANA (Att. 27,765)

### ALBANIA - DENMARK
### 1:0 (1:0)

### 1:0 Pano (3')

ALB: (Coach: Zyber KONÇI)
Shefqet TOPI, Fatbardh DELIALLISI, Skënder HALILI, Ali MEMA, Lin SHLLAKU, Andon ZAHO, Mehdi BUSHATI, Panajot PANO, Pavllo BUKOVIKU, Enver IBËRSHIMI, Fatmir FRASHËRI

DEN: (Coach: Poul PETERSEN)
Erik Lykke SØRENSEN, Kaj JOHANSEN, Jens Jørgen HANSEN, Bent HANSEN, John MADSEN, Jens PETERSEN, Carl BERTELSEN, Kjeld THORST, Ole MADSEN I, John DANIELSEN, Ole SØRENSEN

DENMARK won 4-1 on agg.


11 September 1963    Ref: Arthur BLAVIER (Belgium)
Olympisch Stadion, AMSTERDAM (Att. 36,523)

### NETHERLANDS - LUXEMBOURG

1:1 (1:1)

0:1 Nuninga (5'), 1:1 May (33')

NET: (Coach: Alexandru SCHWARTZ)
Eduard PIETERS GRAAFLAND, Pieter OUDERLAND, Augustinus HAAK, Daniel SCHRIJVERS, Anton PRONK, Jean KLAASSENS, Jesaia SWART, Hendrik GROOT, Klaas NUNINGA, Anthonie VAN DER LINDEN, Coenraad MOULIJN

LUX: (Coach: Robert HEINZ)
Nicolas SCHMITT, Ernest BRENNER, Jean-Pierre HOFFSTETTER, Jean-Pierre FIEDLER, Fernand BROSIUS, François KONTER, Jean KLEIN, Adolphe SCHMIT, Louis PILOT, Paul MAY, Nicolas HOFFMANN


30 October 1963          Ref: Marcel BOIS (France)
Feyenoord Stadion, ROTTERDAM (NETHERLANDS)
(Att. 42,385)

LUXEMBOURG - NETHERLANDS
2:1 (1:1)

0:1 Dimmer (20'), 1:1 Kruiver (35'), 1:2 Dimmer (68')

LUX: (Coach: Robert HEINZ)
Nicolas SCHMITT, Ernest BRENNER, Jean-Pierre HOFFSTETTER, Jean-Pierre FIEDLER, Fernand BROSIUS, François KONTER, Jean KLEIN, Adolphe SCHMIT, Camille DIMMER, Louis PILOT, Henri KLEIN

NET: (Coach: Alexandru SCHWARTZ)
Eduard PIETERS GRAAFLAND, Augustinus HAAK, Cor VELDHOEN, Gerardus VAN WISSEN, Anton PRONK, Marinus BENNAARS, Peter GIESEN, Hendrik GROOT, Pieter KRUIVER, Petrus KEIZER, Peter PETERSEN

**LUXEMBOURG won 3-2 on agg.**


25 September 1963      Ref. Gyula GERE (Hungary)
Praterstadion, VIENNA (Att. 26,741)

### AUSTRIA - REPUBLIC OF IRELAND
### 0:0

AUT: (Coach: Karl DECKER)
Gernot FRAYDL, Peter VARGO, Erich HASENKOPF,
Rudolf OSLANSKY, Walter GLECHNER, Karl
KOLLER, Rudolf FLÖGEL, Erich HOF, Horst NEMEC,
Ernst FIALA, Johann HÖRMAYER

EIR: (Coach: Selection Committee)
Alan KELLY, William BROWNE, Thomas TRAYNOR,
Raymond BRADY, Charles HURLEY, Michael
McGRATH, John GILES, Ronald WHELAN I, Dermot
CURTIS, Ambrose FOGARTY, William TUOHY


13 October 1963      Ref: Åge POULSEN (Denmark)
Dalymount Park, DUBLIN (Att. 39,963)

### REPUBLIC OF IRELAND - AUSTRIA
### 3:2 (1:1)

0:1 Koleznik (38'), 1:1 Cantwell (45'), 2:1 Fogarty (64'),
2:2 Flögel (83'), 3:2 Cantwell (90' pen.)

EIR: (Coach: Selection Committee)
Alan KELLY, Anthony DUNNE, Thomas TRAYNOR,
Raymond BRADY, Charles HURLEY, Michael
McGRATH, John GILES, Andrew McEVOY, Noel
CANTWELL, Ambrose FOGARTY, Joseph HAVERTY

AUT: (Coach: Karl DECKER)
Gernot FRAYDL, Peter VARGO, Erich HASENKOPF,

Johann FRANK, Walter GLECHNER, Karl KOLLER,
Walter KOLEZNIK, Johannes JANK, Johann BUZEK,
Horst NEMEC, Rudolf FLÖGEL

REPUBLIC OF IRELAND won 3-2 on agg.

29 September 1963        Ref: FARUK Talu (Turkey)
Stadion Vasil Levski, SOFIA (Att. 25,947)

BULGARIA - FRANCE
1:0 (1:0)

1:0 Diev (24')

BUL: (Coach: Béla VOLENTIK)
Georgi NAYDENOV II, Aleksandar SHALAMANOV,
Ivan DIMITROV, Ivan VUTSOV, Dobromir ZHECHEV,
Stoyan KITOV, Todor DIEV, Petar VELICHKOV, Georgi
ASPARUHOV, Dimitar YAKIMOV, Ivan KOLEV

FRA: (Coach: Henri GUÉRIN)
Pierre BERNARD, Marcel ADAMCZYK, André
CHORDA, Marcel ARTELESA, Joseph BONNEL,
Yvon DOUIS, Laurent ROBUSCHI, Pierre MICHELIN,
Lucien COSSOU, THEO Szkudlapski, Jean-Louis
BURON

26 October 1963        Ref: José María ORTIZ de
Mendíbil (Spain)
Parc des Princes, PARIS (Att. 32,233)

FRANCE - BULGARIA
3:1 (1:0)

1:0 Goujon (44'), 1:1 Yakimov (75'), 2:1 Herbin (78'),
3:1 Goujon (81')

FRA: (Coach: Henri GUÉRIN)

Pierre BERNARD, Bruno RODZIK, Pierre MICHELIN, Marcel ARTELESA, André CHORDA, Robert HERBIN, Yvon DOUIS, René FERRIER, Georges LECH, Yvon GOUJON, Jean-Louis BURON

BUL: (Coach: Béla VOLENTIK)
Georgi NAYDENOV II, Vasil METODIEV, Ivan DIMITROV, Dobromir ZHECHEV, Ivan VUTSOV, Petar VELICHKOV, Stoyan KITOV, Stefan ABADZHIEV, Georgi ASPARUHOV, Dimitar YAKIMOV, Ivan KOLEV

FRANCE won 3-2 on agg.

13 October 1963          Ref: Ryszard BANASIUK
                                        (Poland)
Tsentralniy Stadion V.I. Lenina, MOSCOW
(Att. 102,358)

USSR - ITALY
2:0 (2:0)

1:0 Ponedelnik (22'), 2:0 Chislenko (42')

URS: (Coach: Konstantin BESKOV)
Ramaz URUSHADZE, Eduard DUBINSKIY, Albert SHESTERNYOV, Anatoliy KRUTIKOV, Valeriy VORONIN, Valeriy KOROLENKOV, Slava METREVELI, Igor CHISLENKO, Viktor PONEDELNIK, Valentin IVANOV, Galimzyan KHUSAINOV

ITA: (Coach: Edmondo FABBRI)
William NEGRI, Cesare MALDINI, Giacinto FACCHETTI, Aristide GUARNERI, Alessandro SALVADORE, Giovanni TRAPATTONI, Giacomo BULGARELLI, Mario CORSO, Angelo SORMANI, Giovanni RIVERA, Ezio PASCUTTI

Red Card: Pascutti (23')

10 November 1963                   Ref: Daniel MELLET
                                        (Switzerland)
Stadio Olimpico, ROME (Att. 69,567)
                    ITALY - USSR
                      1:1 (0:1)

          0:1 Gusarov (33'), 1:1 Rivera (89')

ITA: (Coach: Edmondo FABBRI)
Giuliano SARTI, Tarcisio BURGNICH, Giacinto
FACCHETTI, Aristide GUARNERI, Alessandro
SALVADORE, Giovanni TRAPATTONI, Angelo
DOMENGHINI, Giacomo BULGARELLI, Alessandro
MAZZOLA, Giovanni RIVERA, Giampaolo
MENICHELLI

URS: (Coach: Konstantin BESKOV)
Lev YASHIN, Eduard MUDRIK, Anatoliy KRUTIKOV,
Albert SHESTERNYOV, Valeriy VORONIN, Viktor
SHUSTIKOV, Igor CHISLENKO, Valentin IVANOV,
Gennadiy GUSAROV, Valeriy KOROLENKOV,
Galimzyan KHUSAINOV

USSR won 3-1 on agg.


19 October 1963              Ref: Pyotr BELOV (USSR)
Walter-Ulbricht-Stadion, EAST BERLIN (Att. 33,383)

              EAST GERMANY - HUNGARY
                      1:2 (0:1)

0:1 Bene (18'), 1:1 Nöldner (51'), 1:2 Rákosi (88')

EGR: (Coach: Károly SÓS)
Jürgen HEINSCH, Martin SKABA, Werner HEINE,
Hans-Dieter KRAMPE, Manfred KAISER, Kurt
LIEBRECHT, Rainer NACHTIGALL, Dieter ERLER,
Peter DUCKE, Jürgen NÖLDNER, Hermann STÖCKER

HUN: (Coach: Lajos BARÓTI)
Antal SZENTMIHÁLYI, Kálmán IHÁSZ, Kálmán MÉSZÖLY, László SÁROSI, István NAGY, Ernő SOLYMOSI, Károly SÁNDOR, Gyula RÁKOSI, Flórián ALBERT, Ferenc BENE, Máté FENYVESI

3 November 1963          Ref: Borče NEDELKOVSKI
                                    (Yugoslavia)
Népstadion, BUDAPEST (Att. 35,382)
             HUNGARY - EAST GERMANY
                    3:3 (2:2)

1:0 Bene (7'), 1:1 Heine (12'), 2:1 Sándor (17'), 2:2 R.Ducke (26'), 3:2 Solymosi (51' pen.), 3:3 Erler (81')

HUN: (Coach: Lajos BARÓTI)
Antal SZENTMIHÁLYI, Sándor MÁTRAI, Kálmán MÉSZÖLY, Kálmán IHÁSZ, István NAGY, Ernő SOLYMOSI, Károly SÁNDOR, Gyula RÁKOSI, Flórián ALBERT, Ferenc BENE, Máté FENYVESI

EGR: (Coach: Károly SÓS)
Jürgen HEINSCH, Klaus URBANCZYK, Werner HEINE, Hans-Dieter KRAMPE, Manfred KAISER, Kurt LIEBRECHT, Rainer NACHTIGALL, Jürgen NÖLDNER, Peter DUCKE, Dieter ERLER, Roland DUCKE

HUNGARY won 5-4 on agg.

                  QUARTER-FINALS

4 December 1963          Ref: Pierre SCHWINTE
                                    (France)
Stade Municipal, LUXEMBOURG CITY (Att. 6,921)
             LUXEMBOURG - DENMARK
                    3:3 (2:2)

1:0 Pilot (1'), 1:1 O. Madsen I (9'), 2:1 H. Klein (23'),
2:2 O. Madsen I (30'), 2:3 O. Madsen I (46'), 3:3 H.
Klein (50')

LUX: (Coach: Robert HEINZ)
Nicolas SCHMITT, Ernest BRENNER, Jean-Pierre
HOFFSTETTER, François KONTER, Fernand
BROSIUS, Adolphe SCHMIT, Jean KLEIN, Paul MAY,
Jean LÉONARD, Louis PILOT, Henri KLEIN

DEN: (Coach: Poul PETERSEN)
Erik Lykke SØRENSEN, Kaj JOHANSEN, Jens
Jørgen HANSEN, Bent HANSEN, John MADSEN,
Jens PETERSEN, Carl BERTELSEN, Kjeld THORST,
Ole MADSEN I, John DANIELSEN, Ole SØRENSEN


10 December 1963          Ref: Joseph BARBÉRAN
(France)
Idrætsparken, COPENHAGEN (Att. 36,294)

DENMARK - LUXEMBOURG
2:2 (1:1)

0:1 Léonard (13'), 1:1 O. Madsen I (16'), 2:1
O. Madsen I (70'), 2:2 Schmit (84')

DEN: (Coach: Poul PETERSEN)
Erik Lykke SØRENSEN, Kaj JOHANSEN, Jens Jørgen
HANSEN, Bent HANSEN, John MADSEN, Jens
PETERSEN, Carl BERTELSEN, John DANIELSEN,
Ole MADSEN I, Ole SØRENSEN, Henning ENOKSEN

LUX: (Coach: Robert HEINZ)
Nicolas SCHMITT, Ernest BRENNER, Jean-Pierre
HOFFSTETTER, François KONTER, Fernand
BROSIUS, Adolphe SCHMIT, Jean KLEIN, Paul MAY,
Jean LÉONARD, Louis PILOT, Henri KLEIN

5-5 on agg.

## PLAY-OFF

18 December 1963          Ref: Pieter ROOMER
(Netherlands)
Olympisch Stadion, AMSTERDAM (NETHERLANDS)
(Att. 5,700)

### DENMARK - LUXEMBOURG
### 1:0 (1:0)

1:0 O. Madsen I (43')

DEN: (Coach: Poul PETERSEN)
Erik Lykke SØRENSEN, Kaj JOHANSEN, Jens Jørgen
HANSEN, Bent HANSEN, John MADSEN, Jens
PETERSEN, Carl BERTELSEN, Kjeld THORST, Ole
MADSEN I, Henning ENOKSEN, John DANIELSEN

LUX: (Coach: Robert HEINZ)
Nicolas SCHMITT, Ernest BRENNER, Jean-Pierre
HOFFSTETTER, François KONTER, Fernand
BROSIUS, Adolphe SCHMIT, Jean KLEIN, Paul MAY,
Jean LÉONARD, Louis PILOT, Henri KLEIN

11 March 1964          Ref: Lucien VAN NUFFEL (Belgium)
Estadio Ramón Sánchez Pizjuán, SEVILLE
(Att. 27,137)

### SPAIN - REPUBLIC OF IRELAND
### 5:1 (4:1)

1:0 Amancio (12'), 2:0 Fusté (15'), 2:1 McEvoy (21'), 3:1
Amancio (29'), 4:1 Marcelino (33'), 5:1 Marcelino (88')

SPA: (Coach: José VILLALONGA Llorente)
José Ángel IRIBAR Kortajarena, Feliciano Muñoz
RIVILLA, Ferran OLIVELLA i Pons, Isacio CALLEJA
García, Ignacio ZOCO Esparza, Josep María FUSTÉ
i Blanch, AMANCIO Amaro Varela, Jesús PEREDA

Ruiz de Temiño, MARCELINO Martínez Cao, Juan Manuel VILLA Gutierrez, Carlos LAPETRA Coarasa

EIR: (Coach: Selection Committee)
Alan KELLY, Theodor FOLEY, Thomas TRAYNOR, Raymond BRADY, Charles HURLEY, Michael MEAGAN, John GILES, Andrew MCEVOY, Alfred HALE, Ambrose FOGARTY, Joseph HAVERTY


8 April 1964          Ref: Gérard VERSIJP (Belgium)
Dalymount Park, DUBLIN (Att. 38,027)

### REPUBLIC OF IRELAND - SPAIN
### 0:2 (0:1)

0:1 Zaballa (25'), 0:2 Zaballa (88')

EIR: (Coach: Selection Committee)
Alan KELLY, Anthony DUNNE, William BROWNE, Raymond BRADY, Charles HURLEY, John FULLAM, John GILES, Andrew MCEVOY, Noel CANTWELL, Patrick TURNER, Alfred HALE

SPA: (Coach: José VILLALONGA Llorente)
José Ángel IRIBAR Kortajarena, Feliciano Muñoz RIVILLA, Ferran OLIVELLA i Pons, Isacio CALLEJA García, Ignacio ZOCO Esparza, Josep María FUSTÉ i Blanch, Pedro ZABALLA Barquín, Jesús PEREDA Ruiz de Temiño, MARCELINO Martínez Cao, Juan Manuel VILLA Gutierrez, Carlos LAPETRA Coarasa

SPAIN won 7-1 on agg.


25 April 1964          Ref: Cesare JONNI (Italy)
Stade Olympique Yves-du-Manoir, COLOMBES (Att. 35,274)

### FRANCE - HUNGARY

1:3 (0:2)

0:1 Albert (15'), 0:2 Tichy (16'), 0:3 Tichy (70'), 1:3 Cossou (73')

FRA: (Coach: Henri GUÉRIN)
Pierre BERNARD, Georges CASOLARI, Pierre MICHELIN, Marcel ARTELESA, André CHORDA, Joseph BONNEL, Robert HERBIN, Lucien MULLER, Georges LECH, Nestor COMBIN, Lucien COSSOU

HUN: (Coach: Lajos BARÓTI)
Antal SZENTMIHÁLYI, Sándor MÁTRAI, Kálmán MÉSZÖLY, Ferenc SIPOS, László SÁROSI, János GÖRÖCS, István NAGY, Gyula RÁKOSI, Máté FENYVESI, Flórián ALBERT, Lajos TICHY


23 May 1964          Ref: Concetto LO BELLO (Italy)
Népstadion, BUDAPEST (Att. 70,120)

HUNGARY - FRANCE
2:1 (1:1)

0:1 Combin (2'), 1:1 Sipos (24'), 2:1 Bene (55')

HUN: (Coach: Lajos BARÓTI)
Antal SZENTMIHÁLYI, Sándor MÁTRAI, Kálmán MÉSZÖLY, Ferenc SIPOS, László SÁROSI, István NAGY, Gyula RÁKOSI, Máté FENYVESI, Károly SÁNDOR, Lajos TICHY, Ferenc BENE

FRA: (Coach: Henri GUÉRIN)
Pierre BERNARD, Georges CASOLARI, Marcel ARTELESA, Daniel CHARLES-ALFRED, André CHORDA, Joseph BONNEL, Edouard STAKO, Angel RAMBERT, Georges LECH, Nestor COMBIN, Fleury DI NALLO

HUNGARY won 5-2 on agg.

13 May 1964          Ref: James FINNEY (England)
Råsunda Stadion, SOLNA (Att. 36,937)

SWEDEN - USSR
1:1 (0:0)

0:1 Ivanov (62'), 1:1 Hamrin (87')

SWE: (Coach: Lennart NYMAN)
Arne ARVIDSSON, Hans ROSANDER, Lennart
WING, Orvar BERGMARK, Åke JOHANSSON, Hans
MILD, Kurt HAMRIN, Harry BILD, Agne SIMONSSON,
Örjan MARTINSSON, Örjan PERSSON

URS: (Coach: Konstantin BESKOV)
Lev YASHIN, Eduard MUDRIK, Albert SHESTERNYOV,
Vladimir GLOTOV, Valeriy VORONIN, Alekseiy
KORNEEV, Igor CHISLENKO, Valentin IVANOV,
Gennadiy GUSAROV, Eduard MALOFEYEV, Valeriy
KOROLENKOV


27 May 1964          Ref: Arthur HOLLAND (England)
Tsentralniy Stadion V.I. Lenina, MOSCOW
(Att. 99,609)

USSR - SWEDEN
3:1 (1:0)

1:0 Ponedelnik (32'), 2:0 Ponedelnik (56'), 2:1 Hamrin
(78'), 3:1 Voronin (83')

URS: (Coach: Konstantin BESKOV)
Lev YASHIN, Eduard MUDRIK, Albert SHESTERNYOV,
Vladimir GLOTOV, Valeriy VORONIN, Alekseiy
KORNEEV, Igor CHISLENKO, Valentin IVANOV, Viktor
PONEDELNIK, Gennadiy GUSAROV, Galimzyan
KHUSAINOV

SWE: (Coach: Lennart NYMAN)

Arne ARVIDSSON, Hans ROSANDER, Lennart WING, Orvar BERGMARK, Hans MILD, Anders SVENSSON I, Kurt HAMRIN, Harry BILD, Agne SIMONSSON, Örjan MARTINSSON, Örjan PERSSON

USSR won 4-2 on agg.

# GOALSCORERS

## 11 GOALS

Ole MADSEN I (Denmark)

## 4 GOALS

Lajos TICHY (Hungary), Alberto ORLANDO (Italy), Noel CANTWELL (Republic of Ireland)

## 3 GOALS

Georgi ASPARUHOV (Bulgaria), Lucien COSSOU, Yvon GOUJON (both France), Ferenc BENE (Hungary), Giovanni RIVERA (Italy), AMANCIO Amaro Varela, Vicente GUILLOT Fabián (both Spain), Viktor PONEDELNIK (USSR)

## 2 GOALS

Todor DIEV (Bulgaria), Carl BERTELSEN, Eyvind CLAUSEN, Henning ENOKSEN (all Denmark), Dieter ERLER (East Germany), Maryan WISNIESKI (France), Flórián ALBERT, Károly SÁNDOR (both Hungary), Ríkharður JÓNSSON (Iceland), Camille DIMMER, Henri KLEIN (both Luxembourg), Pieter KRUIVER (Netherlands), HERNÂNI Ferreira da Silva (Portugal), Ambrose FOGARTY, William TUOHY (both Republic of Ireland), MARCELINO Martínez Cao, José Fidalgo VELOSO, Pedro ZABALLA Barquín (all Spain), Kurt HAMRIN, Örjan MARTINSSON, Örjan PERSSON (all Sweden), Josip SKOBLAR, Milan GALIĆ (both Yugoslavia)


## 1 GOAL

Panajot PANO (Albania), Rudolf FLÖGEL, Walter KOLEZNIK (both Austria), Joseph JURION, Jacques STOCKMAN (both Belgium), Hristo ILIEV, Dimitar YAKIMOV (both Bulgaria), Rudolf KUČERA, Václav MAŠEK (both Czechoslovakia), Emil CHRISTIANSEN, Jens PETERSEN (both Denmark), Peter DUCKE, Roland DUCKE, Werner HEINE, Kurt LIEBRECHT, Jürgen NÖLDNER (all East Germany), Ronald FLOWERS, Robert SMITH, Robert TAMBLING (all England), Nestor COMBIN, Yvon DOUIS, Robert HERBIN (all France), Gyula RÁKOSI, Ferenc SIPOS, Ernő SOLYMOSI (all Hungary), Garðar ÁRNASON (Iceland), Angelo SORMANI (Italy), Jean LÉONARD, Paul MAY, Louis PILOT, Adolphe SCHMIT (all Luxembourg), Edward THEOBALD, Joseph URPANI (both Malta), Hendrik GROOT, Klaas NUNINGA, Jesaia SWART, Anthonie VAN DER LINDEN (all Netherlands), William BINGHAM, John CROSSAN, Derek DOUGAN, William HUMPHRIES, William IRVINE (all Northern Ireland), John KROGH (Norway), Mário Esteves COLUNA, ÉUSEBIO da Silva Ferreira (both Portugal), Andrew McEVOY (Republic of Ireland), Gheorghe CONSTANTIN, Cicerone MANOLACHE, Nicolae TĂTARU (all Romania), Enrique COLLAR Monterrubio, Josep María FUSTÉ Blanch, Francisco GENTO López (all Spain), Harry BILD, Leif ERIKSSON (both Sweden), Anton ALLEMANN, Charles HERTIG (both Switzerland), Igor CHISLENKO, Gennadiy GUSAROV, Valentin IVANOV, Valeriy VORONIN (all USSR), Clifford JONES, Terence MEDWIN (both Wales), Velibor VASOVIĆ, Slaven ZAMBATA (both Yugoslavia)

# OWN-GOALS

## Dumitru MACRI (Romania) vs Spain

# FINAL TOURNAMENT

# (SPAIN - 17-21 JUNE 1964)

## VENUES (Stadia)

BARCELONA (Camp Nou), MADRID (Estadio Santiago Bernabéu)

-----

## SEMI-FINALS & THIRD PLACE MATCH

### SPAIN vs HUNGARY

The opening semi-final saw the hosts take on Hungary in Madrid, and it was the guests who had the better of the early exchanges. José Iribar had to be at his best to turn a fierce drive from Imre Komora round the post. Spain then began to get a grip of the game, and they took the lead in the thirty-fifth minute when Jesús Pereda leapt superbly to head home Amancio's cross from the right.

In the second half, the hosts' most influential player, Luis Suárez, was slowed up by injury, and as the game entered the latter stages they were desperately hanging on to their lead – but just six minutes from the end, Hungary equalised, after Iribar failed to hold on to a cross from the right and Ferenc Bene bundled the ball home from a few yards out to force extra time. The additional thirty minutes were very tense and produced nothing of note, until finally, in the 115th minute, Carlos Lapetra's corner was headed into the penalty area by Josép Fusté. Amancio, in acres of space, prodded the ball into the corner of the net to win the match for Spain.

## USSR vs DENMARK

Later that evening, the Soviet Union met Denmark in the second semi-final in Barcelona. The Danes had surprised many by getting this far, but they had had the luck of the draw in getting past relatively easy opposition in the qualifying rounds. Now they were up against the holders, and experience told, as the Soviets ran out comfortable winners.

The opening goal came in the nineteenth minute, when Valeriy Voronin shot high past Leif Nielsen following a corner; then, five misnutes from the interval, Viktor Ponedelnik ran onto a glorious pass from Igor Chislenko to make it 2-0. In the second half the Soviets were content to sit on their lead, but three minutes from the end, Valentin Ivanov went on one of his trademark dribbles past a couple of defenders before shooting low past Nielsen to put a gloss on the scoreline.

## HUNGARY vs DENMARK

The Danes put up a much better performance in the third-place match against Hungary, who were expected to win easily. The game started well enough for the Hungarians, and they took the lead in the eleventh minute through Bene, who latched onto a fine pass from Flórián Albert.

They failed to capitalise on their advantage, though, and were made to pay for their profligacy when Carl Bertelsen got in front of Kálmán Ihász to prod home Ole Sørensen's cross with eight minutes to play. The extra half-hour only came to life in the second period, when two goals in three minutes won the game for Hungary. Both of them were scored by Dezső Novák; firstly from the penalty spot after Albert was floored in the box, then from a free-kick just outside the penalty area.

## FINAL

### SPAIN vs USSR

Four years previously, political intervention had prevented Spain from travelling to the Soviet Union, but by the time both teams stepped onto the pitch at the Santiago Bernabéu stadium for their first ever meeting, diplomatic relations had been tentatively reestablished. There was only one change the teams from their respective semi-final line-ups: Alekseiy Korneev replaced Gennadiy Gusarov in the Soviet midfield.

The hosts commenced on the front foot, and Suárez was just off-target with an early free-kick, but they were celebrating moments later when Suarez's cross was missed by Albert Shesternyov and the ball bounced off Viktor Shustikov nicely into the path of Pereda, who shot past Lev Yashin from eight yards out. Within two minutes, however, the Soviet Union were level. Viktor Anichkin clipped a through ball from midfield that found Galimzyan Khusainov in acres of space, and he ran on to shoot under Iribar from just inside the penalty area. Midway through the half, Yashin made a tremendous point-blank save to deny both Pereda and Fusté; then, five minutes before the break, Iribar parried Chislenko's low shot away for a corner.

In the second half, the Spaniards began to dominate, and Amancio came close to restoring the lead, but he shot into the side netting when well-placed. The winger raced away before finding Marcelino in space, but his effort was tipped over the bar by Yashin. Pereda then ran through to score, but he was penalised for pulling back Shustikov. The Soviets came back into the game, and on the hour mark, Iribar pushed away Ponedelnik's shot. A few minutes later the Soviet forward's low left-wing cross deflected towards goal, but Ignacio Zoco managed to get back to clear just in time.

In the seventy-second minute, Spain thought they had won a penalty, as Pereda was pulled down by Anichkin; but amid vehement Spanish protests, the referee only awarded a free-kick on the edge of the box. With six minutes remaining, though, the hosts scored the winning goal. Feliciano Rivilla fed Pereda on the right wing, who ran towards the byline and crossed into the box, where Marcelino stooped acrobatically to flash a header into the corner of the net past a startled Yashin, who thought the ball was going wide. The Spaniards defended resolutely for the final few minutes to become the new European champions.

# MATCH DETAILS

## SEMI-FINALS

17 June 1964 (20.00)    Ref: Arthur BLAVIER (Belgium
Estadio Santiago Bernabéu, MADRID (Att. 34,713)

### SPAIN - HUNGARY
### 2:1 AET (1:0/1:1)

1:0 Pereda (35'), 1:1 Bene (84'), 2:1 Amancio (115')

SPA: (Coach: José VILLALONGA Llorente)
José Ángel IRIBAR Kortajarena, Feliciano Muñoz
RIVILLA, Ferran OLIVELLA i Pons (Capt.), Isacio
CALLEJA García, Ignacio ZOCO Esparza, Josep
María FUSTÉ i Blanch, AMANCIO Amaro Varela,
MARCELINO Martínez Cao, Luis SUÁREZ
Miramontes, Jesús PEREDA Ruiz de Temiño, Carlos
LAPETRA Coarasa

HUN: (Coach: Lajos BARÓTI)
Antal SZENTMIHÁLYI, Sándor MÁTRAI, Kálmán
MÉSZÖLY, László SÁROSI, István NAGY, Ferenc
SIPOS, Ferenc BENE, Imre KOMORA, Flórián
ALBERT, Lajos TICHY (Capt.), Máté FENYVESI

17 June 1964 (22.30)    Ref: Concetto LO BELLO
(Italy)
Camp Nou, BARCELONA (Att. 38,556)

### USSR - DENMARK
### 3:0 (2:0)

1:0 Voronin (19'), 2:0 Ponedelnik (40'), 3:0 Ivanov (87')

URS: (Coach: Konstantin BESKOV)
Lev YASHIN, Viktor SHUSTIKOV, Albert SHESTERNYOV, Eduard MUDRIK, Valeriy VORONIN, Viktor ANICHKIN, Igor CHISLENKO, Valentin IVANOV (Capt.), Viktor PONEDELNIK, Gennadiy GUSAROV, Galimzyan KHUSAINOV

DEN: (Coach: Poul PETERSEN)
Leif NIELSEN, Jens Jørgen HANSEN, Kaj HANSEN, Bent HANSEN, Birger LARSEN, Erling NIELSEN, Carl BERTELSEN, Ole SØRENSEN, Ole MADSEN I (Capt.), Kjeld THORST, John DANIELSEN

## THIRD PLACE MATCH

20 June 1964 (20.00)          Ref: Daniel MELLET
(Switzerland)
Camp Nou, BARCELONA (Att. 3,869)

### HUNGARY - DENMARK
3:1 AET (1:0/1:1)

1:0 Bene (11'), 1:1 Bertelsen (82'), 2:1 Novák (107' pen.), 3:1 Novák (110')

HUN: (Coach: Lajos BARÓTI)
Antal SZENTMIHÁLYI, Dezső NOVÁK, Kálmán MÉSZÖLY, Kálmán IHÁSZ, Ernő SOLYMOSI, Ferenc SIPOS (Capt.), János FARKAS, Zoltán VARGA, Flórián ALBERT, Ferenc BENE, Máté FENYVESI

DEN: (Coach: Poul PETERSEN)
Leif NIELSEN, Bent WOLMAR, Kaj HANSEN, Bent HANSEN, Birger LARSEN, Erling NIELSEN, Carl BERTELSEN, Ole SØRENSEN, Ole MADSEN I (Capt.), Kjeld THORST, John DANIELSEN

# FINAL

21 June 1964 (18.30)          Ref: Arthur HOLLAND
                                      (England)
Estadio Bernabéu, MADRID (Att. 79,115)

## SPAIN - USSR
## 2:1 (1:1)

1:0 Pereda (6'), 1:1 Khusainov (8'), 2:1 Marcelino (84')

SPA: (Coach: José VILLALONGA Llorente)
José Ángel IRIBAR Kortajarena, Feliciano Muñoz
RIVILLA, Ferran OLIVELLA i Pons (Capt.), Isacio
CALLEJA García, Ignacio ZOCO Esparza, Josep
María FUSTÉ i Blanch, AMANCIO Amaro Varela,
Jesús PEREDA Ruiz de Temiño, MARCELINO
Martínez Cao, Luis SUÁREZ Miramontes, Carlos
LAPETRA Coarasa

URS: (Coach: Konstantin BESKOV)
Lev     YASHIN,     Viktor     SHUSTIKOV,     Albert
SHESTERNYOV, Eduard MUDRIK, Valeriy VORONIN,
Viktor ANICHKIN, Igor CHISLENKO, Valentin IVANOV
(Capt.), Viktor PONEDELNIK, Alekseiy KORNEEV,
Galimzyan KHUSAINOV

# GOALSCORERS

## 2 GOALS

Ferenc BENE, Dezső NOVÁK (both Hungary), Jesús María PEREDA Ruiz de Temiño (Spain)


## 1 GOAL

Carl BERTELSEN (Denmark), AMANCIO Amaro Varela, MARCELINO Martínez Cao (both Spain), Valentin IVANOV, Galimzyan KHUSAINOV, Viktor PONEDELNIK, Valeriy VORONIN (all USSR)

# SQUADS

## DENMARK

### GOALKEEPERS

Leif NIELSEN (28.05.1942/BK Frem København), Svend Aage RASK (14.07.1935/BK 1909 Odense)

### DEFENDERS

John AMDISEN (08.07.1934/Aarhus GF), Bent HANSEN (13.09.1933/BK 1903 København), Jens Jørgen HANSEN (04.01.1939/Esbjerg forenede BK), Kaj HANSEN (16.08.1940/BK Frem København), Birger LARSEN (27.03.1942/BK Frem København), Bent WOLMAR (08.08.1937/Aarhus GF)

### MIDFIELDERS

Carl BERTELSEN (15.11.1937/Esbjerg forenede BK), Leif HARTWING (09.11.1942/BK 1909 Odense), Helge JØRGENSEN (17.09.1937/KFfUM BK (Odense)), Erling NIELSEN (02.01.1935/BK 1909 Odense), Ole SØRENSEN (25.11.1937/Kjøbenhavns BK)

### FORWARDS

John DANIELSEN (13.07.1939/BK 1909 Odense), Ole MADSEN (21.12.1934/Hellerup IK (København)), Jørgen RASMUSSEN (19.02.1937/BK 1913 Odense), Tom SØNDERGAARD (02.01.1944/BK 1893 København), Kjeld THORST (13.05.1940/Aalborg BK)

# HUNGARY

## GOALKEEPERS

József GELEI (29.06.1938/Tatabányai Bányász SC), Antal SZENTMIHÁLYI (13.06.1939/Vasas SC (Budapest))

## DEFENDERS

Kálmán IHÁSZ (06.03.1941/Vasas SC (Budapest)), Sándor MÁTRAI (20.11.1932/Ferencvárosi TC (Budapest)), Kálmán MÉSZÖLY (16.07.1941/ Vasas SC (Budapest)), Dezső NOVÁK (03.02.1939/ Ferencvárosi TC (Budapest)), László SÁROSI (27.02.1932/Vasas SC (Budapest))

## MIDFIELDERS

Imre KOMORA (05.06.1940/Budapesti Honvéd SE), István NAGY (14.04.1939/MTK Budapest), Gyula RÁKOSI (09.10.1938/Ferencvárosi TC (Budapest)), Ferenc SIPOS (13.12.1932/MTK Budapest), Ernő SOLYMOSI (21.06.1940/Újpesti Dózsa SC (Budapest))

## FORWARDS

Flórián ALBERT (15.09.1941/Ferencvárosi TC (Budapest)), Ferenc BENE (17.12.1944/Újpesti Dózsa SC (Budapest)), János FARKAS (27.03.1942/ Vasas SC (Budapest)), Máté FENYVESI (20.09.1933/ Ferencvárosi TC (Budapest)), Lajos TICHY (21.03.1935/Budapesti Honvéd SE), Zoltán VARGA (01.01.1945/Ferencvárosi TC (Budapest))

# SPAIN

## GOALKEEPERS

José Ángel IRIBAR Kortajarena (01.03.1943/Athletic Club Bilbao), José Casas Gris 'PEPÍN' (16.11.1931/ Real Betis Balompié (Seville)), Salvador SADURNÍ i Urpí (03.04.1941/FC Barcelona), José VICENTE Train (19.12.1931/Real Madrid CF)

## DEFENDERS

Isacio CALLEJA García (06.12.1936/Club Atlético de Madrid), Luis María ETXEBERRIA Igartua (24.03.1940/Athletic Club Bilbao), Ferran OLIVELLA i Pons (22.06.1936/FC Barcelona), Severino REIJA Vázquez (25.11.1938/Real Zaragoza), Feliciano Muñoz RIVILLA (21.08.1936/Club Atlético de Madrid)

## MIDFIELDERS

Luis DEL SOL Cascajares (06.04.1935/Juventus FC (Torino (ITALY)), Josep María FUSTÉ Blanch (15.04.1941/FC Barcelona), Jesús María PEREDA Ruiz de Temiño (15.06.1938/FC Barcelona), Juan Manuel VILLA Gutiérrez (26.09.1938/Real Zaragoza), Ignacio ZOCO Esparza (31.07.1939/Real Madrid CF)

## FORWARDS

AMANCIO Amaro Varela (16.10.1939/Real Madrid CF), Vicente GUILLOT Fabián (15.07.1941/Valencia CF), Carlos LAPETRA Coarasa (29.11.1938/Real Zaragoza), MARCELINO Martínez Cao (29.04.1940/ Real Zaragoza), Luis SUÁREZ Miramontes

(02.05.1935/FC Internazionale Milano (ITALY)), Pedro ZABALLA Barquín (29.07.1938/FC Barcelona)

## USSR

### GOALKEEPERS

Ramaz URASHADZE (17.08.1939/FC Torpedo Kutaisi), Lev YASHIN (22.10.1929/FK Dinamo Moskva)

### DEFENDERS

Viktor ANICHKIN (08.12.1941/FK Dinamo Moskva), Eduard DUBINSKIY (06.04.1935/TSKA Moskva), Vladimir GLOTOV (23.01.1937/FK Dinamo Moskva), Eduard MUDRIK (18.07.1939/FK Dinamo Moskva), Albert SHESTERNYOV (20.06.1941/TSKA Moskva), Viktor SHUSTIKOV (28.01.1939/FK Torpedo Moskva)

### MIDFIELDERS

Alekseiy KORNEEV (06.02.1939/FK Spartak Moskva), Yuriy SHIKONOV (08.12.1939/SKA Rostov-na-Donu), Valeriy VORONIN (17.07.1939/FK Torpedo Moskva)

### FORWARDS

Igor CHISLENKO (04.01.1939/FK Dinamo Moskva), Gennadiy GUSAROV (11.03.1937/FK Dinamo Moskva), Valentin IVANOV (19.11.1934/FK Torpedo Moskva), Galimzyan KHUSAINOV (27.06.1937/FK Spartak Moskva), Oleg KOPAYEV (28.11.1937/SKA

Rostov-na-Donu), Eduard MALOFEYEV (02.06.1942/
FK Dinamo Minsk), Viktor PONEDELNIK (22.05.1937/
SKA Rostov-na-Donu)

# 1966-1968

# QUALIFICATION

## GROUP STAGE

For this edition, the competition received a makeover, with a new format and a new name. Round-robin groups were introduced for the qualifying stage, replacing the straight knockout version. In addition, the tournament was now known as the European Championship.

Thirty-one nations took part in eight groups, with the winners of each group progressing to the quarter-finals. Four nations were making their tournament bow, with 1966 World Cup runners-up West Germany finally taking part. Also, Scotland became the last of the British nations to enter, with Cyprus and Finland the other debutants.

## GROUP 1

The holders began their defence of the trophy with a disappointing goalless draw in Dublin; then, after winning the return fixture 2-0, they followed that up with another scoreless tie in Istanbul. Czechoslovakia opened their campaign with a fine 2-0 away success in Dublin, and it was soon clear they would provide the greatest threat to Spain's chances of progressing.

Both teams comfortably beat Turkey at home. Then, in the first meeting between the two sides, the

Czechoslovaks prevailed 1-0 through an Alexander Horváth strike just after the interval. In the return match three weeks later, the Spaniards edged it 2-1. Goals from 'Pirri' and José Gárate had the home side coasting, but Ladislav Kuna's reply fifteen minutes from time had the Spanish hanging on nervously for the final whistle.

With Spain's programme now complete, they had a two point advantage over Czechoslovakia, who had two matches left to overhaul them. The first one ended in a goalless stalemate in Ankara, which left them needing only to draw with the Republic of Ireland in Prague to win the group on goal difference. It was all going to plan when the Czechoslovaks took the lead early in the second half after John Dempsey put through his own goal, but the Irish soon equalised through 'Ray' Treacy. Turlough O'Connor sensationally grabbed a winning goal for the Irish with four minutes remaining, to leave the home side stunned and gift Spain the group.

## GROUP 2

Portugal were the clear favourites after their incredible debut World Cup performance in 1966, where they had finished in third place. They were up against Bulgaria (whom they had comprehensively beaten in the group stage of that World Cup), Sweden and Norway. But in their opening game, the Portuguese suffered a shock 2-1 home reverse to the Swedes. Jaime Graça put the home side ahead midway through the first half, but Inge Danielsson soon levelled, and then the same player netted a sensational winner four minutes from time.

On the same day, Bulgaria started with a comprehensive 4-2 victory over Norway, Nikola Tsanev and Petar

Zhekov both netting a brace. The Portuguese then travelled to Scandinavia for a double header. They were seconds away from avenging their earlier defeat to the Swedes, after Custódio had given them the lead in the nineteenth minute – only for Ingvar Svensson to equalise in the final minute. A week later, however, they defeated Norway 2-1, thanks to a double from Eusébio.

The Bulgarians then undertook trips to both Nordic nations and also came away with three points. They won arguably the harder of the two matches 2-0 in Sweden, then were surprisingly held to a goalless draw in Oslo. Both Bulgaria and Portugal won at home against Sweden and Norway, respectively, to set up the final double header against each other.

Bulgaria held a two-point advantage as well as a far superior goal difference, so Portugal realistically needed to win both games, but in the first meeting in Sofia, a solitary second-half strike from Dinko Dermendzhiev was sufficient to render the return tie obsolete. It ended goalless, in any case, and the Bulgarians cruised to a place in the quarter-finals.


## GROUP 3

Having reached the Final in both of the previous tournaments and been semi-finalists in the 1966 World Cup, the Soviet Union were expected to easily steamroller their opponents. Austria were the likeliest team to offer any resistance, but they suffered an early setback when held to a goalless draw in Finland, who were making their tournament debut. Greece began with a nervy 2-1 home victory over the Finns, with the winner coming four minutes from time; then they earned a point with a 1-1 draw in the return fixture.

A month later, the Soviets commenced their programme in Moscow against Austria, which produced a classic encounter. Eduard Malofeyev fired the Soviets ahead in the twenty-fifth minute, then Anatoliy Byshovets doubled the lead with a fantastic scissor kick. Erich Hof swiftly pulled a goal back, but Igor Chislenko restored the home team's two-goal advantage just before the break. In the second half, the Austrians stormed back to level the match by the seventy-first minute through goals from Franz Wolny and Helmut Siber, but with ten minutes remaining Eduard Streltsov nodded in a cross to win the match for the home side. The Soviets then swatted the Greeks aside, 4-0, in Tbilisi before back-to-back victories over Finland put them on the verge of qualification.

Austria kept their slim hopes alive with a narrow 2-1 home win over Finland, but in their next outing they were soundly thrashed 4-1 by the Greeks in Piraeus, which eliminated them. The Soviets then suffered their first defeat in their penultimate game, going down 1-0 to the Austrians in Vienna. This left Greece still with an outside chance of overhauling them, but they were snuffed out, as Malofeyev's strike just after the break was enough to clinch the group for the Soviet Union when the two sides met in Piraeus.

The final match of the group between Austria and Greece saw the first ever abandonment in the tournament, when crowd trouble in Vienna brought proceedings to a halt in the eighty-third minute, but the 1-1 result was allowed to stand.

## GROUP 4

In the only group with just three teams, 1966 World Cup runners-up, West Germany, opened with a 6-0 thrashing of Albania in Dortmund, with the prolific 'Gerd' Müller bagging four of the goals. However, in their next match they went down 1-0 to Yugoslavia in Belgrade, with Josip Skoblar netting just after the break.

After the Yugoslavs won 2-0 in Albania, they travelled to Hamburg, knowing a draw would likely wrap up the group. The West Germans controlled the first half after 'Hannes' Löhr gave them an early lead, but in the forty-sixth minute, Slaven Zambata levelled. For a period it looked like the visitors would hang on, but two goals in the last twenty minutes from Müller and Uwe Seeler put the West Germans in the box seat.

Yugoslavia, as expected, easily beat Albania 4-0 at home, leaving the West Germans needing only to beat Albania in Tirana to win the group; but it was the Yugoslavs who were celebrating at the end of the match, as the West Germans incredibly failed to find the target, and the game ended goalless.

## GROUP 5

In the opening game, favourites Hungary travelled to Rotterdam to face the Netherlands – who weren't yet the force they would become in the 1970s, but the visitors still had to fight back from 2-0 down to earn a point. Goals from 'Miel' Pijs and 'Johan' Cruijff, who was making his international debut, had the Dutch cruising, but Dezső Molnár reduced the arrears in the seventieth minute before Kálmán Mészöly headed in the leveller two minutes from time.

Both teams then easily beat Denmark at home before the Dutch twice blew a lead away to East Germany. They led 2-0 at the break, thanks to early strikes from

Johan Mulder and 'Piet' Keizer. After Eberhard Vogel and Henning Frenzel had levelled things up, Keizer fired the Dutch ahead once more, midway through the second half, only for Frenzel to net twice in the last twelve minutes to give the East Germans victory in an enthralling match. The next game proved crucial, as the Dutch travelled to Budapest needing to take something, but they came up short despite a spirited second-half display. First-half goals from Mészöly and János Farkas put Hungary in command, then 'Wim' Suurbier pulled a goal back in the sixty-third minute, but the home team held on to win 2-1.

The Hungarians then easily won 2-0 in Denmark, to stand on the brink of qualification. Only East Germany could realistically catch them, but in their next two games away, to Denmark and the Netherlands respectively, they only gained one point. That left them four points behind their Eastern European neighbour going into the decisive clash between the pair in Budapest. Hungary only needed to draw the game, and in the end they won at a canter, with Farkas bagging a hat-trick and Frenzel's reply a mere consolation for the East Germans.

## GROUP 6

Italy were considered favourites, despite their abysmal performance at the 1966 World Cup, where they had been knocked out in the group stage, following their infamous 1-0 defeat to North Korea. The draw had been kind to the Italians when placed with Romania, Switzerland and minnows Cyprus. Romania and Switzerland opened the group when they met in Bucharest, and the home side raced into a 4-0 lead by half-time, which included a treble for Constantin Frăţilă. Although the Swiss rallied in the second period by pulling two goals back, the home side comfortably held on.

The Italians began their campaign against Romania in Naples, where the visitors took an early lead through Nicolae Dobrin, but the *Azzurri* stormed back to lead by half-time, following goals from 'Sandro' Mazzola and Virginio Depaoli. In the second half, Mazzola scored his second, with a superb lob over the keeper to secure the points.

Romania then visited Cyprus, who were making their debut, and the guests found themselves a goal down at the interval, thanks to Kostakis Pieridis' strike in the thirty-second minute. The Romanians responded in the second half by slamming in five unanswered goals, including braces for Frățilă and Mircea Dridea.

Italy found the islanders a tough nut to crack when they met in Nicosia in the next match, and it took until the seventy-sixth minute before Angelo Domenghini forced the breakthrough – then Giacinto Facchetti headed home the clincher in the dying minutes.

The next couple of games produced goal fests, with Romania involved in both. Firstly they dispatched the Cypriots with ease at home, netting seven goals without reply, and Emil Dumitru celebrating a treble this time, but they in turn amazingly conceded seven goals away to the Swiss, although they did bag a consolation near the end.

When the top two met in Bucharest, the Romanians knew that even a victory probably wouldn't be enough to secure qualification in what was their last fixture with the Italians, only a couple of points behind and with three games in hand. In the end, a tight game was settled in Italy's favour by a Mario Bertini effort from the edge of the box in the eighty-first minute.

Switzerland now took up the mantle of challenging the Italians, and after both of them had beaten Cyprus at home by the same 5-0 scoreline, their first group meeting in Berne produced a fantastic match. René-Pierre Quentin gave the Swiss the lead just after the half-hour mark. In the second period, Luigi Riva equalised with a spectacular overhead kick, only for 'Fritz' Künzli to immediately restore the home side's advantage. Just as the Swiss appeared to be contemplating victory, the Italians were awarded a penalty five minutes from the end, which the prolific Riva dispatched with ease. When the sides met on the island of Sardinia for the return tie, the Swiss needed to win in order to stay in the hunt for the qualifying spot. It took only three minutes for the Italians to squash their hopes, though, as they went in front through Mazzola, and by the end, the *Azzurri* had clinched qualification in style by winning 4-0.


## GROUP 7

This looked like being the tightest group to predict a winner when France, Belgium and Poland were drawn together with minnows Luxembourg. France had been the only one of the four to compete at the 1966 World Cup, but they had had a dreadful tournament, being knocked out in the group stage. The Poles got off to a winning start in Szczecin against the Grand Duchy. After a goalless first half, Andrzej Jarosik eventually found the net in the forty-ninth minute, and the home side went on to win comfortably 4-0.

Three weeks later, France began their campaign with a hard-fought win over Poland in Paris. Fleury Di Nallo gave *Les Bleus* the lead midway through the first half; the Poles equalised on the hour mark through a thunderous drive from Ryszard Grzegorczyk, but the home side snatched victory five minutes from time when Georges Lech controlled a cross and swivelled to net on the volley. Belgium entered the fray in the next game when they hosted the French. After a tight first period, the Belgians opened up, and star forward Paul Van Himst netted twice in the first ten minutes of the second half. Although Lech soon pulled a goal back, the home side held on for the points.

The next three games saw Luxembourg host all the other sides, with both Belgium and France winning comfortably 5-0 and 3-0 respectively, but Poland were held to a surprise goalless draw. They bounced back straight away, though, by defeating Belgium 3-1 in Chorzów, with prolific marksman Włodzimierz Lubański getting two of the goals.

The Poles then faced France in Warsaw, where if either side won they would be strong favourites to qualify. It went the way of the French, as, in one of their best ever away performances, they completely dominated the match. 'Roby' Herbin gave them an early lead, then Lucjan Brychczy brought parity briefly before Di Nallo restored the lead for France. Further goals from André Guy and Di Nallo again in the second period gave the French a comprehensive 4-1 victory.

With a game in hand over the French, the Belgians were hoping to put pressure on their neighbour when they hosted Poland, but despite Johan Devrindt twice putting them ahead, the Poles stormed back to triumph 4-2, with Janusz Żmijewski grabbing a treble. Poland now led the group on seven points, but had played all of their games. Both France and Belgium had two games each left, and one or the other would overhaul the Poles.

When the two met in Nantes, the Belgians – two points behind – had to win. They were within six minutes of doing so, after Roger Claessen had put them ahead in the first half, but Herbin popped up with an equaliser in the eighty-fourth minute. Belgium easily won their final game 3-0 at home to Luxembourg, to leave three teams on seven points each, so in the last match, France only needed to avoid defeat in Paris against the Grand Duchy to qualify. That was never in doubt, as Les Bleus eased to a 3-1 victory, with all of their goals coming from Charly Loubet.

## GROUP 8

The group was an all-British affair, with the Home International Championship doubling up as European qualifiers over two seasons. England were overwhelming favourites following their World Cup triumph on home soil in 1966, although Scotland had something to prove after failing to qualify for that tournament. However, the Scots had a disappointing start when they could only draw 1-1 with Wales in Cardiff. The match appeared to be heading for a goalless draw until 'Ron' Davies popped up in the seventy-sixth minute to put Wales ahead, but the predatory Denis Law saved Scotland with an equaliser four minutes from time.

England had a far easier time of it in their opening match, where goals from Roger Hunt and Martin Peters gave them a 2-0 victory away to Northern Ireland. On the next matchday the English cruised to a 5-1 win over Wales, while the Scots had to come from behind in Glasgow against the Northern Irish. 'Jimmy' Nicholson handed the visitors an early lead, but Scotland were ahead by half-time through strikes from 'Bobby' Murdoch and 'Bobby' Lennox, and that was how the match ended.

With the big two meeting in the next game at Wembley, England had the opportunity to put a bit of daylight between themselves and Scotland in the group, but the Scots had other ideas, as they pulled off one of their greatest victories over the 'Auld Enemy' to go top at the midway point. In the first half, Law pounced on a rebound after Gordon Banks had saved William Wallace's shot to fire Scotland ahead, and it stayed that way till the seventy-eighth minute, when Lennox slammed a superb shot past Banks from the edge of the box. 'Jackie' Charlton then pulled a goal back with six minutes remaining, but almost immediately Scotland raced up to the other end, and after some neat interplay, 'Jim' McCalliog, making his international debut, cracked in a third goal for the Scots. There was still time for 'Geoff' Hurst to notch a second goal for England in the last minute – but it was too late to save the match.

Following their fantastic win, the Scots were brought back down to earth six months later as they put in an awful performance where they lost 1-0 to the Irish in Belfast. This handed the initiative back to England, who ran out 3-0 winners in Wales. Both of the big guns won their penultimate matches; England by 2-0 against Northern Ireland, and Scotland coming from behind to beat Wales 3-2, which set up a decider in Glasgow.

Lennox had the ball in the net early on, but it was disallowed for a foul on Banks; then Peters fired England ahead after twenty minutes, but Scotland levelled before the interval with a header from John Hughes. Neither side could find the net in the second half, and the World Champions had done enough to get through to the quarter-finals.

# QUARTER-FINALS

## ENGLAND vs SPAIN

The opening tie pitted the World Champions against the reigning European Champions. The first leg at Wembley was a fairly drab affair, with the home side edging the game from a cleverly taken free-kick six minutes from time. 'Bobby' Moore tapped the ball to 'Bobby' Charlton, who evaded one of the Spaniards charging from the wall and flashed a low shot into the corner of the net.

In the second leg, England defended resolutely in the first half, but they were undone in the forty-eighth minute when Amancio fired past Peter Bonetti. Just seven minutes later, Peters headed home a corner to put England ahead in the tie. Then, with Spain pressing forward, the visitors hit them with a sucker punch in the eighty-first minute, as Norman Hunter's low drive deflected into the net and put England through to the Final Tournament.

## ITALY vs BULGARIA

Italy were strongly fancied to see off Bulgaria, but after an action-packed first leg in Sofia, the *Azzurri* found themselves trailing in the tie. After twelve minutes, the Bulgarians opened the scoring with a soft penalty, which Nikola Kotkov dispatched with ease. The home side held the lead until the hour mark, when Italy equalised through an unfortunate own-goal from Dimitar Penev, but in the next twelve minutes, goals from Dermendzhiev and Zhekov put Bulgaria back in control – only for Pierino Prati to net a second goal for the Italians near the end, leaving the tie finely balanced.

The return leg, staged in the intimidating cauldron of Naples, was expected to be too much for the Bulgarians to handle, and so it proved. Prati levelled the tie on aggregate with a sublime diving header in the fourteenth minute. Dino Zoff, making his debut, did have a couple of anxious moments, but after Domenghini had doubled Italy's lead early in the second period, the home side strolled to a place in the Finals.

## YUGOSLAVIA vs FRANCE

France and Yugoslavia had been involved in some notably tight clashes down the years, and the first leg of their latest meeting was no different. The match only came to life midway through the second half, when Vahidin Musemić rose to head home a free-kick from Dragan Džajić, but Di Nallo saved the French from defeat when he slotted past the keeper twelve minutes from the end.

In contrast, the second leg was anything but tight, as the Yugoslavs destroyed the French in a blistering first-half onslaught. Only three minutes into the game, Ilija Petković shot the opening goal, and not long afterwards, Musemić doubled the lead. Further strikes from Džajić and Petković again put the tie out of sight. Di Nallo did pull a goal back before the break, but near the end Musemić added his second to give Yugoslavia an emphatic 5-1 victory.

## USSR vs HUNGARY

The final quarter-final tie renewed the rivalry between Hungary and the Soviet Union. They'd met at the same stage of the 1966 World Cup, with the Soviets coming out on top, so the Hungarians were out for revenge in the first leg in Budapest – and they got it. Farkas fired the *Magyars* ahead midway through the first half, and later on János Göröcs gave them the cushion of a two-goal lead, with a tap in from six yards out.

In the first half of the return leg, the Hungarians defended stoutly and were behind only to an unfortunate own-goal, when Ernő Solymosi couldn't get out the way of a powerful shot from Anatoliy Banishevskiy and turned the ball into his own net. The Soviets turned up the heat in the second period, and it wasn't long before Murtaz Khurtsilava levelled the tie. In the seventy-second minute, Byshovets ran onto a through pass to net superbly and put the Soviet Union into the Finals for the third consecutive time.

# MATCH DETAILS

<u>GROUP 1</u> (Czechoslovakia, Republic of Ireland,
Spain, Turkey)

23 October 1966     Ref: Hans CARLSSON (Sweden)
Dalymount Park, DUBLIN (Att. 38,877)

### REPUBLIC OF IRELAND - SPAIN
### 0:0

<u>EIR:</u> (Coach: Selection Committee)
Alan KELLY, Séamus BRENNAN, Noel CANTWELL,
Michael MEAGAN, Anthony DUNNE, John GILES,
James CONWAY, Francis O'NEILL, Andrew McEVOY,
Raymond TREACY, Anthony O'CONNELL

<u>SPA:</u> (Coach: José VILLALONGA Llorente)
José Ángel IRIBAR Kortajarena, Manuel SANCHÍS
Martínez, Francisco SANTAMARÍA Mirones, Severino
REIJA Vázquez, Jesús GLARÍA Jordán, José Luis
VIOLETA Lajusticia, Luciano Sánchez Rodríguez
'VAVÁ', Fernando ANSOLA San Martín, LUIS
Aragonés Suárez, MARCIAL Manuel Pina Morales,
Francisco García Gómez 'PAQUITO'

16 November 1966          Ref: Tage SØRENSEN
                                (Denmark)

Dalymount Park, DUBLIN (Att. 22,480)

### REPUBLIC OF IRELAND - TURKEY
### 2:1 (0:0)

1:0 O'Neill (60'), 2:0 McEvoy (74'), 2:1 Ogün (88')

EIR: (Coach: Selection Committee)
Patrick DUNNE, Séamus BRENNAN, Charles HURLEY, Michael MEAGAN, Anthony DUNNE, James CONWAY, Eamon DUNPHY, Francis O'NEILL, John GILES, Andrew McEVOY, Joseph HAVERTY

TUR: (Coach: ADNAN Süvari)
ALI Artuner, TALAT Özkarsli, ERCAN Aktuna, YILMAZ Şen, FEHMI Sağinoğlu, AYHAN Elmastaşoğlu, ŞEREF Has, NEVZAT Güzerlirmak, OGÜN Altiparmak, FEVZI Zemzem, FARUK Karadoğan

7 December 1966          Ref: Pieter ROOMER
                                              (Netherlands)
Estadio Mestalla, VALENCIA (Att. 25,000)

SPAIN - REPUBLIC OF IRELAND
2:0 (2:0)

1:0 José María (21'), 2:0 'Pirri' (35')

SPA: (Coach: Domènec BALMANYA i Perera)
José Ángel IRIBAR Kortajarena, Manuel SANCHÍS Martínez, Francisco Fernández Rodríguez 'GALLEGO', Severino REIJA Vázquez, José Luis VIOLETA Lajusticia, Francisco García Gómez 'PAQUITO', Vicente Anastasio JARA Segovia, José Martínez Sánchez 'PIRRI', Fernando ANSOLA San Martín, LUIS Aragonés Suárez, JOSÉ MARÍA García Lavilla

EIR: (Coach: Selection Committee)
Alan KELLY, Séamus BRENNAN, Charles HURLEY, John DEMPSEY, Anthony DUNNE, Eamon DUNPHY, Michael MEAGAN, Francis O'NEILL, James CONWAY, Alfred HALE, Joseph HAVERTY

1 February 1967          Ref: Gyula GERE (Hungary)
Ali Sami Yen Stadi, ISTANBUL (Att. 27,262)

## TURKEY - SPAIN
### 0:0

TUR: (Coach: ADNAN Süvari)
ALI Artuner, TALAT Özkarsli, YILMAZ Şen, ERCAN Aktuna, YUSUF Tunaoğlu, ŞEREF Has, NEVZAT Güzerlirmak, OGÜN Altiparmak, FEVZI Zemzem, FARUK Karadoğan, FEHMI Sağinoğlu

SPA: (Coach: Domènec BALMANYA i Perera)
José Ángel IRIBAR Kortajarena, Manuel SANCHÍS Martínez, Francisco Fernández Rodríguez 'GALLEGO', José Luis VIOLETA Lajusticia, Severino REIJA Vázquez, José Martínez Sánchez 'PIRRI', Francisco García Gómez 'PAQUITO', Manuel VELÁZQUEZ Villaverde, AMANCIO Amaro Varela, Ramón Moreno GROSSO, JOSÉ MARÍA García Lavilla


22 February 1967          Ref: Dimitar RUMENCHEV
(Bulgaria)
19 Mayis Stadi, ANKARA (Att. 31,063)

## TURKEY - REPUBLIC OF IRELAND
### 2:1 (1:0)

1:0 Ayhan (35'), 2:0 Ogün (79'), 2:1 Cantwell (89')

TUR: (Coach: ADNAN Süvari)
ALI Artuner, ŞÜKRÜ Birant, TALAT Özkarsli, ERCAN Aktuna, FEHMI Sağinoğlu, AYHAN Elmastaşoğlu, ŞEREF Has, ERGÜN Acuner, OGÜN Altiparmak, ABDULLAH Çevrim, FARUK Karadoğan

EIR: (Coach: Selection Committee)
Alan KELLY, Joseph KINNEAR, Charles HURLEY, Alphonse FINUCANE, Michael MCGRATH, Michael

MEAGAN, John GILES, Francis O'NEILL, Charles
GALLAGHER, Noel CANTWELL, Eamon DUNPHY


21 May 1967          Ref: Robert SCHAUT (Belgium)
Dalymount Park, DUBLIN (Att. 6,257)

### REPUBLIC OF IRELAND - CZECHOSLOVAKIA
### 0:2 (0:1)

0:1 Szikora (16'), 0:2 Masný (47')

EIR: (Coach: Selection Committee)
Alan KELLY, Theodor FOLEY, John DEMPSEY,
Alphonse FINUCANE, Charles HURLEY, Michael
MEAGAN, Charles GALLAGHER, Andrew McEVOY,
Raymond TREACY, Eamon DUNPHY, Oliver CONMY

CZE: (Coach: Jozef MARKO)
Ivo VIKTOR, Jan LÁLA, Kamil MAJERNÍK, Ján
POPLUHÁR, Vladimír TÁBORSKÝ, Ján GELETA,
Andrej KVAŠŇÁK, Juraj SZIKORA, Vojtěch MASNÝ,
Jozef ADAMEC, Dušan KABÁT


31 May 1967          Ref: Dittmar HUBER (Switzerland)
Estadio San Mamés, BILBAO (Att. 27,336)

### SPAIN - TURKEY
### 2:0 (0:0)

Grosso (63'), 2:0 Gento (81')

SPA: (Coach: Domènec BALMANYA i Perera)
José Ángel IRIBAR Kortajarena, Manuel SANCHÍS
Martínez, Francisco Fernández Rodríguez 'GALLEGO',
Severino REIJA Vázquez, Francisco García Gómez
'PAQUITO', Jesús GLARÍA Jordán, José Armando
UFARTE Ventoso, ADELARDO Rodríguez Sánchez,
Ramón Moreno GROSSO, JOSÉ MARÍA García
Lavilla, Francisco GENTO López

TUR: (Coach: ADNAN Süvari)
ALI Artuner, ŞÜKRÜ Birant, TALAT Özkarsli, YILMAZ
Şen, FEHMI Sağinoğlu, AYHAN Elmastaşoğlu,
ŞEREF Has, ERGÜN Acuner, OGÜN Altiparmak,
FEVZI Zemzem, FARUK Karadoğan


18 June 1967          Ref: Paul SCHILLER (Austria)
Tehelné pole, BRATISLAVA (Att. 17,839)

CZECHOSLOVAKIA - TURKEY
3:0 (1:0)

1:0 Adamec (25'), 2:0 Adamec (70'), 3:0 Jurkanin (74')

CZE: (Coach: Jozef MARKO)
Ivo VIKTOR, Jan LÁLA, Kamil MAJERNÍK, Ján
POPLUHÁR, Vladimír TÁBORSKÝ, Ján GELETA,
Andrej KVAŠŇÁK, Bohumil VESELÝ, Josef
JURKANIN, Jozef ADAMEC, Dušan KABÁT

TUR: (Coach: ADNAN Süvari)
ALI Artuner, ŞÜKRÜ Birant, HÜSEYIN Yazici, TALAT
Özkarsli, FEHMI Sağinoğlu, ABDULLAH Çevrim,
ŞEREF Has, NEVZAT Güzerlirmak, OGÜN Altiparmak,
FEVZI Zemzem, ERGÜN Acuner


1 October 1967          Ref: Gerhard SCHULENBERG
                                   (West Germany)
Stadión dr. Vacka, PRAGUE (Att. 20,354)

CZECHOSLOVAKIA - SPAIN
1:0 (0:0)

1:0 Horváth (47')

CZE: (Coach: Jozef MARKO)
Ivo VIKTOR, Jan LÁLA, Alexander HORVÁTH, Ján
POPLUHÁR, Vladimír TÁBORSKÝ, Ján GELETA,

Ladislav KUNA, Bohumil VESELÝ, Juraj SZIKORA, Jozef ADAMEC, Dušan KABÁT

SPA: (Coach: Domènec BALMANYA i Perera)
José Ángel IRIBAR Kortajarena, Manuel SANCHÍS Martínez, Antonio Alfonso Moreno 'TONONO', Severino REIJA Vázquez, José Martínez Sánchez 'PIRRI', Francisco Fernández Rodríguez 'GALLEGO', AMANCIO Amaro Varela, Ramón Moreno GROSSO, MARCELINO Martínez Cao, ADELARDO Rodríguez Sánchez, JOSÉ MARÍA García Lavilla

22 October 1967          Ref: Antonio SBARDELLA
                                            (Italy)
Estadio Santiago Bernabéu, MADRID (Att. 25,314)

SPAIN - CZECHOSLOVAKIA
2:1 (1:0)

1:0 'Pirri' (33'), 2:0 Gárate (62'), 2:1 Kuna (75')

SPA: (Coach: Domènec BALMANYA i Perera)
José Ángel IRIBAR Kortajarena, Manuel Fernández OSORIO, Antonio Alfonso Moreno 'TONONO', Francisco Fernández Rodríguez 'GALLEGO', Severino REIJA Vázquez, José Martínez Sánchez 'PIRRI', MARCIAL Manuel Pina Morales, AMANCIO Amaro Varela, LUIS Aragonés Suárez, José Eulogio GÁRATE Ormaechea, JOSÉ MARÍA García Lavilla

CZE: (Coach: Jozef MARKO)
Ivo VIKTOR, Jan LÁLA, Alexander HORVÁTH, Ján POPLUHÁR, Vladimír TÁBORSKÝ, Ján GELETA, Ladislav KUNA, Bohumil VESELÝ, Juraj SZIKORA, Vojtěch MASNÝ, Jaroslav BOROŠ

15 November 1967          Ref: Nicolae MIHĂILESCU
(Romania)
19 Mayis Stadi, ANKARA (Att. 19,760)

## TURKEY - CZECHOSLOVAKIA
## 0:0

TUR: (Coach: ADNAN Süvari)
ALI Artuner, TALAT Özkarsli, YILMAZ Şen, ERCAN
Aktuna, FEHMI Sağinoğlu, NEVZAT Güzerlirmak,
SANLI Sarialioğlu, AYHAN Elmastaşoğlu, OGÜN
Altiparmak, FEVZI Zemzem, FARUK Karadoğan

CZE: (Coach: Jozef MARKO)
Ivo VIKTOR, Jan LÁLA, Andrej KVAŠŇÁK, Ján
POPLUHÁR, Vladimír TÁBORSKÝ, Ján GELETA,
Ladislav KUNA, Vojtěch MASNÝ, Juraj SZIKORA,
Josef JURKANIN, Dušan KABÁT

22 November 1967          Ref: Erwin VETTER
(East Germany)
Stadión dr. Vacka, PRAGUE (Att. 7,615)

## CZECHOSLOVAKIA - REPUBLIC OF IRELAND
## 1:2 (0:0)

1:0Dempsey(57'og),1:1Treacy(65'),1:2O'Connor(86')

CZE: (Coach: Jozef MARKO)
Antonín KRAMERIUS, Jan LÁLA, Alexander
HORVÁTH, Ján POPLUHÁR, Vladimír TÁBORSKÝ,
Ján GELETA, Ladislav KUNA, Jozef LEVICKÝ, Juraj
SZIKORA, Josef JURKANIN, Václav VRÁNA

EIR: (Coach: Selection Committee)
Alan KELLY, Joseph KINNEAR, John DEMPSEY,
Charles HURLEY, Michael MEAGAN, James
CONWAY, Eamon DUNPHY, Edward ROGERS, Oliver
CONMY, Raymond TREACY, Turlough O'CONNOR

| | |
|---|---|
| SPAIN (Q) | (P6, W3, D2, L1, F6, A2, Pts. 8) |
| Czechoslovakia | (P6, W3, D1, L2, F8, A4, Pts. 7) |
| Republic of Ireland | (P6, W2, D1, L3, F5, A8, Pts. 5) |
| Turkey | (P6, W1, D2, L3, F3, A8, Pts. 4) |

GROUP 2 (Bulgaria, Norway, Portugal, Sweden)


13 November 1966          Ref: Jacques COLLING
                                            (Luxembourg)
Estádio Nacional, OEIRAS (Att. 18,244)

PORTUGAL - SWEDEN
1:2 (1:1)

1:0 Graça (21'), 1:1 Danielsson (29'), 1:2 Danielsson (86')

POR: (Coach: Otto Martins GLÓRIA)
José PEREIRA, João Pedro MORAIS, José
Alexandre da Silva BAPTISTA, Jacinto José Martins
Godinho SANTOS, Hilário Rosário da CONCEIÇÃO,
Jaime da Silva GRAÇA, Mário Esteves COLUNA,
JOSÉ AUGUSTO Pinto de Almeida, EUSÉBIO da
Silva Ferreira, António da Silva MENDES, Joaquim
DUARTE Oliveira

SWE: (Coach: Orvar BERGMARK)
Ronney PETTERSSON, Hans SELANDER, Kurt
AXELSSON, Björn NORDQVIST, Rolf BJÖRKLUND,
Jim NILDÉN, Ingvar SVENSSON, Ulf JANSSON, Inge
DANIELSSON, Agne SIMONSSON, Tom TURESSON


13 November 1966          Ref: MUZAFFER Sarvan
                                            (Turkey)
Stadion Vasil Levski, SOFIA (Att. 20,762)

BULGARIA - NORWAY
4:2 (3:0)

1:0 Tsanev (18'), 2:0 Zhekov (42'), 3:0 Tsanev (43'),
3:1 Hasund (59'), 4:1 Zhekov (85'), 4:2 Hasund (86')

BUL: (Coach: Dobromir TASHKOV)
Simeon SIMEONOV, Aleksandar SHALAMANOV,
Boris GAGANELOV, Stoyan ALEKSIEV, Dobromir
ZHECHEV, Ivan DAVIDOV, Dinko DERMENDZHIEV,
Dimitar PENEV, Petar ZHEKOV, Nikola TSANEV,
Aleksandar VASILEV

NOR: (Coach: Ragnar LARSEN)
Kjell KASPERSEN, Roar JOHANSEN, Finn
THORSEN, Trygve BORNØ, Arild MATHISEN, Arne
PEDERSEN, Olav NILSEN, Bjørn BORGEN, Harald
BERG, Per KRISTOFFERSEN, Kjetil HASUND

1 June 1967          Ref: Kevin HOWLEY (England)
Råsunda Stadion, SOLNA (Att. 49,689)

SWEDEN - PORTUGAL
1:1 (0:1)

0:1 Custódio (19'), 1:1 Svensson (90')

SWE: (Coach: Orvar BERGMARK)
Ronney PETTERSSON, Hans SELANDER,
Kurt AXELSSON, Björn NORDQVIST, Rolf
BJÖRKLUND, Jim NILDÉN, Ingvar SVENSSON,
Roger MAGNUSSON, Tom TURESSON, Agne
SIMONSSON, Örjan PERSSON

POR: (Coach: José GOMES da Silva)
Américo LOPES Ferreira, João Pedro MORAIS, Raúl
Martins MACHADO, José CARLOS da Silva, Hilário
Rosário da CONCEIÇÃO, Jaime da Silva GRAÇA,
CUSTÓDIO João Pinto, JOSÉ AUGUSTO Pinto
de Almeida, EUSÉBIO da Silva Ferreira, Manuel
SERAFIM Monteiro Pereira, Fernando PERES da Silva

8 June 1967          Ref: William SYME (Scotland)
Ullevaal Stadion, OSLO (Att. 29,993)

## NORWAY - PORTUGAL
## 1:2 (1:1)

0:1 Eusébio (15'), 1:1 Iversen (35'), 1:2 Eusébio (60')

NOR: (Coach: Wilhelm KMENT)
Kjell KASPERSEN, Arild MATHISEN, Roar JOHANSEN, Finn THORSEN, Nils Arne EGGEN, Trygve BORNØ, Olav NILSEN, Harald SUNDE, Harald BERG, Odd IVERSEN, Leif ERIKSEN

POR: (Coach: José GOMES da Silva)
Américo LOPES Ferreira, João Pedro MORAIS, Raúl Martins MACHADO, José CARLOS da Silva, Hilário Rosário da CONCEIÇÃO, Jaime da Silva GRAÇA, CUSTÓDIO João Pinto, JOSÉ AUGUSTO Pinto de Almeida, EUSÉBIO da Silva Ferreira, José MARIA Júnior, Estêvão Santo MANSIDÃO do Espírito


11 June 1967          Ref: Leo CALLAGHAN (Wales)
Råsunda Stadion, SOLNA (Att. 24,271)

## SWEDEN - BULGARIA
## 0:2 (0:1)

0:1 Zhekov (23'), 0:2 Dermendzhiev (82')

SWE: (Coach: Orvar BERGMARK)
Ronney PETTERSSON, Hans SELANDER, Kurt AXELSSON, Björn NORDQVIST, Rolf BJÖRKLUND, Jim NILDÉN, Ingvar SVENSSON, Inge DANIELSSON, Tom TURESSON, Agne SIMONSSON, Örjan PERSSON

BUL: (Coach: Stefan BOZHKOV)
Simeon SIMEONOV, Aleksandar SHALAMANOV, Ivan

DIMITROV, Boris GAGANELOV, Dobromir ZHECHEV, Dimitar PENEV, Georgi POPOV, Hristo BONEV, Petar ZHEKOV, Dimitar YAKIMOV, Dinko DERMENDZHIEV


29 June 1967          Ref: John ADAIR (Northern Ireland)
Ullevaal Stadion, OSLO (Att. 25,545)

### NORWAY - BULGARIA
### 0:0

NOR: (Coach: Wilhelm KMENT)
Kjell KASPERSEN, Arild MATHISEN, Roar JOHANSEN, Finn THORSEN, Nils Arne EGGEN, Trygve BORNØ, Olav NILSEN, Harald SUNDE, Odd IVERSEN, Harald BERG, Kjetil HASUND

BUL: (Coach: Stefan BOZHKOV)
Simeon SIMEONOV, Aleksandar SHALAMANOV, Ivan DIMITROV, Boris GAGANELOV, Dobromir ZHECHEV, Dimitar PENEV, Vasil MITKOV, Hristo BONEV, Petar ZHEKOV, Dimitar YAKIMOV, Dinko DERMENDZHIEV


3 September 1967          Ref: Jan PAWLIK (Poland)
Ullevaal Stadion, OSLO (Att. 32,151)

### NORWAY - SWEDEN
### 3:1 (1:1)

0:1 Nordahl (19'), 1:1 Berg (23'), 2:1 Birkeland (47'), 3:1 Sunde (80')

NOR: (Coach: Wilhelm KMENT)
Kjell KASPERSEN, Tore BØRREHAUG, Roar JOHANSEN, Finn THORSEN, Nils Arne EGGEN, Trygve BORNØ, Olav NILSEN, Harald SUNDE, Harald BERG, Odd IVERSEN, Sven BIRKELAND

SWE: (Coach: Orvar BERGMARK)

Ronney PETTERSSON, Hans SELANDER, Krister KRISTENSSON, Bertil ELMSTEDT, Rolf BJÖRKLUND, Tommy SVENSSON, Sven LINDMAN, Inge DANIELSSON, Thomas NORDAHL, Leif ERIKSSON, Harry BILD


5 November 1967          Ref: Rudolf GLÖCKNER
                                    (East Germany)
Råsunda Stadion, SOLNA (Att. 14,078)

### SWEDEN - NORWAY
### 5:2 (2:0)

1:0 Turesson (15'), 2:0 Danielsson (39'), 3:0 Eriksson (48'), 3:1 Iversen (57' pen.),4:1 Eriksson (85'), 5:1 Turesson (86'), 5:2 Nilsen (90')

SWE: (Coach: Orvar BERGMARK)
Sven-Gunnar LARSSON, Sven ANDERSSON, Björn NORDQVIST, Bertil ELMSTEDT, Stig JOHANSSON, Sven LINDMAN, Ulf JANSSON, Inge DANIELSSON, Tom TURESSON, Leif ERIKSSON, Ingvar SVAHN

NOR: (Coach: Wilhelm KMENT)
Kjell KASPERSEN, Arild MATHISEN, Per PETTERSEN, Frank OLAFSEN, Nils Arne EGGEN, Trygve BORNØ, Olav NILSEN, Harald SUNDE, Odd IVERSEN, Harald BERG, Kjetil HASUND


12 November 1967          Ref: Michel KITABDJIAN
                                    (France)
Estádio das Antas, OPORTO (Att. 20,500)

### PORTUGAL - NORWAY
### 2:1 (1:1)

1:0 Torres (30'), 1:1 Nilsen (40'), 2:1 Graça (64')

POR: (Coach: José GOMES da Silva)
Américo LOPES Ferreira, Manuel de Sousa RODRIGUES, Raúl Martins MACHADO, José CARLOS da Silva, Hilário Rosário da CONCEIÇÃO, Jaime da Silva GRAÇA, Mário Esteves COLUNA, JOSÉ AUGUSTO Pinto de Almeida, José Augusto da Costa Sénica TORRES, EUSÉBIO da Silva Ferreira, Francisco Lage Pereira de NÓBREGA

NOR: (Coach: Wilhelm KMENT)
Kjell KASPERSEN, Arild MATHISEN, Per PETTERSEN, Tor ALSAKER-NØSTDAHL, Nils Arne EGGEN, Trygve BORNØ, Olav NILSEN, Harald SUNDE, Kai SJØBERG, Harald BERG, Odd IVERSEN

12 November 1967                  Ref: Josip HORVAT
                                       (Yugoslavia)
Stadion Vasil Levski, SOFIA (Att. 16,479)

BULGARIA - SWEDEN
3:0 (2:0)

1:0 Kotkov (43'), 2:0 Mitkov (44'), 3:0 Asparuhov (75')

BUL: (Coach: Stefan BOZHKOV)
Simeon SIMEONOV, Aleksandar SHALAMANOV, Dimitar PENEV, Boris GAGANELOV, Dobromir ZHECHEV, Todor KOLEV, Dinko DERMENDZHIEV, Hristo BONEV, Georgi ASPARUHOV, Nikola KOTKOV, Vasil MITKOV

SWE: (Coach: Orvar BERGMARK)
Sven-Gunnar LARSSON, Sven ANDERSSON, Bertil ELMSTEDT, Björn NORDQVIST, Rolf BJÖRKLUND, Sven LINDMAN, Ulf JANSSON, Inge DANIELSSON, Tom TURESSON, Leif ERIKSSON, Ingvar SVAHN

26 November 1967      Ref: Anvar ZVEREV (USSR)
Stadion Vasil Levski, SOFIA (Att. 39,795)

## BULGARIA - PORTUGAL
### 1:0 (0:0)

### 1:0 Dermendzhiev (63')

BUL: (Coach: Stefan BOZHKOV)
Simeon SIMEONOV, Aleksandar SHALAMANOV,
Dimitar PENEV, Boris GAGANELOV, Dobromir
ZHECHEV, Ivan DAVIDOV, Dinko DERMENDZHIEV,
Hristo BONEV, Georgi ASPARUHOV, Nikola KOTKOV,
Vasil MITKOV

POR: (Coach: José GOMES da Silva)
Américo LOPES Ferreira, Manuel de Sousa
RODRIGUES, Rui Gouveia Pinto RODRIGUES, José
CARLOS da Silva, Hilário Rosário da CONCEIÇÃO,
Jaime da Silva GRAÇA, José Maria de Freitas Pereira
'PEDRAS', JOSÉ AUGUSTO Pinto de Almeida,
EUSÉBIO da Silva Ferreira, José Augusto da Costa
Sénica TORRES, António José SIMÕES da Costa

17 December 1967      Ref: Antonio SBARDELLA (Italy)
Estádio Nacional, OEIRAS (Att. 13,408)

## PORTUGAL - BULGARIA
### 0:0

POR: (José GOMES da Silva)
Américo LOPES Ferreira, Manuel de Sousa
RODRIGUES, Rui Gouveia Pinto RODRIGUES, José
CARLOS da Silva, Hilário Rosário da CONCEIÇÃO,
Jaime da Silva GRAÇA, José Maria de Freitas Pereira
'PEDRAS', JOSÉ AUGUSTO Pinto de Almeida,
EUSÉBIO da Silva Ferreira, José Augusto da Costa
Sénica TORRES, António José SIMÕES da Costa

<u>BUL:</u> (Coach: Stefan BOZHKOV)
Simeon SIMEONOV, Milko GAYDARSKI, Ivan DIMITROV, Boris GAGANELOV, Dimitar PENEV, Dobromir ZHECHEV, Georgi POPOV, Hristo BONEV, Nikola KOTKOV, Dimitar YAKIMOV, Dinko DERMENDZHIEV

| | |
|---|---|
| BULGARIA(Q) | (P6, W4, D2, L0, F10, A2, Pts. 10) |
| Portugal | (P6, W2, D2, L2, F6, A6, Pts. 6) |
| Sweden | (P6, W2, D1, L3, F9, A12, Pts. 5) |
| Norway | (P6, W1, D1, L4, F9, A14, Pts. 3) |

## <u>GROUP 3</u> (Austria, Finland, Greece, USSR)

2 October 1966                  Ref: Peter COATES
                                (Republic of Ireland)
Olympiastadion, HELSINKI (Att. 10,070)

### FINLAND - AUSTRIA
### 0:0

<u>FIN:</u> (Coach: Olavi LAAKSONEN)
Lars NÄSMAN, Pertti MÄKIPÄÄ, Reima NUMMILA, Timo KAUTONEN, Reijo KANERVA, Simo SYRJÄVAARA, Juhani PELTONEN, Matti MÄKELÄ, Tommy LINDHOLM, Markku HYVÄRINEN, Aulis LAINE

<u>AUT:</u> (Coach: Eduard FRÜHWIRTH)
Roman PICHLER, Walter GEBHARDT, Walter GLECHNER, Heinz BINDER, Franz VIEHBÖCK, Horst HIRNSCHRODT, Robert SARA, Rudolf FLÖGEL, Anton FRITSCH, Thomas PARITS, Johann HÖRMAYER

16 October 1966          Ref: Zdeněk VALEŠ
(Czechoslovakia)
Kaftanzoglio stádio, SALONICA (Att. 28,478)

GREECE - FINLAND
2:1 (1:0)

1:0 Alexiadis (39'), 1:1 Mäkipää (57'), 2:1 Alexiadis (86')

GRE: (Coach: Panagiotis MARKOVITS)
Panagiotis    OIKONOMOPOULOS,    Anastasios
VASILIOU, Giorgos SKREKIS, Fotios BALOPOULOS,
Frantsiskos SOURPIS, Stelios SKEVOFILAX, Stathis
HAITAS, Dimitris DOMAZOS, Alexandros ALEXIADIS,
Dimitris PAPAIOANNOU, Giorgos DEDES

FIN: (Coach: Olavi LAAKSONEN)
Lars NÄSMAN, Pertti MÄKIPÄÄ, Reima NUMMILA,
Timo    KAUTONEN,    Reijo    KANERVA,    Simo
SYRJÄVAARA, Juhani PELTONEN, Matti MÄKELÄ,
Arto TOLSA, Markku HYVÄRINEN, Aulis LAINE


10 May 1967      Ref: Pieter ROOMER (Netherlands)
Olympiastadion, HELSINKI (Att. 14,056)

FINLAND - GREECE
1:1 (1:1)

1:0 Peltonen (18'), 1:1 Haitas (39')

FIN: (Coach: Olavi LAAKSONEN)
Martti HALME, Rainer AHO, Timo KAUTONEN, Reijo
KANERVA, Reima NUMMILA, Matti MÄKELÄ, Pertti
MÄKIPÄÄ, Semi NUORANEN, Arto TOLSA, Tommy
LINDHOLM, Juhani PELTONEN

GRE: (Coach: Vasilis PETROPOULOS)
Panagiotis OIKONOMOPOULOS, Mihalis BELLIS,
Hristos ZANTEROGLOU, Alexandros SOFIANIDIS,

Neotakis LOUKANIDIS, Konstantinos POLIHRONIOU, Stathis HAITAS, Nikolaos GIOUTSOS, Dimitris DOMAZOS, Dimitris PAPAIOANNOU, Vasilis BOTINOS


11 June 1967          Ref: Johan BOSTRÖM (Sweden)
Tsentralniy Stadion 'V.I. Lenina', MOSCOW
(Att. 72,142)

### USSR - AUSTRIA
### 4:3 (3:1)

1:0 Malofeyev (25'), 2:0 Byshovets (36'), 2:1 Hof (38'), 3:1 Chislenko (43'), 3:2 Wolny (54'), 3:3 Siber (71'), 4:3 Streltsov (80')


URS: (Coach: Mikhail YAKUSHIN)
Lev YASHIN, Valentin AFONIN, Albert SHESTERNYOV, Murtaz KHURTSILAVA, Aleksandr LENYOV, Valeriy VORONIN, Igor CHISLENKO, Yozhef SABO, Anatoliy BYSHOVETS, Eduard STRELTSOV, Eduard MALOFEYEV

AUT: (Coach: Erwin ALGE/Johann PESSER)
Roman PICHLER, Helmut WARTUSCH, Walter GLECHNER, Gerhard STURMBERGER, Erich FAK, Roland ESCHELMÜLLER, Erich HOF, Rudolf FLÖGEL, Franz WOLNY, Helmut SIBER, Johann HÖRMAYER


16 July 1967          Ref: Birger NILSEN (Norway)
Tsentralniy Stadion 'Dinamo', TBILISI (Att. 28,040)

### USSR - GREECE
### 4:0 (0:0)

1:0 Banishevskiy (50'), 2:0 Sabo (72' pen.), 3:0 Banishevskiy (77'), 4:0 Chislenko (83')

URS: (Coach: Mikhail YAKUSHIN)
Lev YASHIN, Viktor ANICHKIN, Albert SHESTERNYOV, Murtaz KHURTSILAVA, Aleksandr LENYOV, Valeriy VORONIN, Igor CHISLENKO, Yozhef SABO, Anatoliy BANISHEVSKIY, Eduard STRELTSOV, Anatoliy BYSHOVETS

GRE: (Coach: Vasilis PETROPOULOS)
Panagiotis OIKONOMOPOULOS, Dimitris PLESSAS, Neotakis LOUKANIDIS, Mihalis BELLIS, Aristidis KAMARAS, Dimitris DOMAZOS, Konstantinos POLIHRONIOU, Stathis HAITAS, Giorgos SIDERIS, Dimitris PAPAIOANNOU, Vasilis BOTINOS

30 August 1967    Ref: MUZAFFER Sarvan (Turkey)
Tsentralniy Stadion 'V.I. Lenina', MOSCOW
(Att. 20,597)

### USSR - FINLAND
### 2:0 (1:0)

1:0 Khurtsilava (14'), 2:0 Chislenko (80')

URS: (Coach: Mikhail YAKUSHIN)
Anzor KAVAZASHVILI, Valentin AFONIN, Albert SHESTERNYOV, Murtaz KHURTSILAVA, Guram TSKHOVREBOV, Valeriy MASLOV, Igor CHISLENKO, Yozhef SABO, Anatoliy BANISHEVSKIY, Anatoliy BYSHOVETS, Eduard MALOFEYEV

FIN: (Coach: Olavi LAAKSONEN)
Lars NÄSMAN, Pertti MÄKIPÄÄ, Seppo KILPONEN, Timo KAUTONEN, Reima NUMMILA, Juhani PELTONEN, Simo SYRJÄVAARA, Kai PAHLMAN, Matti MÄKELÄ, Arto TOLSA, Aulis LAINE

6 September 1967　　　　Ref: Pavel ŠPOTÁK
(Czechoslovakia)
Kupittaan Stadion, TURKU (Att. 7,793)

### FINLAND - USSR
### 2:5 (2:3)

0:1 Sabo (2'), 0:2 Maslov (14'), 1:2 Peltonen (18' pen.),
2:2 Syrjävaara (25'), 2:3 Banishevskiy (35'), 2:4 Sabo
(56' pen.), 2:5 Malofeyev (63')

FIN: (Coach: Olavi LAAKSONEN)
Lars NÄSMAN, Matti PITKO, Seppo KILPONEN, Pertti
MÄKIPÄÄ, Reima NUMMILA, Matti MÄKELÄ, Simo
SYRJÄVAARA, Aulis LAINE, Arto TOLSA, Juhani
PELTONEN, Semi NUORANEN

URS: (Coach: Mikhail YAKUSHIN)
Yuriy PSHENICHNIKOV (Anzor KAVAZASHVILI 80'),
Valentin AFONIN, Viktor ANICHKIN, Murtaz
KHURTSILAVA, Gennadiy LOGOFET, Valeriy
MASLOV, Igor CHISLENKO, Yozhef SABO, Anatoliy
BANISHEVSKIY, Anatoliy BYSHOVETS, Eduard
MALOFEYEV

24 September 1967　　　　Ref: Milivoje GUGULOVIĆ
(Yugoslavia)
Praterstadion, VIENNA (Att. 25,231)

### AUSTRIA - FINLAND
### 2:1 (1:0)

1:0 Flögel (17'), 1:1 Peltonen (57'), 2:1 Grausam (81')

AUT: (Coach: Erwin ALGE/Johann PESSER)
Gerald FUCHSBICHLER, Walter GEBHARDT,
Walter GLECHNER, Johann EIGENSTILLER, Karl
FRÖHLICH, Gerhard STURMBERGER, Rudolf
FLÖGEL, Helmut MÄTZLER, Franz WOLNY, Leopold
GRAUSAM, Helmut REDL

**FIN:** (Coach: Olavi LAAKSONEN)
Lars NÄSMAN, Matti PITKO, Seppo KILPONEN,
Timo KAUTONEN, Reima NUMMILA, Matti MÄKELÄ,
Simo SYRJÄVAARA, Semi NUORANEN, Tommy
LINDHOLM, Arto TOLSA, Juhani PELTONEN

Red Card: Kautonen 80'


4 October 1967          Ref: Vasile DUMITRESCU
(Romania)
Stádio Georgios Karaiskakis, PIRAEUS (Att. 34,552)

### GREECE - AUSTRIA
### 4:1 (2:0)

1:0 Sideris (28'), 2:0 Sideris (34' pen.), 2:1 Grausam
(62'), 3:1 Sideris (63'), 4:1 Papaioannou (75')

**GRE:** (Coach: Vasilis PETROPOULOS)
Panagiotis       OIKONOMOPOULOS,       Fotios
BALOPOULOS,       Hristos       ZANTEROGLOU,
Konstantinos POLIHRONIOU, Giannis GAITATZIS,
Dimitris DOMAZOS, Neotakis LOUKANIDIS, Vasilis
BOTINOS, Giorgos SIDERIS, Nikolaos GIOUTSOS,
Dimitris PAPAIOANNOU

**AUT:** (Coach: Erwin ALGE/Johann PESSER)
Gerald   FUCHSBICHLER,   Walter   GEBHARDT,
Walter GLECHNER, Johann EIGENSTILLER, Karl
FRÖHLICH, Johann FRANK, Rudolf FLÖGEL, Anton
FRITSCH, Helmut SIBER, Leopold GRAUSAM,
Helmut REDL


15 October 1967     Ref: Todor BECHIROV (Bulgaria)
Praterstadion, VIENNA (Att. 37,400)

### AUSTRIA - USSR
### 1:0 (0:0)

1:0 Grausam (49')

AUT: (Coach: Erwin ALGE/Johann PESSER)
Wilhelm HARREITHER, Walter GEBHARDT, Walter
GLECHNER, Walter STAMM, Karl FRÖHLICH,
Gerhard STURMBERGER, Johann EIGENSTILLER,
Walter KOLEZNIK, Leopold GRAUSAM, Rudolf
FLÖGEL, Helmut SIBER

URS: (Coach: Mikhail YAKUSHIN)
Anzor KAVAZASHVILI, Valentin AFONIN, Albert
SHESTERNYOV, Murtaz KHURTSILAVA, Guram
TSKHOVREBOV, Valeriy MASLOV, Viktor ANICHKIN,
Yozhef SABO, Anatoliy BANISHEVSKIY, Eduard
STRELTSOV, Anatoliy BYSHOVETS


31 October 1967          Ref: Gottfried DIENST
                              (Switzerland)
Stádio Georgios Karaiskakis, PIRAEUS (Att. 33,588)

GREECE - USSR
0:1 (0:0)

0:1 Malofeyev (50')

GRE: (Coach: Vasilis PETROPOULOS)
Nikolaos HRISTIDIS, Fotios BALOPOULOS, Hristos
ZANTEROGLOU, Konstantinos POLIHRONIOU,
Giannis GAITATZIS, Dimitris DOMAZOS, Neotakis
LOUKANIDIS, Stathis HAITAS, Nikolaos GIOUTSOS,
Giorgos SIDERIS, Dimitris PAPAIOANNOU

URS: (Coach: Mikhail YAKUSHIN)
Anzor KAVAZASHVILI, Valentin AFONIN, Albert
SHESTERNYOV, Murtaz KHURTSILAVA, Viktor
ANICHKIN, Valeriy VORONIN, Igor CHISLENKO,
Yozhef SABO, Anatoliy BANISHEVSKIY, Eduard
STRELTSOV, Eduard MALOFEYEV

5 November 1967        Ref: Gyula GERE (Hungary)
Praterstadion, VIENNA (Att. 31,996)

### AUSTRIA - GREECE
### 1:1 (1:0)

1:0 Siber (32'), 1:1 Sideris (71')

AUT: (Coach: Erwin ALGE/Johann PESSER)
Wilhelm HARREITHER, Walter GEBHARDT, Walter
GLECHNER, Walter STAMM, Karl FRÖHLICH, Walter
SKOCIK, Johann EIGENSTILLER, Walter KOLEZNIK,
Helmut SIBER, Leopold GRAUSAM, Helmut REDL

GRE: (Coach: Vasilis PETROPOULOS)
Nikolaos HRISTIDIS, Aristidis KAMARAS, Hristos
ZANTEROGLOU, Konstantinos POLIHRONIOU,
Giannis GAITATZIS, Fotios BALOPOULOS, Dimitris
DOMAZOS, Giorgos KOUDAS, Giorgos SIDERIS,
Dimitris PAPAIOANNOU, Neotakis LOUKANIDIS

Note: The match was abandoned after 83 minutes due
to crowd trouble.

| | |
|---|---|
| USSR (Q) | (P6, W5, D0, L1, F16, A6, Pts. 10) |
| Greece | (P6, W2, D2, L2, F8, A9, Pts. 6) |
| Austria | (P6, W2, D2, L2, F8, A10, Pts. 6) |
| Finland | (P6, W0, D2, L4, F5, A12, Pts. 2) |

GROUP 4 (Albania, West Germany, Yugoslavia)

8 April 1967        Ref: Martti HIRVINIEMI (Finland)
Stadion Rote Erde, DORTMUND (Att. 30,000)

### WEST GERMANY - ALBANIA
### 6:0 (2:0)

1:0 Müller (6'), 2:0 Müller (25'), 3:0 Müller (73'), 4:0
  Löhr (77'), 5:0 Löhr (79'), 6:0 Müller (85' pen.)

WGR: (Coach: Helmut SCHÖN)
Hans TILKOWSKI, Bernhard PATZKE, Horst-Dieter
HÖTTGES, Franz BECKENBAUER, Willi SCHULZ,
Wolfgang WEBER, Bernd DÖRFEL, Lothar ULSAß,
Gerhard MÜLLER, Wolfgang OVERATH, Johannes
LÖHR

ALB: (Coach: Loro BORIÇI)
Mikel JANKU, Fatmir FRASHËRI, Ali MEMA, Teodor
VASO, Ramazan RRAGAMI, Josif KAZANXHI, Nico
XHAÇKA, Skënder HYKA, Panajot PANO, Sabah
BIZI, Bahri ISHKA


3 May 1967       Ref: José María ORTIZ de Mendíbil
                                              (Spain)
Stadion J.N.A., BELGRADE (Att. 48,000)

YUGOSLAVIA - WEST GERMANY
1:0 (0:0)

1:0 Skoblar (64')

YUG: (Coach: Rajko MITIĆ)
Ilija PANTELIĆ, Mirsad FAZLAGIĆ, Fahrudin
JUSUFI, Marijan BRNČIĆ, Branko RAŠOVIĆ, Dragan
HOLCER, Vojislav MELIĆ, Radoslav BEČEJAC,
Mustafa HASANAGIĆ, Josip SKOBLAR, Dragan
DŽAJIĆ

WGR: (Coach: Helmut SCHÖN)
Josef MAIER, Bernhard PATZKE, Hans-Hubert
VOGTS, Franz BECKENBAUER, Willi SCHULZ, Klaus
FICHTEL, Siegfried HELD, Hans KÜPPERS, Gerhard
MÜLLER, Wolfgang OVERATH, Johannes LÖHR

14 May 1967          Ref: Konstantinos XANTHOULIS
(Cyprus)
Stadiumi Qemal Stafa, TIRANA (Att. 18,573)

### ALBANIA - YUGOSLAVIA
### 0:2 (0:1)

0:1 Zambata (23'), 0:2 Zambata (56')

ALB: (Coach: Loro BORIÇI)
Mikel JANKU, Fatmir FRASHËRI, Ali MEMA, Teodor
VASO, Ramazan RRAGAMI, Josif KAZANXHI, Lin
SHLLAKU, Lorenç VORFI, Medin ZHEGA, Panajot
PANO, Gani XHAFA

YUG: (Coach: Rajko MITIĆ)
Miodrag KNEŽEVIĆ, Mirsad FAZLAGIĆ, Marijan
BRNČIĆ, Radoslav BEČEJAC, Branko RAŠOVIĆ,
Dragan HOLCER, Vojislav MELIĆ, Petar NADOVEZA,
Slaven ZAMBATA, Stjepan LAMZA, Dragan DŽAJIĆ


7 October 1967          Ref: Concetto LO BELLO (Italy)
Volksparkstadion, HAMBURG (Att. 70,573)

### WEST GERMANY - YUGOSLAVIA
### 3:1 (1:0)

1:0 Löhr (11'), 1:1 Zambata (46'), 2:1 Müller (71'),
3:1 Seeler (87')

WGR: (Coach: Helmut SCHÖN)
Josef MAIER, Bernhard PATZKE, Horst-Dieter
HÖTTGES, Hans SIEMENSMEYER, Willi SCHULZ,
Wolfgang WEBER, Franz ROTH, Uwe SEELER,
Gerhard MÜLLER, Wolfgang OVERATH, Johannes
LÖHR

YUG: (Coach: Rajko MITIĆ)
Ilija PANTELIĆ, Mirsad FAZLAGIĆ, Marijan BRNČIĆ,

Stevan NEŠTICKI, Branko RAŠOVIĆ, Dragan HOLCER, Slaven ZAMBATA, Radoslav BEČEJAC, Josip SKOBLAR, Ivica OSIM, Dragan DŽAJIĆ


12 November 1967          Ref: Andrei RĂDULESCU
                                              (Romania)
Stadion J.N.A., BELGRADE (Att. 30,000)

### YUGOSLAVIA - ALBANIA
### 4:0 (1:0)

1:0 Srečo (44'), 2:0 Osim (52'), 3:0 Lazarević (70'), 4:0 Osim (81')


YUG: (Coach: Rajko MITIĆ)
Radomir VUKČEVIĆ, Mirsad FAZLAGIĆ, Milan DAMJANOVIĆ, Borivoje ĐORĐEVIĆ, Blagoje PAUNOVIĆ, Dragan HOLCER, Dragan DŽAJIĆ, Ivica OSIM, Vojin LAZAREVIĆ, Edin SPREČO, Krasnodar RORA

ALB: (Coach: Loro BORIÇI)
Jani RAMA, Frederik JORGAQI, Ali MEMA, Teodor VASO, Ramazan RRAGAMI, Foto ANDONI, Niko XHAÇKA, Lin SHLLAKU, Panajot PANO, Sabah BIZI, Medin ZHEGA


17 December 1967          Ref: Ferdinand MARSCHALL
                                              (Austria)
Stadiumi Qemal Stafa, TIRANA (Att. 21,889)

### ALBANIA - WEST GERMANY
### 0:0


ALB: (Coach: Loro BORIÇI)
Koço DINELLA, Frederik JORGAQI, Ali MEMA, Teodor VASO, Ramazan RRAGAMI, Josif KAZANXHI, Frederik GJINALI, Lin SHLLAKU, Panajot PANO,

Sabah BIZI, Medin ZHEGA

WGR: (Coach: Helmut SCHÖN)
Horst WOLTER, Bernhard PATZKE, Horst-Dieter
HÖTTGES, Günter NETZER, Willi SCHULZ, Wolfgang
WEBER, Siegfried HELD, Hans KÜPPERS, Peter
MEYER, Wolfgang OVERATH, Johannes LÖHR


YUGOSLAVIA(Q)     (P4, W3, D0, L1, F8, A3, Pts. 6)
West Germany     (P4, W2, D1, L1, F9, A2, Pts. 5)
Albania     (P4, W0, D1, L3, F0, A12, Pts. 1)


GROUP 5 (Denmark, East Germany, Hungary,
Netherlands)


7 September 1966     Ref: Birger NILSEN (Norway)
Feyenoord Stadion, ROTTERDAM (Att. 61,600)

## NETHERLANDS - HUNGARY
## 2:2 (1:0)

1:0 Pijs (35'), 2:0 Cruijff (52'), 2:1 Molnár (70'), 2:2
Mészöly (88')

NET: (Coach: Georg KEßLER)
Eduard PIETERS GRAAFLAND, Frederik
FLINKEVLEUGEL, Marinus ISRAËL, Daniel
SCHRIJVERS, Cor VELDHOEN, Emil PIJS, Bernardus
MULLER, Jesaia SWART, Johannes CRUIJFF, Klaas
NUNINGA, Petrus KEIZER

HUN: (Coach: Rudolf ILLOVSZKY)
Antal SZENTMIHÁLYI, Benő KÁPOSZTA, Dezső
MOLNÁR, Kálmán MÉSZÖLY, Ferenc SIPOS, Kálmán
IHÁSZ, Zoltán VARGA, Gyula RÁKOSI, Ferenc BENE,
Flórián ALBERT, János FARKAS

21 September 1966          Ref: Petros TZOUVARAS
                                         (Greece)

Népstadion, BUDAPEST (Att. 18,487)

### HUNGARY - DENMARK
### 6:0 (5:0)

1:0 Albert (1'), 2:0 Mészöly (10' pen.), 3:0 Bene (14'),
   4:0 Albert (32'), 5:0 Farkas (37'), 6:0 Varga (83')


HUN: (Coach: Rudolf ILLOVSZKY)
Antal SZENTMIHÁLYI, Benő KÁPOSZTA, Sándor
MÁTRAI, Kálmán IHÁSZ, Imre MATHESZ, Kálmán
MÉSZÖLY, Dezső MOLNÁR, Ferenc BENE, Flórián
ALBERT, Zoltán VARGA, János FARKAS

DEN: (Coach: Poul PETERSEN)
Leif NIELSEN, John HANSEN, John WORBYE, Niels
Erik ANDERSEN, Henning BOEL, Niels MØLLER,
Bent Schmidt HANSEN, René MØLLER, Henning
ENOKSEN, Jens Jørgen HANSEN, Ulrik LE FEVRE


30 November 1966          Ref: Aníbal da Silva OLIVEIRA
                                         (Portugal)
Feyenoord Stadion, ROTTERDAM (Att. 32,000)

### NETHERLANDS - DENMARK
### 2:0 (0:0)

1:0 Swart (58'), 2:0 van der Kuijlen (73')


NET: (Coach: Georg KEßLER)
Eduard   PIETERS   GRAAFLAND,   Wilhelmus
SUURBIER, Marinus ISRAËL, Daniel SCHRIJVERS,
Cor VELDHOEN, Wilhelmus DULLENS, Bernardus
MULLER, Jesaia SWART, Klaas NUNINGA, Wilhelmus
VAN DER KUIJLEN, Petrus KEIZER

DEN: (Coach: Poul PETERSEN)

Leif NIELSEN, John HANSEN, John WORBYE, Leif HARTWIG, Henning BOEL, Henning Munk JENSEN, John Steen OLSEN, Finn WIBERG, Keld BAK, Kjeld THORST, Ulrik LE FEVRE

5 April 1967    Ref: Hannes SIGURÐSSON (Iceland)
Zentralstadion, LEIPZIG (Att. 40,000)

## EAST GERMANY - NETHERLANDS
## 4:3 (0:2)

0:1 Mulder (10'), 0:2 Keizer (12'), 1:2 Vogel (50'), 2:2 Frenzel (62'), 2:3 Keizer (65'), 3:3 Frenzel (78'), 4:3 Frenzel (85')

EGR: (Coach: Károly SÓS)
Horst WEIGANG, Otto FRÄßDORF, Manfred WALTER, Manfred GEISLER, Herbert PANKAU, Gerhard KÖRNER, Dieter ERLER, Roland DUCKE, Henning FRENZEL, Jürgen NÖLDNER, Eberhard VOGEL

NET: (Coach: Georg KEßLER)
Teunis VAN LEEUWEN, Wilhelmus SUURBIER, Emil PIJS, Daniel SCHRIJVERS, Pieter KEMPER, Hendrik GROOT, Pieter DE ZOETE, Jesaia SWART, Klaas NUNINGA, Johan MULDER, Petrus KEIZER

10 May 1967          Ref: Franz MAYER (Austria)
Népstadion, BUDAPEST (Att. 24,352)

## HUNGARY - NETHERLANDS
## 2:1 (2:0)

1:0 Mészöly (7' pen.), 2:0 Farkas (30'), 2:1 Suurbier (63')

HUN: (Coach: Rudolf ILLOVSZKY)
Gyula TAMÁS, Sándor MÁTRAI, Kálmán MÉSZÖLY,

Lajos SZŰCS, Kálmán IHÁSZ, János GÖRÖCS, Flórián ALBERT, Gyula RÁKOSI, Dezső MOLNÁR, Ferenc BENE, János FARKAS

NET: (Coach: Georg KEßLER)
Teunis VAN LEEUWEN (Willem DOESBURG 46'), Marinus ISRAËL, Wilhelmus SUURBIER, Johannes EIJKENBROEK, Cor VELDHOEN, Hendrik GROOT, Bernardus MULLER, Gerard BERGHOLTZ, Johan MULDER, Klaas NUNINGA, Petrus KEIZER

24 May 1967              Ref: William GOW (Wales)
Idrætsparken, COPENHAGEN (Att. 35,200)

DENMARK - HUNGARY
0:2 (0:1)

0:1 Albert (30'), 0:2 Bene (70')

DEN: (Coach: Erik HANSEN/Ernst NETUKA)
Leif NIELSEN, John HANSEN, John WORBYE, Kresten BJERRE, Jens Jørgen HANSEN, Erik SANDVAD, Bent Schmidt HANSEN, Finn LAUDRUP, René MØLLER, Tom SØNDERGAARD, Ulrik LE FEVRE

HUN: (Coach: Rudolf ILLOVSZKY)
Gyula TAMÁS, Sándor MÁTRAI, Kálmán MÉSZÖLY, Kálmán IHÁSZ, Lajos SZŰCS, Dezső MOLNÁR, Ferenc BENE, Flórián ALBERT, János FARKAS, Gyula RÁKOSI, István NAGY

4 June 1967              Ref: Joseph HANNET (Belgium)
Idrætsparken, COPENHAGEN (Att. 23,700)

DENMARK - EAST GERMANY
1:1 (0:1)

0:1 Löwe (5'), 1:1 Bjerre (65' pen.)

DEN: (Coach: Erik HANSEN/Ernst NETUKA)
Leif NIELSEN, John HANSEN, John WORBYE,
Kresten BJERRE, Henning BOEL, Erik SANDVAD,
Bent Schmidt HANSEN, Finn LAUDRUP, René
MØLLER, Tom SØNDERGAARD, Ulrik LE FEVRE

EGR: (Coach: Károly SÓS)
Jürgen CROY, Otto FRÄßDORF, Manfred WALTER,
Manfred GEISLER, Bernd BRANSCH, Harald
IRMSCHER, Gerhard KÖRNER, Roland DUCKE,
Henning FRENZEL, Jürgen NÖLDNER, Wolfram LÖWE

13 September 1967          Ref: Thomas WHARTON
                                      (Scotland)
Olympisch Stadion, AMSTERDAM (Att. 45,000)

NETHERLANDS - EAST GERMANY
1:0 (1:0)

1:0 Cruijff (2')

NET: (Coach: Georg KEßLER)
Eduard PIETERS GRAAFLAND, Wilhelmus
SUURBIER, Marinus ISRAËL, Johannes
EIJKENBROEK, Cor VELDHOEN, Hendrik GROOT,
Bernardus MULLER, Johannes KLIJNJAN, Johannes
CRUIJFF, Klaas NUNINGA, Petrus KEIZER

EGR: (Coach: Károly SÓS)
Wolfgang BLOCHWITZ, Otto FRÄßDORF, Wolfgang
WRUCK, Manfred GEISLER, Bernd BRANSCH,
Herbert PANKAU, Harald IRMSCHER, Roland DUCKE,
Henning FRENZEL, Dieter ERLER, Eberhard VOGEL

27 September 1967          Ref: Tofik BAKHRAMOV
                                      (USSR)
Népstadion, BUDAPEST (Att. 69,871)

## HUNGARY - EAST GERMANY
### 3:1 (1:0)

1:0 Farkas (9'), 2:0 Farkas (48'), 3:0 Farkas (50'),
3:1 Frenzel (58')

HUN: (Coach: Rudolf ILLOVSZKY)
Gyula TAMÁS, Benő KÁPOSZTA, Sándor MÁTRAI,
Lajos SZŰCS, Kálmán IHÁSZ, János GÖRÖCS,
Gyula RÁKOSI, Ferenc BENE, Zoltán VARGA, Flórián
ALBERT, János FARKAS

EGR: (Coach: Károly SÓS)
Jürgen CROY, Otto FRÄßDORF, Herbert PANKAU,
Manfred WALTER, Bernd BRANSCH, Gerhard
KÖRNER, Dieter ERLER, Roland DUCKE, Henning
FRENZEL, Peter DUCKE, Eberhard VOGEL


4 October 1967                Ref: Malcolm WRIGHT
                                (Northern Ireland)
Idrætsparken, COPENHAGEN (Att. 35,200)

## DENMARK - NETHERLANDS
### 3:2 (1:0)

1:0 Bjerre (44' pen.), 2:0 Søndergaard (53'), 3:0 Bjerre
(71'), 3:1 Suurbier (74'), 3:2 Israël (76')

DEN: (Coach: Erik HANSEN/Ernst NETUKA)
Leif NIELSEN, John HANSEN, John WORBYE,
Kresten BJERRE, Henning BOEL, Erik SANDVAD,
John Steen OLSEN, Finn LAUDRUP, Erik
DYREBORG, Tom SØNDERGAARD, Ulrik LE
FEVRE

NET: (Coach: Georg KEßLER)
Eduard PIETERS GRAAFLAND, Marinus ISRAËL,
Anton PRONK, Bernardus MULLER, Hendrik
GROOT, Klaas NUNINGA, Johannes CRUIJFF,

Wilhelmus JANSEN, Petrus KEIZER, Johannes
EIJKENBROEK, Wilhelmus SUURBIER


11 October 1967      Ref: Ryszard BANASIUK (Poland)
Zentralstadion, LEIPZIG (Att. 25,000)

### EAST GERMANY - DENMARK
### 3:2 (1:2)

0:1 Dyreborg (25'), 1:1 Körner (35' pen.), 1:2
Søndergaard (38'), 2:2 Pankau (59'), 3:2 Pankau (73')

EGR: (Coach: Károly SÓS)
Wolfgang BLOCHWITZ, Klaus URBANCZYK, Manfred
WALTER, Bernd BRANSCH, Herbert PANKAU, Jürgen
NÖLDNER, Gerhard KÖRNER, Roland DUCKE,
Henning FRENZEL, Peter DUCKE, Eberhard VOGEL

DEN: (Coach: Erik HANSEN/Ernst NETUKA)
Leif NIELSEN, John HANSEN, John WORBYE,
Kresten BJERRE, Henning BOEL, Erik SANDVAD,
John Steen OLSEN, Finn LAUDRUP, Erik DYREBORG,
Tom SØNDERGAARD, Ulrik LE FEVRE


29 October 1967      Ref: Robert HÉLIÈS (France)
Zentralstadion, LEIPZIG (Att. 48,872)

### EAST GERMANY - HUNGARY
### 1:0 (0:0)

1:0 Frenzel (51')

EGR: (Coach: Károly SÓS)
Wolfgang BLOCHWITZ, Klaus URBANCZYK,
Wolfgang WRUCK, Bernd BRANSCH, Herbert
PANKAU, Harald IRMSCHER, Günter HOGE, Jürgen
NÖLDNER, Henning FRENZEL, Dieter ERLER,
Wolfram LÖWE

<u>HUN:</u> (Coach: Rudolf ILLOVSZKY)
Gyula TAMÁS, Benő KÁPOSZTA, Miklós PÁNCSICS,
Lajos SZŰCS, Kálmán IHÁSZ, Imre MATHESZ, Gyula
RÁKOSI, Ferenc BENE, Zoltán VARGA, Flórián
ALBERT, János FARKAS

| | |
|---|---|
| HUNGARY (Q) | (P6, W4, D1, L1, F15, A5, Pts. 9) |
| East Germany | (P6, W3, D1, L2, F10, A10, Pts. 7) |
| Netherlands | (P6, W2, D1, L3, F11, A11, Pts. 5) |
| Denmark | (P6, W1, D1, L4, F6, A16, Pts. 3) |

<u>GROUP 6</u> (Cyprus, Italy, Romania, Switzerland)

2 November 1966      Ref: James FINNEY (England)
Stadionul Republicii, BUCHAREST (Att. 14,209)

ROMANIA - SWITZERLAND
4:2 (4:0)

1:0 Dridea (8'), 2:0 Frăţilă (11'), 3:0 Frăţilă (25'), 4:0
Frăţilă (38'), 4:1 Künzli (54'), 4:2 Odermatt (70')

<u>ROM:</u> (Coach: Ilie OANĂ)
Mihai IONESCU, Corneliu POPA, Bujor
HĂLMĂGEANU, Dan COE, Mihai MOCANU, Simion
SURDAN, Dumitru POPESCU, Ion PÎRCĂLAB, Mircea
DRIDEA, Constantin FRĂŢILĂ, Mircea LUCESCU

<u>SWI:</u> (Coach: Alfredo FONI)
Mario PROSPERI, Alex MATTER, Heinz BÄNI,
Georges PERROUD, Hans-Rudi FUHRER, Karl
ODERMATT, Richard DÜRR, Vittore GOTTARDI,
Friedrich KÜNZLI, René-Pierre QUENTIN, Bruno
BERNASCONI

26 November 1966     Ref: Gerhard SCHULENBURG
(West Germany)
Stadio San Paolo, NAPLES (Att. 75,000)

## ITALY - ROMANIA
## 3:1 (2:1)

0:1 Dobrin (7'), 1:1 Mazzola (30'), 2:1 Depaoli (43'),
3:1 Mazzola (67')

ITA: (Coach: Ferruccio VALCAREGGI)
Giuliano SARTI, Spartaco LANDINI, Giacinto
FACCHETTI, Ottavio BIANCHI, Aristide GUARNERI,
Armando PICCHI, Angelo DOMENGHINI, Alessandro
MAZZOLA, Virginio DEPAOLI, Antonio JULIANO,
Mario CORSO

ROM: (Coach: Ilie OANĂ)
Ilie DATCU, Corneliu POPA, Ion BARBU, Dan COE,
Augustin DELEANU, Vasile GERGELY, Nicolae
DOBRIN, Ion PÎRCĂLAB, Constantin FRĂȚILĂ,
Mircea DRIDEA, Mircea LUCESCU


3 December 1966      Ref: Arthur LENTINI (Malta)
Stádio G.S.P., NICOSIA (Att. 4,823)

## CYPRUS - ROMANIA
## 1:5 (1:0)

1:0 Pieridis (32'), 1:1 Dridea (49'), 1:2 Lucescu (51'),
1:3 Frăţilă (65'), 1:4 Frăţilă (74'), 1:5 Dridea (82')

CYP: (Coach: Argyris GAVALAS)
Nikolaos ELEUTHERIADIS (Varnavas HRISTOFI
55'), Kyriakos KOUREAS, Ploutis PALLAS, Nikakis
KANTZILIERIS, Kostakis PIERIDIS, Pamboullis
PAPADOPOULOS, Panikos KRYSTALLIS,
Konstantinos PANAYIOTOU, Hristofis HRISTOFI,
Andreas STYLIANOU, Konstantinos HRISTOU

<u>ROM:</u> (Coach: Ilie OANĂ)
Mihai IONESCU, Corneliu POPA, Ion NUNWEILLER, Dan COE, Augustin DELEANU, Vasile GERGELY, Nicolae DOBRIN, Ion PÎRCĂLAB, Constantin FRĂŢILĂ, Mircea DRIDEA, Mircea LUCESCU


22 March 1967      Ref: Atanas KIRYAKOV (Bulgaria)
Stádio G.S.P., NICOSIA (Att. 5,380)

### CYPRUS - ITALY
### 0:2 (0:0)

0:1 Domenghini (76'), 0:2 Facchetti (88')

<u>CYP:</u> (Coach: Argyris GAVALAS)
Varnavas HRISTOFI, Panikos IAKOVOU, Konstantinos PANAYIOTOU, Giorgos KETTENIS, Konstantinos HRISTOU, Ploutis PALLAS, Drosos KALOTHEOU, Kostakis PIERIDIS, Hristofis HRISTOFI, Panikos KRYSTALLIS, Andreas STYLIANOU

<u>ITA:</u> (Coach: Ferruccio VALCAREGGI)
Giuliano SARTI, Tarcisio BURGNICH, Giacinto FACCHETTI, Giovanni LODETTI, Aristide GUARNERI, Armando PICCHI, Angelo DOMENGHINI, Giovanni RIVERA, Renato CAPPELLINI, Antonio JULIANO, Mario CORSO


23 April 1967      Ref: Milivoje GUGULOVIĆ
(Yugoslavia)
Stadionul 23 August, BUCHAREST (Att. 9,412)

### ROMANIA - CYPRUS
### 7:0 (3:0)

1:0 Lucescu (4'), 2:0 Martinovici (15'), 3:0 Dumitru (24'), 4:0 I. Ionescu (47'), 5:0 Dumitru (52'), 6:0 Dumitru (77'), 7:0 I. Ionescu (86')

ROM: (Coach: Ilie OANĂ)
Mihai IONESCU, Corneliu POPA, Ion NUNWEILLER,
Dumitru NICOLAE, Mihai MOCANU, Vasile
GERGELY, Nicolae DOBRIN, Florea MARTINOVICI,
Emil DUMITRU, Ion IONESCU, Mircea LUCESCU

CYP: (Coach: Argyris GAVALAS)
Varnavas HRISTOFI, Panikos IAKOVOU,
Konstantinos HRISTOU, Ploutis PALLAS,
Konstantinos PANAYIOTOU, Giorgos KETTENIS,
Drosos KALOTHEOU, Kostakis PIERIDIS, Panikos
KRYSTALLIS, Andreas STYLIANOU, Hristofis
HRISTOFI


24 May 1967        Ref: Robert LACOSTE (France)
Hardturm Stadion, ZÜRICH (Att. 21,337)

SWITZERLAND - ROMANIA
7:1 (3:0)

1:0 Künzli (12'), 2:0 Quentin (15'), 3:0 Quentin (32'),
4:0 Blättler (46'), 5:0 Blättler (59'), 6:0 Odermatt (63'),
7:0 Künzli (67'), 7:1 Dobrin (70')

SWI: (Coach: Erwin BALLABIO)
Marcel KUNZ, Markus PFIRTER, Ely TACCHELLA,
Bruno MICHAUD, Georges PERROUD, Karl
ODERMATT, Heinz BÄNI, Richard DÜRR, Friedrich
KÜNZLI, Rolf BLÄTTLER, René-Pierre QUENTIN

ROM: (Coach: Ilie OANĂ)
Mihai IONESCU (Ilie DATCU 46'), Corneliu POPA, Ion
NUNWEILLER, Dumitru NICOLAE, Mihai MOCANU,
Vasile GERGELY, Nicolae DOBRIN, Ion PÎRCĂLAB,
Mircea DRIDEA, Ion IONESCU, Mircea LUCESCU


25 June 1967      Ref: Manuel GÓMEZ Arribas (Spain)

Stadionul 23 August, BUCHAREST (Att. 54,300)

## ROMANIA - ITALY
### 0:1 (0:0)

0:1 Bertini (81')

ROM: (Coach: Angelo NICULESCU)
Necula RĂDUCANU, Niculae LUPESCU, Mihai
MOCANU, Vasile GERGELY, Ion NUNWEILLER,
Ion BARBU, Mircea LUCESCU, Emil DUMITRU, Ion
IONESCU, Iuliu NĂFTĂNĂILĂ, Radu NUNWEILLER

ITA: (Coach: Ferruccio VALCAREGGI)
Enrico ALBERTOSI, Adolfo GORI, Giacinto
FACCHETTI, Mario BERTINI, Aristide GUARNERI,
Armando PICCHI, Giovanni RIVERA, Antonio
JULIANO, Gianfranco ZIGONI, Giacomo
BULGARELLI, Ezio PASCUTTI


1 November 1967       Ref: Antoine QUEUDEVILLE
(Luxembourg)
Stadio San Vito, COSENZA (Att. 22,059)

## ITALY - CYPRUS
### 5:0 (2:0)

1:0 Mazzola (12'), 2:0 Mazzola (22'), 3:0 Riva (46'),
4:0 Riva (55'), 5:0 Riva (59')

ITA: (Coach: Ferruccio VALCAREGGI)
Enrico ALBERTOSI, Tarcisio BURGNICH,
Giacinto FACCHETTI, Romano FOGLI, Giancarlo
BERCELLINO, Armando PICCHI, Angelo
DOMENGHINI, Antonio JULIANO, Alessandro
MAZZOLA, Giancarlo DE SISTI, Luigi RIVA

CYP: (Coach: Argyris GAVALAS)
Varnavas HRISTOFI, Konstantinos HRISTOU,

Kyriakos KOUREAS, Panais NIKOLAOU, Konstantinos PANAYIOTOU, Ploutis PALLAS, Pamboullis PAPADOPOULOS, Nikakis KANTZILIERIS, Andreas STYLIANOU, Panikos KRYSTALLIS, Grigoris FILIASTIDIS

8 November 1967    Ref: Robert SCHAUT (Belgium)
Stadio Comunale di Cornaredo, LUGANO (Att. 3,737)

### SWITZERLAND - CYPRUS
### 5:0 (2:0)

1:0 Blättler (32'), 2:0 Künzli (43'), 3:0 Blättler (55'), 4:0 Dürr (58' pen.), 5:0 Odermatt (73')

SWI: (Coach: Alfredo FONI)
Marcel KUNZ, Markus PFIRTER, Bruno MICHAUD, Ely TACCHELLA, Georges PERROUD, Karl ODERMATT, Hans-Rudi FUHRER, Richard DÜRR, Friedrich KÜNZLI, Rolf BLÄTTLER, René-Pierre QUENTIN

CYP: (Coach: Argyris GAVALAS)
Varnavas HRISTOFI, Konstantinos HRISTOU, Kyriakos KOUREAS, Konstantinos PANAYIOTOU, Ploutis PALLAS, Panais NIKOLAOU, Nikakis KANTZILIERIS, Panikos KRYSTALLIS, Pamboullis PAPADOPOULOS, Grigoris FILIASTIDIS, Andreas STYLIANOU

18 November 1967    Ref: István ZSOLT (Hungary)
Wankdorf Stadion, BERNE (Att. 53,137)

### SWITZERLAND - ITALY
### 2:2 (1:0)

1:0 Quentin (34'), 1:1 Riva (66'), 2:1 Künzli (68'), 2:2 Riva (85' pen.)

<u>SWI:</u> (Coach: Alfredo FONI)
Marcel KUNZ, Markus PFIRTER, Ely TACCHELLA,
Bruno MICHAUD, Georges PERROUD, Karl
ODERMATT, Hans-Rudi FUHRER, Richard DÜRR,
Friedrich KÜNZLI, Rolf BLÄTTLER, René-Pierre
QUENTIN

<u>ITA:</u> (Coach: Ferruccio VALCAREGGI)
Enrico ALBERTOSI, Tarcisio BURGNICH,
Giacinto FACCHETTI, Roberto ROSATO,
Giancarlo BERCELLINO, Armando PICCHI,
Angelo DOMENGHINI, Antonio JULIANO, Roberto
BONINSEGNA, Giancarlo DE SISTI, Luigi RIVA

23 December 1967        Ref: Thomas WHARTON
                                     (Scotland)
Stadio Amsicora, CAGLIARI (Att. 28,000)

ITALY - SWITZERLAND
4:0 (3:0)

1:0 Mazzola (3'), 2:0 Riva (13'), 3:0 Domenghini (45'),
4:0 Domenghini (67')

<u>ITA:</u> (Coach: Ferruccio VALCAREGGI)
Enrico ALBERTOSI, Tarcisio BURGNICH,
Giacinto FACCHETTI, Giorgio FERRINI, Giancarlo
BERCELLINO, Armando PICCHI, Angelo
DOMENGHINI, Giovanni RIVERA, Alessandro
MAZZOLA, Antonio JULIANO, Luigi RIVA

<u>SWI:</u> (Coach: Alfredo FONI)
Marcel KUNZ (Karl GROB 84'), Markus PFIRTER, Ely
TACCHELLA, Bruno MICHAUD, Georges PERROUD,
Karl ODERMATT, Hans-Rudi FUHRER, Richard
DÜRR, Bruno BERNASCONI, Friedrich KÜNZLI,
René-Pierre QUENTIN

17 February 1968        Ref: Pavel ŠPOTÁK
(Czechoslovakia)
Stádio G.S.P., NICOSIA (Att. 7,500)

## CYPRUS - SWITZERLAND
## 2:1 (1:1)

0:1 Hristou (9' og), 1:1 Asprou (22'), 2:1 Papadopoulos
(46')


CYP: (Coach: Pamboullis AVRAAMIDES)
Andreas FILOTAS (Mihalakis ALKIVIADIS 46'), Panikos
IAKOVOU, Konstantinos HRISTOU, Giannakis
XIPOLITAS, Konstantinos PANAYIOTOU, Panikos
KRYSTALLIS, Andreas HRISTODOULOU, Panikos
EUTHIMIADIS, Pamboullis PAPADOPOULOS,
Drosos KALOTHEOU, Menelaos ASPROU

SWI: (Coach: Erwin BALLABIO)
Marcel KUNZ, Markus PFIRTER, Bruno MICHAUD,
Renzo BIONDA, Paul MARTI, Karl ODERMATT, Hans-
Rudi FUHRER, Richard DÜRR, Friedrich KÜNZLI,
Rolf BLÄTTLER, René-Pierre QUENTIN


ITALY (Q)        (P6, W5, D1, L0, F17, A3, Pts. 11)
Romania          (P6, W3, D0, L3, F18, A14, Pts. 6)
Switzerland      (P6, W2, D1, L3, F17, A13, Pts. 5)
Cyprus           (P6, W1, D0, L5, F3, A25, Pts. 2)


GROUP 7 (Belgium, France, Luxembourg, Poland)


2 October 1966      Ref: Erwin VETTER (East Germany)
Stadion Pogón, SZCZECIN (Att. 10,840)

## POLAND - LUXEMBOURG
## 4:0 (0:0)

1:0 Jarosik (49'), 2:0 Liberda (54'), 3:0 Grzegorczyk (73'), 4:0 Sadek (88')

POL: (Coach: Selection Committee)
Stanisław MAJCHER, Roman STRZAŁKOWSKI, Paweł ORZECHOWSKI, Henryk BREJZA, Zygmunt ANCZOK, Ryszard GRZEGORCZYK, Zygmunt SCHMIDT, Jerzy SADEK, Jan LIBERDA, Andrzej JAROSIK, Janusz KOWALIK

LUX: (Coach: Robert HEINZ)
Théo STENDEBACH, Erwin KUFFER, Jean-Pierre HOFFSTETTER, Jean HARDT, François KONTER, Fernand JEITZ, René SCHNEIDER, Jean KLEIN, Jean LÉONARD, Nicolas HOFFMANN, Edouard DUBLIN

22 October 1966      Ref: Gerhard SCHULENBURG
(West Germany)
Parc des Princes, PARIS (Att. 23,524)

FRANCE - POLAND
2:1 (1:0)

1:0 Di Nallo (26'), 1:1 Grzegorczyk (61'), 2:1 Lech (85')

FRA: (Coach: Jean SNELLA)
Georges CARNUS, Jean DJORKAEFF, Claude ROBIN, Robert BUDZYNSKI, André CHORDA, Jean-Claude SUAUDEAU, Jacques SIMON, Yves HERBET, Georges LECH, Fleury DI NALLO, Paul COURTIN

POL: (Coach: Selection Committee)
Jan GOMOLA, Roman STRZAŁKOWSKI, Jacek GMOCH, Stanisław OŚLIZŁO, Zygmunt ANCZOK, Piotr SUSKI, Ryszard GRZEGORCZYK, Jerzy SADEK, Włodzimierz LUBAŃSKI, Jan LIBERDA, Andrzej JAROSIK

11 November 1966      Ref: John TAYLOR (England)
Stade du Heysel, BRUSSELS (Att. 43,404)

BELGIUM - FRANCE
2:1 (0:0)

1:0 Van Himst (51'), 2:0 Van Himst (54'), 2:1 Lech (67')

BEL: (Coach: Constant VANDEN STOCK/Raymond
GOETHALS)
Jean NICOLAY, Georges HEYLENS, Pierre HANON,
Jean PLASKIE, Yves BARÉ, Wilfried VAN MOER,
Joseph JURION, John THIO, Raoul LAMBERT, Paul
VAN HIMST, Wilfried PUIS

FRA: (Coach: Jean SNELLA)
Georges CARNUS, Jean DJORKAEFF, Claude
ROBIN, Robert BUDZYNSKI, André CHORDA,
Jacques SIMON, Jean-Claude SUAUDEAU, Bernard
BLANCHET, Hervé REVELLI, Georges LECH, Gérard
HAUSSER

26 November 1966      Ref: Laurens VAN RAVENS
(Netherlands)
Stade Municipal, LUXEMBOURG CITY (Att. 3,465)

LUXEMBOURG - FRANCE
0:3 (0:3)

0:1 Herbet (8'), 0:2 Revelli (40'), 0:3 Lech (41')

LUX: (Coach: Robert HEINZ)
Théo STENDEBACH, Erwin KUFFER, Fernand
JEITZ, Mathias EWEN, Jean-Pierre HOFFSTETTER,
Nicolas HOFFMANN, François KONTER, Edouard
DUBLIN, Jean LÉONARD, Adolphe SCHMIT, Joseph
KIRCHENS

FRA: (Coach: Jean SNELLA)

Georges CARNUS, Jean DJORKAEFF, Marcel ARTELESA, Bernard BOSQUIER, André CHORDA, Joseph BONNEL, Michel WATTEAU, Yves HERBET, Hervé REVELLI, Georges LECH, Laurent ROBUSCHI

19 March 1967     Ref: Karl GÖPPEL (Switzerland)
Stade Municipal, LUXEMBOURG CITY (Att. 9,107)

### LUXEMBOURG - BELGIUM
### 0:5 (0:3)

0:1 Van Himst (20'), 0:2 Stockman (29'), 0:3 Van Himst (36'), 0:4 Stockman (60'), 0:5 Stockman (73')

LUX: (Coach: Robert HEINZ)
Théo STENDEBACH, Erwin KUFFER, Fernand JEITZ, François KONTER, Jean-Pierre HOFFSTETTER, Nicolas HOFFMANN, Mathias EWEN, Louis PILOT, Edouard DUBLIN, Jean LÉONARD, Henri KLEIN

BEL: (Coach: Constant VANDEN STOCK/Raymond GOETHALS)
Jean NICOLAY, Georges HEYLENS, Pierre HANON, Jean PLASKIE, Florent BOHEZ, Wilfried VAN MOER, John THIO, Joseph JURION, Jacques STOCKMAN, Paul VAN HIMST, Wilfried PUIS

16 April 1967     Ref: Einar POULSEN (Denmark)
Stade Municipal, LUXEMBOURG CITY (Att. 7,229)

### LUXEMBOURG - POLAND
### 0:0

LUX: (Coach: Robert HEINZ)
René HOFFMANN, Erwin KUFFER, Fernand JEITZ, Mathias EWEN, Jean-Pierre HOFFSTETTER, Adolphe SCHMIT, François KONTER, Jean KLEIN, Louis PILOT, Jean LÉONARD, Edouard DUBLIN

POL: (Coach: Michał MATYAS)
Konrad KORNEK, Roman STRZAŁKOWSKI, Jacek GMOCH, Stanisław OŚLIZŁO, Zygmunt ANCZOK, Zygmunt SCHMIDT, Zygfryd SZOŁTYSIK, Krzysztof HAUSNER, Włodzimierz LUBAŃSKI, Jerzy MUSIAŁEK, Andrzej JAROSIK

21 May 1967          Ref: Toimi OLKKU (Finland)
Stadion Śląski, CHORZÓW (Att. 57,000)

POLAND - BELGIUM
3:1 (2:0)

1:0 Lubański (28'), 2:0 Lubański (41'), 2:1 Puis (52'),
3:1 Szołtysik (72')

POL: (Coach: Michał MATYAS)
Konrad KORNEK, Paweł KOWALSKI, Roman STRZAŁKOWSKI, Jacek GMOCH, Zygmunt ANCZOK, Zygmunt SCHMIDT, Piotr SUSKI, Jerzy SADEK, Zygfryd SZOŁTYSIK, Włodzimierz LUBAŃSKI, Jan LIBERDA

BEL: (Coach: Constant VANDEN STOCK/Raymond GOETHALS)
Jean NICOLAY, Georges HEYLENS, Albert SULON, Jean PLASKIE, Florent BOHEZ, Prudent BETTENS, Joseph JURION, Wilfried VAN MOER, Jacques STOCKMAN, Paul VAN HIMST, Wilfried PUIS

17 September 1967     Ref: Ferdinand MARSCHALL
(Austria)
Stadion Dziesięciolecia, WARSAW (Att. 51,010)

POLAND - FRANCE
1:4 (1:2)

0:1 Herbin (13'), 1:1 Brychczy (26'), 1:2 Di Nallo (33'),
1:3 Guy (63'), 1:4 Di Nallo (85')

POL: (Coach: Michał MATYAS)
Hubert KOSTKA, Paweł KOWALSKI, Jacek GMOCH, Stanisław OŚLIZŁO, Zygmunt ANCZOK, Lucjan BRYCHCZY, Piotr SUSKI, Eugeniusz FABER, Zygfryd SZOŁTYSIK, Włodzimierz LUBAŃSKI, Robert GADOCHA

FRA: (Coach: Louis DUGAUGUEZ)
Marcel AUBOUR, Jean DJORKAEFF, Roland MITORAJ, Bernard BOSQUIER, Jean BAEZA, Henri MICHEL, Robert HERBIN, Yves HERBET, André GUY, Fleury DI NALLO, Charly LOUBET

8 October 1967   Ref: Juan GARDEAZÁBAL Garay
(Spain)
Stade du Heysel, BRUSSELS (Att. 35,897)

## BELGIUM - POLAND
### 2:4 (2:2)

1:0 Devrindt (15'), 1:1 Żmijewski (26'), 2:1 Devrindt (35'), 2:2 Brychczy (45'), 2:3 Żmijewski (52'), 2:4 Żmijewski (70')

BEL: (Coach: Constant VANDEN STOCK/Raymond GOETHALS)
Jean NICOLAY, Georges HEYLENS, Pierre HANON, Jean PLASKIE, Yves BARÉ, Paul VANDENBERG, John THIO, Alfons HAAGDOREN, Johan DEVRINDT, Paul VAN HIMST, Wilfried PUIS

POL: (Coach: Michał MATYAS)
Hubert KOSTKA, Antoni PIECHNICZEK, Jacek GMOCH, Stanisław OŚLIZŁO, Stefan SZEFER, Henryk BREJZA, Lucjan BRYCHCZY, Zygmunt SCHMIDT, Włodzimierz LUBAŃSKI, Janusz ŻMIJEWSKI, Eugeniusz FABER

Richard Keir

28 October 1967      Ref: Francesco FRANCESCON
(Italy)
Stade Marcel Saupin, NANTES (Att. 14,591)
FRANCE - BELGIUM
1:1 (0:1)

0:1 Claessen (37'), 1:1 Herbin (84')

FRA: (Coach: Louis DUGAUGUEZ)
Marcel AUBOUR, Jean DJORKAEFF, Claude
QUITTET, Bernard BOSQUIER, Jean BAEZA, Yves
HERBET, Henri MICHEL, Robert HERBIN, Fleury DI
NALLO, Hervé REVELLI, Charly LOUBET

BEL: (Coach: Constant VANDEN STOCK/Raymond
GOETHALS)
Fernand BOONE, Georges HEYLENS, André
STASSART, Jean PLASKIE, Jean CORNELIS, Pierre
HANON, Nicolas DEWALQUE, Johan DEVRINDT,
Roger CLAESSEN, Raoul LAMBERT, Wilfried PUIS


22 November 1967          Ref: William O'NEILL
(Northern Ireland)
Albert Dyserynck Stadion, BRUGES (Att. 6,745)
BELGIUM - LUXEMBOURG
3:0 (0:0)

1:0 Thio (62'), 2:0 Claessen (65'), 3:0 Thio (77')

BEL: (Coach: Constant VANDEN STOCK/Raymond
GOETHALS)
Fernand BOONE, Georges HEYLENS, Alfons
PEETERS, Jean PLASKIE, Jean CORNELIS,
Pierre HANON, Jean DOCKX, John THIO, Roger
CLAESSEN, Johan DEVRINDT, Wilfried PUIS

LUX: (Coach: Robert HEINZ)

René HOFFMANN, Erwin KUFFER, Mathias EWEN, Fernand JEITZ, Jean-Pierre HOFFSTETTER, Nicolas HOFFMANN, Louis PILOT, Jean KLEIN, Edouard DUBLIN, Jean LÉONARD, Adolphe SCHMIT


23 December 1967      Ref: Aníbal da Silva OLIVEIRA
(Portugal)

Parc des Princes, PARIS (Att. 7,320)

FRANCE - LUXEMBOURG
3:1 (1:0)

1:0 Loubet (42'), 2:0 Loubet (47'), 3:0 Loubet (53'), 3:1 Klein (85')


FRA: (Coach: Louis DUGAUGUEZ)
Marcel AUBOUR, Jean DJORKAEFF, Claude QUITTET, Bernard BOSQUIER, Jean BAEZA, Richard KRAWCZYK, Henri MICHEL, Robert SZCZEPANIAK, Charly LOUBET, Didier COUÉCOU, Georges BERETA

LUX: (Coach: Robert HEINZ)
René HOFFMANN, Erwin KUFFER, Mathias EWEN, Fernand JEITZ, Jean-Pierre HOFFSTETTER, François KONTER, Louis PILOT, Jean KLEIN, Jean LÉONARD, Edouard DUBLIN, Adolphe SCHMIT


FRANCE (Q)        (P6, W4, D1, L1, F14, A6, Pts. 9)
Belgium           (P6, W3, D1, L2, F14, A9, Pts. 7)
Poland            (P6, W3, D1, L2, F13, A9, Pts. 7)
Luxembourg        (P6, W0, D1, L5, F1, A18, Pts. 1)


GROUP 8 (England, Northern Ireland, Scotland, Wales)

22 October 1966          Ref: Kenneth DAGNALL
                                   (England)

Ninian Park, CARDIFF (Att. 33,269)

WALES - SCOTLAND
1:1 (0:0)

1:0 R. Davies (76'), 1:1 Law (86')

WAL: (Coach: David BOWEN)
Gareth SPRAKE, Peter RODRIGUES, Graham
WILLIAMS, Terrence HENNESSEY, Michael
ENGLAND, Barrington HOLE, Gilbert REECE, Wyn
DAVIES, Ronald DAVIES, Clifford JONES, Alan
JARVIS

SCO: (Coach: Malcolm McDONALD)
Robert FERGUSON, John GREIG, Thomas
GEMMELL, William BREMNER, Ronald McKINNON,
John CLARK, James JOHNSTONE, Denis LAW,
Joseph McBRIDE, James BAXTER, William
HENDERSON


22 October 1966          Ref: Robert DAVIDSON
                                   (Scotland)

Windsor Park, BELFAST (Att. 47,897)

NORTHERN IRELAND - ENGLAND
0:2 (0:1)

0:1 Hunt (40'), 0:2 Peters (60')

NIR: (Coach: Robert PEACOCK)
Patrick JENNINGS (William McFAUL 46'), John
PARKE, Alexander ELDER, Samuel TODD,
Martin HARVEY, William McCULLOUGH, William
FERGUSON, John CROSSAN, William IRVINE,
Derek DOUGAN, George BEST

ENG: (Coach: Alfred RAMSEY)
Gordon BANKS, George COHEN, Ramon WILSON, Norbert STILES, John CHARLTON, Robert MOORE, Alan BALL, Geoffrey HURST, Robert CHARLTON, Roger HUNT, Martin PETERS

Red Card: Ferguson 85'


16 November 1966        Ref: John TAYLOR
(England)

Hampden Park, GLASGOW (Att. 45,281)

SCOTLAND - NORTHERN IRELAND
2:1 (2:1)

0:1 Nicholson (9'), 1:1 Murdoch (14'), 2:1 Lennox (35')

SCO: (Coach: Malcolm McDONALD)
Robert FERGUSON, John GREIG, Thomas GEMMELL, William BREMNER, Ronald McKINNON, John CLARK, William HENDERSON, Robert MURDOCH, Joseph McBRIDE, Stephen CHALMERS, Robert LENNOX

NIR: (Coach: Robert PEACOCK)
Patrick JENNINGS, John PARKE, Alexander ELDER, Martin HARVEY, Terence NEILL, James NICHOLSON, Samuel WILSON, John CROSSAN, William IRVINE, Derek DOUGAN, David CLEMENTS


16 November 1966      Ref: Thomas WHARTON
(Scotland)

Wembley Stadium, LONDON (Att. 75,380)

ENGLAND - WALES
5:1 (3:1)

1:0 Hurst (30'), 2:0 Hurst (34'), 2:1 W. Davies (36'),

3:1 R. Charlton (43'), 4:1 Hennessey (65' og), 5:1 J. Charlton (84')

ENG: (Coach: Alfred RAMSEY)
Gordon BANKS, George COHEN, Ramon WILSON, Norbert STILES, John CHARLTON, Robert MOORE, Alan BALL, Geoffrey HURST, Robert CHARLTON, Roger HUNT, Martin PETERS

WAL: (Coach: David BOWEN)
Anthony MILLINGTON, Colin GREEN, Graham WILLIAMS, Terrence HENNESSEY, Michael ENGLAND, Barrington HOLE, Ronald REES, Wyn DAVIES, Ronald DAVIES, Clifford JONES, Alan JARVIS

12 April 1967　　　Ref: Kevin HOWLEY (England)
Windsor Park, BELFAST (Att. 17,643)

### NORTHERN IRELAND - WALES
### 0:0

NIR: (Coach: Robert PEACOCK)
Roderick MCKENZIE, David CRAIG, Alexander ELDER, Arthur STEWART, Terence NEILL, James NICHOLSON, Eric WELSH, Daniel TRAINOR, Derek DOUGAN, Walter BRUCE, David CLEMENTS

WAL: (Coach: David BOWEN)
Anthony MILLINGTON, Roderick THOMAS, Graham WILLIAMS, Alan JARVIS, Glyn JAMES, Barrington HOLE, Ronald REES, Alan DURBAN, Ronald DAVIES, Royston VERNON, Keith PRING

15 April 1967　　　Ref: Gerhard SCHULENBURG
(West Germany)
Wembley Stadium, LONDON (Att. 99,063)

157

## ENGLAND - SCOTLAND
## 2:3 (0:1)

0:1 Law (27'), 0:2 Lennox (78'), 1:2 J. Charlton (84'),
1:3 McCalliog (87'), 2:3 Hurst (88')

ENG: (Coach: Alfred RAMSEY)
Gordon BANKS, George COHEN, Ramon WILSON,
Norbert STILES, John CHARLTON, Robert MOORE,
Alan BALL, James GREAVES, Robert CHARLTON,
Geoffrey HURST, Martin PETERS

SCO: (Coach: Robert BROWN)
Ronald SIMPSON, Thomas GEMMELL, Edward
MCCREADIE, John GREIG, Ronald McKINNON,
William BREMNER, James McCALLIOG, Denis LAW,
William WALLACE, James BAXTER, Robert LENNOX

21 October 1967        Ref: John GORDON (Scotland)
Ninian Park, CARDIFF (Att. 44,960)

## WALES - ENGLAND
## 0:3 (0:1)

0:1 Peters (34'), 0:2 R. Charlton (87'), 0:3 Ball (90' pen.)

WAL: (Coach: David BOWEN)
Gareth SPRAKE, Peter RODRIGUES, Colin GREEN,
Terrence   HENNESSEY,   Michael   ENGLAND,
Barrington HOLE, Ronald REES, Alan DURBAN,
John MAHONEY, Royston VERNON, Clifford JONES

ENG: (Coach: Alfred RAMSEY)
Gordon BANKS, George COHEN, Keith NEWTON,
Alan MULLERY, John CHARLTON, Robert MOORE,
Alan BALL, Roger HUNT, Robert CHARLTON,
Geoffrey HURST, Martin PETERS

21 October 1967      Ref: James FINNEY (England)
Windsor Park, BELFAST (Att. 55,000)

## NORTHERN IRELAND - SCOTLAND
## 1:0 (0:0)

### 1:0 Clements (67')

NIR: (Coach: William BINGHAM)
Patrick JENNINGS, John PARKE, William McKEAG,
Arthur STEWART, Terence NEILL, David CLEMENTS,
William CAMPBELL, John CROSSAN, Derek
DOUGAN, James NICHOLSON, George BEST

SCO: (Coach: Robert BROWN)
Ronald SIMPSON, Thomas GEMMELL, Edward
McCREADIE, John GREIG, Ronald McKINNON, John
URE, William WALLACE, Robert MURDOCH, James
McCALLIOG, Denis LAW, William MORGAN


22 November 1967      Ref: James FINNEY (England)
Hampden Park, GLASGOW (Att. 57,472)

## SCOTLAND - WALES
## 3:2 (1:1)

1:0 Gilzean (15'), 1:1 R. Davies (18'), 1:2 Durban (55'),
2:2 Gilzean (65'), 3:2 McKinnon (78')

SCO: (Coach: Robert BROWN)
Robert CLARK, James CRAIG, Edward McCREADIE,
John GREIG, Ronald McKINNON, James BAXTER,
James JOHNSTONE, William BREMNER, Alan
GILZEAN, William JOHNSTON, Robert LENNOX

WAL: (Coach: David BOWEN)
Gareth SPRAKE, Peter RODRIGUES, Colin GREEN,
Terrence HENNESSEY, Glyn JAMES, Barrington
HOLE, Ronald REES, Wyn DAVIES, Ronald DAVIES,
Alan DURBAN, Clifford JONES

22 November 1967      Ref: Leo CALLAGHAN (Wales)
Wembley Stadium, LONDON (Att. 83,969)

### ENGLAND - NORTHERN IRELAND
### 2:0 (1:0)

1:0 Hurst (43'), 2:0 R. Charlton (62')

ENG: (Coach: Alfred RAMSEY)
Gordon BANKS, George COHEN, Ramon WILSON,
Alan MULLERY, David SADLER, Robert MOORE,
Peter THOMPSON, Roger HUNT, Robert CHARLTON,
Geoffrey HURST, Martin PETERS

NIR: (Coach: William BINGHAM)
Patrick JENNINGS, John PARKE, Alexander ELDER,
Arthur STEWART, Terence NEILL, Martin HARVEY,
William CAMPBELL, William IRVINE, Samuel
WILSON, James NICHOLSON, David CLEMENTS


24 February 1968      Ref: Laurens VAN RAVENS
                              (Netherlands)
Hampden Park, GLASGOW (Att. 134,461)

### SCOTLAND - ENGLAND
### 1:1 (0:1)

0:1 Peters (20'), 1:1 Hughes (39')

SCO: (Coach: Robert BROWN)
Ronald SIMPSON, Thomas GEMMELL, Edward
McCREADIE, William McNEILL, Ronald McKINNON,
John GREIG, Charles COOKE, William BREMNER,
John HUGHES, William JOHNSTON, Robert LENNOX

ENG: (Coach: Alfred RAMSEY)
Gordon BANKS, Keith NEWTON, Ramon WILSON,
Alan MULLERY, Brian LABONE, Robert MOORE,
Alan BALL, Geoffrey HURST, Michael SUMMERBEE,

Robert CHARLTON, Martin PETERS

28 February 1968          Ref: Robert DAVIDSON
(Scotland)
The Racecourse Ground, WREXHAM (Att. 17,548)

WALES - NORTHERN IRELAND
2:0 (0:0)

1:0 Rees (75'), 2:0 W. Davies (84')

WAL: (Coach: David BOWEN)
Anthony MILLINGTON, Peter RODRIGUES, Colin
GREEN, Terrence HENNESSEY, Michael ENGLAND,
Barrington HOLE, Ronald REES, Wyn DAVIES,
Ronald DAVIES, Alan DURBAN, Graham WILLIAMS

NIR: (Coach: William BINGHAM)
Patrick JENNINGS, David CRAIG, Alexander ELDER,
Martin HARVEY, Samuel TODD, William McKEAG,
William IRVINE, Arthur STEWART, Derek DOUGAN,
James NICHOLSON, Terence HARKIN

ENGLAND (Q)          (P6, W4, D1, L1, F15, A5, Pts. 9)
Scotland             (P6, W3, D2, L1, F10, A8, Pts. 8)
Wales                (P6, W1, D2, L3, F6, A12, Pts. 4)
Northern Ireland     (P6, W1, D1, L4, F2, A8, Pts. 3)

## QUARTER-FINALS

3 April 1968          Ref: Gilbert DROZ (Switzerland)
Wembley Stadium, LONDON (Att. 100,000)

ENGLAND - SPAIN
1:0 (0:0)

## 1:0 R. Charlton (84')

ENG: (Coach: Alfred RAMSEY)
Gordon BANKS, Cyril KNOWLES, Ramon WILSON,
Alan MULLERY, John CHARLTON, Robert MOORE,
Alan BALL, Roger HUNT, Michael SUMMERBEE,
Robert CHARLTON, Martin PETERS

SPA: (Coach: Domènec BALMANYA i Perera)
Salvador SADURNÍ Urpi, José Ignacio SÁEZ Ruiz,
Francisco Fernández Rodríguez 'GALLEGO', Juan
Manuel CANÓS Ferrer, José Martínez Sánchez
'PIRRI', Ignacio ZOCO Esparza, Manuel Polinario
Muñoz 'POLI', AMANCIO Amaro Varela, Fernando
ANSOLA San Martín, Ramón Moreno GROSSO, José
CLARAMUNT Torres


8 May 1968        Ref: Josef KRŇÁVEK
                 (Czechoslovakia)
Estadio Santiago Bernabéu, MADRID (Att. 120,000)

### SPAIN - ENGLAND
### 1:2 (0:0)

1:0 Amancio (48'), 1:1 Peters (55'), 1:2 Hunter (81')

SPA: (Coach: Domènec BALMANYA i Perera)
Salvador SADURNÍ Urpi, José Ignacio SÁEZ Ruiz,
Francisco Fernández Rodríguez 'GALLEGO', Juan
Manuel CANÓS Ferrer, José Martínez Sánchez
'PIRRI', Ignacio ZOCO Esparza, Joaquín RIFÉ
Climent, AMANCIO Amaro Varela, Ramón Moreno
GROSSO, Manuel VELÁZQUEZ Villaverde, Francisco
GENTO López

ENG: (Coach: Alfred RAMSEY)
Peter BONETTI, Keith NEWTON, Ramon WILSON,
Alan MULLERY, Brian LABONE, Robert MOORE,

Alan BALL, Martin PETERS, Robert CHARLTON, Roger HUNT, Norman HUNTER

ENGLAND won 3-1 on agg.

6 April 1968          Ref: Gerhard SCHULENBURG
                      (West Germany)
Stadion Vasil Levski, SOFIA (Att. 70,000)

### BULGARIA - ITALY
### 3:2 (1:0)

1:0 Kotkov (12' pen.), 1:1 Penev (60' og), 2:1 Dermendzhiev (66'), 3:1 Zhekov (73'), 3:2 Prati (83')

BUL: (Coach: Stefan BOZHKOV)
Stancho BONCHEV, Aleksandar SHALAMANOV, Boris GAGANELOV, Dimitar PENEV, Dobromir ZHECHEV, Dimitar YAKIMOV, Georgi POPOV, Petar ZHEKOV, Georgi ASPARUHOV, Nikola KOTKOV, Dinko DERMENDZHIEV

ITA: (Coach: Ferruccio VALCAREGGI)
Enrico ALBERTOSI (Lido VIERI 66'), Tarcisio BURGNICH, Giacinto FACCHETTI, Mario BERTINI, Giancarlo BERCELLINO, Armando PICCHI, Angelo DOMENGHINI, Antonio JULIANO, Alessandro MAZZOLA, Giovanni RIVERA, Pierino PRATI

20 April 1968          Ref: Gottfried DIENST
                       (Switzerland)
Stadio San Paolo, NAPLES (Att. 95,000)

### ITALY - BULGARIA
### 2:0 (1:0)

1:0 Prati (14'), 2:0 Domenghini (55')

ITA: (Coach: Ferruccio VALCAREGGI)
Dino ZOFF, Tarcisio BURGNICH, Giacinto FACCHETTI, Giorgio FERRINI, Aristide GUARNERI, Ernesto CASTANO, Angelo DOMENGHINI, Antonio JULIANO, Alessandro MAZZOLA, Giovanni RIVERA, Pierino PRATI

BUL: (Coach: Stefan BOZHKOV)
Simeon SIMEONOV, Aleksandar SHALAMANOV, Boris GAGANELOV, Dimitar PENEV, Ivan DIMITROV, Dobromir ZHECHEV, Georgi POPOV, Hristo BONEV, Georgi ASPARUHOV, Dimitar YAKIMOV, Dinko DERMENDZHIEV

ITALY won 4-3 on agg.

6 April 1968        Ref: Erwin VETTER (East Germany)
Stade Vélodrome, MARSEILLES (Att. 35,423)

### FRANCE - YUGOSLAVIA
### 1:1 (0:0)

0:1 Musemić (66'), 1:1 Di Nallo (78')

FRA: (Coach: Louis DUGAUGUEZ)
Marcel AUBOUR, Jean DJORKAEFF, Claude QUITTET, Bernard BOSQUIER, Jean BAEZA, Robert HERBIN, Jacques SIMON, Charly LOUBET, Nestor COMBIN, Fleury DI NALLO, Georges BERETA

YUG: (Coach: Rajko MITIĆ)
Ilija PANTELIĆ, Mirsad FAZLAGIĆ, Dragan HOLCER, Borivoje ĐORĐEVIĆ, Blagoje PAUNOVIĆ, Ljubomir MIHAJLOVIĆ, Dzemaludin MUŠOVIĆ, Ivan OSIM, Vahidin MUSEMIĆ, Dobrivoje TRIVIĆ, Dragan DŽAJIĆ

24 April 1968        Ref: Paul SCHILLER (Austria)
Stadion Crvena Zvezda, BELGRADE (Att. 70,900)

## YUGOSLAVIA - FRANCE
### 5:1 (4:1)

1:0 Petković (3'), 2:0 Musemić (12'), 3:0 Džajić (24'),
4:0 Petković (33'), 4:1 Di Nallo (34'), 5:1 Musemić (80')

YUG: (Coach: Rajko MITIĆ)
Ilija PANTELIĆ, Mirsad FAZLAGIĆ, Dragan HOLCER,
Rudolf BELIN, Mladen RAMLJAK, Ljubomir
MIHAJLOVIĆ, Ilija PETKOVIĆ, Dobrivoje TRIVIĆ,
Vahidin MUSEMIĆ, Ivan OSIM, Dragan DŽAJIĆ

FRA: (Coach: Louis DUGAUGUEZ)
Marcel AUBOUR, Vincent ESTÈVE, Claude QUITTET,
Bernard BOSQUIER, Jean BAEZA, Yves HERBET,
Jean DJORKAEFF, Robert SZCZEPANIAK, André
GUY, Charly LOUBET, Fleury DI NALLO


YUGOSLAVIA won 6-2 on agg.


4 May 1968              Ref: Laurens VAN RAVENS
                                    (Netherlands)
Népstadion, BUDAPEST (Att. 80,000)

## HUNGARY - USSR
### 2:0 (1:0)

1:0 Farkas (22'), 2:0 Göröcs (84')

HUN: (Coach: Károly SÓS)
Károly FATÉR, Dezső NOVÁK, Ernő SOLYMOSI,
Kálmán MÉSZÖLY, Kálmán IHÁSZ, János GÖRÖCS,
Lajos SZŰCS, Gyula RÁKOSI, László FAZEKAS,
Zoltán VARGA, János FARKAS

<u>URS:</u> (Coach: Mikhail YAKUSHIN)
Anzor KAVAZASHVILI, Yuriy ISTOMIN, Albert
SHESTERNYOV, Murtaz KHURTSILAVA, Viktor
ANICHKIN, Valeriy VORONIN, Igor CHISLENKO,
Vladimir KAPLICHNIY, Anatoliy BANISHEVSKIY,
Eduard STRELTSOV, Eduard MALOFEYEV


11 May 1968                    Ref: Kurt TSCHENSCHER
                                    (West Germany)
Tsentralniy Stadion 'V.I. Lenina', MOSCOW
(Att. 102,000)

### USSR - HUNGARY
### 3:0 (1:0)

1:0 Solymosi (22' og), 2:0 Khurtsilava (59'), 3:0
Byshovets (72')

<u>URS:</u> (Coach: Mikhail YAKUSHIN)
Yuriy PSHENICHNIKOV, Valentin AFONIN, Albert
SHESTERNYOV, Murtaz KHURTSILAVA, Viktor
ANICHKIN, Valeriy VORONIN, Igor CHISLENKO,
Vladimir KAPLICHNIY, Anatoliy BANISHEVSKIY,
Anatoliy BYSHOVETS, Gennadiy EVRYUZHIKHIN

<u>HUN:</u> (Coach: Károly SÓS)
Gyula TAMÁS, Dezső NOVÁK, Ernő SOLYMOSI,
Kálmán IHÁSZ, Kálmán MÉSZÖLY, Lajos SZŰCS,
Zoltán VARGA, Imre KOMORA, Flórián ALBERT,
János FARKAS, Gyula RÁKOSI


USSR won 3-2 on agg.

Richard Keir

# GOALSCORERS

## 6 GOALS

János FARKAS (Hungary), Luigi RIVA (Italy)

## 5 GOALS

Fleury DI NALLO (France), Henning FRENZEL (East Germany), Gerhard MÜLLER (West Germany), Constantin FRĂȚILĂ (Romania), Friedrich KÜNZLI (Switzerland), Alessandro MAZZOLA (Italy)

## 4 GOALS

Petar ZHEKOV (Bulgaria), Giorgos SIDERIS (Greece), Angelo DOMENGHINI (Italy), Rolf BLÄTTLER (Switzerland), Paul VAN HIMST (Belgium), Robert CHARLTON, Geoffrey HURST, Martin PETERS (all England)

## 3 GOALS

Dinko DERMENDZHIEV (Bulgaria), Inge DANIELSSON (Sweden), Juhani PELTONEN (Finland), Anatoliy BANISHEVSKIY, Igor CHISLENKO, Eduard MALOFEYEV, Iosif SABO (all USSR), Leopold GRAUSAM (Austria), Johannes LÖHR (West Germany), Vahidin MUSEMIĆ, Slaven ZAMBATA (both Yugoslavia), Flórián ALBERT, Kálmán MÉSZÖLY (both Hungary), Kresten BJERRE (Denmark), Mircea DRIDEA, Emil DUMITRU (both Romania), Karl ODERMATT, René-Pierre QUENTIN (both Switzerland), Georges LECH, Charly LOUBET (both France), Jacques STOCKMAN (Belgium), Janusz ŻMIJEWSKI (Poland)

## 2 GOALS

Jozef ADAMEC (Czechoslovakia), José Martínez Sánchez 'PIRRI' (Spain), OGÜN Altiparmak (Turkey), Nikola KOTKOV, Nikola TSANEV (both Bulgaria), Kjetil HASUND, Odd IVERSEN, Olav NILSEN (all Norway), EUSÉBIO da Silva Ferreira, Jaime da Silva GRAÇA (both Portugal), Leif ERIKSSON, Tom TURESSON (both Sweden), Helmut SIBER (Austria), Alexandros ALEXIADIS (Greece), Anatoliy BYSHOVETS, Murtaz KHURTSILAVA (both USSR), Ivan OSIM, Ilija PETKOVIĆ (both Yugoslavia), Tom SØNDERGAARD (Denmark), Herbert PANKAU (East Germany), Ferenc BENE (Hungary), Johannes CRUIJFF, Petrus KEIZER, Wilhelmus SUURBIER (all Netherlands), Nicolae DOBRIN, Ion IONESCU, Mircea LUCESCU (all Romania), Pierino PRATI (Italy), Roger CLAESSEN, Johan DEVRINDT, Johnny THIO (all Belgium), Robert HERBIN (France), Lucjan BRYCHCZY, Ryszard GRZEGORCZYK, Włodzimierz LUBAŃSKI (all Poland), John CHARLTON (England), Alan GILZEAN, Denis LAW, Robert LENNOX (all Scotland), Ronald DAVIES, Wyn DAVIES (both Wales)

## 1 GOAL

Juraj SZIKORA, Vojtěch MASNÝ, Josef JURKANIN, Alexander HORVÁTH, Ladislav KUNA (all Czechoslovakia), Frank O'NEILL, Andrew McEVOY, Noel CANTWELL, Raymond TREACY, Turlough O'CONNOR (all Republic of Ireland), JOSÉ MARÍA García Lavilla, Ramón Moreno GROSSO, Francisco GENTO López, José Eulogio GÁRATE Ormaechea, AMANCIO Amaro Varela (all Spain), AYHAN Elmastasoğlu (Turkey), Georgi ASPARUHOV, Vasil MITKOV (both Bulgaria), Harald BERG, Sven Otto BIRKELAND, Harald SUNDE (all Norway), CUSTÓDIO João Pinto, José Augusto Costa Séneca

TORRES (both Portugal), Thomas NORDAHL, Ingvar SVENSSON (both Sweden), Rudolf FLÖGEL, Erich HOF, Franz WOLNY (all Austria), Pertti MÄKIPÄÄ, Simo SYRJÄVAARA (both Finland), Stathis HAITAS, Dimitris PAPAIOANNOU (both Greece), Valeriy MASLOV, Eduard STRELTSOV (both USSR), Uwe SEELER (West Germany), Dragan DŽAJIĆ, Vojin LAZAREVIĆ, Josip SKOBLAR, Edin SPREČO (all Yugoslavia), Erik DYREBORG (Denmark), Gerhard KÖRNER, Wolfram LÖWE, Eberhard VOGEL (all East Germany), János GÖRÖCS, Dezső MOLNÁR, Zoltán VARGA (all Hungary), Emil PIJS, Marinus ISRAËL, Jesaia SWART, Wilhelmus VAN DER KUIJLEN, Johan MULDER (all Netherlands), Menelaos ASPROU, Pambos PAPADOPOULOS, Kostakis PIERIDIS (all Cyprus), Mario BERTINI, Virginio DEPAOLI, Giacinto FACCHETTI (all Italy), Florea MARTINOVICI (Romania), Richard DÜRR (Switzerland), Wilfried PUIS (Belgium), André GUY, Yves HERBET, Hervé REVELLI (all France), Jean KLEIN (Luxembourg), Andrzej JAROSIK, Jan LIBERDA, Jerzy SADEK, Zygfryd SZOŁTYSIK (all Poland), Alan BALL, Roger HUNT, Norman HUNTER (all England), David CLEMENTS, James NICHOLSON (both Northern Ireland), John HUGHES, James McCALLIOG, Ronald McKINNON, Robert MURDOCH (all Scotland), Alan DURBAN, Ronald REES (both Wales)

OWN-GOALS

Dimitar PENEV (Bulgaria) vs Italy, Konstantinos HRISTOU (Cyprus) vs Switzerland, Ernő SOLYMOSI (Hungary) vs USSR, John DEMPSEY (Republic of Ireland) vs Czechoslovakia, Terrence HENNESSEY (Wales) vs England

# FINAL TOURNAMENT

# (ITALY - 5-10 JUNE 1968)

## VENUES (Stadia)

FLORENCE (Stadio Comunale), NAPLES (Stadio San Paolo), ROME (Stadio Olimpico)

---

## SEMI-FINALS & THIRD PLACE MATCH

### ITALY vs USSR

The opening semi-final in Naples was played amid a constant downpour, which made it difficult for either team to play their preferred passing style of game. The Soviets were further hampered by the loss of three of their certain starters, Viktor Anichkin, Murtaz Khurtsilava and Igor Chislenko, through injury. Not long after the start, the Italians suffered a blow of their own, when 'Gianni' Rivera received a knock in a clash with Valentin Afonin that severely negated his influence on the game. The first real opportunity fell to the hosts when Pierino Prati let fly with a cracking shot from the left-hand side of the box, which Yuriy Pshenichnikov pushed away superbly.

Then, at the other end, Dino Zoff did well to turn a

piledriver from Albert Shesternyov round the post. Chances were few and far between, and the second half continued in the same vein, with 'Sandro' Mazzola coming the closest to breaking the deadlock with a low shot that just rolled past the post. The Soviets' best chance of the half fell to Aleksandr Lenyov, in space just inside the box, but his effort was brilliantly dealt with by Zoff. Extra time produced a little bit more excitement as both teams sought to win the game. Pshenichnikov denied the Italians twice in quick succession; first he parried away a stinging drive from Prati from an acute angle on the right, and as the ball bounced back to the edge of the box, the Soviet keeper was in the right position to gobble up the rebound from Antonio Juliano.

In the second period, Eduard Malofeyev broke through a couple of tackles before fizzing a low shot just past the far post. In the dying moments, Angelo Domenghini latched onto Prati's knockdown, but saw his thunderous drive smack off the inside of the post and rebound to safety – so, for the first and only time in the competition, the winner would be decided by the toss of a coin. Both captains were summoned to the referee's room for the calling of the toss. Shesternyov missed out on calling first, as he didn't understand the official's instruction, whereas Facchetti did. He called heads, which turned out to be the correct decision, and in the most fortunate of circumstances, the *Azzurri* were in the Final.

## YUGOSLAVIA vs ENGLAND

Later that evening, the second semi-final took place in Florence between Yugoslavia and World Champions England. The English were without their midfield enforcer, 'Nobby' Stiles, but they had an able replacement in Alan Mullery. The physical nature of the game was established within the first few minutes, when Dobrivoje Trivić scythed down Alan Ball. In response, Norman Hunter went in late on 'Ivica' Osim, which reduced Yugoslavia's playmaker to a bit-part role for the remainder of the match. Amid the fouling, some football was allowed to be played, and Ball came close with an effort which just cleared the bar.

The second half was a little better, but chances were at a premium. 'Bobby' Charlton had one opportunity when sent through, but he couldn't keep control of the ball and sent his effort well wide. Osim flicked the ball beyond the English defence for Dragan Džajić to run on to, but on his weaker right foot he could only send a tame shot beyond the far post. Extra time was looming, but with three minutes left, the Yugoslavs found the breakthrough when Dragan Holcer surged forward and played the ball out to Vahidin Musemić. His deep cross eluded 'Bobby' Moore, and Džajić stole in behind to chest down and then smash the ball beyond Gordon Banks in one superb movement. England needed a swift response, but they allowed their frustration to get the better of them. After Trivić had committed one foul too many on Mullery, the English midfielder lashed out in retaliation and the referee had no option but to send him off. Mullery thus became the first English player to be dismissed in an international match.

## ENGLAND vs USSR

The third-place match in Rome was played as a precursor to the Final later that day. The Soviet Union fielded an unchanged line-up, but England had Stiles back in midfield and 'Geoff' Hurst to provide a more attacking threat up front. The Soviets, completely exhausted after their energy-sapping semi-final, hardly threatened the English goal, and they allowed England to dominate the game.

'Bobby' Charlton should have shot England in front, but he failed to connect properly from Roger Hunt's knockdown, and Pshenichnikov was able to save easily; but he made no mistake just before the break, when he got on the end of another knockdown to shoot past the Soviet keeper. England continued to control the game after the break, and in the sixty-third minute the match was over as a contest when Martin Peters' deflected shot fell kindly to Hurst, who rounded Pshenichnikov and tapped into an empty net.

## FINAL

## ITALY vs YUGOSLAVIA

By kick-off time, the crowd had swelled to the capacity of 85,000, the vast majority of whom were hoping that the Italians could replicate their success of the 1934 World Cup on home soil. This was the seventh meeting between the sides since 1925, with Italy leading by three wins to two, with one draw. Both teams would be without their most creative player, with 'Gianni' Rivera and 'Ivica' Osim failing to recover from knocks sustained in the semi-finals. Their replacements were both making their international debut: Pietro Anastasi for the *Azzurri* and Jovan Aćimović for the *Plavi*. Italy would also have to cope without Inter's midfield schemer 'Sandro' Mazzola, who had been suffering with a kidney problem; after the gruelling semi-final, it was decided that it was too big a risk to play him. Giovanni Lodetti of city rivals AC Milan took his place.

Italy made all the early running, and they almost opened the scoring when Giorgio Ferrini let fly from about thirty yards. Ilija Pantelić fumbled it, but the keeper redeemed himself by bravely blocking Angelo Domenghini's follow-up before the ball was scrambled to safety. Yugoslavia responded with a long high cross from Dobrivoje Trivić, which found Ilija Petković at the back post, but he failed to connect properly and the ball sailed harmlessly wide. The Yugoslavs began to dominate the play, and just after the half hour mark they opened the scoring. Jovan Aćimović began the move by passing down the inside right channel for Trivić to run onto, and his cut back eluded a couple of players before Dragan Džajić latched onto it. Although his first touch was heavy, he managed to stretch sufficiently to poke the ball beyond Dino Zoff. Just before the break, Italy came mightily close to equalising when Giacinto Facchetti tapped a free-kick from the left side of the box to Domenghini, whose piledriver crashed back off the bar, with Pantelić well beaten.

Just after the restart, the home side should have levelled when Facchetti's corner was headed powerfully towards goal by Antonio Juliano, but unfortunately it struck Anastasi almost on the line and before the debutant could turn the ball home, Trivić nipped in to clear for a corner. Then Yugoslavia had a couple of great opportunities to double their advantage. Firstly Trivić escaped his marker down the right, and Zoff could only parry his effort straight to Džajić, who prodded the rebound goalwards; but Ernesto Castano stepped in to clear in the nick of time. Then Aćimović went on a fantastic run down the left, skipping past a couple of challenges before prodding the ball beyond Zoff – but Musemić, sliding in at the far post, was fractionally too late to connect and the ball agonisingly went inches past.

With only ten minutes remaining, the Italians were awarded a contentious free-kick just outside the box when Blagoje Paunović was adjudged to have barged Lodetti as both went up to challenge for a high ball. As the Yugoslavs attempted to organise their wall, Domenghini ran forward to slam the ball through a gap into the corner of the net to level the match and send the game into extra time. In the additional thirty minutes, Yugoslavia had the best opportunity to win the match when Trivić got away once more and his cross found Musemić, whose effort was magnificently turned away by Zoff, showing superb reflexes. Domenghini had a late chance for Italy from another free-kick, but this time Pantelić was alert, and he saved easily; so the game ended all square, and a replay would be necessary to decide who would become champions.

## FINAL – REPLAY

The replay was staged only two days later, in front of a much smaller attendance of 55,000. The Yugoslavs were surprisingly set to field the same line-up, until Petković pulled up with a stomach complaint during the warm-up and was replaced by Idriz Hošić. The Italians, perhaps grateful to have a second chance, made five changes, including their whole midfield line. Mazzola, well again after a few days' rest, was back and 'Gigi' Riva came in for Pierino Prati up front.

With fresher legs, the *Azzurri* were galvanised from the opening whistle, and Riva had the first chance when he fired in a stinging shot from about twenty yards. Pantelić did well to turn it round the post, then Anastasi somehow missed from point-blank range by poking Riva's knockdown from Roberto Rosato's free-kick past the post; but in the twelfth minute the hosts opened the scoring, as Riva latched onto Domenghini's scuffed shot, and with no defender near him, he simply drilled a left-foot shot into the corner of the net.

A few minutes later, Yugoslavia should have been level when Damjanović's free-kick from the left side of the box was met six yards out by Musemić, but he mistimed his dive and skewed his header wide. That miss would prove costly, as Italy went swiftly upfield, and Domenghini fed Giancarlo De Sisti, who in turn found Anastasi on the edge of the box. The striker's first touch bobbled up, but as the ball fell he swivelled and struck a superb volley beyond Pantelić. The Italians were in full flow now, and the Yugoslav keeper was performing superbly to keep his side in the game.

Riva should have killed the game off early in the second half when he got on the end of another free-kick, but flashed his header wide when it looked easier to score. Yugoslavia threatened, for a period, to get back in the match, but they found Zoff in unbeatable form. One save in particular stood out, when he bravely dived at Musemić's feet from close in to deflect the ball away for a corner. Near the end, Domenghini almost added a third goal from a free-kick, but he sliced the ball just past the post. Moments later the final whistle sounded, and Italy had added the European crown to go with their two World Cup titles.

# MATCH DETAILS

## SEMI-FINALS

5 June 1968 (18.00)     Ref: Kurt TSCHENSCHER
(West Germany)
Stadio San Paolo, NAPLES (Att. 68,582)

### ITALY - USSR
### 0:0 AET

ITALY won on the toss of a coin

ITA: (Coach: Ferruccio VALCAREGGI)
Dino ZOFF, Tarcisio BURGNICH, Giacinto FACCHETTI
(Capt.), Giancarlo BERCELLINO, Ernesto CASTANO,
Giorgio FERRINI, Angelo DOMENGHINI, Antonio
JULIANO, Alessandro MAZZOLA, Giovanni RIVERA,
Pierino PRATI

URS: (Coach: Mikhail YAKUSHIN)
Yuriy PSHENICHNIKOV, Yuriy ISTOMIN, Albert
SHESTERNYOV (Capt.), Vladimir KAPLICHNIY,
Valentin AFONIN, Aleksandr LENYOV, Eduard
MALOFEYEV, Gennadiy LOGOFET, Anatoliy
BANISHEVSKIY, Anatoliy BYSHOVETS, Gennadiy
EVRYUZHIKHIN

5 June 1968 (21.15)     Ref: José María ORTIZ de
Mendíbil (Spain)
Stadio Comunale, FLORENCE (Att. 21,834)

### YUGOSLAVIA - ENGLAND
### 1:0 (0:0)

1:0 Džajić (87')

YUG: (Coach: Rajko MITIĆ)
Ilija PANTELIĆ, Mirsad FAZLAGIĆ (Capt.), Milan DAMJANOVIĆ, Miroslav PAVLOVIĆ, Blagoje PAUNOVIĆ, Dragan HOLCER, Ilija PETKOVIĆ, Ivan OSIM, Vahidin MUSEMIĆ, Dobrivoje TRIVIĆ, Dragan DŽAJIĆ

ENG: (Coach: Alfred RAMSEY)
Gordon BANKS, Keith NEWTON, Ramon WILSON, Alan MULLERY, Brian LABONE, Robert MOORE (Capt.), Alan BALL, Martin PETERS, Robert CHARLTON, Roger HUNT, Norman HUNTER

Red Card: Mullery 89'

## THIRD PLACE MATCH

8 June 1968 (16.45)       Ref: István ZSOLT (Hungary)
Stadio Olimpico, ROME (Att. 68,817)

ENGLAND - USSR
2:0 (1:0)

1:0 Charlton (39'), 2:0 Hurst (63')

ENG: (Coach: Alfred RAMSEY)
Gordon BANKS, Thomas WRIGHT, Ramon WILSON, Norbert STILES, Brian LABONE, Robert MOORE (Capt.), Norman HUNTER, Roger HUNT, Robert CHARLTON, Geoffrey HURST, Martin PETERS

URS: (Coach: Mikhail YAKUSHIN)
Yuriy PSHENICHNIKOV, Yuriy ISTOMIN, Albert SHESTERNYOV (Capt.), Vladimir KAPLICHNIY, Valentin AFONIN, Aleksandr LENYOV, Eduard MALOFEYEV, Gennadiy LOGOFET, Anatoliy

BANISHEVSKIY, Anatoliy BYSHOVETS, Gennadiy EVRYUZHIKHIN

## FINAL

8 June 1968 (21.15)          Ref: Gottfried DIENST
(Switzerland)
Stadio Olimpico, ROME (Att. 85,000)

ITALY - YUGOSLAVIA
1:1 AET (0:1/1:1)

0:1 Džajić (32'), 1:1 Domenghini (80')

ITA: (Coach: Ferruccio VALCAREGGI)
Dino ZOFF, Tarcisio BURGNICH, Giacinto FACCHETTI (Capt.), Giorgio FERRINI, Aristide GUARNERI, Ernesto CASTANO, Angelo DOMENGHINI, Antonio JULIANO, Pietro ANASTASI, Giovanni LODETTI, Pierino PRATI

YUG: (Coach: Rajko MITIĆ)
Ilija PANTELIĆ, Mirsad FAZLAGIĆ (Capt.), Milan DAMJANOVIĆ, Miroslav PAVLOVIĆ, Blagoje PAUNOVIĆ, Dragan HOLCER, Ilija PETKOVIĆ, Dobrivoje TRIVIĆ, Vahidin MUSEMIĆ, Jovan AĆIMOVIĆ, Dragan DŽAJIĆ

## FINAL - REPLAY

10 June 1968 (21.15)          Ref: José María ORTIZ
de Mendíbil (Spain)
Stadio Olimpico, ROME (Att. 55,000)
ITALY - YUGOSLAVIA
2:0 (2:0)

1:0 Riva (12'), 2:0 Anastasi (31')

Richard Keir

179

<u>ITA:</u> (Coach: Ferruccio VALCAREGGI)
Dino ZOFF, Tarcisio BURGNICH, Giacinto FACCHETTI (Capt.), Roberto ROSATO, Aristide GUARNERI, Sandro SALVADORE, Angelo DOMENGHINI, Alessandro MAZZOLA, Pietro ANASTASI, Giancarlo DE SISTI, Luigi RIVA


<u>YUG:</u> (Coach: Rajko MITIĆ)
Ilija PANTELIĆ, Mirsad FAZLAGIĆ (Capt.), Milan DAMJANOVIĆ, Miroslav PAVLOVIĆ, Blagoje PAUNOVIĆ, Dragan HOLCER, Idriz HOŠIĆ, Dobrivoje TRIVIĆ, Vahidin MUSEMIĆ, Jovan AĆIMOVIĆ, Dragan DŽAJIĆ

# GOALSCORERS

## 2 GOALS

Dragan DŽAJIĆ (Yugoslavia)

## 1 GOAL

Robert CHARLTON, Geoffrey HURST (both England), Pietro ANASTASI, Angelo DOMENGHINI, Luigi RIVA (all Italy)

# **SQUADS**

## ENGLAND

## GOALKEEPERS

1 Gordon BANKS (30.12.1937/Stoke City FC), 12 Alexander STEPNEY (18.09.1942/Manchester United FC), 13 Gordon WEST (24.04.1943/Everton FC (Liverpool))

## DEFENDERS

2 Keith NEWTON (23.06.1941/Blackburn Rovers FC), 3 Ramon WILSON (17.12.1934/Everton FC (Liverpool), 5 Brian LABONE (23.01.1940/Everton FC (Liverpool)), 6 Robert MOORE (12.04.1941/West Ham United FC (London)), 15 John CHARLTON (08.05.1935/Leeds United AFC), 16 Thomas WRIGHT (21.10.1944/Everton FC (Liverpool)), 19 Norman HUNTER (29.10.1943/Leeds United AFC)

## MIDFIELDERS

4 Alan MULLERY (23.11.1941/Tottenham Hotspur FC (London)), 7 Alan BALL (12.05.1945/Everton FC (Liverpool)), 9 Robert CHARLTON (11.10.1937/Manchester United FC), 11 Martin PETERS (08.11.1943/West Ham United FC (London)), 14 Cyril KNOWLES (13.07.1944/Tottenham Hotspur FC (London)), 17 Norbert STILES (18.05.1942/Manchester United FC), 20 Colin BELL (26.02.1946/Manchester City FC)

## FORWARDS

8 Roger HUNT (20.07.1938/Liverpool FC), 10 Geoffrey HURST (08.12.1941/West Ham United FC (London)), 18 Michael SUMMERBEE (15.12.1942/Manchester City FC), 21 James GREAVES (20.02.1940/Tottenham Hotspur FC (London)), 22 Peter THOMPSON (27.11.1942/Liverpool FC)

## ITALY

### GOALKEEPERS

1 Enrico ALBERTOSI (02.11.1939/AC Fiorentina (Firenze)), 21 Lido VIERI (16.07.1939/AC Torino), 22 Dino ZOFF (28.02.1942/SSC Napoli)

### DEFENDERS

3 Angelo ANQUILLETTI (25.04.1943/AC Milan), 4 Giancarlo BERCELLINO (09.10.1941/Juventus FC (Torino)), 5 Tarcisio BURGNICH (25.04.1939/ FC Internazionale Milano), 7 Ernesto CASTANO (02.05.1939/Juventus FC (Torino)), 10 Giacinto FACCHETTI (18.07.1942/FC Internazionale Milano), 19 Roberto ROSATO (18.08.1943/AC Milan), 20 Sandro SALVADORE (29.11.1939/Juventus FC (Torino))

### MIDFIELDERS

8 Giancarlo DE SISTI (13.03.1943/AC Fiorentina (Firenze)), 11 Giorgio FERRINI (18.08.1939/AC Torino), 12 Aristide GUARNERI (07.03.1938/Bologna FC), 13 Antonio JULIANO (01.01.1943/SSC Napoli), 14 Giovanni LODETTI (10.08.1942/AC Milan), 18 Giovanni RIVERA (18.08.1943/AC Milan)

## FORWARDS

2 Pietro ANASTASI (07.04.1948/AS Varese), 6 Giacomo BULGARELLI (24.10.1940/Bologna FC), 9 Angelo DOMENGHINI (25.08.1941/FC Internazionale Milano), 15 Alessandro MAZZOLA (08.11.1942/ FC Internazionale Milano), 16 Pierino PRATI (13.12.1946/AC Milan), 17 Luigi RIVA (07.11.1944/ Cagliari Calcio)

## USSR

## GOALKEEPERS

1 Yuriy PSHENICHNIKOV (02.06.1940/TSKA Moskva), 9 Anzor KAVAZASHVILI (19.07.1940/ FK Torpedo Moskva), 14 Evgeniy RUDAKOV (02.01.1942/FK Dinamo Kiev)

## DEFENDERS

3 Valentin AFONIN (22.12.1939/TSKA Moskva), 8 Yuriy ISTOMIN (03.07.1944/TSKA Moskva), 10 Vladimir KAPLICHNIY (26.02.1944/TSKA Moskva), 15 Vladimir LEVCHENKO (18.02.1944/FK Dinamo Kiev), 18 Albert SHESTERNYOV (20.06.1941/TSKA Moskva), 21 Gennadiy LOGOFET (15.04.1942/FK Spartak Moskva)

## MIDFIELDERS

2 Viktor ANICHKIN (08.12.1941/FK Dinamo Moskva), 6 Valeriy VORONIN (17.07.1939/FK Torpedo Moskva), 12 Vladimir MUNTYAN (14.09.1946/FK Dinamo Kiev), 16 Murtaz KHURTSILAVA (05.01.1943/FC Dinamo Tbilisi), 17 Igor CHISLENKO (04.01.1939/FK Dinamo Moskva), 19 Aleksandr LENYOV (25.09.1944/FK

Torpedo Moskva), 20 Kakhi ASATIANI (01.01.1947/ FC Dinamo Tbilisi)

FORWARDS

4 Anatoliy BANISHEVSKIY (23.02.1946/FK Neftchi Baku), 5 Anatoliy BYSHOVETS (23.04.1946/ FK Dinamo Kiev), 7 Gennadiy EVRYUZHIKHIN (04.02.1944/FK Dinamo Moskva), 11 Eduard MALOFEYEV (02.06.1942/FK Dinamo Minsk), 13 Givi NODIYA (02.01.1948/FC Dinamo Tbilisi), 22 Nikolaiy SMOLNIKOV (10.03.1949/FK Neftchi Baku)

YUGOSLAVIA

GOALKEEPERS

1 Ilija PANTELIĆ (02.08.1942/FK Vojvodina Novi Sad), 12 Radomir VUKČEVIĆ (15.09.1944/NK Hajduk Split), 13 Ratomir DUJKOVIĆ (24.02.1946/FK Crvena Zvezda Beograd)

DEFENDERS

2 Mirsad FAZLAGIĆ (04.04.1943/FK Sarajevo), 3 Milan DAMJANOVIĆ (15.10.1943/FK Partizan Beograd), 5 Blagoje PAUNOVIĆ (04.06.1947/FK Partizan Beograd), 6 Dragan HOLCER (19.01.1945/ NK Hajduk Split), 14 Rajko ALEKSIĆ (19.02.1947/ FK Vojvodina Novi Sad), 17 Mladen RAMLJAK (01.07.1945/NK Dinamo Zagreb), 18 Ljubomir MIHAJLOVIĆ (04.09.1943/FK Partizan Beograd)

MIDFIELDERS

4 Borivoje ĐORĐEVIĆ (02.08.1948/FK Partizan

Beograd), 7 Ilija PETKOVIĆ (22.09.1945/OFK Beograd), 8 Ivan OSIM (06.05.1941/FK Željezničar Sarajevo), 10 Rudolf BELIN (04.11.1942/NK Dinamo Zagreb), 15 Miroslav PAVLOVIĆ (23.10.1942/FK Crvena Zvezda Beograd), 16 Jovan AĆIMOVIĆ (21.06.1948/FK Crvena Zvezda Beograd), 19 Ivan BRZIĆ (28.12.1941/FK Vojvodina Novi Sad), 21 Dobrivoje TRIVIĆ (26.10.1943/FK Vojvodina Novi Sad)

## FORWARDS

9 Vahidin MUSEMIĆ (29.10.1946/FK Sarajevo), 11 Dragan DŽAJIĆ (30.05.1946/FK Crvena Zvezda Beograd), 20 Boško ANTIĆ (07.01.1945/FK Sarajevo), 22 Idriz HOŠIĆ (17.02.1944/FK Partizan Beograd)

# 1970-1972

# QUALIFICATION

## GROUP STAGE

After the success of the new tournament set-up in 1968, there was little need to alter the format. Thirty-two nations took part this time, in eight groups of four, with the winners of each group progressing to the quarter-finals. Malta was the only additional country from the previous edition, although they had taken part in 1964. Also, for the first time, outfield substitutions were permitted, having been introduced at the 1970 World Cup, and goal difference would be used to determine group positions in the event of teams being tied on points.

## GROUP 1

Romania and Czechoslovakia renewed acquaintances after being drawn together alongside Finland and Wales. They'd met each other in the 1970 World Cup group stage, where Romania had been the victors on that occasion. Both teams began with a home tie against Finland. The Czechoslovaks fielded an inexperienced team, as some of their major stars were suspended, and although Milan Albrecht gave the home side the lead after half an hour, Finland soon equalised through Matti Paatelainen and the game ended 1-1. In contrast, Romania strolled to a comfortable 3-0 victory over the Finns, including a brace from Florea Dumitrache.

The next couple of matches saw Wales open their campaign. The first one was a frustrating night, as Romania's visit ended goalless in Cardiff. Then in Swansea against Czechoslovakia, the home side looked to be heading for victory after 'Ron' Davies slotted home a penalty shortly after the break, but in a devastating late four-minute spell the visitors scored three times, with Ján Čapkovič bagging two of them. The group leaders then faced off in Bratislava, and after Jozef Adamec had blown a great chance for the hosts by blasting a penalty over the bar, it looked like Romania would hold out for a draw – but in the eighty-eighth minute, František Veselý found space to fire the winner past Necula Răducanu.

Wales then travelled to Finland, and a second-half strike from John Toshack was sufficient to earn the visitors their first win. They gained another two points with a 3-0 victory in the return match in Swansea. In between, both Czechoslovakia and Romania had won convincingly by 4-0 in Finland, and with two games left each, the Czechoslovaks led by two points over both Romania and Wales. The Welsh travelled to Prague, needing to win to stay in contention, but there was to be only disappointment, as they went down to Ladislav Kuna's strike on the hour mark. This meant that Czechoslovakia now only needed to avoid defeat in Bucharest to win the group.

Emerich Dembrovschi put the home side ahead midway through the first half, then the Czechoslovaks drew level shortly after the interval through Ján Čapkovič, but within a minute Nicolae Dobrin put Romania back in front and that was enough to win the game. Romania now had the opportunity to snatch top spot away from Czechoslovakia on goal difference if they could beat Wales at home in the final match, and they took it, with a goal in each half from Nicolae

Lupescu and Mircea Lucescu securing them a place in the quarter-finals.

## GROUP 2

The section looked likely to be a tight affair, with Bulgaria, France and Hungary all evenly matched and Norway expected to make up the numbers. In the opening match, Hungary travelled to Oslo, and by midway through the first half, they led 2-0 through goals from Ferenc Bene and László Nagy. Odd Iversen pulled a goal back just after half time, only for a freak own-goal by the Norwegian keeper Geir Karlsen to gift Hungary a decisive third goal.

France kicked off their campaign with a home match against the Norwegians. Two years earlier the Scandinavians had sensationally won the same fixture 1-0, which had prevented the French from qualifying for the 1970 World Cup, but there was to be no repeat this time round; *Les Bleus* ran out comfortable winners by 3-1.

Norway also provided the opposition for Bulgaria's opening tie in the next game, where Tsvetan Atanasov put the home side ahead after half an hour, but they failed to add to it and Jan Fuglset popped up with a shock equaliser seven minutes from time. The first clash between the main contenders saw Hungary host the French. The first half was a bit cagey, but both teams opened up in the second period and Hervé Revelli fired France ahead in the sixty-fourth minute. Their lead didn't last long, though, as the Hungarians were awarded a penalty six minutes later, which Lajos Kocsis dispatched, and the game finished 1-1. Hungary then travelled to Sofia, hoping to pull ahead in the group, but they performed dreadfully and were soundly thrashed 3-0.

Instead, it was the Bulgarians who took over the leadership of the group in the next match, when they easily won 4-1 in Norway. The French drew level with Bulgaria when they visited Norway and came away with a 3-1 victory. Next, Bulgaria travelled to Budapest knowing that victory would put them in the box seat, but the Hungarians gained revenge for their earlier defeat with two goals in a minute, early in the second half, from Péter Juhász and Csaba Vidáts. Buoyed by this victory, the Hungarians repeated this scoreline when they visited France. This time it was two first-half goals from Bene and Sándor Zámbó that sank the French. In their final match, Hungary brushed aside Norway 4-0 at home, which left them with a four point lead over Bulgaria and France, who still had to play each other twice.

In the first meeting in Nantes, the Bulgarians took the lead early in the second half with a Hristo Bonev penalty kick – but the hosts soon levelled through Georges Lech, and with time running out, Charly Loubet pounced on a rebound to win the game for France. This meant that the French needed to win by at least five clear goals in the return match in Sofia to overtake Hungary on goal difference. It proved to be an impossible task, as the Bulgarians reversed the scoreline to win 2-1, and allowed Hungary to secure the quarter-final berth.

## GROUP 3

England were clear favourites to win when drawn against Switzerland, Greece and Malta. In the opening game, the Maltese almost pulled off a shock victory at home to Greece when William Vassallo gave the minnows the lead midway through the second half, but Mihalis Kritikopoulos spared Greek blushes with an eighty-eighth minute equaliser. Switzerland began with a trip to Greece, and it was the Greeks' turn to face late agony as Kurt Müller grabbed a winner for the visitors five minutes from time. The Swiss then travelled to Malta and ground out another narrow victory, this time by 2-1. The Maltese were also the opponents for England's first game, and again the home side competed valiantly but ultimately lost again to a solitary goal scored by Martin Peters in the thirty-fifth minute. England were far more convincing in their next outing against Greece at Wembley. Martin Chivers put the home side ahead midway through the first half, and from then on England controlled the game. Further goals in the second period from 'Geoff' Hurst and Francis Lee confirmed their superiority.

Both group leaders then walloped the Maltese at home by the same 5-0 scoreline, before the Swiss defeated Greece again by a single goal. Karl Odermatt got the vital strike this time in the seventy-third minute, which left the *Nati* two points ahead of England going into their head-to-head meetings, although the English had a game in hand.

The first match of the double header in Basle was a cracker. Barely a minute had been played when Hurst headed the visitors in front, but the Swiss hit back in the tenth minute through a thunderbolt from Daniel Jeandupeux; then, just two minutes later, Chivers put England back in front with a shot into the top corner from the edge of the box. Just as England thought they'd go in ahead at the interval, 'Fritz' Künzli popped up to level the game again, which brought a breathtaking first half to a close. In the second half, the same level of intensity couldn't be kept up. Although Switzerland had more of the play, they rarely troubled Gordon Banks, and as they tired, England grabbed a winner in the seventy-seventh minute through an unfortunate own-goal, as Anton Weibel diverted a Chivers cross past his own keeper.

In the return match at Wembley a month later, the English again scored early. 'Mike' Summerbee took advantage of a misplaced clearance in the Swiss defence and looped a header over the keeper in the ninth minute, but as in the first meeting, the Swiss were soon level through a fantastic swerving shot from Odermatt that Peter Shilton just failed to keep out. 1-1 was the final score, which left both sides on nine points, but England still had one game left in Greece and they only needed to avoid defeat by at least three goals to go through. That scenario never looked likely, as they eased to a comfortable 2-0 victory through second half strikes from Hurst and Chivers.


## GROUP 4

Two of the three previous winners, Spain and the Soviet Union, were drawn together, along with Northern Ireland and Cyprus. The Spaniards opened the group in style by seeing off Northern Ireland in Seville. Carles Rexach opened the scoring shortly before half-time with a thunderous drive from around thirty yards, and in the second half, 'Pirri' and Luis Aragonés added further goals.

A few days later, the Soviets began their campaign in Nicosia against Cyprus. They appeared to be coasting to victory, after goals from Viktor Kolotov and Gennadiy Evryuzhikhin put them 2-0 up by the sixteenth minute, but the plucky minnows pulled a goal back shortly before the break through 'Nikos' Haralambous. However, five minutes into the second half, Vitaliy Shevchenko restored the Soviet Union's two-goal advantage and that was enough for the visitors. Northern Ireland and Cyprus contested the next two matches, which the Irish won convincingly, 3-0 and 5-0 respectively, George Best grabbing a hat-trick in the latter game.

Spain then won 2-0 in Cyprus, though they had to wait until the eighty-sixth minute for the clinching second goal from José Violeta when 'Pirri' gave them the lead after only three minutes. Three weeks later, the Spaniards faced a much stiffer test when they travelled to Moscow. For eighty minutes they held out comfortably; then they were undone by two quickfire goals from Kolotov and Shevchenko. Rexach did pull a goal back in the dying seconds, but it came too late to save the game. The Soviets then played their other two home games next, predictably thrashing Cyprus 6-1 in the first of them, but they needed a penalty converted by Vladimir Muntyan just before half-time to see off Northern Ireland.

A similar result when the two sides met in Belfast would effectively seal the group for the Soviets, but the Irish had other ideas. 'Jimmy' Nicholson fired the home side ahead in the thirteenth minute, and although Anatoliy Byshovets equalised before the break, the Irish had better opportunities afterwards and were unfortunate not to get a winning goal. This left the Soviet Union five points clear of Spain, who had two games in hand. The Spaniards had to win their three remaining games to qualify, but they faltered at the first hurdle against the Soviets in Seville. They came looking for the point that would win them the group, and they got it in a dour, goalless match.

## GROUP 5

On paper, the group appeared to be one of the most

difficult from which to predict a winner, with Belgium, Portugal and Scotland drawn together along with Denmark, who were capable of producing a shock. However, after they'd lost the opening match in Copenhagen 1-0 to Portugal, they proceeded to lose away to both Scotland and Belgium, 1-0 and 2-0 respectively, which effectively put them out of contention. Following their win over the Danes, the next two games saw Belgium play their other home ties.

Against Scotland in Liège, the final score of 3-0 to the home side suggested an easy victory, but the Scots had been unfortunate in the manner of the goals they had conceded. The first was an own-goal from 'Ronnie' McKinnon, who diverted the ball past 'Jim' Cruickshank just as he was about to gather a cross from Paul Van Himst. In the second half, Van Himst scored with a contentious free-kick, which he won after losing his footing; then Wilfried Van Moer darted into the box before slipping under a challenge, for which the referee awarded a dubious penalty, and Van Himst converted it. Two weeks later it was the turn of the Portuguese to visit Belgium, and they suffered a similar defeat. Raoul Lambert was the tormentor-in-chief this time as he notched the first two goals, with André Denul adding a third late on after rounding the keeper and smashing the ball through a crowd of bodies.

The Portuguese got back on track in their next two games when they defeated Scotland and Denmark 2-0 and 5-0 respectively. Belgium responded with a 2-1 victory away to the Danes, with Johan Devrindt netting both goals for the visitors. Scotland were next up to visit the Scandinavians, but they put in an abysmal performance as they went down 1-0 to a Finn Laudrup strike, which sank their hopes of qualifying and spelled the end of 'Bobby' Brown's tenure as manager.

Both Portugal and Belgium then travelled to Scotland, hoping for the win that might give one of them an advantage going into their final meeting, but both of them would leave empty-handed, as a resurgent Scotland (under new manager 'Tommy' Docherty) won both matches 2-1 and 1-0 respectively. Belgium therefore journeyed to Lisbon for the decisive game with a two-point lead over their hosts. Portugal needed to win by a four-goal margin, but the Belgians were never in any real danger, and indeed they were only seconds away from winning the game after Lambert gave them the lead on the hour mark, only for Fernando Peres to level from the penalty spot with the last kick of the ball.

## GROUP 6

The defending champions, Italy, were drawn in a fairly difficult group along with Austria, Republic of Ireland and Sweden, who they had narrowly beaten in the group stage of the 1970 World Cup en route to finishing runners-up. It was the Republic of Ireland and Sweden who opened proceedings in Dublin, where 'Tommy' Carroll shot the Irish ahead from the penalty spot a minute before half-time, but Dan Brzokoupil equalised for the Swedes just after the hour mark and 1-1 was the final result. Two weeks later, the two sides met again at Solna, and this time Sweden edged the match 1-0, thanks to a Tom Turesson strike in the seventy-fourth minute.

Italy began with a tricky away tie in Vienna, but they came away with a fine 2-1 victory. Giancarlo De Sisti set them on their way with a superb angled drive after twenty-seven minutes, and although Thomas Parits levelled the match with a free-kick, 'Sandro' Mazzola soon restored Italy's advantage in the thirty-fourth minute with a cracking shot into the roof of the net. The Italians followed this up with back-to-back victories over the Republic of Ireland. The first meeting in Florence ended in an easy 3-0 win, but the return in Dublin was a much tighter affair. Roberto Boninsegna gave the *Azzurri* the lead in the fifteenth minute, but that was soon cancelled out by 'Jimmy' Conway. In the second half, the Irish played with a lot of spirit but didn't have a cutting edge, and it was Pierino Prati who notched the winning goal for the visitors just before the hour mark.

Sweden then moved a point behind the Italians after a Jan Olsson goal was sufficient to defeat the Austrians in the next game. Austria finally got points on the board in their next match in Dublin, as they thrashed the Republic of Ireland 4-1. Of greater significance was their meeting with Sweden in Vienna. In the previous group game, the Swedes had missed a great chance to go top after being held to a goalless draw by Italy, so they hoped to go one better in Austria to keep the pressure on the Italians, but they were to be disappointed, as a Josef Stering strike midway through the first half won the match for the Austrians.

That win just about kept Austria in contention with two games left, but they needed Sweden to beat the Italians when the Scandinavians travelled to Milan. It took only three minutes for the home side to squash their hopes, as Luigi Riva tapped in a cross from Mazzola, and further goals from Boninsegna and Riva again gave the Italians a comfortable 3-0 victory and clinched the group with a game to spare.

## GROUP 7

1968 runners-up Yugoslavia were drawn together with an up-and-coming Dutch team, plus the unpredictable East Germans, as well as minnows Luxembourg. The Yugoslavs opened the group with a visit to Rotterdam, and they came away with a creditable 1-1 draw against the Netherlands, who started with five of the Feyenoord players who had won the 1970 European Cup five months earlier. Midway through the first half, Dragan Džajić put Yugoslavia ahead with one of his trademark free-kicks, but the Dutch equalised early in the second half when 'Rinus' Israël converted a penalty given for a pull in the box.

Three days later, the Yugoslavs had an easier time of it away to Luxembourg, although it took until the forty-fourth minute for the deadlock to be broken, with Josip Bukal netting. The same player scored again just after the hour mark to complete a 2-0 victory for the visitors.

East Germany began with a home tie against the Netherlands in Dresden, and they put a huge dent in the qualifying hopes of the Dutch when Peter Ducke headed home the only goal after fifty-six minutes. The East Germans followed this up with a 5-0 thumping of Luxembourg in the Grand Duchy, with Hans-Jürgen Kreische bagging a treble.

The minnows were then hit for six in Rotterdam to give the Netherlands their first win in the group before the Dutch travelled to Yugoslavia. The home side never looked back after taking the lead in the eighth minute through Jurica Jerković, and they made the game safe when Džajić netted with six minutes remaining.

East Germany went top of the group after a narrow 2-1 home win over Luxembourg; they faced a much stiffer test in Leipzig against the Yugoslavs, which looked likely to be the decisive clash as to who would qualify. It was the visitors who took command early on, as they scored twice in the first twenty minutes through Zoran Filipović and Džajić, and although Wolfram Löwe pulled a goal back with twenty minutes remaining, the Yugoslavs held on for a crucial victory. This put them a point ahead of their rivals, with each having two games left.

The Netherlands then entertained the East Germans in Rotterdam, which turned out to be a fantastic match. Eberhard Vogel gave the guests the lead in the tenth minute, but that was cancelled out by 'Barry' Hulshoff midway through the half; then, in the second period, two goals from 'Piet' Keizer put the Dutch in command until Vogel notched his second for the visitors, with eight minutes left to ensure a nervy ending – but the home side held on for the victory. This meant East Germany had to win their final game in Belgrade to keep the group alive, but Yugoslavia were quite content to stifle their opponents, and they obtained the point they required to qualify with a goalless draw.

## GROUP 8

West Germany were clear favourites to win the section. After sensationally failing to qualify last time out, they had gone on to finish third at the 1970 World Cup, and their group opponents Albania, Poland and Turkey weren't expected to cause them any major problems. The Poles kicked off the group with a home tie against Albania. Robert Gadocha fired the home side ahead after nineteen minutes, and two late goals from 'Włodek' Lubański and Zygfryd Szołtysik gave them a comprehensive 3-0 victory.

Three days later, both West Germany and Turkey began their campaign when they met in Cologne. It was the Turks who got off to a fantastic start, when Kamuran Yavuz took advantage of a defensive slip to fire them in front after sixteen minutes, but the hosts were level by the break, courtesy of a penalty from 'Gerd' Müller after he was fouled. The West Germans dominated the second half, but couldn't find a winning goal.

Turkey followed up that fine result by defeating Albania 2-1 at home. The West Germans travelled to Tirana for a rematch with Albania, who had prevented them from qualifying in 1968 when they had been held to a goalless draw. Again, it was a tight affair, but the visitors prevailed this time, with Müller notching the only goal after thirty-eight minutes. The top two then met in Istanbul, and the West Germans strolled to an easy 3-0 victory, with Müller netting a brace either side of half-time and Horst Köppel grabbing the other. Albania then put a spoke in the Poles' wheels by holding them to a 1-1 draw in Tirana. Jan Banaś put the Poles ahead after only seven minutes, but Medin Zhega levelled for the home side in the thirty-second minute.

West Germany took full advantage of the Poles' slip-up when they entertained the Albanians in Karlsruhe, with two first-half goals from Günter Netzer and Jürgen Grabowski securing another two points, which put them four clear of both Poland and Turkey. Poland got back on the winning trail in their next game by thrashing the Turks 5-1 in Kraków, which included a hat-trick for Lubański, before the clash with the West Germans in Warsaw.

The game started well enough for the Poles, as Gadocha latched onto a shocking backpass from Paul

Breitner to open the scoring in the twenty-seventh minute, but the visitors were level within two minutes when Müller got on the end of a Netzer free-kick to head home. Then, midway through the second period, Müller put the West Germans ahead with another simple finish from close in, and a few minutes later Grabowski sealed the win after some terrific interplay set him up to score. Even after this defeat, the Poles could have still qualified if they had won their last two games – but in the first of them in Hamburg, the West Germans were quite content to play out a tame goalless draw to secure the point they needed to clinch a quarter-final berth.

## QUARTER-FINALS

### BELGIUM vs ITALY

In the opening tie, the holders, without Dino Zoff and playmaker 'Gianni' Rivera, couldn't break down a stubborn Belgian defence and were held to a frustrating goalless draw in the first leg in Milan. In the return at Anderlecht's tight ground, the home side, sensing a famous victory could be on the cards, played more expansively and they took the lead midway through the first half when Wilfried Van Moer headed home Léon Semmeling's free-kick.

Just before the interval, though, the goalscorer had to be replaced when he sustained a broken leg after a terrible tackle from Mario Bertini. The Italians came out strongly in the second period but couldn't force an equaliser, and they paid for their profligacy when Raoul Lambert crossed for Paul Van Himst to volley Belgium further ahead in the seventy-first minute.

The *Azzurri* were thrown a lifeline with four minutes remaining when Fabio Capello was tripped in the area and 'Gigi' Riva slotted home the resultant penalty kick, but the Belgians held on to knock the holders out.

## WEST GERMANY vs ENGLAND

The most hotly anticipated quarter-final tie saw England drawn against West Germany, which promised another titanic battle similar to their most recent competitive clashes in the 1966 World Cup Final and the quarter-final at the 1970 Mundial. In the first leg at Wembley, the visitors began the stronger, and they got their reward in the twenty-sixth minute. 'Bobby' Moore was dispossessed by 'Gerd' Müller, who fed 'Sigi' Held to lay the ball off to 'Uli' Hoeneß, who flashed a magnificent drive past Gordon Banks. England played much better in the second half, and eventually they found a way through the West German defence with thirteen minutes remaining.

Colin Bell found a bit of space to crack in a shot that 'Sepp' Maier couldn't hold, and 'Franny' Lee tapped in the rebound. The home side now went in search of a winner, but with five minutes left, they were undone by a classic counter-attack. Rodney Marsh lost possession to Müller on the edge of the West German box, who quickly found Held steaming forward, and he held off Paul Madeley before being brought down inside the box by Moore. Günter Netzer stepped up to take the spot kick, which seemed to lack pace, and, although Banks got both hands to it, he couldn't keep it out.

Then, in the final minute, England shot themselves in the foot again when trying to launch a counter-attack of their own, as Emlyn Hughes stumbled on the ball. Held nipped in to find Hoeneß, who played in Müller with a superb reverse pass, and the striker found the bottom corner of the net to effectively finish the tie.

In the return leg in West Berlin, the visitors tightened up their midfield to negate Netzer's influence on the game without really trying to force a way back into the tie. The West Germans were quite content to play out a goalless draw, and they came the closest to breaking the deadlock when Held's ferocious shot cracked off the bar.


## HUNGARY vs ROMANIA

When Eastern European neighbours Hungary and Romania were drawn together, it was expected to be a tight affair, and that was exactly how it turned out. The Hungarians came flying out the blocks in the first game in Budapest, and they went ahead in the eleventh minute, when István Kocsis played a superb pass for László Branikovits to run onto and he smashed the ball past Răducanu. The same player almost added another shortly afterwards when he latched onto a rebound after Răducanu could only parry László Bálint's piledriver; but the striker saw his effort crash back off the post. Romania came more into the game in the second half, and in the fifty-sixth minute they were level when István Géczi hesitated coming for a cross and Lajos Sătmăreanu headed home.

In the second leg in Bucharest, again it was Hungary who got off to a flyer by opening the scoring after only five minutes. Ferenc Bene fired a shot off the post after a fantastic run through the Romanian defence, and István Szőke was perfectly placed to net the rebound. However, it didn't take long for the home side to respond, as they equalised in the fourteenth minute also from a rebound, Nicolae Dobrin following up to score after Flavius Domide saw his effort crash back off the bar.

Thereafter, the visitors dominated the rest of the half, and it was no surprise when they went back in front in the thirty-sixth minute through Kocsis. Just before the break, however, the same player blew a great chance to virtually seal the tie when Cornel Dinu was penalised for handball, but Kocsis' spot kick was easily saved by Răducanu. Romania came storming back in the second half; for a time it appeared their luck was out, until Alexandru Neagu popped up to equalise with nine minutes remaining. With no further goals, it meant a third game at a neutral venue was necessary to decide which country would go through to the final tournament.

Belgrade was chosen to host the match, and a near-capacity crowd witnessed another tight encounter. Yet again, the Hungarians opened the scoring through a deflected effort from Kocsis in the twenty-sixth minute. The Romanians were level within six minutes, though, as Neagu nipped in ahead of Péter Juhász to get on the end of a low cross and net from eight yards out. 1-1 was still the score as the match entered the final stages, but with extra time looming, the Hungarians snatched a dramatic winner when Sándor Zámbó's cross found Bene inside the box and he squared it to Szőke to fire a shot past Răducanu.

## USSR vs YUGOSLAVIA

The last quarter-final tie paired the Soviet Union and Yugoslavia in a repeat of the 1960 Final. In the opening leg in Belgrade, the visitors set out to stifle their hosts, and they held out quite comfortably to secure a goalless draw. The first half of the return match in Moscow was very cagey, and not surprisingly it was

0-0 at the break, but eight minutes into the second half the Soviets found a breakthrough.

Vladimir Troshkin fed Viktor Kolotov down the left, and he fired a fantastic drive across Enver Marić into the far corner of the net. Then Anatoliy Banishevskiy shot the home side further ahead in the seventy-fourth minute. Yugoslavia were desperate to get back in the game, but they were caught on the break in the final minute after Marić misjudged the bounce of the ball at the edge of the area; Eduard Kozinkevich headed into an empty net, and the Soviet Union were through to yet another Final Tournament.

# MATCH DETAILS

GROUP 1 (Czechoslovakia, Finland, Romania, Wales)


7 October 1970                    Ref: William O'NEIL
                                  (Republic of Ireland)
Letenský stadion, PRAGUE (Att. 5,549)

### CZECHOSLOVAKIA - FINLAND
### 1:1 (1:1)

1:0 Albrecht (31'), 1:1 Paatelainen (41')


CZE: (Coach: Antonín RÝGR)
František SCHMUCKER, Jiří VEČEREK, Jozef
BOMBA, Jozef DESIATNIK (Oldřich URBAN 75'), Peter
MUTKOVIČ, Vladimír MOJŽÍŠ, Dušan BARTOVIČ,
Stanislav ŠTRUNC, Alexander NAGY (František
HOHOLKO 69'), Pavel STRATIL, Milan ALBRECHT


FIN: (Coach: Olavi LAAKSONEN)
Paavo   HEINONEN,   Pertti   MÄKIPÄÄ,   Seppo
KILPONEN, Vilho RAJANTIE, Timo KAUTONEN,
Jouko SUOMALAINEN (Seppo MÄKELÄ 46'), Raimo
TOIVANEN, Pentti TOIVOLA, Olavi LITMANEN, Matti
PAATELAINEN, Pekka HEIKKILÄ


11 October 1970    Ref: Leonidas VAMVAKOPOULOS
                                           (Greece)
Stadionul 23 August, BUCHAREST (Att. 36,584)

### ROMANIA - FINLAND
### 3:0 (2:0)

1:0  Dumitrache  (28'),  2:0  Dumitrache  (42'),  3:0

Nunweiller (77')

ROM: (Coach: Angelo NICULESCU)
Necula RĂDUCANU, Lajos SĂTMĂREANU,
Niculae LUPESCU, Cornel DINU, Iosif VIGU, Ion
DUMITRU, Radu NUNWEILLER, Alexandru NEAGU
(Gheorghe TĂTARU 46'), Nicolae DOBRIN, Florea
DUMITRACHE, Florian DUMITRESCU

FIN: (Coach: Olavi LAAKSONEN)
Paavo HEINONEN, Pertti MÄKIPÄÄ, Seppo
KILPONEN, Vilho RAJANTIE, Timo KAUTONEN,
Jouko SUOMALAINEN (Seppo MÄKELÄ 55'),
Pekka HEIKKILÄ (Olavi LITMANEN 67'), Raimo
SAVIOMAA, Pentti TOIVOLA, Raimo TOIVANEN,
Matti PAATELAINEN


11 November 1970        Ref: Arend VAN GEMERT
                                    (Netherlands)
Ninian Park, CARDIFF (Att. 19,882)

WALES - ROMANIA
0:0

WAL: (Coach: David BOWEN)
Gareth SPRAKE, Peter RODRIGUES, Michael
ENGLAND, David POWELL, Roderick THOMAS,
Alan DURBAN, Graham MOORE, Barrington HOLE,
Richard KRZYWICKI, Wyn DAVIES, Ronald REES

ROM: (Coach: Angelo NICULESCU)
Necula RĂDUCANU, Lajos SĂTMĂREANU, Niculae
LUPESCU, Cornel DINU (Bujor HĂLMĂGEANU 46'),
Mihai MOCANU, Ion DUMITRU, Radu NUNWEILLER,
Alexandru NEAGU, Nicolae DOBRIN (Flavius DOMIDE
76'), Florea DUMITRACHE, Florian DUMITRESCU

Richard Keir

21 April 1971        Ref: Johan BOSTRÖM (Sweden)
Vetch Field, SWANSEA (Att. 12,767)

WALES - CZECHOSLOVAKIA
1:3 (0:0)

1:0 R. Davies (49' pen.), 1:1 Čapkovič (78'), 1:2
Táborský (80'), 1:3 Čapkovič (82')

WAL: (Coach: David BOWEN)
Anthony MILLINGTON, Peter RODRIGUES, Leighton
PHILLIPS, Roderick THOMAS, Edward JAMES,
John WALLEY, Alan DURBAN, Ronald DAVIES, Wyn
DAVIES, John MAHONEY (Arfon GRIFFITHS 46'),
Ronald REES

CZE: (Coach: Ladislav NOVÁK/Ladislav KÁČANI)
Ivo VIKTOR, Karol DOBIAŠ, Vladimír HRIVNÁK, Jozef
DESIATNIK, Vladimír TÁBORSKÝ, Jaroslav POLLÁK,
Ladislav KUNA, Jozef ADAMEC, František VESELÝ,
Pavel STRATIL, Ján ČAPKOVIČ

16 May 1971        Ref: Fernando Nunes dos Santos
                                    LEITE (Portugal)
Tehelné pole, BRATISLAVA (Att. 38, 207)

CZECHOSLOVAKIA - ROMANIA
1:0 (0:0)

1:0 Veselý (88')

CZE: (Coach: Ladislav NOVÁK/Ladislav KÁČANI)
Ivo VIKTOR, Karol DOBIAŠ, Vladimír HRIVNÁK, Jozef
DESIATNIK, Vladimír TÁBORSKÝ, Jaroslav POLLÁK,
Ladislav KUNA, Jozef ADAMEC, František VESELÝ,
Pavel STRATIL (Karol JOKL 72'), Ján ČAPKOVIČ
(Dušan KABÁT 76')

ROM: (Coach: Angelo NICULESCU)

Necula RĂDUCANU, Lajos SĂTMĂREANU, Cornel DINU, Dan COE, Mihai MOCANU, Dan ANCA, Ion DUMITRU, Alexandru NEAGU (Radu NUNWEILLER 61'), Emerich DEMBROVSCHI, Florea DUMITRACHE, Mircea LUCESCU

26 May 1971          Ref: Günter MÄNNIG
(East Germany)
Olympiastadion, HELSINKI (Att. 5,410)

### FINLAND - WALES
0:1 (0:0)

0:1 Toshack (54')

FIN: (Coach: Olavi LAAKSONEN)
Lars NÄSMAN, Timo KAUTONEN, Raimo SAVIOMAA, Vilho RAJANTIE, Jouko SUOMALAINEN, Timo NUMMELIN, Pekka HEIKKILÄ, Raimo TOIVANEN (Jarmo FLINK 46'), Matti PAATELAINEN, Arto TOLSA, Tommy LINDHOLM

WAL: (Coach: David BOWEN)
Anthony MILLINGTON, Malcolm PAGE, Stephen DERRETT, Alan DURBAN, John ROBERTS, Raymond MIELCZAREK, Richard KRZYWICKI, Philip JONES, Ronald REES, John TOSHACK, Gilbert REECE

16 June 1971          Ref: Marian ŚRODECKI
(Poland)
Olympiastadion, HELSINKI (Att. 4,658)

### FINLAND - CZECHOSLOVAKIA
0:4 (0:2)

0:1 Čapkovič (12'), 0:2 Pollák (16'), 0:3 Karkó (84'), 0:4 Karkó (89')

FIN: (Coach: Olavi LAAKSONEN)
Lars NÄSMAN, Timo KAUTONEN, Vilho RAJANTIE, Seppo KILPONEN, Jouko SUOMALAINEN, Timo NUMMELIN, Pekka HEIKKILÄ (Matti PAATELAINEN 46'), Raimo TOIVANEN (Tommy LINDHOLM 65'), Arto TOLSA, Jarmo FLINK, Olavi RISSANEN

CZE: (Coach: Ladislav NOVÁK/Ladislav KÁČANI)
Ivo VIKTOR, Karol DOBIAŠ, Vladimír HRIVNÁK, Jozef DESIATNIK, Vladimír TÁBORSKÝ, Jaroslav POLLÁK, Ladislav KUNA, Jozef ADAMEC (Ivan HRDLIČKA 76'), František VESELÝ (František KARKÓ 76'), Pavel STRATIL, Ján ČAPKOVIČ

22 September 1971      Ref: Pius KAMBER
(Switzerland)
Olympiastadion, HELSINKI (Att. 2,084)

### FINLAND - ROMANIA
### 0:4 (0:2)

0:1 Iordănescu (25'), 0:2 Lupescu (37'), 0:3 Dembrovschi (55'), 0:4 Lucescu (64' pen.)

FIN: (Coach: Olavi LAAKSONEN)
Lars NÄSMAN (Paavo HEINONEN 46'), Jouko SUOMALAINEN, Raimo SAVIOMAA, Ari MÄKYNEN, Esko RANTA, Raimo TOIVANEN (Timo NUMMELIN 57'), Pekka HEIKKILÄ, Miikka TOIVOLA, Timo RAHJA, Antero NIKKANEN, Tommy LINDHOLM

ROM: (Coach: Angelo NICULESCU)
Necula RĂDUCANU, Lajos SĂTMĂREANU, Niculae LUPESCU, Cornel DINU, Mihai MOCANU, Ion DUMITRU, Radu NUNWEILLER, Mircea LUCESCU, Emerich DEMBROVSCHI, Alexandru NEAGU, Anghel IORDĂNESCU (Gheorghe TĂTARU 46')

13 October 1971          Ref: Kaj RASMUSSEN
(Denmark)
Vetch Field, SWANSEA (Att. 10,301)

### WALES - FINLAND
### 3:0 (1:0)

1:0 Durban (10'), 2:0 Toshack (53'), 3:0 Reece (89')

WAL: (Coach: David BOWEN)
Gareth SPRAKE (Anthony MILLINGTON 46'), Peter
RODRIGUES, Roderick THOMAS, John ROBERTS,
Michael ENGLAND, Terrence HENNESSEY, Brian
EVANS, Gilbert REECE, John TOSHACK, Alan
DURBAN, Trevor HOCKEY

FIN: (Coach: Olavi LAAKSONEN)
Lars NÄSMAN, Seppo KILPONEN, Raimo SAVIOMAA,
Ari MÄKYNEN, Pekka KOSONEN, Raimo ELO,
Jarmo FLINK, Miikka TOIVOLA, Heikko SUHONEN
(Henry BERGSTRÖM 46'), Pekka HEIKKILÄ, Tommy
LINDHOLM


27 October 1971      Ref: Mariano MEDINA Iglesias
(Spain)
Letenský stadion, PRAGUE (Att. 20,051)

### CZECHOSLOVAKIA - WALES
### 1:0 (0:0)

1:0 Kuna (60')

CZE: (Coach: Ladislav NOVÁK/Ladislav KÁČANI)
Ivo VIKTOR, Karol DOBIAŠ, Vladimír HRIVNÁK,
Ludovít ZLOCHA, Vladimír TÁBORSKÝ, Jaroslav
POLLÁK, Ladislav KUNA, Karol JOKL (Ondrej DAŇKO
65'), Bohumil VESELÝ (Zdeněk NEHODA 78'), Pavel
STRATIL, Dušan KABÁT

WAL: (Coach: David BOWEN)
Anthony MILLINGTON, Peter RODRIGUES, Leighton
PHILLIPS, Alwyn BURTON, Roderick THOMAS,
Terence YORATH, Terrence HENNESSEY (Ronald
REES 57'), Alan DURBAN, Brian EVANS (Richard
KRZYWICKI 78'), Michael HILL, Leighton JAMES


14 November 1971          Ref: Milivoje GUGULOVIĆ
                                    (Yugoslavia)
Stadionul 23 August, BUCHAREST (Att. 63,583)

ROMANIA - CZECHOSLOVAKIA
2:1 (1:0)

1:0 Dembrovschi (26'), 1:1 Čapkovič (50'), 2:1 Dobrin
(51')

ROM: (Coach: Angelo NICULESCU)
Necula RĂDUCANU, Lajos SĂTMĂREANU, Niculae
LUPESCU, Cornel DINU, Augustin DELEANU, Dan
ANCA, Radu NUNWEILLER, Mircea LUCESCU,
Emerich DEMBROVSCHI (Flavius DOMIDE 72'),
Nicolae DOBRIN, Anghel IORDĂNESCU

CZE: (Coach: Ladislav NOVÁK/Ladislav KÁČANI)
Ivo VIKTOR, Karol DOBIAŠ, Vladimír HRIVNÁK,
Vladimír HAGARA, Vladimír TÁBORSKÝ, Jaroslav
POLLÁK, Ladislav KUNA, Ivan HRDLIČKA, Bohumil
VESELÝ (Zdeněk NEHODA 74'), Pavel STRATIL, Ján
ČAPKOVIČ


24 November 1971          Ref: Alfred DELCOURT
                                    (Belgium)
Stadionul 23 August, BUCHAREST (Att. 35,251)

ROMANIA - WALES
2:0 (1:0)
1:0 Lupescu (9'), 2:0 Lucescu (74')

211

<u>ROM:</u> (Coach: Angelo NICULESCU)
Necula RĂDUCANU, Lajos SĂTMĂREANU, Niculae LUPESCU, Cornel DINU, Augustin DELEANU, Ion DUMITRU, Radu NUNWEILLER, Mircea LUCESCU, Emerich DEMBROVSCHI, Nicolae DOBRIN, Anghel IORDĂNESCU

<u>WAL:</u> (Coach: David BOWEN)
Anthony MILLINGTON, Peter RODRIGUES, Leighton PHILLIPS, Herbert WILLIAMS, Roderick THOMAS, Gilbert REECE, Trevor HOCKEY, Ronald REES, Michael HILL (Cyril DAVIES 46'), Ronald DAVIES, Leighton JAMES

| | |
|---|---|
| ROMANIA(Q) | (P6, W4, D1, L1, F11, A2, Pts. 9) |
| Czechoslovakia | (P6, W4, D1, L1, F11, A4, Pts. 9) |
| Wales | (P6, W2, D1, L3, F5, A6, Pts. 5) |
| Finland | (P6, W0, D1, L5, F1, A16, Pts. 1) |

<u>GROUP 2</u> (Bulgaria, France, Hungary, Norway)

7 October 1970          Ref: Adrianus BOOGAERTS
(Netherlands)
Ullevaal Stadion, OSLO (Att. 16,090)

NORWAY - HUNGARY
1:3 (0:2)

0:1 Bene (6'), 0:2 Nagy (23'), 1:2 Iversen (50'), 1:3 Karlsen (66' og)

<u>NOR:</u> (Coach: Øivind JOHANNESSEN)
Geir KARLSEN, Per PETTERSEN, Finn THORSEN, Thor SPYDEVOLD, Sigbjørn SLINNING, Trygve BORNØ, Olav NILSEN, Svein KVIA, Egil Roger OLSEN, Odd IVERSEN (Kjetil HASUND 86'), Tor FUGLSET (Finn SEEMANN 46')

HUN: (Coach: József HOFFER)
Ádám ROTHERMEL, Ernő NOSKÓ, Kálmán
MÉSZÖLY, Csaba VIDÁTS, Miklós PÁNCSICS,
Sándor MÜLLER, Zoltán HALMOSI, László FAZEKAS,
Lajos KOCSIS, Ferenc BENE, László NAGY


11 November 1970          Ref: António Saldanha
                          RIBEIRO (Portugal)
Stade de Gerland, LYONS (Att. 10,357)

FRANCE - NORWAY
3:1 (1:0)

1:0 Floch (30'), 2:0 Lech (55'), 3:0 Mézy (63'), 3:1
Nilsen (79')

FRA: (Coach: Georges BOULOGNE)
Georges CARNUS, Jean DJORKAEFF, Jacques
NOVI, Bernard BOSQUIER, Jean-Paul ROSTAGNI,
Georges LECH, Henri MICHEL, Jean-Noël HUCK,
Michel MÉZY, Louis FLOCH, Charly LOUBET

NOR: (Coach: Øivind JOHANNESSEN)
Per HAFTORSEN, Per PETTERSEN, Finn
THORSEN, Arild HETLEØEN, Sigbjørn SLINNING,
Trygve BORNØ, Thor SPYDEVOLD, Olav NILSEN,
Harry HESTAD, Egil Roger OLSEN, Finn SEEMANN


15 November 1970          Ref: Mihalis KIRIAKIDIS
                          (Cyprus)
Stadion Vasil Levski, SOFIA (Att. 21,465)

BULGARIA - NORWAY
1:1 (1:0)

1:0 Atanasov (29'), 1:1 Fuglset (83')

BUL: (Coach: Vasil SPASOV)
Yordan FILIPOV, Ivan ZAFIROV, Dobromir ZHECHEV,

Stefan ALADZHOV, Bozhil KOLEV, Georgi DENEV, Tsvetan ATANASOV (Kiril RAYKOV 82'), Hristo BONEV, Atanas MIHAYLOV (Dinko DERMENDZHIEV 46'), Asparuh NIKODIMOV, Vasil MITKOV

NOR: (Coach: Øivind JOHANNESSEN)
Per HAFTORSEN, Per PETTERSEN, Finn THORSEN, Arild HETLEØEN, Sigbjørn SLINNING, Trygve BORNØ, Thor SPYDEVOLD, Olav NILSEN, Egil Roger OLSEN (Arnfinn ESPESETH 83'), Tor FUGLSET, Kjetil HASUND

24 April 1971             Ref: Joaquim Fernandes de
                                    CAMPOS (Portugal)
Népstadion, BUDAPEST (Att. 45,867)

HUNGARY - FRANCE
1:1 (0:0)

0:1 Revelli (64'), 1:1 Kocsis (70' pen.)

HUN: (Coach: József HOFFER)
Ádám ROTHERMEL, Ernő NOSKÓ, Lajos SZŰCS, Miklós PÁNCSICS, Péter JUHÁSZ, László FAZEKAS, Sándor ZÁMBÓ, Flórián ALBERT, Lajos KOCSIS, Ferenc BENE, Mihály KOZMA (László KARSAI 53')

FRA: (Coach: Georges BOULOGNE)
Georges CARNUS, Roger LEMERRE, Francis CAMERINI, Bernard BOSQUIER, Jacques NOVI, Jean DJORKAEFF, Henri MICHEL, Georges LECH, Georges BERETA, Hervé REVELLI, Fleury DI NALLO (Charly LOUBET 46')

19 May 1971         Ref: Tofik BAKHRAMOV (USSR)
Stadion Vasil Levski, SOFIA (Att. 28,342)

BULGARIA - HUNGARY

3:0 (1:0)

1:0 Kolev (38'), 2:0 Petkov (48'), 3:0 Velichkov (72')

BUL: (Coach: Vasil SPASOV)
Stoyan YORDANOV, Milko GAYDARSKI, Dimitar
PENEV, Stefan VELICHKOV, Dobromir ZHECHEV,
Bozhil KOLEV, Georgi VASILEV, Hristo BONEV, Petar
ZHEKOV, Atanas MIHAYLOV (Petko PETKOV 46'),
Mladen VASILEV

HUN: (Coach: József HOFFER)
Ádám ROTHERMEL, Tibor FÁBIÁN, Miklós
PÁNCSICS, Péter JUHÁSZ, Ede DUNAI, Csaba
VIDÁTS, László FAZEKAS (László KARSAI 46'),
Lajos KOCSIS, Flórián ALBERT, Mihály KOZMA
(János NAGY 73'), Sándor ZÁMBÓ

9 June 1971          Ref: William GOW (Wales)
Ullevaal Stadion, OSLO (Att. 22,041)

NORWAY - BULGARIA
1:4 (0:4)

0:1 Bonev (26'), 0:2 Zhekov (29'), 0:3 Vasilev (37'), 0:4
Bonev (42' pen.), 1:4 Iversen (80')

NOR: (Coach: Øivind JOHANNESSEN)
Kjell KASPERSEN, Robert NILSSON, Finn THORSEN,
Frank OLAFSEN (Arild HETLEØEN 82'), Sigbjørn
SLINNING, Tor Egil JOHANSEN (Harald SUNDE 80'),
Per PETTERSEN, Olav NILSEN, Jan FUGLSET, Odd
IVERSEN, Tom LUND

BUL: (Coach: Vasil SPASOV)
Stoyan YORDANOV (Biser MIHAYLOV 59'), Milko
GAYDARSKI, Dimitar PENEV, Stefan VELICHKOV,
Dobromir ZHECHEV, Bozhil KOLEV, Georgi VASILEV
(Georgi GEORGIEV I 68'), Hristo BONEV, Petar

ZHEKOV, Petko PETKOV, Mladen VASILEV

8 September 1971    Ref: John PATERSON (Scotland)
Ullevaal Stadion, OSLO (Att. 16,544)

### NORWAY - FRANCE
### 1:3 (0:2)

0:1 Vergnes (33'), 0:2 Loubet (34'), 0:3 Blanchet (49'),
1:3 Dybwad-Olsen (80')

<u>NOR:</u> (Coach: Øivind JOHANNESSEN)
Geir KARLSEN (Svein OLSEN 51'), Anbjorn
EKELAND, Tore BØRREHAUG, Thor SPYDEVOLD,
Sigbjorn SLINNING, Tom JACOBSEN, Jan
CHRISTIANSEN, Egil OLSEN, Jan FUGLSET, Tom
LUND (Ola DYBWAD-OLSEN 51'), Kjetil HASUND

<u>FRA:</u> (Coach: Georges BOULOGNE)
Georges CARNUS, Jean DJORKAEFF, Jacques
NOVI, Bernard BOSQUIER, Jean-Paul ROSTAGNI,
Henri MICHEL, Michel MÉZY, Georges BERETA,
Bernard BLANCHET (Georges LECH 76'), Jacques
VERGNES, Charly LOUBET

25 September 1971        Ref: Robert DAVIDSON
                                  (Scotland)
Népstadion, BUDAPEST (Att. 67,740)

### HUNGARY - BULGARIA
### 2:0 (0:0)

1:0 P. Juhász (51'), 2:0 Vidáts (52')

<u>HUN:</u> (Coach: Rudolf ILLOVSZKY)
István GÉCZI, Tibor FÁBIÁN, Miklós
PÁNCSICS, Péter JUHÁSZ (Ernő NOSKÓ
79'), Csaba VIDÁTS, Lajos SZŰCS, István
SZŐKE, László FAZEKAS, Ferenc BENE, Antal

DUNAI, Sándor ZÁMBÓ (István JUHÁSZ 76')

BUL: (Coach: Vasil SPASOV)
Biser MIHAYLOV, Milko GAYDARSKI, Dimitar PENEV,
Stefan VELICHKOV, Dobromir ZHECHEV, Bozhil
KOLEV, Mladen VASILEV, Hristo BONEV, Petar
ZHEKOV (Georgi VASILEV 59'), Petko PETKOV,
Dinko DERMENDZHIEV

9 October 1971          Ref: Gaspar PINTADO Viú
                                          (Spain)
Stade Olympique Yves-du-Manoir, COLOMBES
(Att. 21,756)

### FRANCE - HUNGARY
### 0:2 (0:2)

0:1 Bene (35'), 0:2 Zámbó (43')

FRA: (Coach: Georges BOULOGNE)
Georges CARNUS, Jean DJORKAEFF, Jacques
NOVI, Bernard BOSQUIER, Jean-Paul ROSTAGNI,
Georges LECH, Henri MICHEL, Michel MÉZY,
Georges BERETA, Charly LOUBET (Gilbert GRESS
46'), Hervé REVELLI

HUN: (Coach: Rudolf ILLOVSZKY)
István GÉCZI, Ernő NOSKÓ, Miklós PÁNCSICS,
Csaba VIDÁTS, Péter JUHÁSZ, László FAZEKAS,
István JUHÁSZ, Lajos SZŰCS, Sándor ZÁMBÓ,
Ferenc BENE, Antal DUNAI

27 October 1971          Ref: DOĞAN Babacan (Turkey)
Népstadion, BUDAPEST (Att. 29,253)

### HUNGARY - NORWAY
### 4:0 (3:0)

1:0 Bene (22'), 2:0 Dunai (24'), 3:0 Bene (43'), 4:0
Szűcs (63')

HUN: (Coach: Rudolf ILLOVSZKY)
István GÉCZI, Ernő NOSKÓ, Miklós PÁNCSICS,
Csaba VIDÁTS, István JUHÁSZ, Péter JUHÁSZ,
Lajos SZŰCS, László FAZEKAS, Ferenc BENE, Antal
DUNAI, Sándor ZÁMBÓ

NOR: (Coach: Øivind JOHANNESSEN)
Geir KARLSEN, Tore BØRREHAUG, Frank OLAFSEN,
Tor ALSAKER-NØSTDAHL, Sigbjørn SLINNING, Tom
JACOBSEN, Thor SPYDEVOLD, Per PETTERSEN,
Kjetil HASUND, Jan FUGLSET (Egil Roger OLSEN
79'), Roald JENSEN

10 November 1971      Ref: John TAYLOR (England)
Stade Marcel Saupin, NANTES (Att. 9,405)

FRANCE - BULGARIA
2:1 (0:0)

0:1 Bonev (54' pen.), 1:1 Lech (64'), 2:1 Loubet (87')

FRA: (Coach: Georges BOULOGNE)
Georges CARNUS, Francis CAMERINI, Jean
DJORKAEFF, Jacques NOVI, Claude QUITTET,
Michel MÉZY, Bernard BLANCHET, Henri MICHEL,
Hervé REVELLI (Louis FLOCH 82'), Georges LECH,
Charly LOUBET

BUL: (Coach: Vasil SPASOV)
Yordan FILIPOV, Ivan ZAFIROV, Dimitar PENEV,
Stefan VELICHKOV, Dobromir ZHECHEV, Bozhil
KOLEV, Mladen VASILEV, Hristo BONEV, Petko
PETKOV (Georgi TSVETKOV 85'), Georgi DENEV,
Dinko DERMENDZHIEV

4 December 1971      Ref: Kurt TSCHENSCHER
(West Germany)
Stadion Vasil Levski, SOFIA (Att. 18,057)

## BULGARIA - FRANCE
### 2:1 (0:0)

1:0 Zhekov (47'), 2:0 Mihaylov (82'), 2:1 Blanchet (84')

BUL: (Coach: Vasil SPASOV)
Rumyancho GORANOV (Yordan FILIPOV 65'), Milko GAYDARSKI, Dimitar PENEV, Stefan VELICHKOV (VIktor YONOV 46'), Dobromir ZHECHEV, Bozhil KOLEV, Mladen VASILEV, Hristo BONEV, Petar ZHEKOV, Atanas MIHAYLOV, Dinko DERMENDZHIEV

FRA: (Coach: Georges BOULOGNE)
Georges CARNUS, Jean DJORKAEFF, Marius TRÉSOR, Jacques NOVI, Bernard BOSQUIER, Michel MÉZY, Bernard BLANCHET, Henri MICHEL, Georges LECH, Charly LOUBET (Georges BERETA 76'), Hervé REVELLI (Louis FLOCH 60')

| | |
|---|---|
| HUNGARY (Q) | (P6, W4, D1, L1, F12, A5, Pts. 9) |
| Bulgaria | (P6, W3, D1, L2, F11, A7, Pts. 7) |
| France | (P6, W3, D1, L2, F10, A8, Pts. 7) |
| Norway | (P6, W0, D1, L5, F5, A18, Pts. 1) |

## GROUP 3 (England, Greece, Malta, Switzerland)

11 October 1970      Ref: Concetto LO BELLO
(Italy)
Imperu Istadium, GZIRA (Att. 8,689)

## MALTA - GREECE
### 1:1 (0:0)

1:0 Vassallo (66'), 1:1 Kritikopoulos (88')

MAL: (Coach: Carm BORG)
Alfred MIZZI, Joseph GRIMA, Alfred MALLIA (John
PRIVITERA 78'), Emanuele MICALLEF, Anton
CAMILLERI, Ronald COCKS, William VASSALLO,
John BONETT (Charles MICALLEF 70'), Edward
VELLA, Louis ARPA, Edward THEOBALD

GRE: (Coach: Vasilis PETROPOULOS)
Panagiotis OIKONOMOPOULOS, Giorgos SKREKIS,
Aristidis KAMARAS, Apostolos TOSKAS, Nikolaos
STATHOPOULOS, Stathis HAITAS, Konstantinos
ELEFTHERAKIS, Dimitris DOMAZOS, Giorgos
KOUDAS (Mihalis KRITIKOPOULOS 68'), Nikolaos
GIOUTSOS (Antonis ANTONIADIS 68'), Dimitris
PAPAIOANNOU

16 December 1970      Ref: Milivoje GUGULOVIĆ
(Yugoslavia)
Stádio Georgios Karaiskakis, PIRAEUS (Att. 30,699)

GREECE - SWITZERLAND
0:1 (0:0)

0:1 Müller (85')

GRE: (Coach: Vasilis PETROPOULOS)
Nikolaos HRISTIDIS, Giorgos SKREKIS, Aristidis
KAMARAS, Angelos SPIRIDON, Nikolaos
STATHOPOULOS, Stathis HAITAS, Dimitris
DOMAZOS, Konstantinos ELEFTHERAKIS (Mihalis
KRITIKOPOULOS 75'), Giorgos KOUDAS, Nikolaos
GIOUTSOS, Dimitris PAPAIOANNOU

SWI: (Coach: Louis MAURER)
Mario PROSPERI, Peter RAMSEIER, Anton
WEIBEL, Georges PERROUD, Marc BERSET, Karl
ODERMATT, Rolf BLÄTTLER, Jakob KUHN, Kurt
MÜLLER, Friedrich KÜNZLI (Walter BALMER 75'),

Peter WENGER (René-Pierre QUENTIN 46')


20 December 1970      Ref: Gocho RUSEV (Bulgaria)
Imperu Istadium, GZIRA (Att. 4,739)

### MALTA - SWITZERLAND
### 1:2 (0:0)

0:1 Quentin (50'), 1:1 Theobald (57' pen.), 1:2 Künzli (59')

MAL: (Coach: Carm BORG)
Alfred MIZZI, John PRIVITERA, Anton CAMILLERI,
Emanuele MICALLEF, Joseph GRIMA, Alfred DELIA,
Edward THEOBALD (Edward VELLA 75'), William
VASSALLO, Ronald COCKS, Charles MICALLEF,
John BONETT

SWI: (Coach: Louis MAURER)
Marcel KUNZ, Peter RAMSEIER, Anton WEIBEL,
Georges   PERROUD,   Marc   BERSET,   Karl
ODERMATT, Rolf BLÄTTLER, Jakob KUHN, Kurt
MÜLLER, Friedrich KÜNZLI (Walter BALMER 65'),
Peter WENGER (René-Pierre QUENTIN 46')


3 February 1971      Ref: Ferdinand MARSCHALL
(Austria)
Imperu Istadium, GZIRA (Att. 29,751)

### MALTA - ENGLAND
### 0:1 (0:1)

0:1 Peters (35')

MAL: (Coach: Carm BORG)
Alfred  MIZZI,  Joseph  GRIMA,  Alfred  MALLIA,
Emanuele MICALLEF, Anton CAMILLERI, Edward
DARMANIN, Ronald COCKS, William VASSALLO,
Joseph CINI, Edward THEOBALD, Louis ARPA

<u>ENG:</u> (Coach: Alfred RAMSEY)
Gordon BANKS, Paul REANEY, Emlyn HUGHES, Alan
MULLERY, Roy McFARLAND, Norman HUNTER,
Alan BALL, Martin CHIVERS, Joseph ROYLE, Colin
HARVEY, Martin PETERS


21 April 1971          Ref: Martti HIRVINIEMI (Finland)
Wembley Stadium, LONDON (Att. 55,123)

### ENGLAND - GREECE
### 3:0 (1:0)

1:0 Chivers (23'), 2:0 Hurst (68'), 3:0 Lee (87')

<u>ENG:</u> (Coach: Alfred RAMSEY)
Gordon BANKS, Peter STOREY, Emlyn HUGHES,
Alan MULLERY, Roy McFARLAND, Robert MOORE,
Francis LEE, Alan BALL (Ralph COATES 78'), Martin
CHIVERS, Geoffrey HURST, Martin PETERS

<u>GRE:</u> (Coach: Vasilis PETROPOULOS)
Nikolaos HRISTIDIS, Giannis GAITATZIS, Angelos
SPIRIDON, Apostolos TOSKAS, Konstantinos
KAMBAS (Stathis HAITAS 75'), Nikolaos
STATHOPOULOS, Dimitris SYNETOPOULOS,
Giorgos KOUDAS, Giorgos DEDES (Giorgos
DELIKARIS 88'), Dimitris PAPAIOANNOU, Mihalis
KRITIKOPOULOS


21 April 1971          Ref: Gunnar MICHAELSEN
                                          (Denmark)
Allmend Stadion, LUCERNE (Att. 16,470)

### SWITZERLAND - MALTA
### 5:0 (5:0)

1:0 Blättler (14'), 2:0 Künzli (17'), 3:0 Quentin (26'),
4:0 Citherlet (28'), 5:0 Müller (30')

SWI: (Coach: Louis MAURER)
Mario PROSPERI, Pierangelo BOFFI, Peter RAMSEIER (Anton WEIBEL 46'), Roland CITHERLET, Pierre-Albert CHAPUISAT, Karl ODERMATT, Rolf BLÄTTLER, Jakob KUHN, Kurt MÜLLER, Friedrich KÜNZLI, René-Pierre QUENTIN

MAL: (Coach: Carm BORG)
Alfred MIZZI (Vincent BORG BONACI 32'), Joseph GRIMA, Alfred MALLIA, Anton CAMILLERI, Emanuele MICALLEF, Edward DARMANIN, Ronald COCKS, William VASSALLO, Joseph CINI, John BONETT, Louis ARPA (Alfred DELIA 75')


12 May 1971　　　　　Ref: Einar RØED (Norway)
Wembley Stadium, LONDON (Att. 41,534)

### ENGLAND - MALTA
### 5:0 (2:0)

1:0 Chivers (29'), 2:0 Lee (41'), 3:0 Clarke (47' pen.), 4:0 Chivers (48'), 5:0 Lawler (75')

ENG: (Coach: Alfred RAMSEY)
Gordon BANKS, Christopher LAWLER, Terence COOPER, Robert MOORE, Roy McFARLAND, Emlyn HUGHES, Francis LEE, Ralph COATES, Martin CHIVERS, Allan CLARKE, Martin PETERS (Alan BALL 62')

MAL: (Coach: Anthony FORMOSA)
Vincent BORG BONACI (Alfred MIZZI 49'), Louis PACE, Joseph GRIMA, Anton CAMILLERI, Edward DARMANIN, Alfred DELIA, Ronald COCKS, William VASSALLO, John BONETT, Edward THEOBALD, Louis ARPA

12 May 1971          Ref: lorwerth JONES (Wales)/
                     Thomas EDWARDS (Wales (29'))
Wankdorf Stadion, BERNE (Att. 32,770)

### SWITZERLAND - GREECE
### 1:0 (0:0)

1:0 Odermatt (73')

SWI: (Coach: Louis MAURER)
Mario PROSPERI, Peter RAMSEIER, Pierre-Albert
CHAPUISAT, Anton WEIBEL, Georges PERROUD,
Karl ODERMATT, Jakob KUHN, Rolf BLÄTTLER,
Walter BALMER, Friedrich KÜNZLI, Daniel
JEANDUPEUX

GRE: (Coach: Vasilis PETROPOULOS)
Nikolaos HRISTIDIS, Giannis GAITATZIS, Apostolos
TOSKAS, Konstantinos KAMBAS, Apostolos
GLEZOS, Nikolaos STATHOPOULOS, Thanasis
INTZOGLOU (Giorgos KARAFESKOS 77'),
Dimitris PAPAIOANNOU, Giorgos DEDES, Dimitris
HATZIIOANOGLOU (Mihalis KRITIKOPOULOS 74'),
Dimitris SYNETOPOULOS


18 June 1971          Ref: István ZSOLT (Hungary)
Stádio Georgios Karaiskakis, PIRAEUS (Att. 9,561)

### GREECE - MALTA
### 2:0 (0:0)

1:0 Davourlis (60'), 2:0 Aidiniou (80')

GRE: (Coach: Vasilis PETROPOULOS)
Eleftherios POUPAKIS, Giannis GOUNARIS,
Vasilis SIOKOS (Apostolos TOSKAS 85'),
Apostolos GLEZOS, Dimitris ELEFTHERIADIS,
Anastasios PAPPAS (Giorgos KARAFESKOS 48'),
Konstantinos AIDINIOU, Stavros SARAFIS, Mihalis

KRITIKOPOULOS, Konstantinos DAVOURLIS, Haralambos STAVROPOULOS

MAL: (Coach: Anthony FORMOSA)
Vincent BORG BONACI, Louis PACE, Joseph GRIMA, Anton CAMILLERI, Edward DARMANIN (Charles MICALLEF 68'), Edward THEOBALD, Ronald COCKS, William VASSALLO, Joseph CINI, John BONETT, Joseph FARRUGIA (Louis ARPA 46')

13 October 1971      Ref: Vital LORAUX (Belgium)
Sankt Jakob Stadion, BASLE (Att. 47,877)

### SWITZERLAND - ENGLAND
### 2:3 (2:2)

0:1 Hurst (1'), 1:1 Jeandupeux (10'), 1:2 Chivers (12'), 2:2 Künzli (44'), 2:3 Weibel (78' og)

SWI: (Coach: Louis MAURER)
Marcel KUNZ, Pierre-Albert CHAPUISAT (Georges PERROUD 83'), Peter RAMSEIER, Anton WEIBEL, Pirmin STIERLI, Karl ODERMATT, Jakob KUHN, Rolf BLÄTTLER (Kurt MÜLLER 75'), Walter BALMER, Friedrich KÜNZLI, Daniel JEANDUPEUX

ENG: (Coach: Alfred RAMSEY)
Gordon BANKS, Christopher LAWLER, Terence COOPER, Alan MULLERY, Roy McFARLAND, Robert MOORE, Francis LEE, Paul MADELEY, Martin CHIVERS, Geoffrey HURST (John RADFORD 84'), Martin PETERS

10 November 1971     Ref: Constantin BĂRBULESCU
(Romania)
Wembley Stadium, LONDON (Att. 90,423)

### ENGLAND - SWITZERLAND

## 1:1 (1:1)

1:0 Summerbee (9'), 1:1 Odermatt (26')

ENG: (Coach: Alfred RAMSEY)
Peter SHILTON, Paul MADELEY, Terence COOPER, Peter STOREY, Laurence LLOYD, Robert MOORE, Michael SUMMERBEE (Martin CHIVERS 60'), Alan BALL, Geoffrey HURST, Francis LEE (Rodney MARSH 83'), Emlyn HUGHES

SWI: (Coach: Louis MAURER)
Mario PROSPERI, Peter RAMSEIER, Pierre-Albert CHAPUISAT, Georges PERROUD, Pirmin STIERLI, Karl ODERMATT, Rolf BLÄTTLER, Jakob KUHN, Walter BALMER, Friedrich KÜNZLI, Daniel JEANDUPEUX (Peter MEIER 63')


1 December 1971       Ref: José María ORTIZ de Mendíbil (Spain)
Stádio Georgios Karaiskakis, PIRAEUS (Att. 34,014)

### GREECE - ENGLAND
### 0:2 (0:0)

0:1 Hurst (57'), 0:2 Chivers (90')

GRE: (Coach: William BINGHAM)
Nikolaos HRISTIDIS, Theodoros PALLAS, Apostolos TOSKAS, Athanasios ANGELIS, Konstantinos ELEFTHERAKIS, Dimitris DOMAZOS, Konstantinos NIKOLAIDIS (Konstantinos DAVOURLIS 73'), Antonis ANTONIADIS, Dimitris PAPAIOANNOU, Giorgos KOUDAS (Mihalis KRITIKOPOULOS 61'), Anthimos KAPSIS

ENG: (Coach: Alfred RAMSEY)
Gordon BANKS, Paul MADELEY, Emlyn HUGHES, Colin BELL, Roy McFARLAND, Robert MOORE,

Francis LEE, Alan BALL, Martin CHIVERS, Geoffrey HURST, Martin PETERS

| | |
|---|---|
| ENGLAND (Q) | (P6, W5, D1, L0, F15, A3, Pts. 11) |
| Switzerland | (P6, W4, D1, L1, F12, A5, Pts. 9) |
| Greece | (P6, W1, D1, L4, F3, A8, Pts. 3) |
| Malta | (P6, W0, D1, L5, F2, A16, Pts. 1) |

GROUP 4 (Cyprus, Northern Ireland, Spain, USSR)

11 November 1970          Ref: Gyula EMSBERGER
(Hungary)
Estadio Ramón Sánchez Pizjuán, SEVILLE
(Att. 26,215)

### SPAIN - NORTHERN IRELAND
### 3:0 (1:0)

1:0 Rexach (39'), 2:0 'Pirri' (59'), 3:0 Luis (76')

SPA: (Coach: Ladislao KUBALA Stécz)
José Angel IRIBAR Kortajarena, Joaquín RIFÉ Climent, Francisco Fernández Rodríguez 'GALLEGO', Juan Cruz SOL Oria (Juan López HITA 46'), Enrique Álvarez COSTAS, José Luis VIOLETA Lajusticia, Antón María ARIETA-ARAUNABEÑA Piedra, LUIS Aragonés Suárez, Enrique Castro González 'QUINI' (Enrique LORA Millán 46'), José Martínez Sánchez 'PIRRI', Carles REXACH i Cerdà

NIR: (Coach: William BINGHAM)
William McFAUL, David CRAIG, Samuel NELSON, Terence NEILL, Thomas JACKSON, William O'KANE, David SLOAN, George BEST, Derek DOUGAN (Samuel TODD 21'), Terence HARKIN, David CLEMENTS

15 November 1970          Ref: Petar KOSTOVSKI
                                    (Yugoslavia)

Stádio G.S.P., NICOSIA (Att. 8,980)

### CYPRUS - USSR
### 1:3 (1:2)

0:1  Kolotov  (10'),  0:2  Evryuzhikhin  (16'),  1:2
    Haralambous I (42'), 1:3 Shevchenko (50')

CYP: (Coach: Raymond WOOD)
Mihalakis ALKIVIADIS, Konstantinos HRISTOU,
Dimos KAVAZIS, Pashalis FOKKIS, Kyriakos
KOUREAS, Nikolaos HARALAMBOUS, Tasos
KONSTANTINOU (Marios KYTHREOTIS 83'), Michael
THEODOROU (Markos MARKOU 75'), Pamboullis
PAPADOPOULOS, Pavlos VASILIOU, Andreas
STYLIANOU

URS: (Coach: Valentin NIKOLAEV)
Viktor BANNIKOV, Yuriy ISTOMIN, Albert
SHESTERNYOV, Evgeniy LOVCHEV, Vladimir
KAPLICHNIY, Viktor KOLOTOV, Vladimir MUNTYAN,
Boris KOPEIYKIN (Givi NODIYA 70'), Vladimir
FEDOTOV, Vitaliy SHEVCHENKO, Gennadiy
EVRYUZHIKHIN


3 February 1971     Ref: Francesco FRANCESCON
                                    (Italy)

Stádio G.S.P., NICOSIA (Att. 9,119)

### CYPRUS - NORTHERN IRELAND
### 0:3 (0:0)

0:1 Nicholson (53'), 0:2 Dougan (55'), 0:3 Best (86' pen.)

CYP: (Coach: Raymond WOOD)
Herodotos HERODOTOU, Konstantinos HRISTOU
(Michael THEODOROU 75'), Dimos KAVAZIS,
Kyriakos KOUREAS, Stefanis MIHAIL, Kallis

KONSTANTINOU, Nikolaos HARALAMBOUS,
Pamboullis PAPADOPOULOS, Pavlos VASILIOU,
Pashalis FOKKIS, Andreas STYLIANOU

NIR: (Coach: William BINGHAM)
Patrick JENNINGS, David CRAIG, Samuel NELSON,
Allan HUNTER, Terence NEILL, Samuel TODD, Bryan
HAMILTON, Alexander McMORDIE, Derek DOUGAN,
James NICHOLSON, George BEST


21 April 1971    Ref: Jacques COLLING (Luxembourg)
Windsor Park, BELFAST (Att. 19,153)

### NORTHERN IRELAND - CYPRUS
### 5:0 (2:0)

1:0 Dougan (20'), 2:0 Best (44'), 3:0 Best (47'), 4:0
Best (56'), 5:0 Nicholson (85')

NIR: (Coach: William BINGHAM)
Patrick JENNINGS, David CRAIG, David CLEMENTS,
Martin HARVEY, Allan HUNTER, Samuel TODD
(Peter WATSON 86'), Bryan HAMILTON, Alexander
McMORDIE, Derek DOUGAN, James NICHOLSON,
George BEST

CYP: (Coach: Raymond WOOD)
Herodotos HERODOTOU, Kokos MIHAIL (Michael
THEODOROU 54'), Dimos KAVAZIS, Stefanis MIHAIL
(Takis PAPETTAS 65'), Kyriakos KOUREAS, Kallis
KONSTANTINOU, Tasos KONSTANTINOU, Pavlos
VASILIOU, Pamboullis PAPADOPOULOS, Pashalis
FOKKIS, Andreas STYLIANOU


9 May 1971       Ref: Constantin BĂRBULESCU
(Romania)
Stádio G.S.P., NICOSIA (Att. 5,818)

## CYPRUS - SPAIN
## 0:2 (0:1)

0:1 'Pirri' (3'), 0:2 Violeta (86')

CYP: (Coach: Raymond WOOD)
Demos ELEUTHERIADIS, Haris KANTZILIERIS, Kostakis ALEXANDROU, Dimos KAVAZIS, Kokos ANTONIOU, Takis PAPETTAS, Pavlos VASILIOU (Michael THEODOROU 67'), Pashalis FOKKIS, Andreas STYLIANOU, Pamboullis PAPADOPOULOS, Stefanis MIHAIL

SPA: (Coach: Ladislao KUBALA Stécz)
Miguel REINA Santos, José Luis VIOLETA Lajusticia, Gregorio BENITO Rubio, Antonio Alfonso Moreno 'TONONO', Antonio Manuel Martinez Morales 'ANTON', José CLARAMUNT Torres, José Martinez Sanchez 'PIRRI', Fidel URIARTE Macho (Enrique LORA Millán 46'), AMANCIO Amaro Varela, Enrique Castro González 'QUINI', José Ignacio CHURRUCA Sistiaga (Carles REXACH i Cerdà 55')

30 May 1971          Ref: Ferdinand BIWERSI
                     (West Germany)
Tsentralniy Stadion 'V.I. Lenina', MOSCOW
(Att. 81,700)

## USSR - SPAIN
## 2:1 (0:0)

1:0 Kolotov (79'), 2:0 Shevchenko (83'), 2:1 Rexach (88')

URS: (Coach: Valentin NIKOLAEV)
Evgeniy RUDAKOV, Revaz DZODZUASHVILI, Albert SHESTERNYOV, Valeriy ZYKOV, Vladimir KAPLICHNIY, Viktor KOLOTOV, Vladimir MUNTYAN (Vladimir FEDOTOV 57'), Iozhef SABO, Anatoliy BANISHEVSKIY (Givi NODIYA 76'), Vitaliy

SHEVCHENKO, Gennadiy EVRYUZHIKHIN

SPA: (Coach: Ladislao KUBALA Stécz)
José Angel IRIBAR Kortajarena, Juan Cruz SOL Oria
(Antonio Manuel Martínez Morales 'ANTON' 67'),
Antonio Alfonso Moreno 'TONONO', Gregorio BENITO
Rubio, Francisco Fernández Rodríguez 'GALLEGO',
José Luis VIOLETA Lajusticia (Enrique LORA Millán
60'), Carles REXACH i Cerdà, José CLARAMUNT
Torres, AMANCIO Amaro Varela, Fidel URIARTE
Macho, José Ignacio CHURRUCA Sistiaga


7 June 1971          Ref: Erik BEIJAR (Finland)
Tsentralniy Stadion 'V.I. Lenina', MOSCOW
(Att. 21,159)

## USSR - CYPRUS
## 6:1 (3:0)

1:0 Fedotov (4'), 2:0 Evryuzhikhin (23'), 3:0
Evryuzhikhin (38'), 4:0 Kolotov (59'), 4:1 S. Mihail
(75'), 5:1 Banishevskiy (85'), 6:1 Fedotov (86')

URS: (Coach: Valentin NIKOLAEV)
Viktor BANNIKOV (Evgeniy RUDAKOV 46'), Yuriy
ISTOMIN, Albert SHESTERNYOV, Valeriy ZYKOV,
Vladimir KAPLICHNIY, Viktor KOLOTOV, Vladimir
MUNTYAN, Anatoliy BANISHEVSKIY, Vladimir
FEDOTOV, Vitaliy SHEVCHENKO, Gennadiy
EVRYUZHIKHIN (Vitaliy KHMELNITSKIY 64')

CYP: (Coach: Raymond WOOD)
Varnavas HRISTOFI, Kokos MIHAIL, Haris
KANTZILIERIS (Michael THEODOROU 79'), Stefanis
MIHAIL, Dimos KAVAZIS, Kallis KONSTANTINOU,
Pavlos VASILIOU, Andreas KONSTANTINOU I,
Markos MARKOU, Pashalis FOKKIS, Andreas
STYLIANOU (Takis PAPETTAS 52')

22 September 1971          Ref: Ove DAHLBERG
                                              (Sweden)
Tsentralniy Stadion 'V.I. Lenina', MOSCOW
(Att. 51,186)

### USSR - NORTHERN IRELAND
### 1:0 (1:0)

1:0 Muntyan (43' pen.)

URS: (Coach: Valentin NIKOLAEV)
Evgeniy RUDAKOV, Revaz DZODZUASHVILI,
Albert SHESTERNYOV, Valeriy ZYKOV, Murtaz
KHURTSILAVA, Viktor KOLOTOV, Vladimir
MUNTYAN, Oleg DOLMATOV, Vladimir FEDOTOV,
Vitaliy SHEVCHENKO (Levon ISHTOYAN 74'),
Gennadiy EVRYUZHIKHIN

NIR: (Coach: Terence NEILL)
William McFAUL, Daniel HEGAN, Samuel NELSON,
James NICHOLSON, Allan HUNTER, William
O'KANE, David CRAIG (Bryan HAMILTON 60'),
David CLEMENTS, Terence NEILL, Derek DOUGAN,
George BEST

13 October 1971          Ref: Rolf NYHUS (Norway)
Windsor Park, BELFAST (Att. 16,573)

### NORTHERN IRELAND - USSR
### 1:1 (1:1)

1:0 Nicholson (13'), 1:1 Byshovets (32')

NIR: (Coach: Terence NEILL)
Patrick JENNINGS, Patrick RICE, Samuel NELSON,
James NICHOLSON, Allan HUNTER, William
O'KANE, Alexander McMORDIE, Bryan HAMILTON
(Martin O'NEILL 46'), Terence NEILL, Derek DOUGAN
(Thomas CASSIDY 73'), David CLEMENTS

URS: (Coach: Valentin NIKOLAEV)
Evgeniy RUDAKOV, Revaz DZODZUASHVILI, Albert SHESTERNYOV, Evgeniy LOVCHEV, Murtaz KHURTSILAVA, Viktor KOLOTOV, Nikolaiy KISELYOV, Oleg DOLMATOV, Anatoliy KONKOV, Anatoliy BYSHOVETS, Vitaliy SHEVCHENKO (Levon ISHTOYAN 60')


27 October 1971        Ref: Norman BURTENSHAW
(England)
Estadio Ramón Sánchez Pizjuán, SEVILLE
(Att. 40,169)

SPAIN - USSR
0:0

SPA: (Coach: Ladislao KUBALA Stécz)
Miguel REINA Santos, Juan Cruz SOL Oria, Francisco Fernández Rodríguez 'GALLEGO', Antonio Alfonso Moreno 'TONONO', Antonio Manuel Martínez Morales 'ANTON' (MARCIAL Manuel Pina Morales 76'), Enrique LORA Millán, José CLARAMUNT Torres, Enrique Castro González 'QUINI', AMANCIO Amaro Varela, Joaquín Sierra Vallejo 'QUINO', José Ignacio CHURRUCA Sistiaga

URS: (Coach: Valentin NIKOLAEV)
Evgeniy RUDAKOV, Revaz DZODZUASHVILI, Albert SHESTERNYOV, Yuriy ISTOMIN, Murtaz KHURTSILAVA, Viktor KOLOTOV, Vladimir MUNTYAN, Oleg DOLMATOV, Vladimir FEDOTOV (Nikolaiy KISELYOV 80'), Anatoliy BYSHOVETS, Levon ISHTOYAN (Vitaliy SHEVCHENKO 62')


24 November 1971        Ref: Joseph NAUDI (Malta)
Estadio Los Cármenes, GRANADA (Att. 19,176)

## SPAIN - CYPRUS
### 7:0 (3:0)

1:0 'Pirri' (8'), 2:0 'Quino' (15'), 3:0 'Quino' (23'), 4:0 'Pirri' (47' pen.), 5:0 Aguilar (63'), 6:0 Lora (66'), 7:0 Rojo (75')

SPA: (Coach: Ladislao KUBALA Stécz)
José Angel IRIBAR Kortajarena, Juan Cruz SOL Oria, Francisco Fernández Rodríguez 'GALLEGO', Antonio Alfonso Moreno 'TONONO', Juan López HITA, Enrique LORA Millán (José Agustín Aranzábal Ascariba 'GAZTELU' 80'), José Martínez Sánchez 'PIRRI', José CLARAMUNT Torres, AMANCIO Amaro Varela (Francisco Javier AGUILAR García 46'), Joaquín Sierra Vallejo 'QUINO', José Francisco ROJO Arroita

CYP: (Coach: Raymond WOOD)
Herodotos HERODOTOU, Giannis MERTAKKAS (Mihalakis MIHAIL 57'), Pamboullis PARTASIDIS, Stefanis MIHAIL, Dimos KAVAZIS, Kallis KONSTANTINOU, Mihalis ATHINODOROU, Pavlos VASILIOU, Kokos ANTONIOU (Michael THEODOROU 57'), Tasos KONSTANTINOU, Andreas STYLIANOU

16 February 1972     Ref: John TAYLOR (England)
Boothferry Park, KINGSTON-UPON-HULL (ENGLAND) (Att. 19,925)

## NORTHERN IRELAND - SPAIN
### 1:1 (0:1)

0:1 Rojo (41'), 1:1 Morgan (72')

NIR: (Coach: Terence NEILL)
Patrick JENNINGS, Patrick RICE, Samuel NELSON, Terence NEILL, Allan HUNTER, David CLEMENTS, Bryan HAMILTON (Martin O'NEILL 46'), Alexander

McMORDIE, Samuel MORGAN, Samuel McILROY, George BEST

SPA: (Coach: Ladislao KUBALA Stécz)
José Angel IRIBAR Kortajarena, Juan Cruz SOL Oria, Francisco Fernández Rodríguez 'GALLEGO', Enrique Álvarez COSTAS, Antonio Alfonso Moreno 'TONONO', Gregorio BENITO Rubio, Francisco Javier AGUILAR García, Enrique LORA Millán (Miguel Ramos Vargas 'MIGUELI' 55'), Joaquín Sierra Vallejo 'QUINO', Enrique Castro González 'QUINI' (Manuel Ríos Quintanilla 'MANOLETE' 28'), José Francisco ROJO Arroita

| | |
|---|---|
| USSR (Q) | (P6, W4, D2, L0, F13, A4, Pts. 10) |
| Spain | (P6, W3, D2, L1, F14, A3, Pts. 8) |
| Northern Ireland | (P6, W2, D2, L2, F10, A6, Pts. 6) |
| Cyprus | (P6, W0, D0, L6, F2, A26, Pts. 0) |

GROUP 5 (Belgium, Denmark, Portugal, Scotland)

14 October 1970      Ref: Leo CALLAGHAN (Wales)
Idrætsparken, COPENHAGEN (Att. 17,317)

DENMARK - PORTUGAL
0:1 (0:1)

0:1 João (40')

DEN: (Coach: Rudolf STRITTICH)
Kaj PAULSEN, Torben NIELSEN, Poul FREDERIKSEN, Erik SANDVAD, Flemming PEDERSEN, Jens Jørgen HANSEN, Bent OUTZEN, Jan ANDERSEN (Per MADSEN 85'), Kurt PRÆST, Jørgen MARKUSSEN (Poul Erik THYGESEN 69', Keld PEDERSEN

<u>POR:</u> (Coach: José GOMES da Silva)
Vítor Manuel Afonso de Oliveira 'DAMAS', Manuel
Pedro GOMES, Humberto Manuel de Jesus COELHO,
JOSÉ CARLOS da Silva, HILÁRIO Rosario da
Conceição, Fernando PERES da Silva, JOSÉ MARIA
Júnior (Augusto MATINE 72'), António José SIMÕES
da Costa (Jaime da Silva GRAÇA 52'), Artur JORGE
Braga de Melo Teixeira, EUSÉBIO da Silva Ferreira,
Jacinto JOÃO


11 November 1970     Ref: Erich LINEMAYR (Austria)
Hampden Park, GLASGOW (Att. 24,618)

## SCOTLAND - DENMARK
## 1:0 (1:0)

1:0 O'Hare (14')


<u>SCO:</u> (Coach: Robert BROWN)
James CRUICKSHANK, David HAY (William JARDINE
77'), John GREIG, Patrick STANTON, Ronald
McKINNON, Robert MONCUR, James JOHNSTONE,
William CARR, John O'HARE (Peter CORMACK 75'),
William JOHNSTON, Colin STEIN

<u>DEN:</u> (Coach: Rudolf STRITTICH)
Kaj PAULSEN, Torben NIELSEN, Poul FREDERIKSEN,
Erik SANDVAD, Flemming PEDERSEN, Jens Jørgen
HANSEN, Bent OUTZEN, Kristen NYGAARD, Morten
OLSEN (Poul Erik THYGESEN 46'), Keld PEDERSEN,
Benny NIELSEN


25 November 1970     Ref: John CARPENTER
                     (Republic of Ireland)
Albert Dyserynck Stadion, BRUGES (Att. 9,697)

## BELGIUM - DENMARK
## 2:0 (2:0)

1:0 Devrindt (18'), 2:0 Devrindt (35')

BEL: (Coach: Raymond GOETHALS)
Christian PIOT, Georges HEYLENS, Nicolas
DEWALQUE, Léon JECK, Jean THISSEN, Wilfried
VAN MOER (Jan VERHEYEN 70'), Pierre CARTIUS,
Erwin VANDENDAELE, John THIO, Johan DEVRINDT,
Raoul LAMBERT

DEN: (Coach: Rudolf STRITTICH)
Kaj PAULSEN, Torben NIELSEN, Poul FREDERIKSEN,
Erik SANDVAD, Flemming PEDERSEN, Jens Jørgen
HANSEN, Bent OUTZEN, Kristen NYGAARD, Morten
OLSEN (Poul Erik THYGESEN 60'), Keld PEDERSEN,
Benny NIELSEN (Mogens HAASTRUP 70')

3 February 1971      Ref: Antonio SBARDELLA (Italy)
Stade Maurice Dufrasne, LIÈGE (Att. 13,931)

BELGIUM - SCOTLAND
3:0 (1:0)

1:0 McKinnon (34' og), 2:0 Van Himst (55'), 3:0 Van
Himst (83' pen.)

BEL: (Coach: Raymond GOETHALS)
Christian PIOT, Georges HEYLENS, Nicolas
DEWALQUE, Jean PLASKIE, Jean THISSEN,
Wilfried VAN MOER, Erwin VANDENDAELE, Léon
SEMMELING, Henri DEPIREUX, Paul VAN HIMST,
André DENUL

SCO: (Coach: Robert BROWN)
James CRUICKSHANK, David HAY, Thomas
GEMMELL, Patrick STANTON (Anthony GREEN 46'),
Ronald McKINNON, Robert MONCUR, John GREIG,
Colin STEIN (James FORREST 46'), John O'HARE,
Charles COOKE, Archibald GEMMILL

17 February 1971          Ref: Gaspar PINTADO Viu
                                                                (Spain)
Stade Émile Versé, ANDERLECHT (Att. 26,921)

### BELGIUM - PORTUGAL
### 3:0 (1:0)

1:0 Lambert (15'), 2:0 Lambert (63' pen.), 3:0 Denul (80')

BEL: (Coach: Raymond GOETHALS)
Christian PIOT, Georges HEYLENS, Nicolas DEWALQUE, Jean PLASKIE, Jean THISSEN, Wilfried VAN MOER, Erwin VANDENDAELE, Léon SEMMELING (John THIO 46'), Raoul LAMBERT, Paul VAN HIMST, André DENUL

POR: (Coach: José GOMES da Silva)
Vítor Manuel Afonso de Oliveira 'DAMAS', Amandio José MALTA da Silva (Francisco REBELO Moreira da Silva 46'), Humberto Manuel de Jesus COELHO, José ROLANDO Andrade Gonçalves, HILÁRIO Rosario da Conceição, Fernando Pascoal Neves 'PAVÃO', Fernando PERES da Silva, Rui Gouveia Pinto RODRIGUES (Félix Marques GUERREIRO 73'), Vítor Manuel Ferreira BAPTISTA, EUSÉBIO da Silva Ferreira, António José SIMÕES da Costa

21 April 1971          Ref: Michel KITABDJIAN (France)
Estádio da Luz, LISBON (Att. 35,463)

### PORTUGAL - SCOTLAND
### 2:0 (1:0)

1:0 Stanton (22' og), 2:0 Eusébio (82')

POR: (Coach: José GOMES da Silva)
Vítor Manuel Afonso de Oliveira 'DAMAS', Amandio José MALTA da Silva, Humberto Manuel de Jesus COELHO, JOSÉ CARLOS da Silva, Adolfo António

da Luz CALISTO, Rui Gouveia Pinto RODRIGUES, Fernando PERES da Silva, António José SIMÕES da Costa, Tamagnini Manuel Gomes Baptista 'NENÉ' (Fernando Pascoal Neves 'PAVÃO 86'), Vítor Manuel Ferreira BAPTISTA (Artur JORGE Braga de Melo Teixeira 76'), EUSÉBIO da Silva Ferreira

SCO: (Coach: Robert BROWN)
Robert CLARK, David HAY, James BROGAN, Patrick STANTON (Anthony GREEN 75'), Ronald McKINNON, Robert MONCUR, William HENDERSON, James McCALLIOG (Andrew JARVIE 63'), David ROBB, Peter CORMACK, Alan GILZEAN

12 May 1971                    Ref: Malcolm WRIGHT
                                (Northern Ireland)
Estádio das Antas, OPORTO (Att. 16,391)

PORTUGAL - DENMARK
5:0 (2:0)

1:0 Rodrigues (17'), 2:0 Eusébio (42'), 3:0 Baptista (47'), 4:0 Baptista (51'), 5:0 Sandvad (88' og)

POR: (Coach: José GOMES da Silva)
Vítor Manuel Afonso de Oliveira 'DAMAS', Amandio José MALTA da Silva (Francisco REBELO Moreira da Silva 75'), Humberto Manuel de Jesus COELHO, JOSÉ CARLOS da Silva, Adolfo António da Luz CALISTO, Rui Gouveia Pinto RODRIGUES, Fernando PERES da Silva, Tamagnini Manuel Gomes Baptista 'NENÉ', EUSÉBIO da Silva Ferreira, Vítor Manuel Ferreira BAPTISTA (Artur JORGE Braga de Melo Teixeira 83'), António José SIMÕES da Costa

DEN: (Coach: Rudolf STRITTICH)
Erik Lykke SØRENSEN, Henning BOEL, Mogens BERG (Erik NIELSEN 29'), Erik SANDVAD, Jørgen

RASMUSSEN, Finn LAUDRUP, Preben ARENTOFT, Kresten BJERRE, Morten OLSEN, Ole BJØRNMOSE, Benny NIELSEN


26 May 1971          Ref: Kåre SIREVÅG (Norway)
Idrætsparken, COPENHAGEN (Att. 27,266)

### DENMARK - BELGIUM
### 1:2 (0:0)

0:1 Devrindt (65'), 0:2 Devrindt (75'), 1:2 Bjerre (76')

DEN: (Coach: Rudolf STRITTICH)
Erik Lykke SØRENSEN, Henning BOEL, Mogens BERG, Erik SANDVAD, Torben NIELSEN, Finn LAUDRUP, Preben ARENTOFT, Kresten BJERRE, John Steen OLSEN (Keld PEDERSEN 75'), Ole BJØRNMOSE, Benny NIELSEN (Birger PEDERSEN 83')

BEL: (Coach: Raymond GOETHALS)
Christian PIOT, Georges HEYLENS, Erwin VANDENDAELE, Jean PLASKIE, Jean THISSEN, Jan VERHEYEN, Jean DOCKX, Wilfried PUIS, Léon SEMMELING, Johan DEVRINDT, Paul VAN HIMST


9 June 1971          Ref: Wolfgang RIEDEL
                     (East Germany)
Idrætsparken, COPENHAGEN (Att. 37,682)

### DENMARK - SCOTLAND
### 1:0 (1:0)

1:0 Laudrup (43')

DEN: (Coach: Rudolf STRITTICH)
Erik Lykke SØRENSEN, Torben NIELSEN, Mogens BERG, Preben ARENTOFT, Jørgen RASMUSSEN, Kresten BJERRE, Finn LAUDRUP (Bent OUTZEN 75'),

Ulrik LE FEVRE, Benny NIELSEN (Keld PEDERSEN 75'), Jørgen KRISTENSEN, Ole BJØRNMOSE

SCO: (Coach: Robert BROWN)
Robert CLARK, Francis MUNRO, William DICKSON, Patrick STANTON, Ronald McKINNON, Robert MONCUR, Thomas McLEAN, Thomas FORSYTH (David ROBB 46'), Colin STEIN, James FORREST (John SCOTT 75'), Hugh CURRAN


13 October 1971          Ref: Brunon PIOTROWICZ
(Poland)
Hampden Park, GLASGOW (Att. 58,612)
SCOTLAND - PORTUGAL
2:1 (1:0)
1:0 O'Hare (23'), 1:1 Rodrigues (57'), 2:1 Gemmill (58')

SCO: (Coach: Thomas DOCHERTY)
Robert WILSON, William JARDINE, Edmond COLQUHOUN (Martin BUCHAN 87'), Patrick STANTON, David HAY, William BREMNER, Alexander CROPLEY, George GRAHAM, James JOHNSTONE, John O'HARE, Archibald GEMMILL

POR: (Coach: José GOMES da Silva)
Vítor Manuel Afonso de Oliveira 'DAMAS', Amandio José MALTA da Silva, Francisco Antonio Galinho 'CALÓ' (Fernando PERES da Silva 66'), Rui Gouveia Pinto RODRIGUES, Adolfo António da Luz CALISTO, Jaime da Silva GRAÇA, José ROLANDO Andrade Gonçalves, António José SIMÕES da Costa, Tamagnini Manuel Gomes Baptista 'NENÉ', Vítor Manuel Ferreira BAPTISTA, EUSÉBIO da Silva Ferreira (Artur JORGE Braga de Melo Teixeira 46')

10 November 1971    Ref: Johan BOSTRÖM (Sweden)
Pittodrie Park, ABERDEEN (Att. 36,500)

## SCOTLAND - BELGIUM
### 1:0 (1:0)

1:0 O'Hare (5')

SCO: (Coach: Thomas DOCHERTY)
Robert CLARK, William JARDINE, David HAY, William BREMNER, Martin BUCHAN, Patrick STANTON, James JOHNSTONE (John HANSEN 79'), Stephen MURRAY, John O'HARE, Edwin GRAY, Alexander CROPLEY (Kenneth DALGLISH 48')

BEL: (Coach: Raymond GOETHALS)
Christian PIOT, Georges HEYLENS, Nicolas DEWALQUE, André STASSART, Léon DOLMANS, Wilfried VAN MOER (Maurice MARTENS 59'), Erwin VANDENDAELE, Wilfried PUIS (Raoul LAMBERT 68'), Léon SEMMELING, Johan DEVRINDT, Paul VAN HIMST

21 November 1971    Ref: Kenneth BURNS (England)
Estádio da Luz, LISBON (Att. 53,577)

## PORTUGAL - BELGIUM
### 1:1 (0:0)

0:1 Lambert (60'), 1:1 Peres (90' pen.)

POR: (Coach: José GOMES da Silva)
Vítor Manuel Afonso de Oliveira 'DAMAS', Amandio José MALTA da Silva (Octávio Joaquim Coelho MACHADO 46'), Humberto Manuel de Jesus COELHO, Rui Gouveia Pinto RODRIGUES, José de Jesus MENDES, Jaime da Silva GRAÇA, António José SIMÕES da Costa, Tamagnini Manuel Gomes Baptista 'NENÉ' (Artur JORGE Braga de Melo Teixeira 62'),

José Augusto da Costa Sénica TORRES, EUSÉBIO
da Silva Ferreira, Fernando PERES da Silva

BEL: (Coach: Raymond GOETHALS)
Christian PIOT, Georges HEYLENS, Nicolas
DEWALQUE, André STASSART, Léon DOLMANS,
Jean DOCKX, Erwin VANDENDAELE, Maurice
MARTENS (Wilfried PUIS 63'), Léon SEMMELING,
Raoul LAMBERT, Paul VAN HIMST

| | |
|---|---|
| BELGIUM (Q) | (P6, W4, D1, L1, F11, A3, Pts. 9) |
| Portugal | (P6, W3, D1, L2, F10, A6, Pts. 7) |
| Scotland | (P6, W3, D0, L3, F4, A7, Pts. 6) |
| Denmark | (P6, W1, D0, L5, F2, A11, Pts. 2) |

GROUP 6 (Austria, Italy, Republic of Ireland, Sweden)

14 October 1970        Ref: Robert HÉLIÈS (France)
Dalymount Park, DUBLIN (Att. 28,194)

### REPUBLIC OF IRELAND - SWEDEN
### 1:1 (1:0)

1:0 Carroll (44' pen.), 1:1 Brzokoupil (61')

EIR: (Coach: Michael MEAGAN)
Alan KELLY, Thomas CARROLL (Joseph KINNEAR
70'), John DEMPSEY, Anthony BYRNE, Anthony
DUNNE, Eamon DUNPHY, Patrick MULLIGAN,
Mickael LAWLOR, Stephen HEIGHWAY, Daniel
GIVENS (Raymond TREACY 83'), Terence CONROY

SWE: (Coach: Orvar BERGMARK)
Sven-Gunnar LARSSON, Hans SELANDER, Krister
KRISTENSSON, Björn NORDQVIST, Roland GRIP,
Tommy SVENSSON, Leif ERIKSSON, Jan OLSSON,

Inge DANIELSSON (Dan BRZOKOUPIL 46'), Ove GRAHN, Bo LARSSON

28 October 1970      Ref: Pavel KAZAKOV (USSR)
Råsunda Stadion, SOLNA (Att. 11,922)

### SWEDEN - REPUBLIC OF IRELAND
### 1:0 (0:0)

1:0 Turesson (74')

SWE: (Coach: Orvar BERGMARK)
Ronnie HELLSTRÖM, Hans SELANDER, Krister KRISTENSSON, Björn NORDQVIST, Roland GRIP (Claes CRONQVIST 67'), Tommy SVENSSON, Bo LARSSON, Jan OLSSON, Leif ERIKSSON, Ove GRAHN, Dan BRZOKOUPIL (Tom TURESSON 63')

EIR: (Coach: Michael MEAGAN)
Alan KELLY, Séamus BRENNAN, John DEMPSEY, Anthony BYRNE, Patrick DUNNING, Eamon DUNPHY, Alphonse FINUCANE, Mickael LAWLOR, Stephen HEIGHWAY, Raymond TREACY, Terence CONROY

31 October 1970      Ref: Laurens VAN RAVENS (Netherlands)
Praterstadion, VIENNA (Att. 54,953)

### AUSTRIA - ITALY
### 1:2 (1:2)

0:1 De Sisti (27'), 1:1 Parits (29'), 1:2 Mazzola (34')

AUT: (Coach: Leopold ŠTÁSTNÝ)
Friedrich KONCILIA (Herbert RETTENSTEINER 46'), Johann SCHMIDRADNER, Gerhard STURMBERGER, Norbert HOF, Peter PUMM, August STAREK, Johann ETTMAYER, Thomas PARITS,

Josef HICKERSBERGER, Wilhelm KREUZ, Helmut REDL

ITA: (Coach: Ferruccio VALCAREGGI)
Enrico ALBERTOSI, Tarcisio BURGNICH, Giacinto FACCHETTI, Mario BERTINI, Roberto ROSATO, Pierluigi CERA, Angelo DOMENGHINI, Giovanni RIVERA, Alessandro MAZZOLA, Giancarlo DE SISTI, Luigi RIVA (Sergio GORI 76')


8 December 1970                     Ref: Robert SCHAUT
                                              (Belgium)
Stadio Comunale, FLORENCE (Att. 41,092)

ITALY - REPUBLIC OF IRELAND
3:0 (2:0)

1:0 De Sisti (22' pen.), 2:0 Boninsegna (42'), 3:0 Prati (84')

ITA: (Coach: Ferruccio VALCAREGGI)
Enrico ALBERTOSI, Tarcisio BURGNICH, Giacinto FACCHETTI, Mario BERTINI, Roberto ROSATO, Pierluigi CERA, Angelo DOMENGHINI, Alessandro MAZZOLA, Roberto BONINSEGNA, Giancarlo DE SISTI, Pierino PRATI

EIR: (Coach: Michael MEAGAN)
Alan KELLY, Séamus BRENNAN, John DEMPSEY, Anthony BYRNE, Patrick DUNNING, Eamon DUNPHY (Mickael LAWLOR 36'), Alphonse FINUCANE, Edward ROGERS, Terence CONROY, Daniel GIVENS, Raymond TREACY


10 May 1971          Ref: Gerhard SCHULENBURG
                                 (West Germany)
Lansdowne Road, DUBLIN (Att. 22,613)

## REPUBLIC OF IRELAND - ITALY
### 1:2 (1:1)

0:1 Boninsegna (15'), 1:1 Conway (23'), 1:2 Prati (59')

EIR: (Coach: Michael MEAGAN)
Alan KELLY, Joseph KINNEAR, Patrick MULLIGAN,
Anthony BYRNE, Anthony DUNNE, Eamon DUNPHY,
John GILES, Edward ROGERS (Alphonse FINUCANE
46'), Stephen HEIGHWAY, Daniel GIVENS, James
CONWAY

ITA: (Coach: Ferruccio VALCAREGGI)
Dino ZOFF, Tarcisio BURGNICH, Giacinto
FACCHETTI, Mario BERTINI, Roberto ROSATO,
Pierluigi CERA, Pierino PRATI, Alessandro MAZZOLA,
Roberto BONINSEGNA, Giancarlo DE SISTI, Mario
CORSO

26 May 1971    Ref: Stanisław EKSZTAJN (Poland)
Råsunda Stadion, SOLNA (Att. 5,416)

### SWEDEN - AUSTRIA
### 1:0 (0:0)

1:0 Olsson (62')

SWE: (Coach: Georg ERICSON)
Ronnie HELLSTRÖM, Hans SELANDER, Kurt
AXELSSON (Krister KRISTENSSON 46'), Roland
GRIP, Tommy SVENSSON, Jan OLSSON, Bo
LARSSON, Sten PÅLSSON, Bengt JOHANSSON,
Örjan PERSSON (Ove EKLUND 85'), Björn
NORDQVIST

AUT: (Coach: Leopold ŠTÁSTNÝ)
Herbert RETTENSTEINER, Johann SCHMIDRADNER,
Gerhard STURMBERGER, Johann EIGENSTILLER,
Peter PUMM, Josef HICKERSBERGER, August

STAREK, Johann ETTMAYER (Johann GEYER 81'),
Karl KODAT, Wilhelm KREUZ, Alfred GASSNER
(Geza GALLOS 73')


30 May 1971          Ref: Henry ØBERG (Norway)
Dalymount Park, DUBLIN (Att. 14,674)

### REPUBLIC OF IRELAND - AUSTRIA
### 1:4 (0:3)

0:1 Schmidradner (4' pen.), 0:2 Kodat (11'), 0:3 J.
Dunne (30' og), 1:3 Rogers (50' pen.), 1:4 Starek (72')

EIR: (Coach: Michael MEAGAN)
Alan KELLY, Anthony BYRNE, Anthony DUNNE,
Eoin HAND, James DUNNE, Eamon DUNPHY (Noel
CAMPBELL 46'), Edward ROGERS, James CONWAY,
Daniel GIVENS (James HOLMES 74'), Raymond
TREACY, Stephen HEIGHWAY

AUT: (Coach: Leopold ŠTÁSTNÝ)
Herbert RETTENSTEINER, Johann SCHMIDRADNER,
Gerhard STURMBERGER, Johann EIGENSTILLER,
Werner KRIESS (Rainer SCHLAGBAUER 72'), August
STAREK, Norbert HOF, Johann ETTMAYER, Josef
HICKERSBERGER, Wilhelm KREUZ, Karl KODAT


9 June 1971    Ref: Rudolf SCHEURER (Switzerland)
Råsunda Stadion, SOLNA (Att. 36,528)

### SWEDEN - ITALY
### 0:0

SWE: (Coach: Georg ERICSON)
Ronnie HELLSTRÖM, Christer HULT, Krister
KRISTENSSON, Björn NORDQVIST, Roland
GRIP, Tommy SVENSSON, Bo LARSSON, Leif
ERIKSSON, Ove KINDVALL (Jan OLSSON 61'),

Bengt JOHANSSON (Claes CRONQVIST 74'), Örjan PERSSON

ITA: (Coach: Ferruccio VALCAREGGI)
Dino ZOFF, Tarcisio BURGNICH, Giacinto FACCHETTI, Mario BERTINI, Roberto ROSATO (Luciano SPINOSI 54'), Pierluigi CERA, Angelo DOMENGHINI, Alessandro MAZZOLA, Roberto BONINSEGNA, Pierino PRATI, Giancarlo DE SISTI


4 September 1971          Ref: Rudolf GLÖCKNER
(East Germany)
Praterstadion, VIENNA (Att. 38,274)

AUSTRIA - SWEDEN
1:0 (1:0)

1:0 Stering (23')

AUT: (Coach: Leopold ŠTÁSTNÝ)
HerbertRETTENSTEINER,JohannSCHMIDRADNER, Gerhard STURMBERGER, Johann EIGENSTILLER, Peter PUMM, August STAREK, Norbert HOF, Johann ETTMAYER (Alois JAGODIC 68'), Karl KODAT, Josef STERING (Josef HICKERSBERGER 60'), Johann PIRKNER

SWE: (Coach: Georg ERICSON)
Ronnie HELLSTRÖM, Christer HULT, Krister KRISTENSSON, Kurt AXELSSON, Roland GRIP, Björn NORDQVIST, Bo LARSSON, Jan OLSSON, Sten PÅLSSON (Hans SELANDER 60'), Roland SANDBERG (Dan BRZOKOUPIL 73'), Sven LINDMAN


9 October 1971          Ref: Roger MACHIN (France)
Stadio San Siro, MILAN (Att. 65,582)

ITALY - SWEDEN

3:0 (2:0)

1:0 Riva (3'), 2:0 Boninsegna (41'), 3:0 Riva (83')

ITA: (Coach: Ferruccio VALCAREGGI)
Dino ZOFF (Enrico ALBERTOSI 46'), Tarcisio
BURGNICH, Giacinto FACCHETTI, Mario BERTINI,
Roberto ROSATO, Pierluigi CERA, Alessandro
MAZZOLA (Mario CORSO 81'), Romeo BENETTI,
Roberto BONINSEGNA, Giovanni RIVERA, Luigi
RIVA

SWE: (Coach: Georg ERICSON)
Ronnie HELLSTRÖM, Christer HULT (Claes
CRONQVIST 52'), Björn NORDQVIST, Krister
KRISTENSSON (Hans NILSSON 59'), Roland
GRIP, Thomas NORDAHL, Kurt OLSBERG, Bo
LARSSON, Inge DANIELSSON, Ove GRAHN, Roland
SANDBERG


10 October 1971                    Ref: Karl GÖPPEL
                                      (Switzerland)
Linzer Stadion, LINZ (Att. 15,050)

AUSTRIA - REPUBLIC OF IRELAND
6:0 (3:0)

1:0 Jara (12'), 2:0 Pirkner (40' pen.), 3:0 Parits (45'),
    4:0 Parits (52'), 5:0 Jara (85'), 6:0 Parits (90')

AUT: (Coach: Leopold ŠTÁSTNÝ)
Adolf ANTRICH, Johann SCHMIDRADNER, Gerhard
STURMBERGER, Johann EIGENSTILLER, Peter
PUMM, Rudolf HORVATH, Norbert HOF, Johann
ETTMAYER, Johann PIRKNER, Thomas PARITS,
Kurt JARA

EIR: (Coach: William TUOHY)
Patrick ROCHE, Michael GANNON, Alphonse

FINUCANE, Thomas McCONVILLE, John HERRICK, Michael KEARIN (Damien RICHARDSON 53'), Patrick MULLIGAN (Michael MARTIN 69'), Alfred HALE, Frank O'NEILL, Michael LEECH, Turlough O'CONNOR

20 November 1971        Ref: Gyula EMSBERGER
(Hungary)
Stadio Olimpico, ROME (Att. 58,752)

ITALY - AUSTRIA
2:2 (1:1)

1:0 Prati (10'), 1:1 Jara (36'), 1:2 Sara (59'), 2:2 De Sisti (75')

ITA: (Coach: Ferruccio VALCAREGGI)
Dino ZOFF, Tazio ROVERSI, Giacinto FACCHETTI, Mario BERTINI (Gianfranco BEDIN 46'), Aldo BET, Sergio SANTARINI, Pierino PRATI, Romeo BENETTI (Claudio SALA 65'), Roberto BONINSEGNA, Giancarlo DE SISTI, Luigi RIVA

AUT: (Coach: Leopold ŠTÁSTNÝ)
Adolf ANTRICH, Johann SCHMIDRADNER, Rudolf HORVATH, Johann EIGENSTILLER, Peter PUMM, Robert SARA, Norbert HOF, Johann ETTMAYER, Helmut KÖGLBERGER, Johann PIRKNER, Kurt JARA

| | |
|---|---|
| ITALY (Q) | (P6, W4, D2, L0, F12, A4, Pts. 10) |
| Austria | (P6, W3, D1, L2, F14, A6, Pts. 7) |
| Sweden | (P6, W2, D2, L2, F3, A5, Pts. 6) |
| Republic of Ireland | (P6, W0, D1, L5, F3, A17, Pts. 1) |

GROUP 7 (East Germany, Luxembourg, Netherlands, Yugoslavia)

11 October 1970     Ref: William MULLAN (Scotland)
Feyenoord Stadion, ROTTERDAM (Att. 56,200)

### NETHERLANDS - YUGOSLAVIA
### 1:1 (0:1)

0:1 Džajić (22'), 1:1 Israël (49' pen.)

NET: (Coach: František FADRHONC)
Jan VAN BEVEREN, Pleun STRIK, Theodorus LASEROMS, Marinus ISRAËL, Theodorus VAN DUIVENBODE, Wilhelmus JANSEN, Willem VAN HANEGEM, Reinier RIJNDERS, Johannes KLIJNJAN, Wilhelmus VAN DER KUIJLEN (Hendrikus WERY 35'), Wietse VEENSTRA (Wietze COUPERUS 52')

YUG: (Coach: Rajko MITIĆ)
Ivan ĆURKOVIĆ, Anđelko TEŠAN, Dragoslav STEPANOVIĆ, Miroslav PAVLOVIĆ (Jovan AĆIMOVIĆ 25' (Branko OBLAK 82')), Dragan HOLCER, Ilija PETKOVIĆ, Vahidin MUSEMIĆ, Blagoje PAUNOVIĆ, Dušan BAJEVIĆ, Jurica JERKOVIĆ, Dragan DŽAJIĆ

14 October 1970     Ref: Vital LORAUX (Belgium)
Stade Municipal, LUXEMBOURG CITY (Att. 5,163)

### LUXEMBOURG - YUGOSLAVIA
### 0:2 (0:1)

0:1 Bukal (44'), 0:2 Bukal (62')

LUX: (Coach: Ernst MELCHIOR)
René HOFFMANN, Erwin KUFFER (René FLENGHI 46'), Louis PILOT, Fernand JEITZ, Johny HOFFMANN, Norbert LESZCZYNSKI, Adolphe SCHMIT, Paul

PHILIPP, Nicolas BRAUN, Johny LÉONARD, Joseph KIRCHENS

YUG: (Coach: Rajko MITIĆ)
Dragomir MUTIBARIĆ, Anđelko TEŠAN, Dragoslav STEPANOVIĆ, Borivoje ĐORĐEVIĆ, Blagoje PAUNOVIĆ, Dragan HOLCER, Ilija PETKOVIĆ, Josip BUKAL, Dušan BAJEVIĆ, Jurica JERKOVIĆ, Dragan DŽAJIĆ


11 November 1970                Ref: Curt LIEDBERG
                                      (Sweden)
Rudolf-Harbig-Stadion, DRESDEN (Att. 30,089)

EAST GERMANY - NETHERLANDS
1:0 (0:0)

1:0 Ducke (56')

EGR: (Coach: Georg BUSCHNER)
Jürgen CROY, Peter ROCK, Michael STREMPEL, Klaus SAMMER, Lothar KURBJUWEIT, Frank GANZERA, Otto FRÄßDORF, Henning FRENZEL (Harald IRMSCHER 54'), Hans-Jürgen KREISCHE, Peter DUCKE, Eberhard VOGEL

NET: (Coach: František FADRHONC)
Jan VAN BEVEREN, Wilhelmus SUURBIER, Marinus ISRAËL, Pleun STRIK, Einert DROST, Wilhelmus JANSEN, Johannes NEESKENS, Reinier RIJNDERS, Willem VAN HANEGEM, Johannes KLIJNJAN, Petrus KEIZER (Hendrikus WERY 69')


15 November 1970                Ref: Anton BUCHELI
                                    (Switzerland)
Stade Municipal, LUXEMBOURG CITY (Att. 3,795)

LUXEMBOURG - EAST GERMANY

0:5 (0:4)

0:1 Vogel (21'), 0:2 Kreische (29'), 0:3 Kreische (36'),
0:4 Kreische (39'), 0:5 Kreische (78')

LUX: (Coach: Ernst MELCHIOR)
René HOFFMANN (Jeannot MOES 32'), Erwin
KUFFER, René FLENGHI, Fernand JEITZ, Johny
HOFFMANN, Jeannot KRECKÉ, Louis PILOT, Johny
LÉONARD, Adolphe SCHMIT (Nicolas BRAUN 46'),
Louis TRIERWEILER, Joseph KIRCHENS

EGR: (Coach: Georg BUSCHNER)
Jürgen CROY, Peter ROCK, Lothar KURBJUWEIT,
Michael STREMPEL, Frank GANZERA, Harald
IRMSCHER, Henning FRENZEL (Jürgen
SPARWASSER 63'), Klaus SAMMER, Hans-Jürgen
KREISCHE, Peter DUCKE (Rainer SCHLUTTER 77'),
Eberhard VOGEL


24 February 1971        Ref: Faik BAJRAMI (Albania)
Feyenoord Stadion, ROTTERDAM (Att. 38,117)

NETHERLANDS - LUXEMBOURG
6:0 (1:0)

1:0 Lippens (26'), 2:0 Keizer (53'), 3:0 Cruijff (59'), 4:0
Cruijff (69'), 5:0 Keizer (80'), 6:0 Suurbier (83')

NET: (Coach: František FADRHONC)
Jan VAN BEVEREN, Wilhelmus SUURBIER, Marinus
ISRAËL, Johannes NEESKENS, Einert DROST,
Wilhelmus JANSEN, Willem VAN HANEGEM,
Theodorus PAHLPLATZ, Willem LIPPENS, Johannes
CRUIJFF, Petrus KEIZER

LUX: (Coach: Ernst MELCHIOR)
René HOFFMANN, Léon SCHMIT, Louis PILOT,
René FLENGHI, Fernand JEITZ, Johny HOFFMANN,

Nicolas HOFFMANN, Gilbert DUSSIER, Nicolas BRAUN, Paul PHILIPP, Joseph KIRCHENS

4 April 1971                          Ref: Kurt TSCHENSCHER
(West Germany)
Stadion Stari plac, SPLIT (Att. 15,563)

YUGOSLAVIA - NETHERLANDS
2:0 (1:0)

1:0 Jerković (8'), 2:0 Džajić (84')

YUG: (Coach: Vujadin BOŠKOV)
Radomir VUKČEVIĆ, Miroslav PAVLOVIĆ, Dragoslav STEPANOVIĆ, Zoran ANTONIJEVIĆ (Ljubiša RAJKOVIĆ 65'), Blagoje PAUNOVIĆ, Dragan HOLCER, Ilija PETKOVIĆ, Jurica JERKOVIĆ, Josip BUKAL (Nenad BJEKOVIĆ 65'), Jovan AĆIMOVIĆ, Dragan DŽAJIĆ

NET: (Coach: František FADRHONC)
Jan VAN BEVEREN, Wilhelmus SUURBIER, Johannes NEESKENS, Pleun STRIK, Einert DROST (Johannes KLIJNJAN 76'), Wilhelmus JANSEN, Gerardus MÜHREN, Willem VAN HANEGEM, Hendrikus WERY, Petrus KEIZER, Everardus MULDERS

24 April 1971                          Ref: Hugh WILSON
(Northern Ireland)
Stadion der Freundschaft, GERA (Att. 11,276)

EAST GERMANY - LUXEMBOURG
2:1 (1:0)

1:0 Kreische (31'), 2:0 Frenzel (88'), 2:1 Dussier (90')

EGR: (Coach: Georg BUSCHNER)
Jürgen CROY, Klaus SAMMER, Frank GANZERA, Michael STREMPEL, Bernd BRANSCH, Konrad

WEISE, Helmut STEIN, Rainer SCHLUTTER, Jürgen SPARWASSER (Frank RICHTER 85'), Henning FRENZEL, Hans-Jürgen KREISCHE

LUX: (Coach: Ernst MELCHIOR)
René HOFFMANN, Jean-Pierre HOFFMANN, Fernand JEITZ, René FLENGHI, Johny HOFFMANN, Louis TRIERWEILER, Nicolas HOFFMANN, Gilbert DUSSIER, Dominique DI GENOVA, Nicolas BRAUN, Joseph KIRCHENS


9 May 1971          Ref: Paul SCHILLER (Austria)
Zentralstadion, LEIPZIG (Att. 94,876)

### EAST GERMANY - YUGOSLAVIA
### 1:2 (0:2)

0:1 Filipović (11'), 0:2 Džajić (20'), 1:2 Löwe (70')

EGR: (Coach: Georg BUSCHNER)
Jürgen CROY, Konrad WEISE, Klaus SAMMER, Michael STREMPEL, Bernd BRANSCH, Rainer SCHLUTTER, Helmut STEIN, Hans-Jürgen KREISCHE, Henning FRENZEL (Harald IRMSCHER 77'), Peter DUCKE, Eberhard VOGEL (Wolfram LÖWE 66')

YUG: (Coach: Vujadin BOŠKOV)
Radomir VUKČEVIĆ, Miroslav PAVLOVIĆ, Mladen RAMLJAK, Zoran ANTONIJEVIĆ, Blagoje PAUNOVIĆ, Dragan HOLCER, Ilija PETKOVIĆ (Nenad BJEKOVIĆ 72'), Branko OBLAK (Vladislav BOGIĆEVIĆ 63'), Zoran FILIPOVIĆ, Jovan AĆIMOVIĆ, Dragan DŽAJIĆ


10 October 1971     Ref: Concetto LO BELLO (Italy)
Feyenoord Stadion, ROTTERDAM (Att. 48,037)

### NETHERLANDS - EAST GERMANY

## 3:2 (1:1)

0:1 Vogel (10'), 1:1 Hulshoff (25'), 2:1 Keizer (52'), 3:1
Keizer (72'), 3:2 Vogel (82')

**NET:** (Coach: František FADRHONC)
Jan VAN BEVEREN, Johannes VENNEKER, Marinus
ISRAËL, Bernardus HULSHOFF, Pleun STRIK,
Wilhelmus JANSEN, Willem VAN HANEGEM,
Hendrikus WERY, Dirk VAN DIJK (Jan JEURING 71'),
Johannes CRUIJFF, Petrus KEIZER

**EGR:** (Coach: Georg BUSCHNER)
Jürgen CROY, Bernd BRANSCH, Michael
STREMPEL, Konrad WEISE, Gerd KISCHE, Hans-
Jürgen KREISCHE, Jürgen SPARWASSER (Harald
IRMSCHER 68'), Klaus SAMMER, Joachim STREICH,
Peter DUCKE (Wolfram LÖWE 80'), Eberhard VOGEL

16 October 1971      Ref: John TAYLOR (England)
Stadion J.N.A., BELGRADE (Att. 2,340)

### YUGOSLAVIA - EAST GERMANY
### 0:0

**YUG:** (Coach: Vujadin BOŠKOV)
Ratomir DUJKOVIĆ, Ljubiša RAJKOVIĆ, Dragoslav
STEPANOVIĆ, Miroslav PAVLOVIĆ, Blagoje
PAUNOVIĆ, Dragan HOLCER, Ilija PETKOVIĆ, Branko
OBLAK (Petar NIKEZIĆ 62'), Josip BUKAL (Zoran
FILIPOVIĆ 67'), Jovan AĆIMOVIĆ, Dragan DŽAJIĆ

**EGR:** (Coach: Georg BUSCHNER)
Jürgen CROY, Bernd BRANSCH, Michael
STREMPEL, Klaus SAMMER, Konrad WEISE, Gerd
KISCHE, Helmut STEIN (Wolfram LÖWE 80'), Hans-
Jürgen KREISCHE (Harald IRMSCHER 71'), Joachim
STREICH, Peter DUCKE, Eberhard VOGEL

27 October 1971          Ref: MUZAFFER Sarvan
                                          (Turkey)
Stadion pod Goricom, TITOGRAD (Att. 10,022)

### YUGOSLAVIA - LUXEMBOURG
### 0:0

YUG: (Coach: Vujadin BOŠKOV)
Ratomir DUJKOVIĆ, Ljubiša RAJKOVIĆ (Zoran
FILIPOVIĆ 60'), Dragoslav STEPANOVIĆ, Miroslav
PAVLOVIĆ, Blagoje PAUNOVIĆ, Dragan HOLCER,
Ilija PETKOVIĆ, Branko OBLAK (Jurica JERKOVIĆ
33'), Josip BUKAL, Jovan AĆIMOVIĆ, Nenad
BJEKOVIĆ

LUX: (Coach: Ernst MELCHIOR)
Jeannot MOES, Jean-Pierre HOFFMANN, René
KOLLWELTER, René FLENGHI, Johny HOFFMANN,
Jeannot KRECKÉ, Nicolas HOFFMANN, Gilbert
DUSSIER, Nicolas BRAUN, Paul PHILIPP, Joseph
KIRCHENS


17 November 1971            Ref: Michal JURSA
                                    (Czechoslovakia)
Philips Stadion, EINDHOVEN (NETHERLANDS)
(Att. 12,561)

### LUXEMBOURG - NETHERLANDS
### 0:8 (0:5)

0:1 Cruijff (4'), 0:2 Keizer (7'), 0:3 Pahlplatz (12'), 0:4
Cruijff (14'), 0:5 Hulshoff (37'), 0:6 Hoekema (54'), 0:7
Cruijff (60'), 0:8 Israël (82')

LUX: (Coach: Ernst MELCHIOR)
Jeannot MOES (Théo STENDEBACH 46'), Jean-
Pierre HOFFMANN, René KOLLWELTER, René
FLENGHI, Johny HOFFMANN, Jeannot KRECKÉ,
Nicolas HOFFMANN, Gilbert DUSSIER, Nicolas

BRAUN, Paul PHILIPP, Joseph KIRCHENS

NET: (Coach: František FADRHONC)
Jan VAN BEVEREN, Johannes VENNEKER, Marinus ISRAËL, Bernardus HULSHOFF, Rudolf KROL, Gerardus MÜHREN, Wilhelmus JANSEN, Theodorus PAHLPLATZ, Uilke HOEKEMA, Johannes CRUIJFF, Petrus KEIZER

| | |
|---|---|
| YUGOSLAVIA(Q) | (P6, W3, D3, L0, F7, A2, Pts. 9) |
| Netherlands | (P6, W3, D1, L2, F18, A6, Pts. 7) |
| East Germany | (P6, W3, D1, L2, F11, A6, Pts. 7) |
| Luxembourg | (P6, W0, D1, L5, F1, A23, Pts. 1) |

GROUP 8 (Albania, Poland, Turkey, West Germany)

14 October 1970          Ref: Andreas KOUNIAIDES
                                          (Cyprus)
Stadion Śląski, CHORZÓW (Att. 8,507)

POLAND - ALBANIA
3:0 (1:0)

1:0 Gadocha (19'), 2:0 Lubański (83'), 3:0 Szołtysik (90')

POL: (Coach: Ryszard KONCEWICZ)
Piotr CZAJA, Władysław STACHURSKI, Jerzy WYROBEK, Jerzy GORGOŃ, Adam MUSIAŁ, Zygfryd SZOŁTYSIK, Kazimierz DEYNA, Bronisław BULA, Joachim MARX, Włodzimierz LUBAŃSKI, Robert GADOCHA

ALB: (Coach: Loro BORIÇI)
Koço DINELLA, Fatmir FRASHËRI, Gëzim KASMI, Bujar ÇANI, Perikli DHALES, Lin SHLLAKU, Iljaz

ÇEÇO, Ramazan RRAGAMI, Sabah BIZI, Panajot PANO, Medin ZHEGA


17 October 1970          Ref: Paul BONETT (Malta)
Müngersdorferstadion, COLOGNE (Att. 52,204)

### WEST GERMANY - TURKEY
### 1:1 (1:1)

0:1 Kamuran (16'), 1:1 Müller (36' pen.)

WGR: (Coach: Helmut SCHÖN)
Josef MAIER, Hans-Hubert VOGTS, Horst-Dieter HÖTTGES, Franz BECKENBAUER, Klaus-Dieter SIELOFF (Josef HEYNCKES 66'), Wolfgang WEBER, Reinhard LIBUDA, Klaus FICHTEL, Gerhard MÜLLER, Wolfgang OVERATH, Jürgen GRABOWSKI

TUR: (Coach: CIHAT Arman)
ALI Artuner, ERGÜN Acuner, MUZAFFER Sipahi, ERCAN Aktuna, ALPASLAN Eratli, KAMURAN Yavuz, ZIYA Şengül, SANLI Sarialioğlu, METIN Kurt, CEMIL Turan (YAŞAR Mumcuoğlu 46'), ENDER Konca


13 December 1970          Ref: János BIRÓCZKY
                                        (Hungary)
Mithatpaşa Stadi, ISTANBUL (Att. 39,000)

### TURKEY - ALBANIA
### 2:1 (2:1)

1:0 Metin (3'), 1:1 Ziu (22'), 2:1 Cemil (43')

TUR: (Coach: CIHAT Arman)
ALI Artuner, ERGÜN Acuner, ERCAN Aktuna, MUZAFFER Sipahi, ALPASLAN Eratli, KAMURAN Yavuz, SANLI Sarialioğlu, ZIYA Şengül, METIN Kurt, CEMIL Turan, ENDER Konca (YAŞAR Mumcuoğlu 80')

<u>ALB:</u> (Coach: Loro BORIÇI)
Koço DINELLA (Jani RAMA 46'), Perikli DHALES,
Safet BERISHA, Bujar ÇANI, Astrit ZIU, Ramazan
RRAGAMI, Teodor VASO, Sabah BIZI, Iljaz ÇEÇO,
Panajot PANO, Medin ZHEGA


17 February 1971          Ref: Todor BECHIROV
                                    (Bulgaria)
Stadiumi Qemal Stafa, TIRANA (Att. 18,082)

ALBANIA - WEST GERMANY
0:1 (0:1)

0:1 Müller (38')


<u>ALB:</u> (Coach: Loro BORIÇI)
Koço DINELLA, Mihal GJIKA, Perikli DHALES, Bujar
ÇANI, Gëzim KASMI, Ramazan RRAGAMI, Teodor
VASO, Sabah BIZI, Astrit ZIU, Iljaz ÇEÇO, Panajot
PANO

<u>WGR:</u> (Coach: Helmut SCHÖN)
Josef MAIER, Hans-Hubert VOGTS, Bernhard PATZKE
(Michael BELLA 67'), Karl-Heinz SCHNELLINGER,
Wolfgang WEBER, Franz BECKENBAUER, Wolfgang
OVERATH, Jürgen GRABOWSKI, Günter NETZER,
Gerhard MÜLLER, Josef HEYNCKES


25 April 1971        Ref: Karlo KRUASHVILI (USSR)
Mithatpaşa Stadi, ISTANBUL (Att. 38,097)

TURKEY - WEST GERMANY
0:3 (0:1)

0:1 Müller (43'), 0:2 Müller (47'), 0:3 Köppel (72')

<u>TUR:</u> (Coach: CIHAT Arman)
ALI Artuner, MEHMET Işikal (ZEKERIYA Alp 61'),

MUZAFFER Sipahi, ERCAN Aktuna, ALPASLAN Eratli, KAMURAN Yavuz, SANLI Sarialioğlu (FETHI Heper 73'), ZIYA Şengül, MEHMET Oğuz, CEMIL Turan, ENDER Konca

WGR: (Coach: Helmut SCHÖN)
Josef MAIER, Hans-Hubert VOGTS, Bernhard PATZKE, Wolfgang WEBER, Franz BECKENBAUER, Herbert WIMMER, Horst KÖPPEL (Heinz FLOHE 77'), Günter NETZER, Jürgen GRABOWSKI, Gerhard MÜLLER, Josef HEYNCKES

12 May 1971          Ref: Robert HÉLIÈS (France)
Stadiumi Qemal Stafa, TIRANA (Att. 18,182)
ALBANIA - POLAND
1:1 (1:1)
0:1 Banaś (7'), 1:1 Zhega (32')

ALB: (Coach: Loro BORIÇI)
Koço DINELLA, Mihal GJIKA, Perikli DHALES, Bujar ÇANI, Gëzim KASMI, Teodor VASO (Safet BERISHA 46'), Ramazan RRAGAMI, Sabah BIZI, Iljaz ÇEÇO, Panajot PANO, Medin ZHEGA

POL: (Coach: Kazimierz GÓRSKI)
Władysław GROTYŃSKI, Jan WRAŻY, Jerzy WYROBEK, Walter WINKLER, Zygmunt ANCZOK, Zygfryd SZOŁTYSIK, Kazimierz DEYNA (Lesław ĆMIKIEWICZ 69'), Bernard BLAUT, Jan BANAŚ, Włodzimierz LUBAŃSKI, Robert GADOCHA (Marian KOZERSKI 46')

12 June 1971          Ref: Timoleon LATSIOS (Greece)
Wildparkstadion, KARLSRUHE (Att. 44,833)
WEST GERMANY - ALBANIA

2:0 (2:0)

1:0 Netzer (18'), 2:0 Grabowski (44')

WGR: (Coach: Helmut SCHÖN)
Josef MAIER, Hans-Georg SCHWARZENBECK, Hans-Hubert VOGTS (Hartwig BLEIDICK 90'), Franz BECKENBAUER, Herbert WIMMER, Günter NETZER, Jürgen GRABOWSKI, Wolfgang OVERATH (Siegfried HELD 73'), Horst KÖPPEL, Josef HEYNCKES, Klaus-Dieter SIELOFF

ALB: (Coach: Loro BORIÇI)
Bashkim MUHEDINI, Mihal GJIKA, Safet BERISHA, Bujar ÇANI, Astrit ZIU, Faruk SEJDINI, Ramazan RRAGAMI, Vladimir BALLUKU (Teodor VASO 53'), Sabah BIZI, Panajot PANO, Medin ZHEGA


22 September 1971      Ref: Antoine QUEUDEVILLE
(Luxembourg)
Stadion Wisła, KRAKÓW (Att. 20,241)

POLAND - TURKEY
5:1 (1:0)

1:0 Bula (33'), 2:0 Lubański (62'), 3:0 Gadocha (69'), 4:0 Lubański (73'), 4:1 Nihat (83'), 5:1 Lubański (90')

POL: (Coach: Kazimierz GÓRSKI)
Jan GOMOLA, Zygmunt ANCZOK, Andrzej ZYGMUNT, Jerzy GORGOŃ, Adam MUSIAŁ, Zygfryd SZOŁTYSIK, Kazimierz DEYNA (Andrzej JAROSIK 46'), Bronisław BULA, Jan BANAŚ, Włodzimierz LUBAŃSKI, Robert GADOCHA

TUR: (Coach: CIHAT Arman)
ALI Artuner, ABDURRAHMAN Temel, MUZAFFER Sipahi, ERCAN Aktuna, ZEKERIYA Alp, KAMURAN Yavuz, YUSUF Tunaoğlu (SANLI Sarialioğlu 78'),

VAHAP Özbayar, METIN Kurt, FETHI Heper, CEMIL Turan (NIHAT Yayöz 46')


10 October 1971          Ref: Ferdinand MARSCHALL
                                              (Austria)
Stadion Dziesięciolecia, WARSAW (Att. 63,300)

### POLAND - WEST GERMANY
### 1:3 (1:1)

1:0 Gadocha (27'), 1:1 Müller (29'), 1:2 Müller (64'),
1:3 Grabowski (70')


POL: (Coach: Kazimierz GÓRSKI)
Jan TOMASZEWSKI, Adam MUSIAŁ, Stanisław OŚLIZŁO, Jerzy GORGOŃ, Zygmunt ANCZOK, Zygfryd SZOŁTYSIK, Bronisław BULA (Antoni KOT 46'), Zygmunt MASZCZYK, Jan BANAŚ (Jerzy SADEK 80'), Włodzimierz LUBAŃSKI, Robert GADOCHA

WGR: (Coach: Helmut SCHÖN)
Josef MAIER, Paul BREITNER, Franz BECKENBAUER, Klaus FICHTEL, Hans-Georg SCHWARZENBECK, Herbert WIMMER, Horst KÖPPEL, Günter NETZER, Gerhard MÜLLER, Josef HEYNCKES, Jürgen GRABOWSKI


14 November 1971          Ref: Iván PLÁČEK
                                              (Czechoslovakia)
Stadiumi Qemal Stafa, TIRANA (Att. 18,159)

### ALBANIA - TURKEY
### 3:0 (1:0)

1:0 Përnaska (22'), 2:0 Pano (50'), 3:0 Përnaska (53')


ALB: (Coach: Loro BORIÇI)
Bashkim MUHEDINI, Mihal GJIKA, Safet BERISHA, Bujar ÇANI, Astrit ZIU, Faruk SEJDINI, Iljaz ÇEÇO,

Sabah BIZI, Ilir PËRNASKA, Panajot PANO, Maksut LESHTENI (Rifat IBËRSHIMI 70')

TUR: (Coach: CIHAT Arman)
ALI Artuner, VAHIT Kolukisa (ALPASLAN Eratli 67'), MUZAFFER Sipahi, ERCAN Aktuna, ZEKERIYA Alp, MEHMET Oğuz, KAMURAN Yavuz, VEDAT Okyar, METIN Kurt, OSMAN Arpacioğlu, NECATI Göçmen

17 November 1971          Ref: William MULLAN
(Scotland)
Volksparkstadion, HAMBURG (Att. 60,448)

WEST GERMANY - POLAND
0:0

WGR: (Coach: Helmut SCHÖN)
Josef MAIER, Horst-Dieter HÖTTGES, Franz BECKENBAUER, Wolfgang WEBER, Hans-Georg SCHWARZENBECK, Herbert WIMMER (Horst KÖPPEL 75'), Klaus FICHTEL, Wolfgang OVERATH, Reinhard LIBUDA, Gerhard MÜLLER, Jürgen GRABOWSKI

POL: (Coach: Kazimierz GÓRSKI)
Marian SZEJA, Antoni SZYMANOWSKI, Marian OSTAFIŃSKI, Jerzy GORGOŃ, Zygmunt ANCZOK (Jerzy WYROBEK 68'), Zygfryd SZOŁTYSIK, Kazimierz DEYNA, Bernard BLAUT, Joachim MARX, Grzegorz LATO (Bronisław BULA 83'), Włodzimierz LUBAŃSKI

5 December 1971     Ref: Petar NIKOLOV (Bulgaria)
Atatürk Stadi, IZMIR (Att. 57,794)

TURKEY - POLAND
1:0 (0:0)

1:0 Cemil (52')

<u>TUR:</u> (Coach: Nicolae PETRESCU)
YASIN Özdenak, EKREM Günalp, MUZAFFER Sipahi,
ÖZER Yurteri, ZEKERIYA Alp (VAHIT Kolukisa 83'),
MEHMET Oğuz, VEDAT Okyar, METIN Kurt, CEMIL
Turan, ENDER Konca (ÇETIN Erdoğan 30'), AYFER
Elmastaşoğlu

<u>POL:</u> (Coach: Kazimierz GÓRSKI)
Marian SZEJA, Antoni SZYMANOWSKI, Marian
OSTAFIŃSKI, Jerzy GORGOŃ, Adam MUSIAŁ,
Zygfryd SZOŁTYSIK, Kazimierz DEYNA (Bronisław
BULA 70'), Bernard BLAUT, Joachim MARX, Grzegorz
LATO, Robert GADOCHA (Andrzej JAROSIK 63')

WESTGERMANY(Q) (P6,W4,D2,L0,F10,A2,Pts.10)
Poland             (P6,W2,D2,L2,F10,A6,Pts.6)
Turkey             (P6,W2,D1,L3,F5,A13,Pts.5)
Albania            (P6,W1,D1,L4,F5,A9,Pts.3)

## QUARTER-FINALS

29 April 1972          Ref: Petar NIKOLOV (Bulgaria)
Stadio San Siro, MILAN (Att. 63,549)

### ITALY - BELGIUM
### 0:0

<u>ITA:</u> (Coach: Ferruccio VALCAREGGI)
Enrico ALBERTOSI, Tarcisio BURGNICH, Giacinto
FACCHETTI, Gianfranco BEDIN, Roberto ROSATO,
Pierluigi CERA, Angelo DOMENGHINI (Franco
CAUSIO 46'), Alessandro MAZZOLA, Pietro
ANASTASI, Giancarlo DE SISTI, Luigi RIVA

<u>BEL</u>: (Coach: Raymond GOETHALS)
Christian PIOT, Georges HEYLENS, Erwin VANDENDAELE, Jean THISSEN, Maurice MARTENS (Léon DOLMANS 49'), Wilfried VAN MOER, Jan VERHEYEN, Jean DOCKX, Léon SEMMELING, Paul VAN HIMST, Raoul LAMBERT


13 May 1972          Ref: Paul SCHILLER (Austria)
Stade Émile Versé, ANDERLECHT (Att. 26,561)

### BELGIUM - ITALY
### 2:1 (1:0)

1:0 Van Moer (23'), 2:0 Van Himst (71'), 2:1 Riva (86' pen.)

<u>BEL</u>: (Coach: Raymond GOETHALS)
Christian PIOT, Georges HEYLENS, Erwin VANDENDAELE, Jean THISSEN, Léon DOLMANS, Jean DOCKX, Jan VERHEYEN, Wilfried VAN MOER (Odilon POLLEUNIS 46'), Léon SEMMELING, Raoul LAMBERT, Paul VAN HIMST

<u>ITA</u>: (Coach: Ferruccio VALCAREGGI)
Enrico ALBERTOSI, Tarcisio BURGNICH, Giacinto FACCHETTI, Luciano SPINOSI, Pierluigi CERA, Alessandro MAZZOLA, Romeo BENETTI, Mario BERTINI (Fabio CAPELLO 46'), Roberto BONINSEGNA, Giancarlo DE SISTI, Luigi RIVA

BELGIUM won 2-1 on agg.


29 April 1972          Ref: Robert HÉLIÈS (France)
Wembley Stadium, LONDON (Att. 96,800)

### ENGLAND - WEST GERMANY
### 1:3 (0:1)

Richard Keir

0:1 Hoeneß (26'), 1:1 Lee (77'), 1:2 Netzer (85' pen.),
1:3 Müller (88')

ENG: (Coach: Alfred RAMSEY)
Gordon BANKS, Paul MADELEY, Colin BELL, Robert
MOORE, Emlyn HUGHES, Francis LEE, Alan BALL,
Martin CHIVERS, Geoffrey HURST (Rodney MARSH
60'), Martin PETERS, Norman HUNTER

WGR: (Coach: Helmut SCHÖN)
Josef MAIER, Horst-Dieter HÖTTGES, Paul
BREITNER, Franz BECKENBAUER, Hans-Georg
SCHWARZENBECK, Herbert WIMMER, Jürgen
GRABOWSKI, Günter NETZER, Ulrich HOENEß,
Gerhard MÜLLER, Siegfried HELD


13 May 1972                Ref: Milivoje GUGULOVIĆ
                                (Yugoslavia)
Olympiastadion, WEST BERLIN (Att. 76,122)
              WEST GERMANY - ENGLAND
                      0:0

WGR: (Coach: Helmut SCHÖN)
Josef MAIER, Horst-Dieter HÖTTGES, Franz
BECKENBAUER, Hans-Georg SCHWARZENBECK,
Paul BREITNER, Heinz FLOHE, Günter NETZER,
Herbert WIMMER, Ulrich HOENEß (Josef HEYNCKES
51'), Gerhard MÜLLER, Siegfried HELD

ENG: (Coach: Alfred RAMSEY)
Gordon BANKS, Paul MADELEY, Emlyn HUGHES,
Peter STOREY, Robert MOORE, Alan BALL, Colin
BELL, Martin CHIVERS, Rodney MARSH (Michael
SUMMERBEE 20'), Norman HUNTER (Martin
PETERS 57'), Roy McFARLAND

WEST GERMANY won 3-1 on agg.

29 April 1972        Ref: David SMITH (England)
Népstadion, BUDAPEST (Att. 68,585)

### HUNGARY - ROMANIA
### 1:1 (1:0)

1:0 Branikovits (11'), 1:1 Sătmăreanu (56')

HUN: (Coach: Rudolf ILLOVSZKY)
István GÉCZI, Tibor FÁBIÁN, Miklós PÁNCSICS, László BÁLINT, Péter VÉPI, Lajos KOCSIS (Ferenc BENE 59'), Lajos SZŰCS, László FAZEKAS, László BRANIKOVITS, Antal DUNAI, Sándor ZÁMBÓ

ROM: (Coach: Angelo NICULESCU)
Necula RĂDUCANU, Lajos SĂTMĂREANU, Niculae LUPESCU, Cornel DINU, Augustin DELEANU, Ion DUMITRU, Radu NUNWEILLER, Mircea LUCESCU, Emerich DEMBROVSCHI, Flavius DOMIDE, Anghel IORDĂNESCU

14 May 1972        Ref: Kurt TSCHENSCHER
                              (West Germany)
Stadionul 23 August, BUCHAREST (Att. 60,300)

### ROMANIA - HUNGARY
### 2:2 (1:2)

0:1 Szőke (5'), 1:1 Dobrin (14'), 1:2 Kocsis (36'), 2:2 Neagu (81')

ROM: (Coach: Angelo NICULESCU)
Necula RĂDUCANU, Lajos SĂTMĂREANU, Niculae LUPESCU, Cornel DINU, Augustin DELEANU, Ion DUMITRU, Radu NUNWEILLER, Flavius DOMIDE, Emerich DEMBROVSCHI (Mircea LUCESCU 74'), Nicolae DOBRIN, Anghel IORDĂNESCU (Alexandru NEAGU 66')

HUN: (Coach: Rudolf ILLOVSZKY)
István GÉCZI, Tibor FÁBIÁN, Miklós PÁNCSICS,
László BÁLINT, Péter JUHÁSZ, István JUHÁSZ, Lajos
KOCSIS (Lajos KŰ 66'), Lajos SZŰCS, István SZŐKE
(Antal DUNAI 66'), Ferenc BENE, Sándor ZÁMBÓ

3-3 on agg.

## PLAY-OFF

17 May 1972          Ref: Hristos MIHAS (Greece)
Stadion J.N.A., BELGRADE (Att. 32,130)

### HUNGARY - ROMANIA
### 2:1 (1:1)

1:0 Kocsis (26'), 1:1 Neagu (32'), 2:1 Szőke (89')

HUN: (Coach: Rudolf ILLOVSZKY)
Ádám ROTHERMEL, Tibor FÁBIÁN, Miklós
PÁNCSICS, László BÁLINT, István JUHÁSZ, Péter
JUHÁSZ, Lajos KOCSIS, Sándor ZÁMBÓ, István
SZŐKE, Ferenc BENE, Lajos KŰ

ROM: (Coach: Angelo NICULESCU)
Necula RĂDUCANU, Lajos SĂTMĂREANU, Niculae
LUPESCU, Cornel DINU, Augustin DELEANU
(Bujor HĂLMĂGEANU 52'), Ion DUMITRU, Radu
NUNWEILLER, Mircea LUCESCU, Nicolae DOBRIN,
Alexandru NEAGU, Flavius DOMIDE

30 April 1972          Ref: Rudolf SCHEURER
                              (Switzerland)
Stadion Crvena Zvezda, BELGRADE (Att. 58,312)

### YUGOSLAVIA - USSR
### 0:0

<u>YUG:</u> (Coach: Vujadin BOŠKOV)
Enver MARIĆ, Mladen RAMLJAK, Dragoslav
STEPANOVIĆ, Miroslav PAVLOVIĆ, Blagoje
PAUNOVIĆ, Dragan HOLCER, Božidar JANKOVIĆ,
Branko OBLAK, Josip BUKAL (Dušan BAJEVIĆ 84'),
Jovan AĆIMOVIĆ, Dragan DŽAJIĆ

<u>URS:</u> (Coach: Nikolaiy GULYAEV)
Evgeniy RUDAKOV, Revaz DZODZUASHVILI, Murtaz
KHURTSILAVA, Vladimir KAPLICHNIY, Yuriy ISTOMIN,
Aleksandr MAKHOVIKOV (Vladimir TROSHKIN
62'), Oleg DOLMATOV, Anatoliy BAIYDACHNIY,
Anatoliy BANISHEVSKIY, Anatoliy KONKOV, Eduard
KOZINKEVICH (Gennadiy EVRYUZHIKHIN 75')

13 May 1972          Ref: Aurelio ANGONESE (Italy)
Tsentralniy Stadion 'V.I. Lenina', MOSCOW
(Att. 90,300)

USSR - YUGOSLAVIA
3:0 (0:0)

1:0 Kolotov (53'), 2:0 Banishevskiy (74'), 3:0
Kozinkevich (90')

<u>URS:</u> (Coach: Nikolaiy GULYAEV)
Evgeniy RUDAKOV, Revaz DZODZUASHVILI, Murtaz
KHURTSILAVA, Nikolaiy ABRAMOV, Yuriy ISTOMIN,
Viktor KOLOTOV, Vladimir TROSHKIN, Anatoliy
BAIYDACHNIY (Boris KOPEIYKIN 66'), Anatoliy
BANISHEVSKIY, Anatoliy KONKOV, Gennadiy
EVRYUZHIKHIN (Eduard KOZINKEVICH 46')

<u>YUG:</u> (Coach: Vujadin BOŠKOV)
Enver MARIĆ, Mladen RAMLJAK, Dragoslav
STEPANOVIĆ, Miroslav PAVLOVIĆ, Blagoje
PAUNOVIĆ, Dragan HOLCER (Ilija PETKOVIĆ
57'), Zoran ANTONIJEVIĆ, Branko OBLAK (Jurica

JERKOVIĆ 71'), Jovan AĆIMOVIĆ, Dragan DŽAJIĆ,
Božidar JANKOVIĆ

USSR won 3-0 on agg.

# GOALSCORERS

## 7 GOALS

Gerhard MÜLLER (West Germany)

## 5 GOALS

Hans-Jürgen KREISCHE (East Germany), Martin CHIVERS (England), Johannes CRUIJFF, Petrus KEIZER (both Netherlands)

## 4 GOALS

Jan ČAPKOVIČ (Czechoslovakia), Ferenc BENE (Hungary), José Martínez Sánchez 'PIRRI' (Spain), George BEST (Northern Ireland), Viktor KOLOTOV (USSR), Johan DEVRINDT (Belgium), Thomas PARITS (Austria), Włodzimierz LUBAŃSKI (Poland)

## 3 GOALS

Hristo BONEV (Bulgaria), Lajos KOCSIS (Hungary), Geoffrey HURST, Francis LEE (both England), Friedrich KÜNZLI (Switzerland), James NICHOLSON (Northern Ireland), Gennadiy EVRYUZHIKHIN (USSR), Raoul LAMBERT, Paul VAN HIMST (both Belgium), John O'HARE (Scotland), Kurt JARA (Austria), Roberto BONINSEGNA, Giancarlo DE SISTI, Pierino PRATI, Luigi RIVA (all Italy), Eberhard VOGEL (East Germany), Dragan DŽAJIĆ (Yugoslavia), Robert GADOCHA (Poland)

## 2 GOALS

František KARKÓ (Czechoslovakia), Emerich

DEMBROVSCHI, Nicolae DOBRIN, Florea
DUMITRACHE, Mircea LUCESCU, Nicolae
LUPESCU, Alexandru NEAGU (all Romania), John
TOSHACK (Wales), Petar ZHEKOV (Bulgaria),
Bernard BLANCHET, Georges LECH, Charly LOUBET
(all France), Odd IVERSEN (Norway), István SZŐKE
(Hungary), Kurt MÜLLER, Karl ODERMATT, René-
Pierre QUENTIN (all Switzerland), Derek DOUGAN
(Northern Ireland), Joaquín Sierra Vallejo 'QUINO',
Carles REXACH i Cerdà, José Francisco ROJO
Arroitia (all Spain), Anatoliy BANISHEVSKIY, Vitaliy
SHEVCHENKO, Vladimir FEDOTOV (all USSR),
EUSÉBIO da Silva Ferreira, Rui Gouveia Pinto
RODRIGUES, Vitor Manuel Ferreira BAPTISTA (all
Portugal), Bernardus HULSHOFF, Marinus ISRAËL
(both Netherlands), Josip BUKAL (Yugoslavia), Ilir
PËRNASKA (Albania), CEMIL Turan (Turkey), Jürgen
GRABOWSKI, Günter NETZER (both West Germany)

1 GOAL

Milan ALBRECHT, Ladislav KUNA, Jaroslav POLLÁK,
Vladimír TÁBORSKÝ, František VESELÝ (all
Czechoslovakia), Matti PAATELAINEN (Finland),
Anghel IORDĂNESCU, Radu NUNWEILLER, Lajos
SĂTMĂREANU (all Romania), Ronald DAVIES,
Alan DURBAN, Gilbert REECE (all Wales), Tsvetan
ATANASOV, Bojil KOLEV, Atanas MIHAYLOV, Petko
PETKOV, Mladen VASILEV, Stefan VELICHKOV
(all Bulgaria), Louis FLOCH, Michel MÉZY, Hervé
REVELLI, Jacques VERGNES (all France), László
BRANIKOVITS, Antal DUNAI, Péter JUHÁSZ, László
NAGY, Lajos SZŰCS, Csaba VIDÁTS, Sándor
ZÁMBÓ (all Hungary), Ola DYBWAD-OLSEN,
Jan FUGLSET, Olav NILSEN (all Norway), Allan
CLARKE, Christopher LAWLER, Martin PETERS,
Michael SUMMERBEE (all England), Konstantinos
AIDINIOU, Konstantinos DAVOURLIS, Mihalis

KRITIKOPOULOS (all Greece), Edward THEOBALD,
William VASSALLO (both Malta), Rolf BLÄTTLER,
Roland CITHERLET, Daniel JEANDUPEUX (all
Switzerland), Nikolaos HARALAMBOUS I, Stefanis
MIHAIL (both Cyprus), Samuel MORGAN (Northern
Ireland), Francisco AGUILAR García, Enrique LORA
Millán, LUIS Aragonés Suárez, José Luis VIOLETA
Lajusticia (all Spain), Anatoliy BYSHOVETS, Eduard
KOZINKEVICH, Vladimir MUNTYAN (all USSR), André
DE NUL, Wilfried VAN MOER (both Belgium), Kresten
BJERRE, Finn LAUDRUP (both Denmark), Jacinto
JOÃO, Fernando PERES da Silva (both Portugal),
Archibald GEMMILL (Scotland), Karl KODAT, Johann
PIRKNER, Robert SARA, Johann SCHMIDRADNER,
August STAREK, Josef STERING (all Austria),
Alessandro MAZZOLA (Italy), Thomas CARROLL,
Terence CONROY, Eamonn ROGERS (all Republic
of Ireland), Dan BRZOKOUPIL, Jan OLSSON, Tom
TURESSON (all Sweden), Peter DUCKE, Henning
FRENZEL, Wolfram LÖWE (all East Germany),
Gilbert DUSSIER (Luxembourg), Uilke HOEKEMA,
Willi LIPPENS, Theodorus PAHLPLATZ, Wilhelmus
SUURBIER (all Netherlands), Zoran FILIPOVIĆ,
Jurica JERKOVIĆ (both Yugoslavia), Panajot PANO,
Medin ZHEGA, Astrit ZIU (all Albania), Jan BANAŚ,
Bronisław BULA, Zygfryd SZOŁTYSIK (all Poland),
KAMURAN Yavuz, METIN Kurt, NIHAT Yayöz (all
Turkey), Ulrich HOENEß, Horst KÖPPEL (both West
Germany)

## OWN-GOALS

Geir KARLSEN (Norway) vs Hungary, Anton WEIBEL
(Switzerland) vs England, Ronald McKINNON
(Scotland) vs Belgium, Patrick STANTON (Scotland)
vs Portugal, Erik SANDVAD (Denmark) vs Portugal,
James DUNNE (Republic of Ireland) vs Austria

# FINAL TOURNAMENT

# (BELGIUM - 14-18 JUNE 1972)

## VENUES (Stadia)

ANDERLECHT (Stade Émile Versé), ANTWERP (Bosuilstadion), BRUSSELS (Stade du Heysel), LIÈGE (Stade Maurice Dufrasne)

---

## SEMI-FINALS & THIRD PLACE MATCH

### BELGIUM vs WEST GERMANY

The West Germans began brightly, with Erwin Kremers, winning only his second cap, tormenting the experienced Georges Heylens down the left wing before testing in the Belgian goal Christian Piot, who got down smartly to stop his effort. Gradually, the Belgians came into the game, but midway through the half they were undone when Günter Netzer clipped a delightful cross towards the six yard area. 'Gerd' Müller leaped ahead of Jean Thissen to head past Piot, who had come out for the cross but was way too late, and the ball sailed beyond him into an empty net.

Just before the interval, the Belgians thought they'd equalised when Léon Semmeling headed in a cross from Paul Van Himst, but it was disallowed for offside. The hosts pressed forward in the early stages of the second half, and Van Himst had a sight of goal after playing a neat one-two with Erwin Vandendaele, but he failed to connect properly with his volley inside the box, and 'Sepp' Maier saved comfortably at his near post. Georges Heylens got on the end of a poor defensive header from a free-kick and let fly from the right-hand edge of the area, which clipped the top of the bar, Maier well beaten.

But, in the seventy-first minute, the West Germans doubled their lead after another deadly Netzer-Müller combination. Jürgen Grabowski started the move just inside the West German half and passed to Netzer, who spun away from one tackle before lofting the ball over the Belgian defence, and Müller ghosted in behind to prod the ball beyond the advancing Piot. The hosts needed a response, and they got it with seven minutes remaining when Jean Dockx chipped a speculative ball to the edge of the box and it broke kindly off Herbert Wimmer for Odilon Polleunis to smash home on the half volley. Moments later they nearly grabbed an equaliser as Vandendaele rose to meet a corner but headed just wide; then, in the final minute, Josef Heynckes almost added a third for the West Germans, but he shot over the bar.

## USSR vs HUNGARY

The other semi-final was played in front of a half-empty Anderlecht stadium, understandably, due to Belgium's match being played at the same time. The opening half was a bit of a slow burner, with neither side showing any attacking ambition, and the crowd had to wait until just before the break for the first real opportunity, when István Géczi saved superbly from Anatoliy Banishevskiy.

The game badly needed a goal, and early in the second half, the Soviets obliged. Anatoliy Baiydachniy's corner from the right was headed away by Miklós Páncsics, but it fell nicely to Anatoliy Konkov, who volleyed from the edge of the box, and it flew past Géczi via a slight deflection off Péter Juhász. The Hungarians responded by bringing on Flórián Albert and Antal Dunai to inject a more attacking threat, and a few minutes before the end, they were handed a great opportunity to level when Dunai was bundled over in the box by Revaz Dzodzuashvili. Sándor Zámbó was entrusted with the penalty, but his weak shot was parried by Evgeniy Rudakov, and István Szőke could only smack the rebound off the outside of the post. The Soviets held on to reach their third final.


## BELGIUM vs HUNGARY

After the disappointment of their semi-final loss to the West Germans, a sparse crowd turned up in Liège to see if the hosts could take the bronze medal in the third-place match against Hungary. They began well enough, and deservedly went ahead in the twenty-fourth minute when Raoul Lambert weaved past a couple of defenders before unleashing a cracking drive from the edge of the box, which flew past Géczi. Four minutes later, they were gifted a second goal as Lambert intercepted Tibor Fabián's pass. He sprinted away from the full-back before sending a low cross into the box, which Páncsics and Géczi left to each other, and they both let the ball roll past, leaving Van Himst with a simple tap in.

At the break, the Hungarians brought on Lajos Szűcs for the ineffectual Zámbó, and early in the second half they were back in the game when Mihály Kozma floated a cross from the right, which Dunai was about to pounce on, until he was barged off the ball by Heylens. Lajos Kű took the resultant penalty and slotted it into the right-hand corner of the net as Piot hardly moved. Hungary tried desperately in the remainder of the match to find an equaliser, but Belgium clung on to claim third place.

## FINAL

## WEST GERMANY vs USSR

The final in Brussels' Heysel Stadium felt like a home game for the West Germans, as the crowd was predominantly full of their own supporters. This was the sixth meeting between the sides, with West Germany leading by three wins to two in the head-to-head – including a 4-1 victory in Munich only three weeks previously – and neither side made any changes to their respective semi-final line-ups.

The Soviet Union kicked off, and spent the first few minutes mainly in their opponents' half. However, as soon as the West Germans gained decent possession they almost carved out an opening when Murtaz Khurtsilava slipped as he tried to intercept a long through ball from Netzer, and Rudakov had to sprint out to clear the danger before Müller could get onto it. Moments later, Müller got his first sniff of goal when Kremers' deflected shot broke to him six yards out, but Rudakov spread himself superbly to block his effort. Netzer curled a ball over the Soviet defence, and Rudakov again did well to hold Heynckes' cross-shot, as Müller waited to pounce on any slip-up.

The Soviets then had their first effort on goal when Yuriy Istomin cut inside Wimmer and found some space just outside the box, but he couldn't get enough curl on his shot and it went wide. West Germany were soon back on the offensive, and Paul Breitner went on a superb run before playing a one-two with Heynckes, but he put too much power on his cross and it fizzed over the head of the waiting Müller. 'Uli' Hoeneß came mightily close to opening the scoring when he got on the end of Kremers' cross, but he saw his header crash back off the bar.

The inevitable opening goal arrived after twenty-seven minutes. Franz Beckenbauer started the move by advancing a few yards forward before finding Heynckes, whose pass to Müller spun up kindly for Netzer, whose scissor volley smacked off the bar. Istomin's headed clearance only found Heynckes on the right-hand edge of the box, and his swerving shot was pushed away by Rudakov straight to the predatory Müller, who slotted the rebound into the corner of the net. It was the Bayern Munich striker's fiftieth international goal in only his forty-first appearance – a phenomenal strike rate. Ten minutes from the break, Rudakov once more came to the rescue as he kept out Heynckes' point-blank header from a Netzer free-kick, then Maier was at last tested as he turned over a rasping drive from Dzodzuashvili.

The Soviet Union started the second half like the first, with lots of possession, but never looking likely to penetrate the West German defence, and seven minutes into the half the West Germans doubled their lead. Netzer passed to Heynckes, who threaded a superb ball with the outside of his foot to Wimmer, whose cross-shot bobbled over the outstretched arm of Rudakov into the far corner of the net. For the next few minutes, the West Germans were guilty of some sloppy play, but the Soviets couldn't take advantage; then, just before the hour mark, the West Germans put the result beyond doubt with another lightning attack.

Breitner found Hans-Georg Schwarzenbeck in acres of space and he surged forward, passing to Müller, who quickly fed Heynckes. His chip into the box bounced off Schwarzenbeck into the path of Müller, who had run on behind the Soviet defence, and he curled the ball beyond Rudakov from eight yards out. The Soviets should have pulled a goal back a couple of minutes later when Vladimir Troshkin's cross bounced up off Horst-Dieter Höttges into the path of Baiydachniy, but he headed over from just a couple of yards out. Although too late to make any difference to the outcome, they were now creating some openings, and next to try his luck was Khurtsilava, who let fly from fully thirty yards – only to see the ball spank off the bar, with Maier well beaten. With fifteen minutes left, the skipper sent in another searing drive from distance, which Maier spilled, but he managed to get to the ball before the onrushing Soviet forwards could capitalise on his error.

West Germany should have then had a fourth goal when Beckenbauer passed to Heynckes, who spun away from Dzodzuashvili, but he shot tamely at Rudakov, who saved easily. There were incredible scenes in the closing minutes, as the West German fans encircled the touchline in anticipation of the final whistle. Some even encroached onto the pitch, which earned them a rebuke from coach Helmut Schön, but the authorities managed to get them off to allow play to continue; then Ferdinand Marschall blew for full-time, and the players were surrounded by jubilant supporters and struggled to get off the pitch. After a few minutes, Franz Beckenbauer was able to lead his victorious team-mates up the steps to collect the trophy, and West Germany became the fourth nation to win the European crown. Few would have bet against them becoming World Champions on home soil two years hence.

# MATCH DETAILS

## SEMI-FINALS

14 June 1972 (20.00)          Ref: William MULLAN
                                    (Scotland)

Bosuilstadion, ANTWERP (Att. 55,669)

### BELGIUM - WEST GERMANY
### 1:2 (0:1)

0:1 Müller (24'), 0:2 Müller (71'), 1:2 Polleunis (83')

BEL: (Coach: Raymond GOETHALS)
Christian PIOT, Georges HEYLENS, Erwin
VANDENDAELE, Jean THISSEN, Léon DOLMANS,
Jean DOCKX, Jan VERHEYEN, Maurice MARTENS
(Odilon POLLEUNIS 65'), Léon SEMMELING, Raoul
LAMBERT, Paul VAN HIMST (Capt.)

WGR: (Coach: Helmut SCHÖN)
Josef MAIER, Horst-Dieter HÖTTGES,
Franz BECKENBAUER (Capt.), Hans-Georg
SCHWARZENBECK, Paul BREITNER, Ulrich
HOENEß (Jürgen GRABOWSKI 59'), Herbert
WIMMER, Günter NETZER, Josef HEYNCKES,
Gerhard MÜLLER, Erwin KREMERS

14 June 1972 (20.00)          Ref: Rudolf GLÖCKNER
                                    (East Germany)

Stade Émile Versé, ANDERLECHT (Att. 16,590)

### USSR - HUNGARY
### 1:0 (0:0)

1:0 Konkov (53')

URS: (Coach: Aleksandr PONOMARYOV)
Evgeniy RUDAKOV, Revaz DZODZUASHVILI,
Vladimir KAPLICHNIY, Murtaz KHURTSILAVA
(Capt.), Yuriy ISTOMIN, Viktor KOLOTOV, Vladimir
TROSHKIN, Anatoliy BAIYDACHNIY, Anatoliy
BANISHEVSKIY (Givi NODIYA 70'), Anatoliy
KONKOV, Vladimir ONISCHENKO

HUN: (Coach: Rudolf ILLOVSZKY)
István GÉCZI, Tibor FABIÁN, Miklós PÁNCSICS,
Péter JUHÁSZ, István JUHÁSZ, László BÁLINT,
István SZŐKE, Lajos KOCSIS (Flórián ALBERT
60'), Ferenc BENE (Capt. (Antal DUNAI 60'), Sándor
ZÁMBÓ, Lajos KŰ

## THIRD PLACE MATCH

17 June 1972 (20.00)        Ref: Einar BOSTRÖM
(Sweden)
Stade Maurice Dufrasne, LIÈGE (Att. 6,184)

BELGIUM - HUNGARY
2:1 (2:0)

1:0 Lambert (24'), 2:0 Van Himst (28'), 2:1 KŰ (53' pen.)

BEL: (Coach: Raymond GOETHALS)
Christian PIOT, Georges HEYLENS, Erwin
VANDENDAELE, Jean THISSEN, Léon DOLMANS,
Jean DOCKX, Jan VERHEYEN, Odilon POLLEUNIS,
Léon SEMMELING, Paul VAN HIMST (Capt.), Raoul
LAMBERT

HUN: (Coach: Rudolf ILLOVSZKY)
István GÉCZI, Tibor FABIÁN, Miklós PÁNCSICS

(Capt.), László BÁLINT, Péter JUHÁSZ, István
JUHÁSZ, Lajos KŰ, Mihály KOZMA, Antal DUNAI,
Sándor ZÁMBÓ (Lajos SZŰCS 46'), Flórián ALBERT

## FINAL

18 June 1972 (16.00)    Ref: Ferdinand MARSCHALL
(Austria)
Stade du Heysel, BRUSSELS (Att. 43,437)

### WEST GERMANY - USSR
### 3:0 (1:0)

1:0 Müller (27'), 2:0 Wimmer (52'), 3:0 Müller (58')

WGR: (Coach: Helmut SCHÖN)
Josef     MAIER,     Horst-Dieter     HÖTTGES,
Franz    BECKENBAUER    (Capt.),    Hans-Georg
SCHWARZENBECK,    Paul    BREITNER,    Ulrich
HOENEß, Günter NETZER, Herbert WIMMER, Josef
HEYNCKES, Gerhard MÜLLER, Erwin KREMERS

URS: (Coach: Aleksandr PONOMARYOV)
Evgeniy    RUDAKOV,    Revaz    DZODZUASHVILI,
Vladimir   KAPLICHNIY,   Murtaz   KHURTSILAVA
(Capt.), Yuriy ISTOMIN, Viktor KOLOTOV, Anatoliy
BAIYDACHNIY,    Vladimir    TROSHKIN,    Anatoliy
BANISHEVSKIY   (Eduard   KOZINKEVICH   66'),
Anatoliy KONKOV (Oleg DOLMATOV 46'), Vladimir
ONISCHENKO

# GOALSCORERS

## 4 GOALS

Gerhard MÜLLER (West Germany)


## 1 GOAL

Raoul LAMBERT, Odilon POLLEUNIS, Paul VAN HIMST (all Belgium), Lajos KŰ (Hungary), Anatoliy KONKOV (USSR), Herbert WIMMER (West Germany)

# SQUADS

## BELGIUM

### GOALKEEPERS

1 Christian PIOT (06.10.1947/Royal Standard de Liège), 12 Luc SANDERS (06.10.1945/Club Brugge KV)

### DEFENDERS

2 Georges HEYLENS (08.08.1941/RSC Anderlechtois), 3 Léon DOLMANS (06.04.1945/Royal Standard de Liège), 4 Jean THISSEN (21.04.1946/Royal Standard de Liège), 8 Maurice MARTENS (05.06.1947/Royal Racing White Club de Bruxelles), 13 Gilbert VAN BINST (05.07.1951/RSC Anderlechtois)

### MIDFIELDERS

5 Erwin VANDENDAELE (05.03.1945/Club Brugge KV), 7 Leon SEMMELING (04.01.1940/Royal Standard de Liège), 11 Jan VERHEYEN (09.07.1944/RSC Anderlechtois), 16 John THIO (02.09.1944/Club Brugge KV)

### FORWARDS

6 Jean DOCKX (24.05.1941/RSC Anderlechtois), 9 Raoul LAMBERT (20.01.1944/Club Brugge KV), 10 Paul VAN HIMST (02.10.1943/RSC Anderlechtois), 14 Odilon POLLEUNIS (01.05.1943/K Sint-Truidense VV (Sint-Truiden)), 15 Jacques TEUGELS (03.08.1946/Royal Racing White Club de Bruxelles), 21 Frans JANSSENS (25.09.1945/K Lierse SK (Lier))

# HUNGARY

## GOALKEEPERS

1 István GÉCZI (13.06.1944/Ferencvárosi TC (Budapest)), 22 Imre RAPP (15.09.1937/Pécsi Dózsa SC (Pécs))

## DEFENDERS

2 Tibor FABIÁN (26.07.1946/Vasas SC (Budapest)), 3 Miklós PÁNCSICS (04.02.1944/Ferencvárosi TC (Budapest)), 4 Péter JUHÁSZ (03.08.1948/Újpesti Dózsa SC (Budapest)), 6 László BÁLINT (01.02.1948/ Ferencvárosi TC (Budapest))

## MIDFIELDERS

7 István SZŐKE (13.02.1947/Ferencvárosi TC (Budapest)), 8 Lajos KOCSIS (17.06.1947/Budapesti Honvéd SE), 10 Lajos KŰ (05.07.1948/Ferencvárosi TC (Budapest)), 12 István JUHÁSZ (17.07.1945/ Ferencvárosi TC (Budapest)), 16 József KOVÁCS (03.04.1949/Videoton SC (Székesfehérvár)), 20 Mihály KOZMA (01.11.1949/Budapesti Honvéd SE), 24 Flórián ALBERT (15.09.1941/Ferencvárosi TC (Budapest))

## FORWARDS

5 Lajos SZŰCS (10.12.1943/Budapesti Honvéd SE), 9 Ferenc BENE (17.12.1944/Újpesti Dózsa SC (Budapest)), 11 Sándor ZÁMBÓ (10.10.1944/Újpesti Dózsa SC (Budapest)), 15 Antal DUNAI (21.03.1943/ Újpesti Dózsa SC (Budapest))

## USSR

### GOALKEEPERS

1 Evgeniy RUDAKOV (02.01.1942/FK Dinamo Kiev),
19 Vladimir PILGUIY (26.01.1948/FK Dinamo Moskva)

### DEFENDERS

2 Revaz DZODZUASHVILI (10.04.1945/FC Dinamo
Tbilisi), 4 Nikolaiy ABRAMOV (05.01.1950/FK Spartak
Moskva), 5 Viktor MATVIENKO (09.11.1948/FK
Dinamo Kiev), 7 Vladimir TROSHKIN (28.09.1947/FK
Dinamo Kiev), 12 Vladimir KAPLICHNIY (26.02.1944/
TSKA Moskva), 13 Yuriy ISTOMIN (03.07.1944/TSKA
Moskva)

### MIDFIELDERS

3 Murtaz KHURTSILAVA (05.01.1943/FC Dinamo
Tbilisi), 6 Viktor KOLOTOV (03.07.1949/FK Dinamo
Kiev), 8 Anatoliy BAIYDACHNIY (01.10.1952/FK
Dinamo Moskva), 10 Vladimir MUNTYAN (14.09.1946/
FK Dinamo Kiev), 11 Oleg DOLMATOV (29.11.1948/FK
Dinamo Moskva), 14 Anatoliy KONKOV (19.09.1949/
FK Shakhtar Donetsk)

### FORWARDS

9 Anatoliy BANISHEVSKIY (23.02.1946/FK Neftchi
Baku), 15 Eduard KOZINKEVICH (23.05.1949/SKA
Lvov), 16 Givi NODIYA (02.01.1948/FC Dinamo
Tbilisi), 18 Vladimir ONISCHENKO (28.10.1949/FK
Zarya Voroshilovgrad)

Richard Keir

# WEST GERMANY

## GOALKEEPERS

1 Josef MAIER (28.02.1944/FC Bayern München), 22 Wolfgang KLEFF (16.11.1946/VfL Borussia Mönchengladbach)

## DEFENDERS

2 Horst-Dieter HÖTTGES (10.09.1943/SV Werder Bremen), 3 Paul BREITNER (05.09.1951/FC Bayern München), 4 Hans-Georg SCHWARZENBECK (03.04.1948/FC Bayern München), 5 Franz BECKENBAUER (11.09.1945/FC Bayern München), 14 Hans-Hubert VOGTS (30.12.1946/VfL Borussia Mönchengladbach), 16 Michael BELLA (29.09.1945/ MSV Duisburg)

## MIDFIELDERS

8 Ulrich HOENEß (05.01.1952/FC Bayern München), 10 Günter NETZER (14.09.1944/VfL Borussia Mönchengladbach), 15 Rainer BONHOF (29.03.1952/ VfL Borussia Mönchengladbach), 18 Horst KÖPPEL (17.05.1948/VfL Borussia Mönchengladbach)

## FORWARDS

6 Herbert WIMMER (09.11.1944/VfL Borussia Mönchengladbach), 7 Jürgen GRABOWSKI (07.07.1944/Eintracht Frankfurt), 9 Josef HEYNCKES (09.05.1945/VfL Borussia Mönchengladbach), 11 Erwin KREMERS (23.03.1949/FC Schalke 04 Gelsenkirchen), 13 Gerhard MÜLLER (03.11.1945/FC Bayern München), 17 Johannes LÖHR (05.07.1942/1. FC Köln)

# 1974-1976

## QUALIFICATION

### GROUP STAGE

Again, thirty-two nations competed in eight groups of four teams, with the winners of each group advancing to the quarter-finals. Iceland took part for the first time since 1964, while Albania decided not to enter.

### GROUP 1

After failing to qualify for the 1974 World Cup, which had ended Sir 'Alf' Ramsey's tenure as manager, England were hoping to bounce back under new coach, 'Don' Revie. They were handed a fairly modest draw, with Czechoslovakia and Portugal their main rivals for qualification, alongside minnows Cyprus. England hosted the Czechoslovaks at Wembley in the opening game, where the visitors defended stoutly, until 'Mick' Channon finally broke the deadlock with a header in the seventy-second minute. Colin Bell then scored twice in the next ten minutes to give the home side an emphatic 3-0 victory. The following month it was the turn of the Portuguese to visit Wembley, where they proved to be harder to break down; on this occasion England couldn't find a way past an inspired Vítor Damas in the visitors' goal, and the game ended goalless.

England then played their final home match, walloping Cyprus 5-0, with Malcolm McDonald equalling a national record for most goals in a match by netting all five of them. Four days later, Czechoslovakia got their first points on the board when they too saw off the Cypriots at home by 4-0, with Antonín Panenka notching a hat-trick. Of greater significance was their next match, where they sensationally thrashed Portugal 5-0 in Prague to move to within a point of England. However, England moved three points clear again, as an early Kevin Keegan strike was enough to secure the points away to Cyprus.

The next match was virtually a group decider when Czechoslovakia hosted England in Bratislava, where the home side had to win. The game was abandoned, however, after only seventeen minutes as fog descended over the pitch, with no goals having being scored. Twenty-four hours later, the match was replayed, and it was England who struck first when Keegan set up Channon through the middle to lob the ball over Ivo Viktor in the twenty-sixth minute. However, the Czechoslovaks levelled right on half-time when Zdeněk Nehoda headed in Marián Masný's corner. Just two minutes into the second half they were ahead, as the English defence had allowed Masný to stride through towards the byline and his cross was headed home by Dušan Galis. The hosts were never really threatened thereafter, and 2-1 was the final result. The Czechoslovaks then had a chance to go top in their penultimate game in Oporto against Portugal, but despite going ahead early on through Anton Ondruš, they were pegged back almost immediately, as 'Nené' levelled. It could have got worse for the visitors, had the same player not missed a penalty late on.

A week later it was England's turn to visit Portugal, where a win would leave Czechoslovakia needing at least a three-goal margin of victory in Cyprus to win the group. Keegan had the ball in the net early on, but he was flagged for offside; then, in the sixteenth minute, 'Nené' fell to the ground theatrically under pressure from Paul Madeley, some thirty-five yards from goal. Rui Rodrigues strode forward and smacked the resultant free-kick with tremendous force into the top corner of the net.

Portugal had a couple of chances to increase their lead, particularly when 'Nené' was clean through, but he sliced his effort wide. England drew level three minutes before the break, also from a free-kick. The Portuguese wall refused to retreat the full ten yards and it rebounded on them, as Channon's shot took a wicked deflection and the ball sailed beyond the wrong-footed Damas. In the second half, Clemence came to England's rescue on a couple of occasions as the home side pressed for a winner, but the game ended all square. This left Czechoslovakia needing only to win in Cyprus, and they duly did so, with three first-half goals taking them through to the quarter-finals.

## GROUP 2

Wales were hopeful of qualifying after being drawn alongside Austria and Hungary, who were both rebuilding their squads after some pretty lean years, as well as minnows Luxembourg. In the opening fixture, the Welsh started superbly in Vienna by taking the lead in the thirty-fifth minute when Arfon Griffiths took advantage of a misplaced header from 'Eddy' Krieger to nod home; but after the interval, incessant Austrian pressure paid off just after the hour mark. 'Willy' Kreuz volleyed in from 'Gusti' Starek's cross, then 'Hans' Krankl stabbed home the winner from close range with sixteen minutes remaining.

Hungary commenced their campaign in Luxembourg, where they went a goal down after fifteen minutes, with Gilbert Dussier netting. The *Magyars* were soon level, however, through József Horváth. Not long afterwards, László Nagy fired the visitors ahead, only for Dussier to net again for the Grand Duchy from the penalty spot just before the break. In the second half, the visitors stepped it up, and they netted twice more without reply through Nagy and László Bálint to win 4-2.

Hungary then travelled to Wales, where, after a tense first half, the *Dragons* opened the scoring in the fifty-seventh minute when Griffiths latched onto a rebound to slot home. A couple of minutes from time, Leighton James' cross found John Toshack unmarked to head into an empty net and seal the victory. The Welsh then went top of the group with a 5-0 thrashing of Luxembourg at home, five different players sharing the goals. The Austrians also travelled to Luxembourg, where they scraped a narrow win with two second-half goals from Helmut Köglberger and Krankl, after 'Nico' Braun had put the minnows ahead in the twelfth minute. Austria then edged a point ahead of the Welsh when held to a goalless draw by Hungary in a disappointing game in Vienna.

With all of their home fixtures to come, the Hungarians looked well placed to take control of the group; but in the first of them against Wales, despite dominating possession, they went down to a 2-1 defeat. Toshack set the visitors on their way a minute from the break with a simple tap in from James' cross, having earlier been denied an opening goal when Ferenc Mészáros saved his penalty kick. In the second half the Welsh continued to soak up the pressure, and they went further ahead in the sixty-ninth minute when Brian Flynn sent a superb through ball for John Mahoney to slot home. The home side did pull a goal back thirteen minutes from time when László Branikovits got in behind the Welsh defence to coolly finish from Sándor Pintér's fine pass, but they couldn't force an equaliser, and Wales held on for a famous victory.

Two weeks later, the Welsh moved onto eight points with a straightforward 3-1 win in Luxembourg in their penultimate game, and at the same time eliminated the Hungarians, who in turn did Wales a huge favour by defeating Austria 2-1 in Budapest in the next match. In their penultimate game, the Austrians came from behind to eventually stroll to a 6-2 victory over Luxembourg, leaving them a point behind Wales going into the decisive match between the sides in Wrexham.

Needing only a point to qualify, the home side might have been expected to keep it tight, but they took the game to the Austrians. They nearly took the lead from James' inswinging corner, which almost caught out 'Friedl' Koncilia, but the keeper managed to keep it out with the help of the crossbar. In the second half, the Welsh finally got the goal they deserved in the sixty-ninth minute; 'Rod' Thomas played a delightful pass to Griffiths, who thrashed his shot beyond Koncilia to put the *Dragons* through to the quarter-finals.


## GROUP 3

Sweden and Yugoslavia renewed rivalries, having met in the 1974 World Cup, where the Swedes had come out on top on that occasion. They were joined by Northern Ireland and Norway, who met each other in the opening match in Oslo, and the visitors got off to a dream start when 'Tom' Finney fired them ahead after only three minutes – but in the second half, the Norwegians hit back with two goals from star forward Tom Lund to win the game.

The following month, both Sweden and Yugoslavia commenced their campaigns with contrasting fortunes. The Yugoslavs entertained Norway, where Lund struck first for the guests in the thirty-sixth minute, but Momčilo Vukotić soon equalised, and two goals after the break from Josip Katalinski eased the home side to a 3-1 victory. Northern Ireland made their second group visit to Scandinavia more in hope than expectation, but in one of their best ever performances they came away from Sweden with a superb 2-0 win, thanks to first-half goals from 'Chris' Nicholl and Martin O'Neill.

They followed up by defeating Yugoslavia in Belfast, with the only goal coming midway through the first half from Bryan Hamilton's close-range header. The Yugoslavs then travelled to Scandinavia for a double-header in the space of five days. During the first of them, in Sweden, they found themselves a goal down early on through Ralf Edström, but Katalinski levelled just before half-time; then, thirteen minutes from time, Zvonko Ivezić netted a winning goal for the visitors. They found things much easier in Oslo, where they raced into a three-goal lead by the twenty-fifth minute. The Yugoslavs eased off after that, and Norway grabbed a consolation midway through the second half.

Sweden then brought themselves into contention with home and away wins over Norway, before putting a dent in Northern Ireland's chances with a comeback 2-1 win in Belfast. The Swedes were now level on points with Yugoslavia, who had a game in hand going into their meeting in Zagreb. Swedish hopes soon evaporated when Branko Oblak fired the home side ahead in the eighteenth minute, and further strikes from Franjo Vladić and Dragutin Vabec gave Yugoslavia a comfortable 3-0 win and put them on the brink of qualification.

Two weeks later, Northern Ireland kept their chances alive when two goals in the first five minutes from 'Sammy' Morgan and 'Sammy' McIlroy sent them on their way to an easy 3-0 victory over Norway in Belfast, setting up a final day decider with the Yugoslavs in Belgrade. The Irish had to win by at least two goals to overhaul their hosts on goal difference, but a single goal from Oblak after twenty-one minutes was sufficient for Yugoslavia to proceed to the quarter-finals.

## GROUP 4

Scotland were considered to be slight favourites to win the section, having been the only one of the four nations to have taken part at the 1974 World Cup, where they had been unfortunate to go out at the group stage. Denmark and Spain opened proceedings when they met in Copenhagen, and it was the visitors who got off to the perfect start with a 2-1 victory, thanks to first half goals from José Claramunt from the penalty spot, and Roberto Martínez. Kristen Nygaard pulled a goal back with a penalty shortly after the break, but even though Claramunt was sent off, the home side couldn't find an equaliser. The Danes fared a little better in their next outing by holding Romania to a goalless draw at home.

Scotland began their campaign against the Spaniards in Glasgow, where they got off to a flyer when 'Billy' Bremner put them ahead in the 11th minute. However,

'Tommy' Hutchison blew a great chance to double the lead when he missed a penalty kick, and the visitors took advantage of this let-off when 'Quini' levelled nine minutes before the break. The same player stunned the Scots by netting a second goal just after the hour mark to give the Spanish another away win. The two sides met again three months later in Valencia. The Scots again struck first blood when 'Joe' Jordan netted with barely sixty seconds on the clock, but they were pegged back as Alfredo Megido equalised midway through the second half.

Spain then entertained Romania in Madrid, and Manuel Velázquez put the home side ahead in the sixth minute, but again they had to settle for a 1-1 draw, as Zoltán Crişan levelled with twenty minutes remaining. The Romanians followed up that fine result by thrashing the Danes 6-1 in Bucharest, which included doubles for Crişan and Dudu Georgescu. They were only a minute away from another home success in their next game against Scotland after Georgescu headed them in front midway through the first half, only for Gordon McQueen to pop up with a fantastic shot which flew past Răducanu to give the Scots a share of the spoils.

Scotland then got their first victories with back-to-back wins over Denmark, while in between, the Spaniards also beat the Danes 2-0 in Barcelona, which left them needing only a point in their last match in Bucharest to qualify. With a game in hand, the Romanians could still win the group if they won their two matches, but Spain started strongly. They opened the scoring on the half-hour through Ángel Villar, then, twelve minutes into the second half, went further ahead when 'Santillana' struck a superb volley from Vicente Del Bosque's cross. The home side pulled a goal back from the penalty spot with eighteen minutes left through Georgescu, then in the eightieth minute Iordănescu equalised with a deflected shot; but in the remaining minutes, the visitors held firm to secure the draw they needed to progress.

## GROUP 5

This was by far the most difficult group from which to predict a winner, with 1974 World Cup runners-up Holland joined by Poland, who had performed magnificently and finished in third place, and Italy, who had gone out at the group stage, and also Finland, who made up the foursome. The Finns kicked off the group at home to Poland, and they took a surprise lead when Timo Rahja netted after only three minutes. However, the Poles soon got into their stride, and Andrzej Szarmach levelled midway through the half before 1974 World Cup top goalscorer Grzegorz Lato grabbed the winner five minutes after the break. The Dutch also began their campaign with a trip to Helsinki, and a similar pattern ensued; again Rahja put the home side ahead, only for 'Johan' Cruijff to net twice before the interval, then 'Johan' Neeskens wrapped up the points for the visitors with a penalty kick in the fifty-first minute.

The Poles then easily brushed aside Finland at home with a 3-0 victory. The Italians began with a visit to Rotterdam, where they got off to a cracking start when Roberto Boninsegna headed in a Giancarlo Antognoni cross after only five minutes, but 'Rob' Rensenbrink equalised in the twenty-fourth minute from 'Ruud' Krol's centre before two second-half goals from Cruijff gave the Dutch a comprehensive victory. The *Azzurri* were then held to a disappointing goalless draw by the Poles in Rome before they gained their first win with a narrow 1-0 victory in Finland, thanks to Giorgio Chinaglia's first-half penalty.

The Netherlands then went top of the group with another comeback win over Finland in Nijmegen; after Matti Paatelainen had put the visitors in front, the Dutch stormed back to win 4-1, with 'Willy' van der Kuijlen notching a hat-trick. They were hoping to consolidate their position at the top when they travelled to Poland, but the home side produced a fantastic display of attacking football to blow away the Dutch. Lato put the Poles ahead in the fourteenth minute as he took advantage of a poor backpass to head home; then, a minute before the interval, Robert Gadocha latched onto a quickly taken free-kick from 'Kazu' Deyna to knock in the second. Szarmach added two further goals in the second period, and the only response the Dutch could muster was a late consolation from 'René' van de Kerkhof.

The Italians were then sensationally held to a goalless draw by the Finns in Rome, before the Dutch exacted revenge on Poland when they met in Amsterdam. Neeskens opened the scoring after sixteen minutes with a superb diving header from 'Wim' Suurbier's cross. Early in the second half, the goalscorer turned provider, as his free-kick was glanced home by 'Ruud' Geels, before 'Frans' Thijssen added some gloss to a polished display with the third goal on the hour mark. In their final match, the Poles suffered a setback when held to another goalless draw at home by the Italians, in a match where both goalkeepers were the stars, making a series of fine stops.

This left the Poles level on eight points with the Dutch, who had a superior goal difference, going into their final match against Italy in Rome. For Poland to qualify they needed the Italians to win by four clear goals, but that outcome never looked likely, and after conceding a twentieth minute goal when Fabio Capello bulleted a header beyond 'Piet' Schrijvers from a Franco Causio free-kick, the Dutch were content to see out the rest of the game without further loss.

## GROUP 6

The Soviet Union, who had been to every Final Tournament thus far, were strong favourites to emerge victorious when drawn against the Republic of Ireland, Switzerland and Turkey, but they got off to a disastrous start against the Irish in Dublin. After twenty-two minutes, 'Joe' Kinnear crossed for 'Don' Givens to powerfully head past Vladimir Pilguiy; then Givens added a second on the half-hour after a defensive mix-up, before completing his hat-trick twenty minutes from time when he got on the end of 'Johnny' Giles' free-kick to head home. The Irish followed up with a fine point away to Turkey. After going behind to an own-goal from 'Tony' Dunne early in the second half, Givens struck an equaliser on the hour mark. The Swiss kicked off their campaign with a trip to Izmir, where they began well – taking the lead through Hanspeter Schild – but İsmail Arca soon levelled for the Turks, and five minutes from time, Mehmet Oğuz struck a winning goal for the home side.

Turkey then travelled to Kiev to take on the Soviet Union under new coach Valeriy Lobanovskiy, whose entire team was made up of Dynamo Kiev players, and their familiarity proved significant; the home side ran out easy 3-0 winners, with Viktor Kolotov netting two from the penalty spot and Oleg Blokhin notching the third. Meanwhile, the Swiss were virtually eliminated after only drawing 1-1 at home to the Turks, then losing 2-1 away to the Republic of Ireland. A week after beating Switzerland, the Irish travelled to Kiev for a crunch match against the Soviets, which the home side had to win – and they got it, thanks to first half goals from Blokhin and Kolotov. Eoin Hand did pull a goal back for the visitors, but the Soviet Union held out for the victory.

The Irish travelled straight to Switzerland for their next game three days later, where they suffered another defeat, with 'Rudi' Elsener scoring the only goal fifteen minutes from time to blow the group wide open. The next match took place five months later with the Swiss hosting the Soviet Union, and it was the visitors who came away with a priceless win, thanks to Vladimir Muntyan's seventy-eighth minute strike to go top of the group.

In their final game, the Republic of Ireland thrashed Turkey 4-0 in Dublin, which put paid to the visitors' qualification hopes and also kept the pressure on the Soviets, who needed at least two points from their last two matches to take top spot. Fortunately they got them in the first one in Kiev against Switzerland, whose defending was woeful; the home side cantered to a 4-1 victory, meaning that their 1-0 defeat to Turkey in their final game was rendered obsolete.

## GROUP 7

This section looked finely balanced on paper, with Belgium, East Germany and France drawn together with Iceland. It was the Icelanders who got the group underway when they hosted Belgium. They'd met in the previous World Cup preliminaries, where the Belgians had won both games easily, but they had it much tougher this time. Wilfried Van Moer put the *Diables Rouges* ahead after thirty-eight minutes, but they had to wait until three minutes from time to seal the points when Jacques Teugels converted a penalty kick. Iceland then travelled to Magdeburg and came away with a fantastic point. Martin Hoffmann opened the scoring for the East Germans after only seven minutes, but Matthías Hallgrímsson levelled midway through the half, and that was the way it finished. On the same day, France kicked off with a visit to Belgium, where the home side took an early lead when Maurice Martens beat Dominique Baratelli in the French goal from a tight angle. However, Christian Coste soon equalised and a draw looked likely, until François Van der Elst took advantage of some dreadful defending to slam home a winner for the Belgians.

In their next game at home to East Germany, only a stirring fightback saved the French from another defeat after goals from Jürgen Sparwasser and Hans-Jürgen Kreische had put the visitors two up early in the second half. With ten minutes remaining, Jean-Marc Guillou reduced the deficit, then Jean Gallice headed home a dramatic last minute equaliser. East Germany then blew a great chance to draw level with the Belgians when the two sides met in Leipzig, where the visitors held out for a goalless draw. Surprisingly, that was the scoreline when the French travelled to Iceland five months later – then, just two weeks after that, the Icelanders created an even bigger shock as the East Germans were humbled 2-1 in Reykjavík. They were brought back down to earth, though, in their next match, as the French coasted to a 3-0 victory in Nantes.

The Belgians edged closer to qualifying with a nervy 1-0 win over Iceland in Liège, thanks to a Raoul Lambert strike just before the interval. Belgium now only required a point from their last two games to progress, but at home to East Germany, they were sensationally defeated 2-1. The East Germans came from behind in their final match to beat France 2-1, with the winning goal coming from a controversial penalty thirteen minutes from the end, which Eberhard Vogel converted. This result ended the hopes of the French, who had nothing to play for in the final group game at home to Belgium, who could afford to lose by one goal and still go through, and in the end both sides appeared content to play out a goalless draw.

## GROUP 8

The holders appeared to be given an easy path to the quarter-finals when drawn alongside Bulgaria, Greece and Malta. The Bulgarians and the Greeks commenced proceedings when they met in Sofia, and the home side got off to a flyer when Hristo Bonev netted after only two minutes. Then, near the half hour mark, three goals were scored in as many minutes, with Georgi Denev notching a double and Antonis Antoniadis replying for Greece in between. It stayed that way until the eighty-sixth minute, when, remarkably, the visitors struck twice in two minutes through Dimitris Papaioannou and Apostolos Glezos to snatch an unlikely draw. In the next game it was Greece's turn to suffer late agony in Piraeus against West Germany, where they led twice, with the visitors' second equaliser coming in the eighty-third minute through Herbert Wimmer. However, in their next game, they managed to hold out against a late Bulgarian fightback to win 2-1 at home.

West Germany's less than impressive start continued in their next game in Malta, where they struggled to a single goal victory, courtesy of a 'Bernd' Cullmann strike just before the interval. The shock result of the group occurred in the next match, as the hitherto unbeaten Greeks suffered a 2-0 reverse in Malta, while Bulgaria and West Germany shared the spoils in a 1-1 draw in Sofia with both goals coming from the penalty spot.

Greece then got their revenge over the Maltese in the return fixture by winning comprehensively 4-0, and a week later the minnows suffered another thumping as Bulgaria put five past them without reply.

For their final match the Greeks travelled to Düsseldorf, where they needed an improbable win to put some daylight between them and their hosts. In the end they got a point after going behind when 'Jupp' Heynckes latched onto a Paul Breitner pass to net in the sixty-eighth minute. Ten minutes later, an uncharacteristic error from Franz Beckenbauer allowed Giorgos Delikaris to run through unopposed, round 'Sepp' Maier and slot home the equaliser. Greece thus finished on seven points, with both West Germany and Bulgaria having two games left to overtake them. Those two met in the next match in Stuttgart, and it was Heynckes who was in the right place to take advantage of a ricochet inside the box; he coolly placed the ball beyond Yordan Filipov for the only goal after sixty-four minutes. The West Germans were still behind Greece on goal difference, but they were left with the simple task of taking care of Malta in Dortmund to go through – which they did with consummate ease, winning 8-0.

## QUARTER-FINALS

## CZECHOSLOVAKIA vs USSR

The opening quarter-final pitted Czechoslovakia against the Soviet Union, who were bidding to make the Final Tournament for a fifth successive time, but that scenario looked a long way off after the first leg in Bratislava, where the home side took firm control of the tie. Jozef Móder opened the scoring after thirty-four minutes with a fine strike; then, just a couple of minutes into the second half, Antonín Panenka blasted an unstoppable free-kick from the edge of the area to double the lead.

In the return leg in Kiev, the Soviets were more competitive, but it was the visitors who broke the deadlock through Móder right on half-time, though Leonid Buryak levelled things up soon after the break. The Soviet Union continued to press, but they were hit on the break seven minutes from time when Móder scored again to kill off the tie. There was still time for Oleg Blokhin to notch a second goal for the home side and avoid another defeat.

## WEST GERMANY vs SPAIN

The draw paired the holders with Spain, who hosted the first match in Madrid, where they had the better of the opening half and deservedly took the lead in the twenty-first minute – a long ball fell into the path of 'Santillana', who poked the ball beyond 'Sepp' Maier on the half-volley. However, after the interval the West Germans came more into the game, and on the hour mark Erich Beer struck a fabulous equaliser from fully thirty yards which José Iribár couldn't keep out.

In the second leg in Munich, it was the Spaniards who came closest to scoring early on when 'Quini' struck the bar, but the home side soon got into their stride, and they took the lead in the seventeenth minute when Beer crossed for 'Uli' Hoeneß to score with a spectacular volley. The same player should have doubled the advantage soon afterwards, as he surged past several tackles, only to shoot off the post with only the keeper to beat. The decisive second goal arrived just before half-time, when Franz Beckenbauer's effort was parried straight into the path of Klaus Toppmöller, who tapped into the empty net to put the holders through.

## YUGOSLAVIA vs WALES

Wales' reward for getting through the group stage was a tie against Yugoslavia, and in the first leg in Zagreb they got off to the worst possible start when they conceded a goal in the first minute. Dragutin Vabec fired in a shot which deflected straight to Momčilo Vukotić, who slotted home. The Welsh came into the game more but rarely threatened an equaliser, and in the fifty-fourth minute the Yugoslavs went further ahead when Branko Oblak's cross was headed back across goal by 'Ivica' Šurjak for Danilo Popivoda to score.

A capacity crowd in Cardiff greeted the teams for the return match, hoping for an early Welsh goal to put them back in the tie; Brian Flynn went close early on, but in the nineteenth minute Popivoda was clumsily brought down in the box by Malcolm Page, and Josip Katalinski sent 'Dai' Davies the wrong way from the resultant penalty. The Welsh surged forward after this, and, after Flynn had hit the post with one effort, they got a deserved equaliser seven minutes before the break, when Ian Evans netted from Flynn's corner. In the second half the home side were incensed after John Toshack had two goals disallowed; near the end they got a penalty when Toshack was upended by Enver Marić, but the keeper atoned for his lapse by easily saving 'Terry' Yorath's weak effort.

## NETHERLANDS vs BELGIUM

Neighbours Belgium and the Netherlands met in the last quarter-final tie. Their most recent meetings had been two 0-0 draws in the qualifiers for the 1974 World Cup, but this time the tie was all over after the opening leg in Rotterdam. The visitors' defensive game plan backfired after seventeen minutes when 'Johan' Cruijff nudged a free-kick to 'Wim' Rijsbergen, who cracked a low drive into the bottom corner of the net. Ten minutes later, 'Rob' Rensenbrink doubled the lead when he got in front of Christian Piot to head in a Cruijff corner. In the second half, the Dutch continued to pour forward, and Rensenbrink soon made it 3-0 when he rounded Piot before tapping into an empty net. Georges Leekens punched away 'Willy' van de Kerkhof's lob, and 'Johan' Neeskens coolly converted the resultant spot kick. With five minutes left, Rensenbrink headed the fifth goal, and his third, to complete a memorable night for him.

The Belgians had only pride to play for in the second leg, but they could have been behind early on had Neeskens not missed a penalty – they took advantage of that let-off by taking the lead in the twenty-seventh minute, when Roger Van Gool scored with a fantastic free-kick. However, in the second period, the Dutch came storming back, and just after the hour mark, 'Johnny' Rep equalised after Cruijff set him up with a sublime backheel. With thirteen minutes remaining, Cruijff grabbed a winner for the visitors, with a superb chip into the far corner.

# MATCH DETAILS

<u>GROUP 1</u> (Cyprus, Czechoslovakia, England, Portugal)

30 October 1974          Ref: Michel KITABDJIAN
(France)

Wembley Stadium, LONDON (Att. 83,858)

ENGLAND - CZECHOSLOVAKIA
3:0 (0:0)

1:0 Channon (72'), 2:0 Bell (80'), 3:0 Bell (83')

<u>ENG:</u> (Coach: Donald REVIE)
Raymond CLEMENCE, Paul MADELEY, Emlyn HUGHES, Martin DOBSON (Trevor BROOKING 64'), David WATSON I, Norman HUNTER, Colin BELL, Gerald FRANCIS, Frank WORTHINGTON (David THOMAS 64'), Michael CHANNON, Kevin KEEGAN

<u>CZE:</u> (Coach: Václav JEŽEK)
Ivo VIKTOR, Ján PIVARNÍK, Anton ONDRUŠ, Jozef ČAPKOVIČ (Rostislav VOJÁČEK 64'), Vojtěch VARADÍN, Přemysl BIČOVSKÝ (Ladislav KUNA 70'), Ivan PEKÁRIK, Miroslav GAJDŮŠEK, Marián MASNÝ, Ján ŠVEHLÍK, Pavel STRATIL

20 November 1974          Ref: Anton BUCHELI
(Switzerland)

Wembley Stadium, LONDON (Att. 84,461)

ENGLAND - PORTUGAL
0:0

ENG: (Coach: Donald REVIE)
Raymond CLEMENCE, Paul MADELEY, David
WATSON I, Emlyn HUGHES, Terence COOPER (Colin
TODD 23'), Trevor BROOKING, Gerald FRANCIS,
Colin BELL, David THOMAS, Michael CHANNON,
Allan CLARKE (Frank WORTHINGTON 70')

POR: (Coach: José Maria Carvalho PEDROTO)
Vítor Manuel Afonso de Oliveira 'DAMAS', Artur
Manuel Soares CORREIA, Humberto Manuel de Jesus
COELHO, CARLOS Alexandre Fortes ALHINHO,
Firmino da Graça Sardinha 'OSVALDINHO', Adelino
de Jesus TEIXEIRA, Octávio Joaquim Coelho
MACHADO, Vítor Manuel Rosa MARTINS, João
António Ferreira Resende ALVES, Francisco Delfim
Dias FARIA (ROMEU Fernando Fernandes da Silva
76'), Tamagnini Manuel Gomes Baptista 'NENÉ'
(António Luís Alves Ribeiro OLIVEIRA 76')

16 April 1975      Ref: Martti HIRVINIEMI (Finland)
Wembley Stadium, LONDON (Att. 68,245)

ENGLAND - CYPRUS
5:0 (2:0)

1:0   MacDonald   (2'),   2:0   MacDonald   (35'),
3:0   MacDonald   (48'),   4:0   MacDonald   (53'),
5:0 MacDonald (86')

ENG: (Coach: Donald REVIE)
Peter SHILTON, Paul MADELEY, David WATSON
I, Colin TODD, Kevin BEATTIE, Colin BELL, Alan
HUDSON, Michael CHANNON (David THOMAS 58'),
Malcolm MACDONALD, Kevin KEEGAN

CYP: (Coach: Pamboullis AVRAAMIDES)
Mihalakis ALKIVIADIS (Andreas KONSTANTINOU II
58'), Hristakis KOVIS, Kyriakos KOUREAS, Stefanis

MIHAIL, Nikolaos PANTZIARAS, Dimitris KYZAS, Gregory SAVVA, Michael THEODOROU, Andreas STYLIANOU, Nikolaos HARALAMBOUS I (Andreas KONSTANTINOU I 46'), Markos MARKOU

20 April 1975    Ref: Heinz EINBECK (East Germany)
Letenský stadion, PRAGUE (Att. 4,994)

CZECHOSLOVAKIA - CYPRUS
4:0 (2:0)

1:0 Panenka (10'), 2:0 Panenka (35'), 3:0 Panenka (50' pen.), 4:0 Masný (78')

CZE: (Coach: Václav JEŽEK)
Ivo VIKTOR, Ján PIVARNÍK, Anton ONDRUŠ, Jozef ČAPKOVIČ (Ladislav PETRÁŠ 75'), Miroslav GAJDŮŠEK, Přemysl BIČOVSKÝ, Antonín PANENKA, Marián MASNÝ, Ján ŠVEHLÍK, Zdeněk KOUBEK, Zdeněk NEHODA

CYP: (Coach: Pamboullis AVRAAMIDES)
Fanos STYLIANOU, Hristakis KOVIS, Nikolaos PANTZIARAS, Stavros STYLIANOU, Stefanis MIHAIL (Panikos YIOLITIS 82'), Dimitris KYZAS, Nikolaos HARALAMBOUS I, Gregory SAVVA, Markos MARKOU, Menelaos ASPROU (Panikos EUTHIMIADIS 64'), Andreas STYLIANOU

30 April 1975          Ref: Ferdinand BIWERSI
                                    (West Germany)
Letenský stadion, PRAGUE (Att. 12,034)

CZECHOSLOVAKIA - PORTUGAL
5:0 (3:0)

1:0 Bičovský (11'), 2:0 Bičovský (22'), 3:0 Nehoda (25'), 4:0 Nehoda (46'), 5:0 Petráš (52')

<u>CZE:</u> (Coach: Václav JEŽEK)
Ivo VIKTOR, Ján PIVARNÍK, Anton ONDRUŠ, Jozef
ČAPKOVIČ, Zdeněk KOUBEK (Jindřich SVOBODA
76'), Přemysl BIČOVSKÝ, Lubomír KNAPP (Ján
MEDVID 80'), Miroslav GAJDŮŠEK, Marián MASNÝ,
Ladislav PETRÁŠ, Zdeněk NEHODA

<u>POR:</u> (Coach: José Maria Carvalho PEDROTO)
Vítor Manuel Afonso de Oliveira 'DAMAS', Francisco
REBELO Moreira da Silva, Humberto Manuel de
Jesus COELHO, Carlos Alexandre Fortes ALHINHO,
Antonio Monteiro Teixeira de BARROS, António
José da Conceição Oliveira 'TONI' (Minervino
José Lopes PIETRA 49'), Octávio Joaquim Coelho
MACHADO, João António Ferreira Resende ALVES,
Samuel Ferreira FRAGUITO, Mário da Silva Mateus
'MARINHO', Tamagnini Manuel Gomes Baptista
'NENÉ' (Fernando Mendes Soares GOMES 64')

11 May 1975        Ref: Tsvetan STANEV (Bulgaria)
Stádio Tsirio, LIMASSOL (Att. 15,708)

CYPRUS - ENGLAND
0:1 (0:1)

0:1 Keegan (6')

<u>CYP:</u> (Coach: Pamboullis AVRAAMIDES)
Andreas KONSTANTINOU II, Hristakis KOVIS, Stavros
STYLIANOU, Dimitris KYZAS, Nikolaos PANTZIARAS,
Stefanis MIHAIL, Tasos KONSTANTINOU, Andros
MIAMILIOTIS (Takis PAPETTAS 78'), Gregory SAVVA,
Nikolaos HARALAMBOUS I, Dimitris PANAYIOTOU
(Kokos ANTONIOU 56')

<u>ENG:</u> (Coach: Donald REVIE)
Raymond CLEMENCE, Stephen WHITWORTH, Kevin
BEATTIE (Emlyn HUGHES 43'), David WATSON I,

Colin TODD, Colin BELL, David THOMAS, Alan BALL, Michael CHANNON, Malcolm MACDONALD, Kevin KEEGAN (Dennis TUEART 73')


8 June 1975     Ref: Gheorghe LIMONA (Romania)
Stádio Tsirio, LIMASSOL (Att. 8,615)

### CYPRUS - PORTUGAL
### 0:2 (0:1)

0:1 'Nené' (25'), 0:2 Moínhos (87')

CYP: (Coach: Pamboullis AVRAAMIDES)
Andreas KONSTANTINOU II, Hristakis KOVIS, Stavros STYLIANOU, Nikolaos PANTZIARAS, Dimitris KYZAS, Stefanis MIHAIL, Gregory SAVVA, Markos MARKOU, Nikolaos HARALAMBOUS I (Dimitris EKONOMOU 65'), Andros SAVVA, Takis PAPETTAS (Andreas KANARIS 72')

POR: (Coach: José Maria Carvalho PEDROTO)
Vítor Manuel Afonso de Oliveira 'DAMAS', Artur Manuel Soares CORREIA, Humberto Manuel de Jesus COELHO, Fernando José António FREITAS Alexandrino, António Monteiro Teixeira de BARROS, António José da Conceição Oliveira 'TONI', Octávio Joaquim Coelho MACHADO, João António Ferreira Resende ALVES, Vítor Manuel da Cruz GODINHO, Mário da Silva Mateus 'MARINHO' (FRANCISCO MÁRIO Pinto da Silva 76'), Tamagnini Manuel Gomes Baptista 'NENÉ' (Mário Jorge MOÍNHOS Matos 55')


30 October 1975     Ref: Alberto MICHELOTTI (Italy)
Tehelné pole, BRATISLAVA (Att. 50,651)

### CZECHOSLOVAKIA - ENGLAND
### 2:1 (1:1)

0:1 Channon (26'), 1:1 Nehoda (45'), 2:1 Galis (47')

CZE: (Coach: Václav JEŽEK)
Ivo VIKTOR, Ján PIVARNÍK, Anton ONDRUŠ,
Ladislav JURKEMIK, Koloman GÖGH (Karol DOBIAŠ
62'), Přemysl BIČOVSKÝ, Jaroslav POLLÁK, Lubomír
KNAPP, Marián MASNÝ, Dušan GALIS, Zdeněk
NEHODA

ENG: (Coach: Donald REVIE)
Raymond CLEMENCE, Paul MADELEY, Ian
GILLARD, Gerald FRANCIS, Roy McFARLAND
(David WATSON I 46'), Colin TODD, Kevin KEEGAN,
Michael CHANNON (David THOMAS 74'), Malcolm
MACDONALD, Allan CLARKE, Colin BELL


12 November 1975        Ref: Charles CORVER
                                    (Netherlands)
Estádio das Antas, OPORTO (Att. 38,000)

PORTUGAL - CZECHOSLOVAKIA
1:1 (1:1)

0:1 Ondruš (7'), 1:1 'Nené' (8')

POR: (Coach: José Maria Carvalho PEDROTO)
Vítor Manuel Afonso de Oliveira 'DAMAS', Francisco
REBELO Moreira da Silva, Humberto Manuel de
Jesus COELHO, Fernando José António FREITAS
Alexandrino, Artur Manuel Soares CORREIA, Octávio
Joaquim Coelho MACHADO, João António Ferreira
Resende ALVES, António José da Conceição Oliveira
'TONI', Mário Jorge MOÍNHOS Matos, Vítor Manuel
Ferreira BAPTISTA, Tamagnini Manuel Gomes
Baptista 'NENÉ' (António Luís Alves Ribeiro OLIVEIRA
46' (Mário da Silva Mateus 'MARINHO' 66'))

CZE: (Coach: Václav JEŽEK)

Ivo VIKTOR, Ján PIVARNÍK, Anton ONDRUŠ, Ladislav JURKEMIK, Koloman GÖGH, Přemysl BIČOVSKÝ, Jaroslav POLLÁK, Jozef MÓDER, Marián MASNÝ (Karol DOBIAŠ 89'), Dušan GALIS (František VESELÝ 62'), Zdeněk NEHODA

19 November 1975    Ref: Erich LINEMAYR (Austria)
Estádio José Alvalade, LISBON (Att. 60,000)

### PORTUGAL - ENGLAND
### 1:1 (1:1)

1:0 Rodrigues (16'), 1:1 Channon (42')

POR: (Coach: José Maria Carvalho PEDROTO)
Vítor Manuel Afonso de Oliveira 'DAMAS', Francisco REBELO Moreira da Silva (António Carlos Sousa Laranjeira 'TAI' 46'), Rui Gouveia Pinto RODRIGUES (Álvaro CAROLINO do Nascimento 48'), Fernando José António FREITAS Alexandrino, Artur Manuel Soares CORREIA, Octávio Joaquim Coelho MACHADO, João António Ferreira Resende ALVES, António José da Conceição Oliveira 'TONI', Tamagnini Manuel Gomes Baptista 'NENÉ', Vítor Manuel Ferreira BAPTISTA, Mário Jorge MOÍNHOS Matos

ENG: (Coach: Donald REVIE)
Raymond CLEMENCE, Stephen WHITWORTH, Kevin BEATTIE, Gerald FRANCIS, David WATSON I, Colin TODD, Kevin KEEGAN, Michael CHANNON, Malcolm MACDONALD (David THOMAS 74'), Trevor BROOKING, Paul MADELEY (Allan CLARKE 74')

23 November 1975    Ref: Sándor PETRI (Hungary)
Stádio Tsirio, LIMASSOL (Att. 13,000)

### CYPRUS - CZECHOSLOVAKIA
### 0:3 (0:3)

0:1 Nehoda (9'), 0:2 Bičovský (27'), 0:3 Masný (33')

CYP: (Coach: Pamboullis AVRAAMIDES)
Mihalakis ALKIVIADIS, Giannis MERTAKKAS,
Stefanis MIHAIL, Stavros STYLIANOU, Nikolaos
PANTZIARAS, Pashalis FOKKIS (Kallis
KONSTANTINOU 89'), Gregory SAVVA, Sotiris
KAIAFAS (Andros MIAMILIOTIS 35'), Markos
MARKOU, Andreas KANARIS, Takis PAPETTAS

CZE: (Coach: Václav JEŽEK)
Ivo VIKTOR, Ján PIVARNÍK, Anton ONDRUŠ, Ladislav
JURKEMIK, Koloman GÖGH, Přemysl BIČOVSKÝ,
Jaroslav POLLÁK (Ján MEDVID 67'), Jozef MÓDER,
Marián MASNÝ, Ján ŠVEHLÍK (František VESELÝ
71'), Zdeněk NEHODA

3 December 1975        Ref: Richard CASHA (Malta)
Estádio do Bonfim, SETÚBAL (Att. 4,000)

PORTUGAL - CYPRUS
1:0 (1:0)

1:0 Alves (20')

POR: (Coach: José Maria Carvalho PEDROTO)
Antonio José da Silva BOTELHO, Artur Manuel Soares
CORREIA, José de Jesus MENDES, Fernando José
António FREITAS Alexandrino, António Carlos Sousa
Laranjeira 'TAI', Octávio Joaquim Coelho MACHADO,
João António Ferreira Resende ALVES, António José
da Conceição Oliveira 'TONI', António Luís Alves
Ribeiro OLIVEIRA, Vítor Manuel Ferreira BAPTISTA,
Mário Jorge MOÍNHOS Matos (Manuel José Tavares
FERNANDES 46')

CYP: (Coach: Pamboullis AVRAAMIDES)
Fanos STYLIANOU, Stavros STYLIANOU, Kallis

KONSTANTINOU, Nikolaos PANTZIARAS, Giannis MERTAKKAS, Stefanis MIHAIL, Andros MIAMILIOTIS, Gregory SAVVA, Markos MARKOU, Takis PAPETTAS (Panikos EUTHIMIADIS 62'), Andreas KANARIS (Dimitris PANAYIOTOU 75')


CZECHOSLOVAKIA(Q)  (P6,W4,D1,L1,F15,A5,Pts.9)
England             (P6, W3, D2, L1, F11, A3, Pts. 8)
Portugal            (P6, W2, D3, L1, F5, A7, Pts. 7)
Cyprus              (P6, W0, D0, L6, F0, A16, Pts. 0)


GROUP 2 (Austria, Hungary, Luxembourg, Wales)


4 September 1974      Ref: DOĞAN Babacan (Turkey)
Praterstadion, VIENNA (Att. 30,795)

AUSTRIA - WALES
2:1 (0:1)

0:1 Griffiths (35'), 1:1 Kreuz (63'), 2:1 Krankl (74')

AUT: (Coach: Leopold ŠTÁSTNÝ)
Herbert RETTENSTEINER, Johann EIGENSTILLER, Johannes WINKLBAUER, Eduard KRIEGER, Werner KRIESS, Werner WALZER, August STAREK, Rainer SCHLAGBAUER (Helmut KÖGLBERGER 61'), Josef STERING, Wilhelm KREUZ, Johann KRANKL

WAL: (Coach: David BOWEN)
Gareth SPRAKE, Philip ROBERTS, Leighton PHILLIPS, David ROBERTS, John ROBERTS, Terence YORATH, John MAHONEY, Arfon GRIFFITHS, Gilbert REECE, John TOSHACK, Leighton JAMES

13 October 1974          Ref: Magnus PÉTURSSON
                                   (Iceland)
Stade Municipal, LUXEMBOURG CITY (Att. 3,326)

### LUXEMBOURG - HUNGARY
### 2:4 (2:2)

1:0 Dussier (15'), 1:1 Horváth (18'), 1:2 Nagy (29'), 2:2
Dussier (43' pen.), 2:3 Nagy (55'), 2:4 Bálint (71')

LUX: (Coach: Gilbert LEGRAND)
Jeannot MOES, Roger FANDEL, Joseph HANSEN,
René FLENGHI, Robert DA GRAVA, Jean ZUANG,
Louis TRIERWEILER, Paul PHILIPP, Gilbert
DUSSIER, Nicolas BRAUN, Pierrot LANGERS

HUN: (Coach: Ede MOÓR)
Ferenc MÉSZÁROS, Péter TÖRÖK, László
HARSÁNYI, József HORVÁTH, Mihály KÁNTOR,
László BÁLINT, László FAZEKAS, András TÓTH,
Mihály PÉNZES, Tibor KISS, László NAGY

30 October 1974      Ref: António da Silva GARRIDO
                                   (Portugal)
Ninian Park, CARDIFF (Att. 8,445)

### WALES - HUNGARY
### 2:0 (0:0)
1:0 Griffiths (57'), 2:0 Toshack (88')

WAL: (Coach: Michael SMITH)
Gareth SPRAKE (John PHILLIPS 83'), Roderick
THOMAS, Philip ROBERTS, John MAHONEY, Michael
ENGLAND, Leighton PHILLIPS, Arfon GRIFFITHS,
Terence YORATH, Gilbert REECE, John TOSHACK,
Leighton JAMES

HUN: (Coach: Ede MOÓR)
Ferenc MÉSZÁROS, Péter TÖRÖK, László BÁLINT,

József MUCHA, Mihály KÁNTOR, Zoltán HALMOSI, László FAZEKAS, András TÓTH (József PÓCZIK 63'), László FEKETE, Tibor KISS, László NAGY


20 November 1974   Ref: Preben CHRISTOPHERSEN
(Denmark)
Vetch Field, SWANSEA (Att. 10,539)

## WALES - LUXEMBOURG
### 5:0 (1:0)

1:0 Toshack (34'), 2:0 England (53'), 3:0 Roberts (70'), 4:0 Griffiths (73'), 5:0 Yorath (75')

WAL: (Coach: Michael SMITH)
Gareth SPRAKE, Roderick THOMAS, Michael ENGLAND, Philip ROBERTS, Leighton PHILLIPS, John MAHONEY (Brian FLYNN 77'), Terence YORATH, Arfon GRIFFITHS, Leighton JAMES, Gilbert REECE, John TOSHACK

LUX: (Coach: Gilbert LEGRAND)
Lucien THILL, Roger FANDEL, René FLENGHI, Joseph HANSEN, Robert DA GRAVA (Henri ROEMER 73'), Jean ZUANG, Louis PILOT, Louis TRIERWEILER, Pierrot LANGERS (Jean-Paul MARTIN 64'), Paul PHILIPP, Gilbert DUSSIER


16 March 1975     Ref: Leonardus VAN DER KROFT
(Netherlands)
Stade Municipal, LUXEMBOURG CITY (Att. 5,340)

## LUXEMBOURG - AUSTRIA
### 1:2 (1:0)

1:0 Braun (12'), 1:1 Köglberger (58'), 1:2 Krankl (75')

LUX: (Coach: Gilbert LEGRAND)

Jeannot MOES, Roger FANDEL, Joseph HANSEN, Louis PILOT, Jean-Louis MARGUE, Louis TRIERWEILER, Paul PHILIPP, Jean ZUANG, Gilbert ZENDER (Jean-Paul GOERRES 77'), Gilbert DUSSIER, Nicolas BRAUN

AUT: (Coach: Leopold ŠTÁSTNÝ)
Friedrich KONCILIA, Roland HATTENBERGER, Egon PAJENK, Norbert HOF, Johann EIGENSTILLER, Josef HICKERSBERGER, Herbert PROHASKA, Manfred GOMBASCH, Josef STERING, Kurt WELZL (Helmut KÖGLBERGER 46'), Johann KRANKL

2 April 1975          Ref: John TAYLOR (England)
Praterstadion, VIENNA (Att. 65,674)

AUSTRIA - HUNGARY
0:0

AUT: (Coach: Leopold ŠTÁSTNÝ)
Friedrich KONCILIA, Johann EIGENSTILLER, Johannes WINKLBAUER, Erich OBERMAYER, Heinrich STRASSER, Roland HATTENBERGER, Wilhelm KREUZ, Herbert PROHASKA, Helmut KÖGLBERGER (Johann PIRKNER 69'), Johann KRANKL, Alfred RIEDL

HUN: (Coach: Ede MOÓR)
Ferenc MÉSZÁROS, Péter TÖRÖK, János NAGY, László BÁLINT, József TÓTH, Károly CSAPÓ, Lajos KOCSIS, József HORVÁTH, András TÓTH (Sándor PINTÉR 68'), Ferenc BENE, László BRANIKOVITS (László FEKETE 68')

16 April 1975    Ref: Pablo Augusto SÁNCHEZ Ibáñez
(Spain)
Népstadion, BUDAPEST (Att. 21,080)

## HUNGARY - WALES
### 1:2 (0:1)

0:1 Toshack(44'), 0:2 Mahoney(69'), 1:2 Branikovits(77')

HUN: (Coach: János SZŐCS)
Ferenc MÉSZÁROS, Péter TÖRÖK, János NAGY, László BÁLINT, József TÓTH, Károly CSAPÓ (Ferenc BENE 56'), Lajos KOCSIS, József HORVÁTH (Sándor PINTÉR 46'), Mihály KOZMA, Lászlo BRANIKOVITS, János MÁTÉ

WAL: (Coach: Michael SMITH)
William DAVIES, Roderick THOMAS, Malcolm PAGE, Leighton PHILLIPS, John ROBERTS, Terence YORATH, John MAHONEY, Arfon GRIFFITHS, Gilbert REECE (David SMALLMAN 82'), John TOSHACK, Leighton JAMES (Brian FLYNN 59')


1 May 1975          Ref: Jan PEETERS (Belgium)
Stade Municipal, LUXEMBOURG CITY (Att. 3,289)

### LUXEMBOURG - WALES
### 1:3 (1:2)

0:1 Reece (24'), 0:2 James (32'), 1:2 Philipp (39' pen.), 1:3 James (83' pen.)

LUX: (Coach: Gilbert LEGRAND)
Jeannot MOES, Roger FANDEL, Joseph HANSEN, Louis PILOT, Jean-Louis MARGUE, Louis TRIERWEILER, Paul PHILIPP, Jean ZUANG, Jean-Paul MARTIN (Jeannot KRECKÉ 50' (Henry ROEMER 80')), Nicolas BRAUN, Gilbert ZENDER

WAL: (Coach: Michael SMITH)
William DAVIES, Malcolm PAGE, Terence YORATH, David ROBERTS, John MAHONEY, Leighton PHILLIPS, Arfon GRIFFITHS (Brian FLYNN 58'),

Gilbert REECE, John TOSHACK, Leighton JAMES, Roderick THOMAS

24 September 1975　　　Ref: René VIGLIANI (France)
Népstadion, BUDAPEST (Att. 31,270)
## HUNGARY - AUSTRIA
## 2:1 (2:1)
1:0 Nyilasi (3'), 1:1 Krankl (16' pen.), 2:1 Pusztai (35')

HUN: (Coach: Lajos BARÓTI)
László KOVÁCS, János NAGY, László BÁLINT, Tibor RAB, Sándor LUKÁCS, Tibor NYILASI, Lajos KOCSIS, András TÓTH (Sándor PINTÉR 75'), László PUSZTAI, László FAZEKAS, László NAGY (Béla VÁRADY 46')

AUT: (Coach: Leopold ŠTÁSTNÝ)
Friedrich KONCILIA, Robert SARA, Bruno PEZZEY, Erich OBERMAYER (Johannes WINKLBAUER 46'), Werner KRIESS, Peter KONCILIA, Herbert PROHASKA (Manfred STEINER 46'), Kurt JARA, Günter RINKER, Kurt WELZL, Johann KRANKL

15 October 1975　　　　　　Ref: Miroslav KOPAL
(Czechoslovakia)
Praterstadion, VIENNA (Att. 14,499)
## AUSTRIA - LUXEMBOURG
## 6:2 (3:2)
1:0 Welzl (1'), 1:1 Braun (4'), 1:2 Philipp (32'), 2:2 Krankl (38'), 3:2 Jara (41'), 4:2 Welzl (46'), 5:2 Krankl (76' pen.), 6:2 Prohaska (80')

AUT: (Coach: Branko ELSNER)
Friedrich KONCILIA, Werner KRIESS, Johannes WINKLBAUER, Bruno PEZZEY, Heinrich STRASSER,

Herbert PROHASKA, Peter KONCILIA, Johann ETTMAYER, Kurt WELZL, Johann KRANKL, Kurt JARA

LUX: (Coach: Gilbert LEGRAND)
René HOFFMANN, Emile LAHURE, Joseph HANSEN, Louis PILOT, Jean-Louis MARGUE, Jean ZUANG, Louis TRIERWEILER, Paul PHILIPP, Pierrot LANGERS (Jeannot KRECKÉ 75'), Gilbert DUSSIER (François HAUER 65'), Nicolas BRAUN


19 October 1975        Ref: Nikola DUDIN (Bulgaria)
Stadion Rohonci Úti, SZOMBATHELY (Att. 7,503)

### HUNGARY - LUXEMBOURG
### 8:1 (4:0)

1:0 Pintér (13'), 2:0 Nyilasi (21'), 3:0 Nyilasi (32'), 4:0 Nyilasi (44'), 5:0 Nyilasi (57'), 6:0 Nyilasi (67'), 7:0 Wollek (78'), 7:1 Dussier (83'), 8:1 Várady (84')

HUN: (Coach: Lajos BARÓTI)
Ádám ROTHERMEL, János NAGY, Lászlo BÁLINT, Tibor RAB, Sándor LUKÁCS, József KOVÁCS, Tibor NYILASI, Sándor PINTÉR, László FAZEKAS, Béla VÁRADY, László NAGY (Tibor WOLLEK 39')

LUX: (Coach: Gilbert LEGRAND)
Raymond ZENDER, Léon SCHMIT, Joseph HANSEN, Louis PILOT, Emile LAHURE, Jean ZUANG, Louis TRIERWEILER (René FLENGHI 50'), Paul PHILIPP, Pierrot LANGERS (Jeannot KRECKÉ 70'), Nicolas BRAUN, Gilbert DUSSIER


19 November 1975       Ref: Sergio GONELLA (Italy)
The Racecourse Ground, WREXHAM (Att. 27,578)

### WALES - AUSTRIA
### 1:0 (0:0)

Richard Keir

1:0 Griffiths (69')

<u>WAL:</u> (Coach: Michael SMITH)
Brian LLOYD, Roderick THOMAS, Joseph JONES,
John MAHONEY, Ian EVANS, Leighton PHILLIPS,
Arfon GRIFFITHS, Brian FLYNN, Terence YORATH,
David SMALLMAN, Leighton JAMES

<u>AUT:</u> (Coach: Branko ELSNER)
Friedrich KONCILIA, Robert SARA, Johannes
WINKLBAUER, Bruno PEZZEY, Werner KRIESS
(Heinrich STRASSER 29'), Herbert PROHASKA,
Manfred STEINER, Johann ETTMAYER, Kurt WELZL
(Josef STERING 70'), Johann KRANKL, Kurt JARA

| | |
|---|---|
| WALES (Q) | (P6, W5, D0, L1, F14, A4, Pts. 10) |
| Hungary | (P6, W3, D1, L2, F15, A8, Pts. 7) |
| Austria | (P6, W3, D1, L2, F11, A7, Pts. 7) |
| Luxembourg | (P6, W0, D0, L6, F7, A28, Pts. 0) |

<u>GROUP 3</u> (Northern Ireland, Norway, Sweden, Yugoslavia)

4 September 1974          Ref: Alfred DELCOURT
                                              (Belgium)
Ullevaal Stadion, OSLO (Att. 7,192)

NORWAY- NORTHERN IRELAND
2:1 (0:1)

0:1 Finney (3'), 1:1 Lund (50'), 2:1 Lund (72')

<u>NOR:</u> (Coach: Nils Arne EGGEN)
Geir KARLSEN, Reidar GOA, Jan BIRKELUND, Torkild
BRAKSTAD, Svein GRØNDALEN, Egil AUSTBØ, Tor
Egil JOHANSEN, Svein KVIA, Jan FUGLSET, Tom
LUND, Harry HESTAD

323

<u>NIR:</u> (Coach: Terence NEILL)
Patrick JENNINGS, Patrick RICE, David CRAIG (Hugh DOWD 46'), William O'KANE, Allan HUNTER, David CLEMENTS, Bryan HAMILTON, Thomas CASSIDY, Thomas FINNEY, Samuel McILROY, Christopher McGRATH (Thomas JACKSON 67')


30 October 1974          Ref: Theodorus BOOSTEN
                                        (Netherlands)
Råsunda Stadion, SOLNA (Att. 18,131)

SWEDEN - NORTHERN IRELAND
0:2 (0:2)

0:1 Nicholl (7'), 0:2 O'Neill (23')

<u>SWE:</u> (Coach: Georg ERICSON)
Ronnie HELLSTRÖM, Roland ANDERSSON, Kent KARLSSON, Björn NORDQVIST, Björn ANDERSSON, Staffan TAPPER, Ove KINDVALL (Thomas NORDAHL 78'), Bo LARSSON, Conny TORSTENSSON (Jan MATTSSON 46'), Ralf EDSTRÖM, Roland SANDBERG

<u>NIR:</u> (Coach: Terence NEILL)
Patrick JENNINGS, William O'KANE, Samuel NELSON (Ronald BLAIR 46'), Hugh DOWD, Allan HUNTER, Christopher NICHOLL, Thomas JACKSON, Martin O'NEILL, Samuel MORGAN, Samuel McILROY, Bryan HAMILTON


30 October 1974          Ref: Antoine QUEUDEVILLE
                                        (Luxembourg)
Stadion J.N.A., BELGRADE (Att. 15,000)

YUGOSLAVIA - NORWAY
3:1 (1:1)

0:1 Lund (36'), 1:1 Vukotić (43'), 2:1 Katalinski (58'),
3:1 Katalinski (72')

YUG: (Coach: Ante MLADINIĆ)
Ognjen PETROVIĆ, Vilson DŽONI, Džemal
HADŽIABDIĆ, Ivan BULJAN, Josip KATALINSKI,
Ivan ŠURJAK, Slaviša ŽUNGUL, Momčilo VUKOTIĆ,
Franjo VLADIĆ (Ljubiša RAJKOVIĆ 46'), Jurica
JERKOVIĆ, Dragan DŽAJIĆ

NOR: (Coach: Nils Arne EGGEN)
Geir KARLSEN, Øystein WORMDAL, Jan BIRKELUND,
Torkild BRAKSTAD, Svein GRØNDALEN, Egil
AUSTBØ, Tor Egil JOHANSEN (Jan FUGLSET 72'),
Svein KVIA, Terje OLSEN, Tom LUND, Harry HESTAD


16 April 1975          Ref: Robert WURTZ (France)
Windsor Park, BELFAST (Att. 25,847)

### NORTHERN IRELAND - YUGOSLAVIA
### 1:0 (1:0)

1:0 Hamilton (23')

NIR: (Coach: David CLEMENTS)
Patrick JENNINGS, Patrick RICE, Samuel NELSON,
Christopher NICHOLL, Allan HUNTER, David
CLEMENTS, Bryan HAMILTON, Martin O'NEILL,
Derek SPENCE, Samuel McILROY, Thomas
JACKSON

YUG: (Coach: Ante MLADINIĆ)
Ognjen PETROVIĆ, Luka PERUZOVIĆ, Džemal
HADŽIABDIĆ, Ivan BULJAN, Josip KATALINSKI,
Dražen MUŽINIĆ, Slobodan JANKOVIĆ, Momčilo
VUKOTIĆ (Franjo VLADIĆ 46'), Branko OBLAK, Jurica
JERKOVIĆ (Ivica MILJKOVIĆ 77'), Ivan ŠURJAK

4 June 1975          Ref: Vital LORAUX (Belgium)
Råsunda Stadion, SOLNA (Att. 27,250)

SWEDEN - YUGOSLAVIA
1:2 (1:1)

1:0 Edström (16'), 1:1 Katalinski (41'), 1:2 Ivezić (77')

SWE: (Coach: Georg ERICSON)
Ronnie HELLSTRÖM (Göran HAGBERG 46'),
Kent KARLSSON, Björn NORDQVIST, Jörgen
AUGUSTSSON, Ove GRAHN, Eine FREDRIKSSON,
Ralf EDSTRÖM, Roland SANDBERG, Thomas
SJÖBERG (Thomas NORDAHL 65'), Roland
ANDERSSON, Benny WENDT

YUG: (Coach: Ante MLADINIĆ)
Ognjen PETROVIĆ, Ivan BULJAN, Džemal
HADŽIABDIĆ, Dražen MUŽINIĆ, Josip KATALINSKI,
Vladislav BOGIĆEVIĆ, Danilo POPIVODA, Branko
OBLAK, Dušan SAVIĆ (Zvonko IVEZIĆ 53'), Franjo
VLADIĆ, Ivan ŠURJAK

9 June 1975       Ref: Edgar PEDERSEN (Denmark)
Ullevaal Stadion, OSLO (Att. 21,843)

NORWAY - YUGOSLAVIA
1:3 (0:3)

0:1 Buljan (12'), 0:2 Bogićević (13'), 0:3 Šurjak (25'),
1:3 Thunberg (65')

NOR: (Coach: Nils Arne EGGEN)
Erik JOHANNESSEN (Geir KARLSEN 74'), Erling
MEIRIK, Reidar GOA (Trond PEDERSEN 40'),
Jan BIRKELUND, Svein GRØNDALEN, Tor Egil
JOHANSEN, Svein KVIA, Harry HESTAD, Stein
THUNBERG, Tom LUND, Gabriel HØYLAND

YUG: (Coach: Ante MLADINIĆ)
Ognjen PETROVIĆ, Ivan BULJAN, Džemal HADŽIABDIĆ, Dražen MUŽINIĆ, Josip KATALINSKI, Vladislav BOGIĆEVIĆ, Danilo POPIVODA, Branko OBLAK, Ivan ŠURJAK, Franjo VLADIĆ (Vladimir PETROVIĆ 77'), Zvonko IVEZIĆ

30 June 1975          Ref: Rudolf GLÖCKNER
(East Germany)
Råsunda Stadion, SOLNA (Att. 9,580)

SWEDEN - NORWAY
3:1 (1:0)

1:0 Nordahl (33'), 1:1 Olsen (54' pen.), 2:1 Nordahl (56'), 3:1 Grahn (65' pen.)

SWE: (Coach: Georg ERICSON)
Ronnie HELLSTRÖM, Roland ANDERSSON, Roy ANDERSSON, Kent KARLSSON, Jörgen AUGUSTSSON, Anders LINDEROTH, Ove GRAHN, Eine FREDRIKSSON (Kurt OLSBERG 60'), Roland SANDBERG, Thomas NORDAHL, Benny WENDT (Jan MATTSSON 65')

NOR: (Coach: Nils Arne EGGEN)
Erik JOHANNESSEN (Tore ANTONSEN 80'), Erling MEIRIK, Helge KARLSEN, Svein GRØNDALEN, Trond PEDERSEN, Tor Egil JOHANSEN, Svein KVIA, Frode LARSEN (Stein THUNBERG 70'), Helge SKUSETH, Gabriel HØYLAND, Erik OLSEN

13 August 1975          Ref: Anders MATTSSON
(Finland)
Ullevaal Stadion, OSLO (Att. 18,011)

NORWAY - SWEDEN
0:2 (0:1)

0:1 Sandberg (29'), 0:2 Sjöberg (53')

<u>NOR:</u> (Coach: Nils Arne EGGEN)
Tore ANTONSEN, Trond PEDERSEN, Helge KARLSEN, Svein GRØNDALEN, Sigbjørn SLINNING, Jan HANSEN, Svein KVIA, Stein THUNBERG (Tor Egil JOHANSEN 80'), Frode LARSEN, Helge SKUSETH, Gabriel HØYLAND (Svein MATHISEN 68')

<u>SWE:</u> (Coach: Georg ERICSON)
Ronnie HELLSTRÖM, Roland ANDERSSON, Kent KARLSSON, Björn NORDQVIST, Jörgen AUGUSTSSON, Anders LINDEROTH, Ove GRAHN, Ralf EDSTRÖM, Roland SANDBERG, Thomas SJÖBERG, Benny WENDT (Jan MATTSSON 72')

3 September 1975      Ref: Hans-Joachim WEYLAND
(West Germany)
Windsor Park, BELFAST (Att. 14,622)

NORTHERN IRELAND - SWEDEN
1:2 (1:1)
1:0 Hunter (32'), 1:1 Sjöberg (44'), 1:2 Torstensson (55')

<u>NIR:</u> (Coach: David CLEMENTS)
Patrick JENNINGS, Patrick RICE, Samuel NELSON, David CLEMENTS, Allan HUNTER, Christopher NICHOLL, Ronald BLAIR, Bryan HAMILTON (Samuel MORGAN 70'), Derek SPENCE, Samuel McILROY, Thomas JACKSON

<u>SWE:</u> (Coach: Georg ERICSON)
Ronnie HELLSTRÖM, Roland ANDERSSON, Kent KARLSSON, Björn NORDQVIST, Jörgen AUGUSTSSON, Eine FREDRIKSSON, Conny TORSTENSSON, Anders LINDEROTH, Kurt OLSBERG (Staffan TAPPER 46'), Thomas SJÖBERG, Jan MATTSSON

15 October 1975      Ref: Walter HUNGERBÜHLER
(Switzerland)
Stadion Maksimir, ZAGREB (Att. 29,836)

YUGOSLAVIA - SWEDEN
3:0 (1:0)

1:0 Oblak (18'), 2:0 Vladić (50'), 3:0 Vabec (83')

YUG: (Coach: Ante MLADINIC)
Ognjen PETROVIĆ, Ivan BULJAN, Džemal
HADŽIABDIĆ, Branko OBLAK, Josip KATALINSKI,
Dražen MUŽINIĆ, Dragutin VABEC, Jurica JERKOVIĆ,
Ivan ŠURJAK, Franjo VLADIĆ, Dragan DŽAJIĆ

SWE: (Coach: Georg ERICSON)
Ronnie HELLSTRÖM, Roland ANDERSSON,
Kent KARLSSON, Björn NORDQVIST, Jörgen
AUGUSTSSON, Anders LINDEROTH, Staffan
TAPPER, Conny TORSTENSSON, Roland
SANDBERG, Thomas SJÖBERG (Jan MATTSSON
65'), Ralf EDSTRÖM


29 October 1975      Ref: Guðjón FINNBOGASON
(Iceland)
Windsor Park, BELFAST (Att. 8,923)

NORTHERN IRELAND - NORWAY
3:0 (2:0)

1:0 Morgan (2'), 2:0 McIlroy (5'), Hamilton (53')

NIR: (Coach: David CLEMENTS)
Patrick JENNINGS, Patrick RICE, Samuel NELSON,
Christopher NICHOLL, Allan HUNTER, Thomas
JACKSON, Bryan HAMILTON, Samuel McILROY,
Samuel MORGAN (Terence COCHRANE 59'), John
JAMISON, Thomas FINNEY

NOR: (Coach: Nils Arne EGGEN)
Geir KARLSEN (Tom Rüsz JACOBSEN 64'), Trond
PEDERSEN, Helge KARLSEN, Svein GRØNDALEN
(Børge JOSEFSEN 35'), Sigbjørn SLINNING, Jan
HANSEN, Svein KVIA, Helge SKUSETH, Gabriel
HØYLAND, Pål JACOBSEN, Harry HESTAD


19 November 1975        Ref: Antonio CAMACHO
                              Jiménez (Spain)
Stadion J.N.A., BELGRADE (Att. 21,545)

YUGOSLAVIA - NORTHERN IRELAND
1:0 (1:0)

1:0 Oblak (21')

YUG: (Coach: Ante MLADINIC)
Ognjen PETROVIĆ, Ivan BULJAN, Džemal
HADŽIABDIĆ, Branko OBLAK, Josip KATALINSKI,
Dražen MUŽINIĆ, Jurica JERKOVIĆ, Momčilo
VUKOTIĆ, Ivan ŠURJAK, Franjo VLADIĆ, Dragan
DŽAJIĆ

NIR: (Coach: David CLEMENTS)
Patrick JENNINGS, Patrick RICE, Peter SCOTT,
Christopher NICHOLL, Allan HUNTER, David
CLEMENTS, Bryan HAMILTON, Samuel McILROY,
Samuel MORGAN, Thomas JACKSON (Martin
O'NEILL 31'), Thomas FINNEY


YUGOSLAVIA(Q)        (P6,W5,D0,L1,F12,A4,Pts.10)
Northern Ireland        (P6,W3,D0,L3,F8,A5,Pts.6)
Sweden                (P6,W3,D0,L3,F8,A9,Pts.6)
Norway                (P6,W1,D0,L5,F5,A15,Pts.2)

# GROUP 4 (Denmark, Romania, Scotland, Spain)

25 September 1974         Ref: John CARPENTER
(Republic of Ireland)
Idrætsparken, COPENHAGEN (Att. 27,300)

## DENMARK - SPAIN
### 1:2 (0:2)

0:1 Claramunt (28' pen.), 0:2 Martínez (41'), 1:2 Nygaard (48' pen.)

DEN: (Coach: Rudolf STRITTICH)
Benno LARSEN, Flemming MORTENSEN, Henning Munk JENSEN, Keld SENECA, Jørgen RASMUSSEN, Niels SORENSEN (Jørgen JØRGENSEN 70'), Morten OLSEN, Kristen NYGAARD, Allan SIMONSEN, Henning JENSEN, Niels-Christian HOLMSTRØM (Ove Flindt BJERG 46')

SPA: (Coach: Ladislao KUBALA Stécz)
José Angel IRIBAR Kortajarena, Juan Cruz SOL Oria, Gregorio BENITO Rubio, José Luis CAPÓN González, Jesús MARTÍNEZ Rivadeneira, Ángel CASTELLANOS Céspedes, Juan Roberto MARTÍNEZ Martínez (Juan Antonio GARCÍA SORIANO 61'), José CLARAMUNT Torres, Enrique Castro González 'QUINI', Juan Manuel ASENSI Ripoll, MARCIAL Manuel Pina Morales

Red Card: Claramunt 62'

13 October 1974         Ref: Ferdinand BIWERSI
(West Germany)
Idrætsparken, COPENHAGEN (Att. 15,700)

## DENMARK - ROMANIA
### 0:0

<u>DEN:</u> (Coach: Rudolf STRITTICH)
Benno LARSEN, Flemming MORTENSEN, Henning Munk JENSEN, Steen DANIELSEN, Jørgen RASMUSSEN, Morten OLSEN, Jørgen JØRGENSEN, Ulrik LE FEVRE, Flemming LUND, Niels-Christian HOLMSTRØM, Benny NIELSEN

<u>ROM:</u> (Coach: Valentin STĂNESCU)
Necula RĂDUCANU, Florin CHERAN, Dumitru ANTONESCU, Alexandru SĂTMĂREANU, Teodor ANGHELINI, Ion DUMITRU, Cornel DINU, Anghel IORDĂNESCU, Mircea LUCESCU (Radu TROI 80'), Atila KUN, Radu NUNWEILLER

20 November 1974      Ref: Erich LINEMAYR (Austria)
Hampden Park, GLASGOW (Att. 94,331)

SCOTLAND - SPAIN
1:2 (1:1)

1:0 Bremner (11'), 1:1 'Quini' (36'), 1:2 'Quini' (61')

<u>SCO:</u> (Coach: William ORMOND)
David HARVEY, William JARDINE, Alexander FORSYTH, Gordon McQUEEN, Kenneth BURNS, William BREMNER, Graeme SOUNESS, Thomas HUTCHISON (Kenneth DALGLISH 64'), James JOHNSTONE, John DEANS (Peter LORIMER 64'), Joseph JORDAN

<u>SPA:</u> (Coach: Ladislao KUBALA Stécz)
José Angel IRIBAR Kortajarena, Ángel CASTELLANOS Céspedes, Gregorio BENITO Rubio, José Luis CAPÓN González, Miguel Bernardo Bianquetti 'MIGUELI' (Juan Cruz SOL Oria 75'), Enrique Álvarez COSTAS, Juan Roberto MARTÍNEZ Martínez, Ángel María VILLAR Llona, Enrique Castro González 'QUINI', Javier PLANAS Abad, Carles REXACH i Cerdà

5 February 1975    Ref: Alfred DELCOURT (Belgium)
Estadio Luís Casanova, VALENCIA (Att. 40,952)

## SPAIN - SCOTLAND
### 1:1 (0:1)

0:1 Jordan (1'), 1:1 Megido (67')

SPA: (Coach: Ladislao KUBALA Stécz)
José Angel IRIBAR Kortajarena, Juan Cruz SOL Oria,
Gregorio BENITO Rubio, José Antonio CAMACHO
Alfaro, Enrique Álvarez COSTAS (Miguel Bernardo
Bianquetti 'MIGUELI' 70'), José CLARAMUNT Torres,
Enrique Castro González 'QUINI', Ángel María VILLAR
Llona, José Eulogio GÁRATE Ormaechea (Alfredo
MEGIDO Sánchez 66'), Juan Manuel ASENSI Ripoll,
Carles REXACH i Cerdà

SCO: (Coach: William ORMOND)
David    HARVEY,    William    JARDINE,    Gordon
McQUEEN, Martin BUCHAN, Daniel McGRAIN,
William BREMNER, Charles COOKE, Thomas
HUTCHISON, Kenneth DALGLISH, Joseph JORDAN
(Derek PARLANE 80'), Kenneth BURNS (Paul
WILSON 75')


17 April 1975    Ref: Charles CORVER (Netherlands)
Estadio Santiago Bernabéu, MADRID (Att. 54,660)

## SPAIN - ROMANIA
### 1:1 (1:0)

1:0 Velázquez (6'), 1:1 Crişan (70')

SPA: (Coach: Ladislao KUBALA Stécz)
José Angel IRIBAR Kortajarena, José Antonio
CAMACHO Alfaro, Gregorio BENITO Rubio, José Luis
CAPÓN González, José Martínez Sánchez 'PIRRI',
Vicente DEL BOSQUE González, Carles REXACH

i Cerdà, Manuel VELÁZQUEZ Villaverde (Javier Iruretagoyena Amiano 'IRURETA' 46'), Carlos Alonso González 'SANTILLANA', José Eulogio GÁRATE Ormaechea, José Francisco ROJO Arroita

<u>ROM:</u> (Coach: Valentin STĂNESCU)
Necula RĂDUCANU, Florin CHERAN, Gabriel SANDU, Alexandru SĂTMĂREANU, Teodor ANGHELINI, Ilie BALACI, Ion DUMITRU, Dudu GEORGESCU, Radu NUNWEILLER (Zoltan CRIŞAN 42'), Atila KUN (Anghel IORDĂNESCU 42'), Mircea LUCESCU

11 May 1975     Ref: Nikolaos ZLATANOS (Greece)
Stadionul 23 August, BUCHAREST (Att. 60,000)

### ROMANIA - DENMARK
### 6:1 (2:0)

1:0 Georgescu (28'), 2:0 Crişan (40'), 3:0 Crişan (59'), 4:0 Georgescu (76'), 5:0 Lucescu (83'), 6:0 Dinu (85'), 6:1 Dahl (86')

<u>ROM:</u> (Coach: Valentin STĂNESCU)
Necula RĂDUCANU, Florin CHERAN, Alexandru SĂTMĂREANU, Gabriel SANDU, Teodor ANGHELINI, Ion DUMITRU (Ilie BALACI 80'), Cornel DINU, Dudu GEORGESCU, Zoltan CRIŞAN, Nicolae DOBRIN (Atila KUN 80'), Mircea LUCESCU

<u>DEN:</u> (Coach: Rudolf STRITTICH)
Benno LARSEN (Per POULSEN 21'), Flemming MORTENSEN, Henning Munk JENSEN, Lars LARSEN, Jørgen RASMUSSEN, Niels SØRENSEN (Frank NIELSEN 63'), Morten OLSEN, Jørgen JØRGENSEN, Birger MAURITZEN, Peter DAHL, Eigil NIELSEN

1 June 1975          Ref: ERTUĞRUL Dilek (Turkey)
Stadionul 23 August, BUCHAREST (Att. 52,203)

ROMANIA - SCOTLAND
1:1 (1:0)

1:0 Georgescu (21'), 1:1 McQueen (89')

ROM: (Coach: Valentin STĂNESCU)
Necula RĂDUCANU, Florin CHERAN, Alexandru
SĂTMĂREANU, Gabriel SANDU, Teodor ANGHELINI,
Ion DUMITRU, Cornel DINU, Dudu GEORGESCU
(Ilie BALACI 38'), Zoltan CRIȘAN, Nicolae DOBRIN
(Atila KUN 82'), Mircea LUCESCU

SCO: (Coach: William ORMOND)
James BROWN, Daniel McGRAIN, Alexander
FORSYTH, Francis MUNRO, Gordon McQUEEN,
Bruce RIOCH (Thomas HUTCHISON 66'), Kenneth
DALGLISH, William MILLER, Derek PARLANE, Luigi
MACARI (Robert ROBINSON 66'), Arthur DUNCAN


3 September 1975      Ref: Robert SCHAUT (Belgium)
Idrætsparken, COPENHAGEN (Att. 40,300)

DENMARK - SCOTLAND
0:1 (0:0)
0:1 Harper (51')

DEN: (Coach: Rudolf STRITTICH)
Birger JENSEN, Flemming MORTENSEN, Henning
Munk JENSEN, Lars LARSEN, Niels TUNE, Ove
Flindt BJERG, Ole BJØRNMOSE, Benny NIELSEN,
Allan SIMONSEN, Henning JENSEN, Ulrik LE FEVRE

SCO: (Coach: William ORMOND)
David HARVEY, Daniel McGRAIN, Alexander
FORSYTH, William BREMNER, Gordon McQUEEN,
Martin BUCHAN, Peter LORIMER, Kenneth

DALGLISH, Joseph HARPER, Bruce RIOCH, Thomas
HUTCHISON (Arthur DUNCAN 70')


12 October 1975          Ref: Paul BONETT (Malta)
Estadio Sarriá, BARCELONA (Att. 6,869)

### SPAIN - DENMARK
### 2:0 (1:0)

1:0 'Pirri' (40'), 2:0 Capón (85')

SPA: (Coach: Ladislao KUBALA Stécz)
MIGUEL ÁNGEL González Suárez, José Antonio
RAMOS Huete, Gregorio BENITO Rubio, José Luis
CAPÓN González, Miguel Bernardo Bianquetti
'MIGUELI', MARCIAL Manuel Pina Morales, Daniel
SOLSONA Puig, José Martínez Sánchez 'PIRRI',
Carlos Alonso González 'SANTILLANA', Vicente DEL
BOSQUE González (Juan Manuel ASENSI Ripoll 46'),
Carles REXACH i Cerdà (José Ignacio CHURRUCA
Sistiaga 66')

DEN: (Coach: Rudolf STRITTICH)
Benno LARSEN, John HANSEN, Henning Munk
JENSEN, Lars LARSEN, John ANDERSEN, Niels
SØRENSEN (Carsten NIELSEN 46'), Ove Flindt
BJERG, Heino HANSEN, Ole RASMUSSEN, Lars
BASTRUP, Peter DAHL


29 October 1975          Ref: Rolf NYHUS (Norway)
Hampden Park, GLASGOW (Att. 48,021)

### SCOTLAND - DENMARK
### 3:1 (0:1)

0:1 Bastrup (20'), 1:1 Dalglish (48'), 2:1 Rioch (54'),
3:1 MacDougall (61')

SCO: (Coach: William ORMOND)
David HARVEY, Daniel McGRAIN, Stewart
HOUSTON, John GREIG, Colin JACKSON, Bruce
RIOCH, Peter LORIMER, Kenneth DALGLISH,
Edward MACDOUGALL (Derek PARLANE 85'),
Richard HARTFORD, Archibald GEMMILL

DEN: (Coach: Rudolf STRITTICH)
Benno LARSEN, John ANDERSEN, Henning Munk
JENSEN, Lars LARSEN, John HANSEN, Heino
HANSEN, Niels TUNE (Frank NIELSEN 70'), Niels
SØRENSEN, Kristen NYGAARD, Lars BASTRUP,
Jens KOLDING

16 November 1975     Ref: Hans-Joachim WEYLAND
(West Germany)
Stadionul 23 August, BUCHAREST (Att. 45,381)

ROMANIA - SPAIN
2:2 (0:1)

0:1 Villar (29'), 0:2 'Santillana' (57'), 1:2 Georgescu
(72' pen.),  2:2 Iordănescu (80')

ROM: (Coach: Valentin STĂNESCU)
Necula RĂDUCANU, Teodor ANGHELINI, Alexandru
SĂTMĂREANU, Gabriel SANDU, Teodor LUCUȚĂ,
Dudu GEORGESCU, Cornel DINU, Nicolae
DOBRIN, Mircea LUCESCU, Mircea SANDU (Anghel
IORDĂNESCU 46'), Constantin ZAMFIR (Zoltan
CRIȘAN 61')

SPA: (Coach: Ladislao KUBALA Stécz)
MIGUEL ÁNGEL González Suárez, Juan Cruz SOL
Oria, Gregorio BENITO Rubio, José Antonio CAMACHO
Alfaro, Miguel Bernardo Bianquetti 'MIGUELI', José
Martínez Sánchez 'PIRRI', Enrique Castro González
'QUINI' (Jesús María SATRÚSTEGUI Azpiroz 88'),

Ángel María VILLAR Llona, Carlos Alonso González 'SANTILLANA', Vicente DEL BOSQUE González, José Francisco ROJO Arroita (Francisco FORTES Calvo 76')


17 December 1975          Ref: Adolf PROKOP
                                              (East Germany)
Hampden Park, GLASGOW (Att. 11,375)

### SCOTLAND - ROMANIA
### 1:1 (1:0)

1:0 Rioch (39'), 1:1 Crişan (74')

SCO: (Coach: William ORMOND)
James CRUICKSHANK, John BROWNLIE, William DONACHIE, Martin BUCHAN, Colin JACKSON, Bruce RIOCH, John DOYLE (Peter LORIMER 73'), Richard HARTFORD, Andrew GRAY, Kenneth DALGLISH (Edward MACDOUGALL 73'), Archibald GEMMILL

ROM: (Coach: Cornel DRĂGUŞIN)
Necula RĂDUCANU, Florin CHERAN, Alexandru SĂTMĂREANU, Gabriel SANDU, Teodor ANGHELINI, Mihai ROMILĂ (Iuliu HAJNAL 58'), Ladislau BÖLÖNI, Mircea LUCESCU (Zoltan CRIŞAN 60'), Dudu GEORGESCU, Anghel IORDĂNESCU, Cornel DINU


| | |
|---|---|
| SPAIN (Q) | (P6, W3, D3, L0, F10, A6, Pts. 9) |
| Romania | (P6, W1, D5, L0, F11, A6, Pts. 7) |
| Scotland | (P6, W2, D3, L1, F8, A6, Pts. 7) |
| Denmark | (P6, W0, D1, L5, F3, A14, Pts. 1) |


GROUP 5 (Finland, Italy, Netherlands, Poland)


1 September 1974          Ref: John PATERSON

Richard Keir
(Scotland)

Olympiastadion, HELSINKI (Att. 18,759)

## FINLAND - POLAND
## 1:2 (1:1)

1:0 Rahja (3'), 1:1 Szarmach (23'), 1:2 Lato (50')

FIN: (Coach: Olavi LAAKSONEN)
Pertti ALAJA, Henry FORSSELL, Arto TOLSA, Erkki
VIHTILÄ, Esko RANTA, Jouko SUOMALAINEN, Timo
RAHJA (Antero NIKKANEN 81'), Aki HEISKAINEN,
Miikka TOIVOLA, Matti PAATELAINEN (Jarmo
MANNINEN 64'), Juha-Pekka LAINE

POL: (Coach: Kazimierz GÓRSKI)
Jan TOMASZEWSKI, Antoni SZYMANOWSKI, Jerzy
GORGOŃ, Mirosław BULZACKI, Adam MUSIAŁ,
Henryk KASPERCZAK (Marek KUSTO 77'), Lesław
ĆMIKIEWICZ, Zygmunt MASZCZYK, Grzegorz LATO,
Andrzej SZARMACH, Robert GADOCHA

25 September 1974          Ref: Wolfgang RIEDEL
(East Germany)
Olympiastadion, HELSINKI (Att. 20,449)

## FINLAND - NETHERLANDS
## 1:3 (1:2)

1:0 Rahja (16'), 1:1 Cruijff (28'), 1:2 Cruijff (40'), 1:3
Neeskens (51' pen.)

FIN: (Coach: Olavi LAAKSONEN)
Harri HOLLI, Raimo SAARI, Arto TOLSA, Erkki
VIHTILÄ, Esko RANTA, Jouko SUOMALAINEN,
Aki HEISKAINEN (Olavi RISSANEN 60'), Raimo
HUKKA (Miikka TOIVOLA 54'), Timo RAHJA, Rutger
PETTERSON, Juha-Pekka LAINE

NET: (Coach: Georg KNOBEL)

Jan JONGBLOED, Cornelius VAN IERSSEL, Adrianus HAAN, Theodorus DE JONG, Rudolf KROL, Wilhelmus JANSEN, Johannes NEESKENS, Willem VAN HANEGEM (Reinirus NOTTEN 46'), Peter RESSEL, Johannes CRUIJFF, John REP (Geertruida GEELS 66')


9 October 1974        Ref: Dušan MAKSIMOVIĆ
(Yugoslavia)
Stadion Warty, POZNAŃ (Att. 38,724)

### POLAND - FINLAND
### 3:0 (2:0)

1:0 Kasperczak (12'), 2:0 Gadocha (14'), 3:0 Lato (53')


POL: (Coach: Kazimierz GÓRSKI)
Jan TOMASZEWSKI, Antoni SZYMANOWSKI, Marian OSTAFIŃSKI, Jerzy WYROBEK, Piotr DRZEWIECKI, Henryk KASPERCZAK (Roman JAKÓBCZAK 53'), Kazimierz DEYNA, Bronisław BULA, Grzegorz LATO, Andrzej SZARMACH (Joachim MARX 74'), Robert GADOCHA

FIN: (Coach: Olavi LAAKSONEN)
Harri HOLLI, Raimo SAARI, Arto TOLSA, Erkki VIHTILÄ, Esko RANTA, Jouko SUOMALAINEN, Aki HEISKAINEN (Rutger PETTERSON 46'), Timo RAHJA, Miikka TOIVOLA, Matti PAATELAINEN (Juha-Pekka LAINE 46'), Olavi RISSANEN


20 November 1974      Ref: Pavel KAZAKOV (USSR)
Feyenoord Stadion, ROTTERDAM (Att. 58,463)

### NETHERLANDS - ITALY
### 3:1 (1:1)

0:1 Boninsegna (5'), 1:1 Rensenbrink (24'), 2:1 Cruijff

Richard Keir

(64'), 3:1 Cruijff (80')

NET: (Coach: Georg KNOBEL)
Jan JONGBLOED, Wilhelmus SUURBIER, Rudolf KROL, Johannes NEESKENS, Wilhelmus RIJSBERGEN, Adrianus HAAN, John REP (Wilhelmus VAN DE KERKHOF 46'), Wilhelmus VAN DER KUIJLEN, Johannes CRUIJFF, Willem VAN HANEGEM, Robert RENSENBRINK

ITA: (Coach: Fulvio BERNARDINI)
Dino ZOFF, Francesco ROCCA, Moreno ROGGI, Andrea ORLANDINI, Francesco MORINI, Luciano ZECCHINI, Franco CAUSIO, Antonio JULIANO, Roberto BONINSEGNA, Giancarlo ANTOGNONI, Pietro ANASTASI

19 April 1975          Ref: Robert HÉLIÈS (France)
Stadio Olimpico, ROME (Att. 66,048)
ITALY - POLAND
0:0

ITA: (Coach: Fulvio BERNARDINI)
Dino ZOFF, Claudio GENTILE, Francesco ROCCA, Franco CORDOVA, Mauro BELLUGI, Giacinto FACCHETTI, Francesco GRAZIANI, Giorgio MORINI, Giorgio CHINAGLIA, Giancarlo ANTOGNONI, Paolo PULICI

POL: (Coach: Kazimierz GÓRSKI)
Jan TOMASZEWSKI, Antoni SZYMANOWSKI, Jerzy GORGOŃ, Władysław ŻMUDA, Henryk WAWROWSKI, Zygmunt MASZCZYK, Kazimierz DEYNA, Henryk KASPERCZAK (Lesław ĆMIKIEWICZ 46'), Grzegorz LATO, Andrzej SZARMACH, Robert GADOCHA

5 June 1975               Ref: Walter ESCHWEILER
                                    (West Germany)
Olympiastadion, HELSINKI (Att. 17,732)

FINLAND - ITALY
0:1 (0:1)

0:1 Chinaglia (26' pen.)

FIN: (Coach: Aulis RYTKÖNEN)
Göran ENCKELMAN, Erkki VIHTILÄ, Arto TOLSA, Matti
PAATELAINEN, Esko RANTA, Jouko SUOMALAINEN,
Pauno KYMÄLÄINEN (Olavi RISSANEN 46'), Jarmo
MANNINEN, Juha-Pekka LAINE (Kalle NIEMINEN
77'), Miikka TOIVOLA, Aki HEISKAINEN

ITA: (Coach: Fulvio BERNARDINI)
Dino ZOFF, Claudio GENTILE, Francesco ROCCA,
Franco CORDOVA (Andrea ORLANDINI 46'),
Mauro BELLUGI, Giacinto FACCHETTI, Francesco
GRAZIANI, Giancarlo ANTOGNONI, Giorgio
CHINAGLIA, Fabio CAPELLO, Roberto BETTEGA

3 September 1975               Ref: Eric SMYTON
                                    (Northern Ireland)
Goffertstadion, NIJMEGEN (Att. 19,189)

NETHERLANDS - FINLAND
4:1 (2:1)

0:1 Paatelainen (9'), 1:1 Van der Kuijlen (29'), 2:1 Van der
Kuijlen (35'),  3:1 Lubse (48'), 4:1 Van der Kuijlen (55')

NET: (Coach: Georg KNOBEL)
Jan VAN BEVEREN, Wilhelmus SUURBIER, Adrianus
VAN KRAAIJ, Cornelis OVERWEG, Rudolf KROL,
Wilhelmus JANSEN, Johannes PETERS, Willem VAN
HANEGEM, Reinier VAN DE KERKHOF, Heinricus
LUBSE, Wilhelmus VAN DER KUIJLEN

FIN: (Coach: Aulis RYTKÖNEN)
Göran ENCKELMAN, Erkki VIHTILÄ, Matti PAATELAINEN, Henry FORSSELL, Esko RANTA, Jouko SUOMALAINEN, Aki HEISKAINEN (Pertti JANTUNEN 78'), Olavi RISSANEN, Ari MÄKYNEN, Eero RISSANEN, Hannu HÄMÄLÄINEN (Juha-Pekka LAINE 50')

10 September 1975          Ref: Patrick PARTRIDGE
                                          (England)
Stadion Śląski, CHORZÓW (Att. 70,409)

POLAND - NETHERLANDS
4:1 (2:0)

1:0 Lato (14'), 2:0 Gadocha (44'), 3:0 Szarmach (63'),
    4:0 Szarmach (77'), 4:1 Van de Kerkhof (80')

POL: (Coach: Kazimierz GÓRSKI)
Jan TOMASZEWSKI, Antoni SZYMANOWSKI, Władysław ŻMUDA, Mirosław BULZACKI, Henryk WAWROWSKI, Henryk KASPERCZAK, Kazimierz DEYNA, Zygmunt MASZCZYK, Grzegorz LATO, Andrzej SZARMACH, Robert GADOCHA

NET: (Coach: Georg KNOBEL)
Jan VAN BEVEREN, Wilhelmus SUURBIER, Adrianus VAN KRAAIJ, Cornelis OVERWEG, Rudolf KROL, Wilhelmus JANSEN, Willem VAN HANEGEM (Geertruida GEELS 46'), Johannes NEESKENS, Wilhelmus VAN DER KUIJLEN, Johannes CRUIJFF, Reinier VAN DE KERKHOF

27 September 1975   Ref: Konstantinos XANTHOULIS
                                          (Cyprus)
Stadio Olimpico, ROME (Att. 29,203)

ITALY - FINLAND

## 0:0

ITA: (Coach: Vicenzo BEARZOT)
Dino ZOFF, Francesco ROCCA, Moreno ROGGI, Romeo BENETTI, Mauro BELLUGI, Giacinto FACCHETTI, Francesco GRAZIANI, Eraldo PECCI, Giuseppe SAVOLDI, Giancarlo ANTOGNONI, Giorgio MORINI

FIN: (Coach: Aulis RYTKÖNEN)
Göran ENCKELMAN, Erkki VIHTILÄ, Matti PAATELAINEN, Arto TOLSA, Esko RANTA, Jouko SUOMALAINEN, Aki HEISKAINEN, Pertti JANTUNEN, Olavi RISSANEN (Hannu HÄMÄLÄINEN 1'), Ari MÄKYNEN (Timo KAUTONEN 28'), Miikka TOIVOLA

15 October 1975       Ref: Károly PALOTAI (Hungary)
Olympisch Stadion, AMSTERDAM (Att. 56,030)

### NETHERLANDS - POLAND
### 3:0 (1:0)

1:0 Neeskens (16'), 2:0 Geels (47'), 3:0 Thijssen (59')

NET: (Coach: Georg KNOBEL)
Pieter SCHRIJVERS, Wilhelmus SUURBIER, Adrianus VAN KRAAIJ, Cornelus KRIJGH, Rudolf KROL, Wilhelmus JANSEN, Franciscus THIJSSEN, Johannes NEESKENS, Geertruida GEELS, Johannes CRUIJFF, Reinier VAN DE KERKHOF

POL: (Coach: Kazimierz GÓRSKI)
Jan TOMASZEWSKI, Antoni SZYMANOWSKI, Mirosław BULZACKI, Władysław ŻMUDA, Henryk WAWROWSKI, Henryk KASPERCZAK, Kazimierz DEYNA, Zygmunt MASZCZYK (Bronisław BULA 67'), Grzegorz LATO, Andrzej SZARMACH, Robert GADOCHA

26 October 1975      Ref: Paul SCHILLER (Austria)
Stadion Dziesięciolecia, WARSAW (Att. 59,773)

### POLAND - ITALY
### 0:0

POL: (Coach: Kazimierz GÓRSKI)
Jan  TOMASZEWSKI,  Antoni  SZYMANOWSKI,
Marian OSTAFIŃSKI, Władysław ŻMUDA, Henryk
WAWROWSKI, Henryk KASPERCZAK, Kazimierz
DEYNA, Bronisław BULA (Joachim MARX 59'),
Grzegorz  LATO,  Andrzej  SZARMACH,  Robert
GADOCHA (Kazimierz KMIECIK 78')

ITA: (Coach: Vicenzo BEARZOT)
Dino ZOFF, Claudio GENTILE, Francesco ROCCA,
Antonello CUCCUREDDU, Mauro BELLUGI, Giacinto
FACCHETTI, Franco CAUSIO, Romeo BENETTI,
Pietro ANASTASI (Roberto BETTEGA 67'), Giancarlo
ANTOGNONI (Renato ZACCARELLI 87'), Paolo
PULICI


22 November 1975     Ref: Robert SCHAUT (Belgium)
Stadio Olimpico, ROME (Att. 33,307)

### ITALY - NETHERLANDS
### 1:0 (1:0)

1:0 Capello (20')

ITA: (Coach: Vicenzo BEARZOT)
Dino  ZOFF,  Claudio  GENTILE,  Francesco
ROCCA,  Romeo  BENETTI,  Mauro  BELLUGI,
Giacinto FACCHETTI, Franco CAUSIO, Giancarlo
ANTOGNONI, Giuseppe SAVOLDI, Fabio CAPELLO,
Paolo PULICI

NET: (Coach: Georg KNOBEL)
Pieter SCHRIJVERS, Wilhelmus SUURBIER, Rudolf

KROL, Wilhelmus JANSEN, Cornelus KRIJGH, Adrianus VAN KRAAIJ, Wilhelmus VAN DE KERKHOF (Reinirus NOTTEN 70'), Johannes PETERS, Geertruida GEELS, Franciscus THIJSSEN, Reinier VAN DE KERKHOF

| | |
|---|---|
| NETHERLANDS(Q) | (P6,W4,D0,L2,F14,A8,Pts.8) |
| Poland | (P6, W3, D2, L1, F9, A5, Pts. 8) |
| Italy | (P6, W2, D3, L1, F3, A3, Pts. 7) |
| Finland | (P6, W0, D1, L5, F3, A13, Pts. 1) |

### GROUP 6 (Republic of Ireland, Switzerland, Turkey, USSR)

30 October 1974          Ref: Erik AXELRYD (Sweden)
Dalymount Park, DUBLIN (Att. 31,758)

### REPUBLIC OF IRELAND - USSR
### 3:0 (2:0)

1:0 Givens (22'), 2:0 Givens (30'), 3:0 Givens (70')

EIR: (Coach: John GILES)
Patrick ROCHE, Joseph KINNEAR, Patrick MULLIGAN, Terence MANCINI, James HOLMES, Michael MARTIN, John GILES, William BRADY, Stephen HEIGHWAY, Raymond TREACY, Daniel GIVENS

URS: (Coach: Konstantin BESKOV)
Vladimir PILGUIY, Sergeiy NIKULIN, Sergeiy OLSHANSKIY, Viktor MATVIENKO, Vladimir KAPLICHNIY, Evgeniy LOVCHEV, Vladimir FEDOTOV (Vladimir FYODOROV 59'), Vladimir ONISHCHENKO, Viktor KOLOTOV, Vladimir VEREMEEV, Oleg BLOKHIN

Red Card: Mancini 32'; Kaplichniy 32'

20 November 1974          Ref: Marian SRODECKI
                                        (Poland)
Atatürk Stadi, IZMIR (Att. 67,500)

### TURKEY - REPUBLIC OF IRELAND
### 1:1 (0:0)

1:0 Dunne (54' og), 1:1 Givens (61')

TUR: (Coach: COŞKUN Özari)
YASIN Özdenak, ALPASLAN Eratli, ISMAIL Arca,
ZIYA Şengül, ZEKERIYA Alp, SELÇUK Yalçıntaş,
ENGIN Verel, MEHMET Türken (OSMAN Arpacioğlu
80'), MEHMET Oğuz, CEMIL Turan, METIN Kurt

EIR: (Coach: John GILES)
Patrick   ROCHE,   Joseph   KINNEAR,   Patrick
MULLIGAN, Eoin HAND, Anthony DUNNE, Michael
MARTIN, John GILES, William BRADY, Stephen
HEIGHWAY, Daniel GIVENS, Terence CONROY
(Jeremiah DENNEHY 86')


1 December 1974          Ref: Milivoje GUGULOVIĆ
                                        (Yugoslavia)
Atatürk Stadi, IZMIR (Att. 51,410)

### TURKEY - SWITZERLAND
### 2:1 (1:1)

0:1 Schild (18'), 1:1 İsmail (21'), 2:1 Mehmet Oğuz (85')

TUR: (Coach: COŞKUN Özari)
YASIN Özdenak, ALPASLAN Eratli, ISMAIL Arca,
ZIYA Şengül, ZEKERIYA Alp, ENGIN Verel, MEHMET
Özgül, SELÇUK Yalçıntaş (RAŞIT Karasu 46'),
OSMAN Arpacioğlu (MEHMET Oğuz 75'), CEMIL
Turan, METIN Kurt

SWI: (Coach: René HÜSSY)

Erich BURGENER, Gilbert GUYOT, René HASLER, Lucio BIZZINI, René BOTTERON, Hanspeter SCHILD, Jakob KUHN, Rudolf SCHNEEBERGER, Hans-Jörg PFISTER (Ernst RUTSCHMANN 58'), Daniel JEANDUPEUX, Kurt MÜLLER

2 April 1975        Ref: Robert DAVIDSON (Scotland)
Tsentralniy Stadion, KIEV (Att. 74,223)

### USSR - TURKEY
### 3:0 (1:0)

1:0 Kolotov (25' pen.), 2:0 Kolotov (56' pen.), 3:0 Blokhin (75')

URS: (Coach: Valeriy LOBANOVSKIY)
Evgeniy RUDAKOV, Anatoliy KONKOV (Leonid BURYAK 65'), Viktor MATVIENKO, Mikhail FOMENKO, Stefan RESHKO, Vladimir TROSHKIN, Vladimir MUNTYAN, Vladimir ONISHCHENKO (Vladimir FYODOROV 80'), Viktor KOLOTOV, Vladimir VEREMEEV, Oleg BLOKHIN

TUR: (Coach: COŞKUN Özari)
SABRI Dino, KEMAL Batmaz, ISMAIL Arca, ZIYA Şengül, ALPASLAN Eratli, ZAFER Göncüler, ENGIN Verel, RAŞIT Karasu, ALI KEMAL Denizci, CEMIL Turan, METIN Kurt (TUNCAY Temeller 69')

30 April 1975        Ref: Riccardo LATTANZI (Italy)
Hardturm Stadion, ZÜRICH (Att. 21,965)

### SWITZERLAND - TURKEY
### 1:1 (1:0)

1:0 İsmail (43' og), 1:1 Alpaslan (54')

SWI: (Coach: René HÜSSY)

Hans KÜNG, Gilbert GUYOT, Max HEER, Lucio BIZZINI, Pius FISCHBACH, Ernst RUTSCHMANN (Hans-Jörg PFISTER 70'), René HASLER (Hanspeter SCHILD 70'), René BOTTERON, Kurt MÜLLER, Daniel JEANDUPEUX, Rudolf ELSENER

TUR: (Coach: COŞKUN Özari)
YASIN Özdenak, ALPASLAN Eratli, ISMAIL Arca, ZIYA Şengül, ZEKERIYA Alp, FATIH Terim, NIKO Kovi, ENGIN Verel, ALI KEMAL Denizci (AYDIN Çelik 46'), GÖKMEN Özdenak, CEMIL Turan


10 May 1975          Ref: Paul SCHILLER (Austria)
Lansdowne Road, DUBLIN (Att. 48,074)

### REPUBLIC OF IRELAND - SWITZERLAND
### 2:1 (2:0)

1:0 Martin (2'), 2:0 Treacy (28'), 2:1 Müller (74')

EIR: (Coach: John GILES)
Patrick ROCHE, Joseph KINNEAR, Patrick MULLIGAN, Eoin HAND, Anthony DUNNE, Michael MARTIN, John GILES, William BRADY, Terence CONROY, Raymond TREACY, Daniel GIVENS

SWI: (Coach: René HÜSSY)
Erich BURGENER, Gilbert GUYOT, René HASLER, Lucio BIZZINI, Max HEER, René BOTTERON, Jakob KUHN, Ernst RUTSCHMANN, Hanspeter SCHILD, Daniel JEANDUPEUX, Kurt MÜLLER


18 May 1975          Ref: René VIGLIANI (France)
Tsentralniy Stadion, KIEV (Att. 84,480)

### USSR - REPUBLIC OF IRELAND
### 2:1 (2:0)

1:0 Blokhin (13'), 2:0 Kolotov (29'), 2:1 Hand (79')

<u>URS:</u> (Coach: Valeriy LOBANOVSKIY)
Evgeniy RUDAKOV, Anatoliy KONKOV, Viktor MATVIENKO, Mikhail FOMENKO, Leonid BURYAK, Vladimir TROSHKIN, Vladimir MUNTYAN (Stefan RESHKO 46'), Vladimir ONISHCHENKO, Viktor KOLOTOV, Vladimir VEREMEEV (Vladimir FYODOROV 84'), Oleg BLOKHIN

<u>EIR:</u> (Coach: John GILES)
Patrick ROCHE, Joseph KINNEAR, Patrick MULLIGAN, Eoin HAND, Anthony DUNNE, Michael MARTIN, John GILES, William BRADY, Stephen HEIGHWAY, Daniel GIVENS, Terence CONROY


21 May 1975          Ref: César da Luz Dias CORREIA
(Portugal)

Wankdorf Stadion, BERNE (Att. 12,793)

SWITZERLAND - REPUBLIC OF IRELAND
1:0 (0:0)

1:0 Elsener (75')

<u>SWI:</u> (Coach: René HUSSY)
Erich BURGENER, Gilbert GUYOT, Lucio BIZZINI, Serge TRINCHERO, Pius FISCHBACH, Jakob KUHN, René HASLER, René BOTTERON, Ernst RUTSCHMANN (Hans-Jörg PFISTER 46'), Kurt MÜLLER (Rudolf ELSENER 70'), Daniel JEANDUPEUX

<u>EIR:</u> (Coach: John GILES)
Patrick ROCHE, Anthony DUNNE, Patrick MULLIGAN, Eoin HAND, James HOLMES, Michael MARTIN, John GILES (Gerard DALY 79'), William BRADY, Terence CONROY, Raymond TREACY, Daniel GIVENS

Richard Keir

12 October 1975    Ref: Leonardus VAN DER KROFT
(Netherlands)
Hardturm Stadion, ZÜRICH (Att. 17,887)

SWITZERLAND - USSR
0:1 (0:0)

0:1 Muntyan (78')

SWI: (Coach: René HÜSSY)
Erich BURGENER, Gilbert GUYOT, Lucio BIZZINI,
Serge TRINCHERO (Rudolf SCHNEEBERGER 75'),
Pius FISCHBACH, Kurt MÜLLER, Jakob KUHN, René
BOTTERON (Alfred SCHEIWILER 75'), Hans-Jörg
PFISTER, Peter RISI, Daniel JEANDUPEUX

URS: (Coach: Valeriy LOBANOVSKIY)
Evgeniy RUDAKOV, Anatoliy KONKOV, Evgeniy
LOVCHEV, Mikhail FOMENKO, Viktor ZVYAGINTSEV,
Vladimir TROSHKIN (Stefan RESHKO 31'), Vladimir
MUNTYAN, Vladimir ONISHCHENKO, Leonid
BURYAK (Vladimir SAKHAROV 68'), Vladimir
VEREMEEV, Oleg BLOKHIN


29 October 1975      Ref: Ángel FRANCO Martínez
(Spain)
Dalymount Park, DUBLIN (Att. 25,000)

REPUBLIC OF IRELAND - TURKEY
4:0 (3:0)

1:0 Givens (26'), 2:0 Givens (33'), 3:0 Givens (38'),
4:0 Givens (89')

EIR: (Coach: John GILES)
Patrick ROCHE, Anthony DUNNE (Joseph KINNEAR
83'), Patrick MULLIGAN, Eoin HAND, James
HOLMES, Michael MARTIN, John GILES, William
BRADY, Stephen HEIGHWAY (Terence CONROY
46'), Raymond TREACY, Daniel GIVENS

TUR: (Coach: COŞKUN Özari)
YASIN Özdenak (RASIM Kara 39'), SABAHATTIN Erbuğa, FATIH Terim, ISMAIL Arca (ZAFER Göncüler 34'), ENGIN Verel, NECATI Özçağlayan, ALI KEMAL Denizci, GÖKMEN Özdenak, CEMIL Turan, KADRI Özcan, ALPASLAN Eratli

Red Card: Martin 79'; Alpaslan 79'


12 November 1975             Ref: Klaus OHMSEN
                                    (West Germany)
Tsentralniy Stadion, KIEV (Att. 24,581)

### USSR - SWITZERLAND
### 4:1 (2:1)

1:0 Konkov (13'), 2:0 Onischenko (14'), 2:1 Risi (45'), 3:1 Onischenko (68'), 4:1 Veremeev (81')

URS: (Coach: Valeriy LOBANOVSKIY)
Evgeniy RUDAKOV, Anatoliy KONKOV (Vladimir SAKHAROV 75'), Evgeniy LOVCHEV, Mikhail FOMENKO, Viktor ZVYAGINTSEV, Vladimir TROSHKIN, Vladimir MUNTYAN (Viktor KOLOTOV 65'), Vladimir ONISHCHENKO, Leonid BURYAK, Vladimir VEREMEEV, Oleg BLOKHIN

SWI: (Coach: René HUSSY)
Erich BURGENER, Gilbert GUYOT, Lucio BIZZINI, Serge TRINCHERO, Pius FISCHBACH, René BOTTERON, Jakob KUHN, Rudolf SCHNEEBERGER, Kurt MÜLLER, Peter RISI, Daniel JEANDUPEUX


23 November 1975             Ref: Petar NIKOLOV
                                    (Bulgaria)
Atatürk Stadi, IZMIR (Att. 21,325)

## TURKEY - USSR
### 1:0 (1:0)

1:0 Reshko (22' og)

TUR: (Coach: COŞKUN Özari)
RASIM Kara, TURGAY Semercioğlu, SABAHATTIN
Erbuğa, ISMAIL Arca, KADRI Özcan, ALI Yavaş,
MEHMET Türken (ORHAN Özselek 90'), FATIH Terim,
GÖKMEN Özdenak (NURI HÜSEYIN Tok 89'), CEMIL
Turan, ALI KEMAL Denizci

URS: (Coach: Valeriy LOBANOVSKIY)
Evgeniy RUDAKOV, Anatoliy KONKOV, Valeriy
ZUEV, Mikhail FOMENKO, Stefan RESHKO, Viktor
ZVYAGINTSEV, Vladimir MUNTYAN (Leonid BURYAK
61'), Vladimir ONISHCHENKO, Viktor KOLOTOV,
Vladimir VEREMEEV, Oleg BLOKHIN

| | |
|---|---|
| USSR (Q) | (P6, W4, D0, L2, F10, A6, Pts. 8) |
| Republic of Ireland | (P6, W3, D1, L2, F11, A5, Pts. 7) |
| Turkey | (P6, W2, D2, L2, F5, A10, Pts. 6) |
| Switzerland | (P6, W1, D1, L4, F5, A10, Pts. 3) |

GROUP 7 (Belgium, East Germany, France, Iceland)

8 September 1974          Ref: Thomas REYNOLDS
(Wales)
Laugardalsvöllur, REYKJAVÍK (Att. 7,540)

### ICELAND - BELGIUM
### 0:2 (0:1)

0:1 Van Moer (38'), 0:2 Teugels (87' pen.)

ICE: (Coach: Anthony KNAPP)
Þorsteinn ÓLAFSSON, Gísli TORFASON, Jón

PÉTURSSON, Marteinn GEIRSSON, Jóhannes
EÐVALDSSON, Karl HERMANNSSON, Guðgeir
LEIFSSON, Grétar MAGNÚSSON, Ásgeir ELÍASSON
(Matthías HALLGRÍMSSON 50'), Teitur ÞÓRÐARSON,
Ásgeir SIGURVINSSON

BEL: (Coach: Raymond GOETHALS)
Christian PIOT, Gilbert VAN BINST, Hugo BROOS,
Erwin VANDENDAELE, Ludo COECK (Julien COOLS
46'), Jan VERHEYEN, Wilfried VAN MOER, Paul VAN
HIMST, François VAN DER ELST, Jean JANSSENS
(Jacques TEUGELS 84'), Roger HENROTAY


12 October 1974      Ref: Svein Inge THIME (Norway)
Ernst-Grube-Stadion, MAGDEBURG (Att. 15,800)

### EAST GERMANY - ICELAND
### 1:1 (1:1)

1:0 Hoffmann (7'), 1:1 Hallgrímsson (25')

EGR: (Coach: Georg BUSCHNER)
Ulrich SCHULZE, Manfred ZAPF, Konrad WEISE,
Bernd BRANSCH, Siegmar WÄTZLICH (Hans-
Jürgen DÖRNER 55'), Lothar KURBJUWEIT, Jürgen
POMMERENKE (Eberhard VOGEL 71'), Klaus
DECKER, Joachim STREICH, Peter DUCKE, Martin
HOFFMANN

ICE: (Coach: Anthony KNAPP)
Þorsteinn ÓLAFSSON, Gísli TORFASON (Eiríkur
ÞORSTEINSSON 67'), Jón PÉTURSSON, Marteinn
GEIRSSON, Jóhannes EÐVALDSSON, Guðgeir
LEIFSSON, Grétar MAGNÚSSON, Ásgeir ELÍASSON,
Ásgeir SIGURVINSSON, Teitur ÞÓRÐARSON (Atli
HÉÐINSSON 83'), Matthías HALLGRÍMSSON

12 October 1974        Ref: Kenneth BURNS (England)
Stade du Heysel, BRUSSELS (Att. 32,108)

### BELGIUM - FRANCE
### 2:1 (1:1)

1:0 Martens (12'), 1:1 Coste (16'), 2:1 Van der Elst (75')

BEL: (Coach: Raymond GOETHALS)
Christian PIOT, Gilbert VAN BINST, Hugo BROOS,
Erwin VANDENDAELE, Maurice MARTENS, Wilfried
VAN MOER, Jan VERHEYEN, Paul VAN HIMST
(Jean DOCKX 71'), François VAN DER ELST, Raoul
LAMBERT, Jacques TEUGELS

FRA: (Coach: Ştefan KOVÁCS)
Dominique BARATELLI, Jean-François JODAR, Jean-
Pierre ADAMS, Marius TRÉSOR, François BRACCI,
Jean-Noël HUCK, Henri MICHEL, Jean-Marc
GUILLOU, Christian COSTE, Bernard LACOMBE
(Jean GALLICE 83'), Georges BERETA


16 November 1974        Ref: Pablo Augusto SÁNCHEZ
                               Ibáñez (Spain)
Parc des Princes, PARIS (Att. 45,381)

### FRANCE - EAST GERMANY
### 2:2 (0:1)

0:1 Sparwasser (25'), 0:2 Kreische (57'), 1:2 Guillou
(79'), 2:2 Gallice (89')

FRA: (Coach: Ştefan KOVÁCS)
Jean-Paul BERTRAND-DEMANES, Jean-François
JODAR, Jean-Pierre ADAMS, Marius TRÉSOR,
François BRACCI, Jean-Noël HUCK, Henri MICHEL
(Christian SYNAEGHEL 65'), Jean-Marc GUILLOU,
Gérard SOLER, Christian COSTE (Jean GALLICE
46'), Georges BERETA

EGR: (Coach: Georg BUSCHNER)
Jürgen CROY, Hans-Jürgen DÖRNER, Gerd KISCHE,
Konrad WEISE, Siegmar WÄTZLICH, Reinhard
HÄFNER, Lothar KURBJUWEIT, Reinhard LAUCK,
Hans-Jürgen KREISCHE (Wolfgang SEGUIN 83'),
Jürgen SPARWASSER, Martin HOFFMANN

Red Card: Soler 86'


7 December 1974          Ref: Sergio GONELLA (Italy)
Zentralstadion, LEIPZIG (Att. 20,557)

### EAST GERMANY - BELGIUM
### 0:0

EGR: (Coach: Georg BUSCHNER)
Jürgen CROY, Hans-Jürgen DÖRNER, Gerd
KISCHE, Konrad WEISE, Siegmar WÄTZLICH (Hans-
Jürgen KREISCHE 70'), Reinhard LAUCK, Reinhard
HÄFNER, Lothar KURBJUWEIT, Martin HOFFMANN,
Joachim STREICH, Eberhard VOGEL

BEL: (Coach: Raymond GOETHALS)
Christian PIOT, Gilbert VAN BINST, Hugo BROOS,
Erwin VANDENDAELE, Maurice MARTENS, Julien
COOLS, Nicolas DEWALQUE, Jan VERHEYEN, Paul
VAN HIMST (François VAN DER ELST 15'), Raoul
LAMBERT, Jacques TEUGELS


25 May 1975                Ref: Malcolm WRIGHT
                              (Northern Ireland)
Laugardalsvöllur, REYKJAVÍK (Att. 7,613)

### ICELAND - FRANCE
### 0:0

ICE: (Coach: Anthony KNAPP)
Sigurður DAGSSON, Gísli TORFASON, Jón
PÉTURSSON, Marteinn GEIRSSON, Jóhannes
EÐVALDSSON, Karl HERMANNSSON (Grétar
MAGNÚSSON 76'), Guðgeir LEIFSSON, Ásgeir
SIGURVINSSON, Ólafur JÚLÍUSSON, Teitur
ÞÓRÐARSON, Matthías HALLGRÍMSSON (Elmar
GEIRSSON 60')

FRA: (Coach: Ştefan KOVÁCS)
Dominique BARATELLI, Christian LOPEZ, Jean-Pierre
ADAMS, Marius TRÉSOR, François BRACCI (Jean
GALLICE 75'), Patrick PARIZON, Henri MICHEL,
Jean-Michel LARQUÉ, Jean-Marc GUILLOU, Marc
BERDOLL, Georges BERETA


5 June 1975          Ref: Ian FOOTE (Scotland)
Laugardalsvöllur, REYKJAVÍK (Att. 10,373)

ICELAND - EAST GERMANY
2:1 (2:0)

1:0 Eðvaldsson (12'), 2:0 Sigurvinsson (32'), 2:1
Pommerenke (48')

ICE: (Coach: Anthony KNAPP)
Sigurður DAGSSON, Gísli TORFASON, Jón
PÉTURSSON, Marteinn GEIRSSON, Jóhannes
EÐVALDSSON, Hörður HILMARSSON (Karl
HERMANNSSON 77'), Guðgeir LEIFSSON, Ásgeir
SIGURVINSSON, Ólafur JÚLÍUSSON, Elmar
GEIRSSON (Matthías HALLGRÍMSSON 85'), Teitur
ÞÓRÐARSON

EGR: (Coach: Georg BUSCHNER)
Jürgen CROY, Manfred ZAPF (Hans-Jürgen
RIEDIGER 83'), Gerd KISCHE, Konrad WEISE,
Siegmar WÄTZLICH, Jürgen POMMERENKE,

Rüdiger SCHNUPHASE (Hans-Jürgen DÖRNER 55'),
Lothar KURBJUWEIT, Martin HOFFMANN, Joachim
STREICH, Eberhard VOGEL

3 September 1975     Ref: Albert VICTOR (Luxembourg)
Stade Marcel Saupin, NANTES (Att. 25,418)

### FRANCE - ICELAND
### 3:0 (1:0)

1:0 Guillou (20'), 2:0 Guillou (74'), 3:0 Berdoll (87')

FRA: (Coach: Ştefan KOVÁCS)
Dominique BARATELLI, Raymond DOMENECH,
Jean-Pierre ADAMS, Marius TRÉSOR, François
BRACCI, Jean-Noël HUCK, Henri MICHEL, Dominique
ROCHETEAU, Marc MOLITOR (Marc BERDOLL 46'),
Albert EMON, Jean-Marc GUILLOU

ICE: (Coach: Anthony KNAPP)
Árni STEFÁNSSON, Ólafur SIGURVINSSON, Jón
PÉTURSSON, Marteinn GEIRSSON, Jóhannes
EÐVALDSSON, Gísli TORFASON, Hörður
HILMARSSON (Karl ÞÓRÐARSON 61'), Guðgeir
LEIFSSON, Ásgeir SIGURVINSSON, Teitur
ÞÓRÐARSON, Matthías HALLGRÍMSSON (Elmar
GEIRSSON 75')

6 September 1975     Ref: Henning LUND SØRENSEN
(Denmark)
Stade Maurice Dufrasne, LIÈGE (Att. 9,371)

### BELGIUM - ICELAND
### 1:0 (1:0)

1:0 Lambert (43')

BEL: (Coach: Raymond GOETHALS)

Christian PIOT, Gilbert VAN BINST, Hugo BROOS, Nicolas DEWALQUE, Maurice MARTENS, Julien COOLS, Jan VERHEYEN (Ludo COECK 61'), Odilon POLLEUNIS, Johan DEVRINDT, Raoul LAMBERT, Jacques TEUGELS

ICE: (Coach: Anthony KNAPP)
Árni STEFÁNSSON, Ólafur SIGURVINSSON, Björn LÁRUSSON, Jón PÉTURSSON, Marteinn GEIRSSON, Guðgeir LEIFSSON, Elmar GEIRSSON, Ásgeir SIGURVINSSON, Teitur ÞÓRÐARSON (Árni SVEINSSON 75'), Matthías HALLGRÍMSSON, Gísli TORFASON

27 September 1975          Ref: Nicolae RAINEA
(Romania)
Stade Émile Versé, ANDERLECHT (Att. 17,281)

BELGIUM - EAST GERMANY
1:2 (0:0)

0:1 Ducke (50'), 1:1 Puis (60'), 1:2 Häfner (71')

BEL: (Coach: Raymond GOETHALS)
Christian PIOT, Eric GERETS, Nicolas DEWALQUE, Erwin VANDENDAELE, Maurice MARTENS, Julien COOLS, Ludo COECK, Odilon POLLEUNIS (Jean JANSSENS 78'), Wilfried PUIS, Johan DEVRINDT, Jacques TEUGELS

EGR: (Coach: Georg BUSCHNER)
Jürgen CROY (Hans-Ulrich GRAPENTHIN 88'), Hans-Jürgen DÖRNER, Joachim FRITSCHE, Konrad WEISE, Lothar KURBJUWEIT, Reinhard HÄFNER, Reinhard LAUCK, Gerd WEBER, Hans-Jürgen RIEDIGER, Peter DUCKE, Martin HOFFMANN

12 October 1975          Ref: Erik FREDRIKSSON
(Sweden)

Zentralstadion, LEIPZIG (Att. 28,544)

### EAST GERMANY - FRANCE
### 2:1 (0:0)

0:1 Bathenay (50'), 1:1 Streich (55'), 2:1 Vogel (77' pen.)

EGR: (Coach: Georg BUSCHNER)
Jürgen CROY, Hans-Jürgen DÖRNER, Gerd WEBER,
Konrad WEISE, Joachim FRITSCHE, Reinhard
HÄFNER, Hartmut SCHADE, Reinhard LAUCK,
Joachim STREICH (Martin HOFFMANN 75'), Peter
DUCKE, Eberhard VOGEL

FRA: (Coach: Ştefan KOVÁCS)
Dominique BARATELLI, Gérard JANVION, Jean-
Pierre ADAMS, Marius TRÉSOR, François BRACCI,
Henri MICHEL, Jean GALLICE, Jean-Marc GUILLOU,
Dominique BATHENAY, Dominique ROCHETEAU,
Albert EMON


15 November 1975   Ref: Robert DAVIDSON (Scotland)
Parc des Princes, PARIS (Att. 35,547)

### FRANCE - BELGIUM
### 0:0

FRA: (Coach: Ştefan KOVÁCS)
Dominique BARATELLI, Raymond DOMENECH,
Charles ORLANDUCCI, Marius TRÉSOR, François
BRACCI, Jean-Noël HUCK (Jean-Michel LARQUÉ
46'), Henri MICHEL, Jean-Marc GUILLOU, Dominique
ROCHETEAU, Christian COSTE (Jean GALLICE 78'),
Albert EMON

BEL: (Coach: Raymond GOETHALS)
Christian PIOT, Gilbert VAN BINST, Erwin

VANDENDAELE, Georges LEEKENS, Jean DOCKX, Julien COOLS, Ludo COECK, Jan VERHEYEN, René VANDEREYCKEN, Roger VAN GOOL, Raoul LAMBERT (Jacques TEUGELS 78')

Red Card: Larqué 67'

| | |
|---|---|
| BELGIUM (Q) | (P6, W3, D2, L1, F6, A3, Pts. 8) |
| East Germany | (P6, W2, D3, L1, F8, A7, Pts. 7) |
| France | (P6, W1, D3, L2, F7, A6, Pts. 5) |
| Iceland | (P6, W1, D2, L3, F3, A8, Pts. 4) |

GROUP 8 (Bulgaria, Greece, Malta, West Germany)

13 October 1974      Ref: Alberto MICHELOTTI (Italy)
Stadion Vasil Levski, SOFIA (Att. 14,291)

BULGARIA - GREECE
3:3 (3:1)

1:0 Bonev (2'), 2:0 Denev (27'), 2:1 Antoniadis (28'), 3:1 Denev (29'), 3:2 Papaioannou (86'), 3:3 Glezos (88')

BUL: (Coach: Manol MANOLOV)
Stoyan YORDANOV, Ivan ZAFIROV, Dimitar PENEV, Borislav DIMITROV, Bozhil KOLEV, Krasimir BORISOV, Voyn VOYNOV, Hristo BONEV, Traycho SOKOLOV (Pavel PANOV 74'), Georgi DENEV, Chavdar TSVETKOV (Todor BARZOV 58')

GRE: (Coach: Alketas PANAGOULIAS)
Panagiotis OIKONOMOPOULOS, Theodoros PALLAS, Giorgos FOIROS, Apostolos GLEZOS, Konstantinos IOSIFIDIS, Konstantinos ELEFTHERAKIS, Dimitris DIMITRIOU (Stavros SARAFIS 58'), Hristos TERZANIDIS, Giorgos DELIKARIS, Antonis ANTONIADIS, Dimitris PAPAIOANNOU

20 November 1974    Ref: Nicolae RAINEA (Romania)
Stádio Georgios Karaiskakis, PIRAEUS (Att. 11,425)

## GREECE - WEST GERMANY
## 2:2 (1:0)

1:0 Delikaris (13'), 1:1 Cullmann (51'), 2:1 Eleftherakis
(70'), 2:2 Wimmer (83')

GRE: (Coach: Alketas PANAGOULIAS)
Panagiotis OIKONOMOPOULOS, Giannis
KYRASTAS, Vasilis SIOKOS, Apostolos GLEZOS
(Giorgos FOIROS 62'), Konstantinos IOSIFIDIS,
Konstantinos ELEFTHERAKIS, Dimitris DOMAZOS,
Stavros SARAFIS, Dimitris PAPAIOANNOU (Ahileas
ASLANIDIS 68'), Giorgos DELIKARIS, Hristos
TERZANIDIS

WGR: (Coach: Helmut SCHÖN)
Josef MAIER, Hans-Hubert VOGTS, Helmut
KREMERS, Hans-Georg SCHWARZENBECK, Franz
BECKENBAUER, Bernhard CULLMANN (Hans-Josef
KAPELLMANN 78'), Reiner GEYE, Herbert WIMMER,
Bernhard HÖLZENBEIN, Ulrich HOENEß, Josef
HEYNCKES (Josef PIRRUNG 81')


18 December 1974    Ref: Paul SCHILLER (Austria)
Stádio Georgios Karaiskakis, PIRAEUS (Att. 22,328)

## GREECE - BULGARIA
## 2:1 (2:0)

1:0 Sarafis (4'), 2:0 Antoniadis (40'), 2:1 Kolev (89')

GRE: (Coach: Alketas PANAGOULIAS)
Vasilis KONSTANTINOU, Dimitris ELEFTHERIADIS,
Vasilis SIOKOS, Apostolos GLEZOS, Theodoros
PALLAS, Konstantinos ELEFTHERAKIS, Hristos
TERZANIDIS, Stavros SARAFIS, Dimitris
PAPAIOANNOU (Giannis KYRASTAS 71'), Ahileas

ASLANIDIS, Antonis ANTONIADIS

BUL: (Coach: Stoyan ORMANDZHIEV)
Yordan FILIPOV, Tsonyo VASILEV, Kiril IVKOV,
Stefan ALADZHOV, Bozhil KOLEV, Kiril STANKOV,
Voyn VOYNOV (Boris ANGELOV 46'), Hristo BONEV,
Nikola HRISTOV (Chavdar TSVETKOV 69'), Georgi
DENEV, Nikolay KURBANOV

22 December 1974        Ref: Gyula EMSBERGER
(Hungary)
Imperu Istadium, GZIRA (Att. 12,528)

MALTA - WEST GERMANY
0:1 (0:1)

0:1 Cullmann (44')

MAL: (Coach: Terenzio POLVERINI)
Alfred DEBONO, Joseph BORG, Edward VELLA,
Edward DARMANIN, John HOLLAND, William
VASSALLO, Vincent MAGRO, Raymond XUEREB,
Toninu CAMILLERI, Edward AQUILINA (Richard
AQUILINA 51'), Carlo SEYCHELL

WGR: (Coach: Helmut SCHÖN)
Norbert NIGBUR, Hans-Hubert VOGTS, Karl-
Heinz KORBEL, Franz BECKENBAUER, Bernard
DIETZ, Rainer BONHOF, Heinz FLOHE, Bernhard
CULLMANN (Rudolf SELIGER 74'), Josef PIRRUNG
(Bernd NICKEL 46'), Erwin KOSTEDDE, Bernhard
HÖLZENBEIN

23 February 1975        Ref: Robert MATTHEWSON
(England)
Imperu Istadium, GZIRA (Att. 8,621)

MALTA - GREECE

2:0 (1:0)

1:0 Aquilina (33'), 2:0 Magro (79')

MAL: (Coach: Terenzio POLVERINI)
Robert GATT, George CIANTAR, Edward VELLA,
Edward DARMANIN, John HOLLAND, William
VASSALLO, Vincent MAGRO, David AZZOPARDI
(Carlo SEYCHELL 46'), Raymond XUEREB, Richard
AQUILINA, Toninu CAMILLERI

GRE: (Coach: Alketas PANAGOULIAS)
Vasilis KONSTANTINOU, Theodoros PALLAS,
Konstantinos IOSIFIDIS, Vasilis SIOKOS, Giorgos
FOIROS, Dimitris DOMAZOS, Stavros SARAFIS,
Dimitris DIMITRIOU (Dimitris PARIDIS 29' (Pantelis
NIKOLAOU 75')), Mihalis KRITIKOPOULOS, Antonis
ANTONIADIS, Dimitris PAPAIOANNOU


27 April 1975        Ref: Jean DUBACH (Switzerland)
Stadion Vasil Levski, SOFIA (Att. 47,200)

BULGARIA - WEST GERMANY
1:1 (0:0)

1:0 Kolev (71' pen.), 1:1 Ritschel (75' pen.)

BUL: (Coach: Stoyan ORMANDZHIEV)
Yordan FILIPOV, Ivan ZAFIROV, Todor MAREV,
Milcho EVTIMOV, Bozhil KOLEV, Angel RANGELOV,
Atanas ALEKSANDROV (Radoslav ZDRAVKOV 60'),
Borislav DIMITROV, Andrey ZHELYAZKOV, Pavel
PANOV, Georgi DENEV

WGR: (Coach: Helmut SCHÖN)
Josef MAIER, Hans-Hubert VOGTS, Paul
BREITNER, Hans-Georg SCHWARZENBECK,
Franz BECKENBAUER, Rainer BONHOF, Manfred
RITSCHEL, Ulrich HOENEß (Karl-Heinz KÖRBEL 74'),

Wolfgang SEEL, Günter NETZER, Josef HEYNCKES
(Bernhard HÖLZENBEIN 34')


4 June 1975          Ref: Marijan RAUŠ (Yugoslavia)
Stádio Toúmbas, SALONIKA (Att. 16,545)

### GREECE - MALTA
### 4:0 (2:0)

1:0 Mavros (32'), 2:0 Antoniadis (34' pen.), 3:0 Iosifidis
(47'), 4:0 Papaioannou (50')

GRE: (Coach: Alketas PANAGOULIAS)
Stelios PAPAFLORATOS, Theodoros PALLAS,
Konstantinos IOSIFIDIS, Giorgos FOIROS, Filotas
PELLIOS (Pantelis NIKOLAOU 72'), Kyriakos
APOSTOLIDIS, Thomas MAVROS, Antonis
ANTONIADIS (Nikolaos KALAMBAKAS 67'), Dimitris
PAPAIOANNOU, Ahileas ASLANIDIS, Angelos
ANASTASIADIS

MAL: (Coach: Terenzio POLVERINI)
Robert GATT (Alfred DEBONO 55'), Joseph BORG,
Edwin FARRUGIA, William VASSALLO, Edward
DARMANIN, John HOLLAND, Vincent MAGRO, David
AZZOPARDI, Raymond XUEREB, Richard AQUILINA,
Carlo SEYCHELL (Toninu CAMILLERI 46')


11 June 1975          Ref: Michal JURSA
(Czechoslovakia)
Stadion Vasil Levski, SOFIA (Att. 27,560)

### BULGARIA - MALTA
### 5:0 (3:0)

1:0 Dimitrov (2'), 2:0 Denev (22'), 3:0 Panov (25'), 4:0
Bonev (68' pen.), 5:0 Milanov (71')

BUL: (Coach: Stoyan ORMANDZHIEV)

Yordan FILIPOV, Ivan ZAFIROV, Todor MAREV, Milcho
EVTIMOV, Konstantinos ISAKIDIS (Kiril MILANOV
59'), Nikolay KURBANOV (Atanas ALEKSANDROV
46'), Hristo BONEV, Andrey ZHELYAZKOV, Pavel
PANOV, Georgi DENEV, Borislav DIMITROV

MAL: (Coach: Terenzio POLVERINI)
Alfred DEBONO, George CIANTAR, Edwin
FARRUGIA, Edward VELLA, John HOLLAND, Edward
DARMANIN, Vincent MAGRO, Joseph BORG,
Edward AQUILINA (Raymond XUEREB 68'), William
VASSALLO, Richard AQUILINA


11 October 1975          Ref: Clive THOMAS (Wales)
Rheinstadion, DÜSSELDORF (Att. 61,252)

WEST GERMANY - GREECE
1:1 (0:0)

1:0 Heynckes (68'), 1:1 Delikaris (78')

WGR: (Coach: Helmut SCHÖN)
Josef MAIER, Hans-Hubert VOGTS, Franz
BECKENBAUER, Karl-Heinz KÖRBEL, Manfred
KALTZ, Paul BREITNER, Günter NETZER, Erich
BEER, Bernhard HÖLZENBEIN, Erwin KOSTEDDE,
Josef HEYNCKES

GRE: (Coach: Alketas PANAGOULIAS)
Panagiotis KELESIDIS, Giannis KYRASTAS,
Theodoros PALLAS, Dimitris SYNETOPOULOS
(Kyriakos APOSTOLIDIS 46'), Hristos TERZANIDIS,
Stavros SARAFIS, Giorgos KOUDAS (Ahileas
ASLANIDIS 86'), Mihalis KRITIKOPOULOS,
Dimitris PAPAIOANNOU, Giorgos FOIROS, Giorgos
DELIKARIS

19 November 1975          Ref: Alistair McKENZIE
                                                    (Scotland)
Neckarstadion, STUTTGART (Att. 68,819)

### WEST GERMANY - BULGARIA
### 1:0 (0:0)

1:0 Heynckes (64')

WGR: (Coach: Helmut SCHÖN)
Josef  MAIER,  Hans-Hubert  VOGTS,  Bernard
DIETZ,  Hans-Georg  SCHWARZENBECK,  Franz
BECKENBAUER,  Dietmar  DANNER,  Bernhard
HÖLZENBEIN, Herbert WIMMER, Erich BEER, Ulrich
STIELIKE, Josef HEYNCKES

BUL: (Coach: Stoyan ORMANDZHIEV)
Yordan FILIPOV, Ivan ZAFIROV, Kiril IVKOV, Tsonyo
VASILEV, Bozhil KOLEV (Pavel PANOV 75'), Boris
ANGELOV, Atanas ALEKSANDROV (Voyn VOYNOV
76'), Hristo BONEV, Kiril MILANOV, Angel RANGELOV,
Chavdar TSVETKOV


21 December 1975          Ref: Norbert ROLLES
                                                 (Luxembourg)
Imperu Istadium, GZIRA (Att. 7,174)

### MALTA - BULGARIA
### 0:2 (0:0)

0:1 Panov (69'), 0:2 Yordanov (83')

MAL: (Coach: Terenzio POLVERINI)
Alfred DEBONO, Sunny GOUDER (Edward VELLA
90'), Edwin FARRUGIA, John HOLLAND, Edward
DARMANIN, William VASSALLO, Vincent MAGRO
(Christopher VELLA 46'), David AZZOPARDI, Richard
AQUILINA, Edward AQUILINA, Carlo SEYCHELL

<u>BUL:</u> (Coach: Stoyan ORMANDZHIEV)
Georgi TIHANOV, Ivan ZAFIROV (Yordan YORDANOV
46'), Kiril IVKOV, Tsonyo VASILEV, Boris ANGELOV,
Angel RANGELOV, Voyn VOYNOV, Hristo BONEV,
Kiril MILANOV, Pavel PANOV, Chavdar TSVETKOV
(Atanas ALEKSANDROV 68')


28 February 1976      Ref: Marian KUSTOŃ (Poland)
Westfalenstadion, DORTMUND (Att. 52,248)

### WEST GERMANY - MALTA
### 8:0 (4:0)

1:0 Worm (5'), 2:0 Worm (27'), 3:0 Heynckes (34'), 4:0
Beer (41' pen.), 5:0 Heynckes (58'), 6:0 Beer (77'), 7:0
Vogts (82'), 8:0 Hölzenbein (87')

<u>WGR:</u> (Coach: Helmut SCHÖN)
Josef MAIER, Hans-Hubert VOGTS, Bernard
DIETZ,      Hans-Georg      SCHWARZENBECK,
Franz BECKENBAUER, Erich BEER, Bernhard
HÖLZENBEIN, Herbert WIMMER (Hans BONGARTZ
57'), Ronald WORM, Ulrich STIELIKE (Bernhard
CULLMANN 46'), Josef HEYNCKES

<u>MAL:</u> (Coach: Terenzio POLVERINI)
Charles  SCIBERRAS,  Olivier  LOSCO,  John
HOLLAND, Sunny GOUDER, Edwin FARRUGIA,
Richard AQUILINA, William VASSALLO, Dennis
FENECH, Vincent MAGRO (Carlo SEYCHELL 46'),
Raymond XUEREB, Mario LOPORTO (Edward
AQUILINA 28')


WEST GERMANY (Q)  (P6, W3, D3, L0, F14, A4, Pts. 9)
Greece            (P6, W2, D3, L1, F12, A9, Pts. 7)
Bulgaria          (P6, W2, D2, L2, F12, A7, Pts. 6)
Malta             (P6, W1, D0, L5, F2, A20, Pts. 2)

# QUARTER-FINALS

24 April 1976              Ref: HILMI Ok (Turkey)
Tehelné pole, BRATISLAVA (Att. 47,621)

## CZECHOSLOVAKIA - USSR
### 2:0 (1:0)

1:0 Móder (34'), 2:0 Panenka (47')

CZE: (Coach: Václav JEŽEK)
Ivo VIKTOR, Karol DOBIAŠ, Anton ONDRUŠ, Jozef
ČAPKOVIČ, Koloman GÖGH, Jozef MÓDER (Lubomír
KNAPP 76'), Jaroslav POLLÁK, Antonín PANENKA,
Marián MASNÝ, Ladislav PETRÁŠ (Karel KROUPA
17'), Zdeněk NEHODA

URS: (Coach: Valeriy LOBANOVSKIY)
Aleksandr   PROKHOROV,   Anatoliy   KONKOV,
Viktor ZVYAGINTSEV, Mikhail FOMENKO, Stefan
RESHKO, Viktor MATVIENKO, Evgeniy LOVCHEV
(Vladimir VEREMEEV 57'), Vladimir ONISHCHENKO
(Leonid NAZARENKO 68'), Viktor KOLOTOV, Vladimir
TROSHKIN, Oleg BLOKHIN

22 May 1976      Ref: Alistair McKENZIE (Scotland)
Tsentralniy Stadion, KIEV (Att. 76,495)

## USSR - CZECHOSLOVAKIA
### 2:2 (0:1)

0:1 Móder (45'), 1:1 Buryak (53'), 1:2 Móder (82'), 2:2
Blokhin (87')

URS: (Coach: Valeriy LOBANOVSKIY)
Evgeniy RUDAKOV, Anatoliy KONKOV (Aleksandr
MINAYEV 54'), Evgeniy LOVCHEV, Mikhail FOMENKO,
Viktor ZVYAGINTSEV, Vladimir TROSHKIN, Vladimir

MUNTYAN, Vladimir ONISHCHENKO, Leonid BURYAK, Vladimir VEREMEEV, Oleg BLOKHIN

CZE: (Coach: Václav JEŽEK)
Ivo VIKTOR, Koloman GÖGH, Karol DOBIAŠ, Anton ONDRUŠ, Ján PIVARNÍK, Jozef ČAPKOVIČ (Ladislav JURKEMIK 80'), Marián MASNÝ, Jozef MÓDER, Dušan GALIS (Ján ŠVEHLÍK 87'), Zdeněk NEHODA, Jaroslav POLLÁK

CZECHOSLOVAKIA won 4-2 on agg.

24 April 1976          Ref: John TAYLOR (England)
Estadio Vicente Calderón, MADRID (Att. 51,771)

SPAIN - WEST GERMANY
1:1 (1:0)

1:0 'Santillana' (21'), 1:1 Beer (60')

SPA: (Coach: Ladislao KUBALA Stécz)
José Angel IRIBAR Kortajarena, Juan Cruz SOL Oria, Gregorio BENITO Rubio, José Luis CAPÓN González, Miguel Bernardo Bianquetti 'MIGUELI' (Sebastián ALABANDA González 81'), José Antonio CAMACHO Alfaro, Enrique Castro González 'QUINI' (Jesús María SATRÚSTEGUI Azpiroz 81'), Carlos Alonso González 'SANTILLANA', Vicente DEL BOSQUE González, José Ignacio CHURRUCA Sistiaga, Ángel María VILLAR Llona

WGR: (Coach: Helmut SCHÖN)
Josef MAIER, Hans-Hubert VOGTS, Hans-Georg SCHWARZENBECK (Bernhard CULLMANN 46'), Bernard DIETZ (Peter REICHEL 81'), Rainer BONHOF, Dietmar DANNER, Bernhard HÖLZENBEIN, Herbert WIMMER, Erich BEER, Ronald WORM, Franz BECKENBAUER

22 May 1976          Ref: Robert WURTZ (France)
Olympiastadion, MUNICH (Att. 77,673)

### WEST GERMANY - SPAIN
### 2:0 (2:0)

1:0 Hoeneß (17'), 2:0 Toppmöller (43')

WGR: (Coach: Helmut SCHÖN)
Josef MAIER, Hans-Hubert VOGTS, Bernard
DIETZ, Hans-Georg SCHWARZENBECK, Franz
BECKENBAUER, Rainer BONHOF, Bernhard
HÖLZENBEIN, Ulrich HOENEß, Herbert WIMMER,
Klaus TOPPMÖLLER, Erich BEER

SPA: (Coach: Ladislao KUBALA Stécz)
MIGUEL ÁNGEL González Suárez, José Luis CAPÓN
González, Juan Cruz SOL Oria (Inaxio KORTABARRIA
Abarrategi 17'), José Martínez Sánchez 'PIRRI', José
Antonio CAMACHO Alfaro, Ángel María VILLAR Llona
(José Antonio RAMOS Huete 46'), Vicente DEL BOSQUE
González, Juan Manuel ASENSI Ripoll, Enrique
Castro González 'QUINI', Carlos Alonso González
'SANTILLANA', José Ignacio CHURRUCA Sistiaga

WEST GERMANY won 3-1 on agg.


24 April 1976          Ref: Paul SCHILLER (Austria)
Stadion Maksimir, ZAGREB (Att. 36,917)

### YUGOSLAVIA - WALES
### 2:0 (1:0)

1:0 Vukotić (1'), 2:0 Popivoda (54')

YUG: (Coach: Ante MLADINIĆ)
Ognjen PETROVIĆ, Ivan BULJAN, Džemal
HADŽIABDIĆ, Branko OBLAK, Josip KATALINSKI,
Dražen MUŽINIĆ, Dragutin VABEC, Danilo

POPIVODA, Momčilo VUKOTIĆ (Jurica JERKOVIĆ 60'), Jovan AĆIMOVIĆ, Ivan ŠURJAK

WAL: (Coach: Michael SMITH)
William DAVIES, Roderick THOMAS, Malcolm PAGE, John MAHONEY, Leighton PHILLIPS, Ian EVANS, Leighton JAMES (Alan CURTIS 85'), Brian FLYNN, Terence YORATH, John TOSHACK, Arfon GRIFFITHS


22 May 1976          Ref: Rudolf GLÖCKNER
                              (East Germany)
Ninian Park, CARDIFF (Att. 30,346)

## WALES - YUGOSLAVIA
### 1:1 (1:1)

0:1 Katalinski (19' pen.), 1:1 Evans (38')

WAL: (Coach: Michael SMITH)
William DAVIES, Leighton PHILLIPS, David ROBERTS, Ian EVANS, Malcolm PAGE, Arfon GRIFFITHS (Alan CURTIS 46'), Terence YORATH, John MAHONEY, Brian FLYNN, John TOSHACK, Leighton JAMES

YUG: (Coach: Ante MLADINIĆ)
Enver MARIĆ, Ivan BULJAN, Džemal HADŽIABDIĆ, Branko OBLAK, Josip KATALINSKI, Dražen MUŽINIĆ, Slaviša ŽUNGUL (Franjo VLADIĆ 61'), Danilo POPIVODA, Borislav ĐORĐEVIĆ, Jurica JERKOVIĆ, Ivan ŠURJAK

YUGOSLAVIA won 3-1 on agg.


25 April 1976     Ref: Jean DUBACH (Switzerland)
Feyenoord Stadion, ROTTERDAM (Att. 48,706)

## NETHERLANDS - BELGIUM
### 5:0 (2:0)

1:0 Rijsbergen (17'), 2:0 Rensenbrink (27'), 3:0 Rensenbrink (58'), 4:0 Neeskens (79' pen.) 5:0 Rensenbrink (85')

NET: (Coach: Georg KNOBEL)
Pieter SCHRIJVERS, Wilhelmus SUURBIER, Adrianus VAN KRAAIJ, Wilhelmus RIJSBERGEN, Rudolf KROL, Wilhelmus JANSEN, Johannes NEESKENS (Johannes PETERS 84'), Wilhelmus VAN DE KERKHOF, John REP, Johannes CRUIJFF, Robert RENSENBRINK

BEL: (Coach: Raymond GOETHALS)
Christian PIOT, Eric GERETS, Georges LEEKENS, Gilbert VAN BINST, Maurice MARTENS, Jan VERHEYEN, Julien COOLS (François VAN DER ELST 46'), Ludo COECK, René VANDEREYCKEN, Roger VAN GOOL, Raoul LAMBERT (Jacques TEUGELS 81')

22 May 1976        Ref: Alberto MICHELOTTI (Italy)
Stade du Heysel, BRUSSELS (Att. 19,050)

BELGIUM - NETHERLANDS
1:2 (1:0)

1:0 Van Gool (27'), 1:1 Rep (61'), 1:2 Cruijff (77')

BEL: (Coach: Guy THYS)
Jean-Marie PFAFF, Gilbert VAN BINST, Michel RENQUIN, Robert DALVING, Maurice MARTENS, Julien COOLS, François VAN DER ELST, René VERHEYEN, Willy WELLENS, René VANDEREYCKEN, Roger VAN GOOL (Hervé DELESIE 66')

NET: (Coach: Georg KNOBEL)
Pieter SCHRIJVERS, Wilhelmus SUURBIER, Adrianus VAN KRAAIJ, Wilhelmus RIJSBERGEN, Rudolf

KROL, Wilhelmus VAN DE KERKHOF, Johannes
NEESKENS, Willem VAN HANEGEM (Johannes
PETERS 82'), John REP, Johannes CRUIJFF, Robert
RENSENBRINK

NETHERLANDS won 7-1 on agg.

# GOALSCORERS

## 8 GOALS

Daniel GIVENS (Republic of Ireland)

## 6 GOALS

Tibor NYILASI (Hungary)

## 5 GOALS

Malcolm MACDONALD (England), Johann KRANKL (Austria), Johannes CRUIJFF (Netherlands)

## 4 GOALS

Zdeněk NEHODA, Antonín PANENKA (both Czechoslovakia), Arfon GRIFFITHS (Wales), Josip KATALINSKI (Yugoslavia), Zoltan CRIŞAN, Dudu GEORGESCU (both Romania), Robert RENSENBRINK (Netherlands), Josef HEYNCKES (West Germany)

## 3 GOALS

Přemysl BIČOVSKÝ, Jozef MÓDER (both Czechoslovakia), Michael CHANNON (England), Gilbert DUSSIER (Luxembourg), John TOSHACK (Wales), Tom LUND (Norway), Johannes NEESKENS, Wilhelmus VAN DER KUIJLEN (both Netherlands), Grzegorz LATO, Andrzej SZARMACH (both Poland), Oleg BLOKHIN, Viktor KOLOTOV (both USSR), Jean-Marc GUILLOU (France), Georgi DENEV (Bulgaria), Antonis

ANTONIADIS (Greece), Erich BEER (West Germany)

## 2 GOALS

Marián MASNÝ (Czechoslovakia), Colin BELL (England), Tamagnini Manuel Gomes Baptista 'NENÉ' (Portugal), Kurt WELZL (Austria), László NAGY (Hungary), Nicolas BRAUN, Paul PHILIPP (both Luxembourg), Leighton JAMES (Wales), Bryan HAMILTON (Northern Ireland), Thomas NORDAHL, Thomas SJÖBERG (both Sweden), Branko OBLAK, Momčilo VUKOTIĆ (both Yugoslavia), Bruce RIOCH (Scotland), Enrique Castro González 'QUINI', Carlos Alonso González 'SANTILLANA' (both Spain), Timo RAHJA (Finland), Robert GADOCHA (Poland), Vladimir ONISCHENKO (USSR), Hristo BONEV, Bozhil KOLEV, Pavel PANOV (all Bulgaria), Giorgos DELIKARIS, Dimitris PAPAIOANNOU (both Greece), Bernhard CULLMANN, Ronald WORM (both West Germany)

## 1 GOAL

Dušan GALIS, Anton ONDRUŠ, Ladislav PETRÁŠ (all Czechoslovakia), Kevin KEEGAN (England), João António Ferreira Resende ALVES, Mário Jorge MOÍNHOS Matos, Rui Gouveia Pinto RODRIGUES (all Portugal), Kurt JARA, Helmut KÖGLBERGER, Wilhelm KREUZ, Herbert PROHASKA (all Austria), László BRANIKOVITS, László BÁLINT, József HORVÁTH, László PUSZTAI, Sándor PINTÉR, Béla VÁRADY, Tibor WOLLEK (all Hungary), Michael ENGLAND, Ian EVANS, John MAHONEY, Gilbert REECE, Philip ROBERTS, Terence YORATH (all Wales), Thomas FINNEY, Allan HUNTER, Samuel MORGAN, Samuel McILROY, Christopher NICHOLL, Martin O'NEILL (all Northern Ireland), Erik Just OLSEN, Stein THUNBERG (both Norway), Ralf EDSTRÖM, Ove GRAHN, Roland

SANDBERG, Conny TORSTENSSON (all Sweden), Vladislav BOGIĆEVIĆ, Ivan BULJAN, Zvonko IVEZIĆ, Danilo POPIVODA, Ivan ŠURJAK, Dragutin VABEC, Franjo VLADIĆ (all Yugoslavia), Lars BASTRUP, Peter DAHL, Kristen NYGAARD (all Denmark), Cornel DINU, Anghel IORDĂNESCU, Mircea LUCESCU (all Romania), William BREMNER, Kenneth DALGLISH, Joseph HARPER, Joseph JORDAN, Edward MACDOUGALL, Gordon McQUEEN (all Scotland), José Luis CAPÓN González, José CLARAMUNT Torres, Roberto MARTÍNEZ Martínez, Alfredo MEGIDO Sánchez, José Martínez Sánchez 'PIRRI', Manuel VELÁZQUEZ Villaverde, Ángel María VILLAR Llona (all Spain), Matti PAATELAINEN (Finland), Roberto BONINSEGNA, Fabio CAPELLO, Giorgio CHINAGLIA (all Italy), Geertruida GEELS, Heinricus LUBSE, John REP, Wilhelmus RIJSBERGEN, Franciscus THIJSSEN, Reinier VAN DE KERKHOF (all Netherlands), Henryk KASPERCZAK (Poland), Eoin HAND, Michael MARTIN, Raymond TREACY (all Republic of Ireland), Rudolf ELSENER, Kurt MÜLLER, Peter RISI, Hanspeter SCHILD (all Switzerland), ALPASLAN Eratli, İSMAIL Arca, MEHMET Oğuz (all Turkey), Leonid BURYAK, Anatoliy KONKOV, Vladimir MUNTYAN, Vladimir VEREMEEV (all USSR), Raoul LAMBERT, Maurice MARTENS, Wilfried PUIS, Jacques TEUGELS, François VAN DER ELST, Roger VAN GOOL, Wilfried VAN MOER (all Belgium), Peter DUCKE, Reinhard HÄFNER, Martin HOFFMANN, Hans-Jürgen KREISCHE, Jürgen POMMERENKE, Jürgen SPARWASSER, Joachim STREICH, Eberhard VOGEL (all East Germany), Dominique BATHENAY, Marc BERDOLL, Christian COSTE, Jean GALLICE (all France), Jóhannes EÐVALDSSON, Matthías HALLGRÍMSSON, Ásgeir SIGURVINSSON (all Iceland), Borislav DIMITROV, Kiril MILANOV, Yordan YORDANOV (all Bulgaria), Konstantinos ELEFTHERAKIS, Apostolos GLEZOS, Konstantinos

IOSIFIDIS, Thomas MAVROS, Stavros SARAFIS (all Greece), Richard AQUILINA, Vincent MAGRO (both Malta), Ulrich HOENEß, Bernd HÖLZENBEIN, Manfred RITSCHEL, Klaus TOPPMÖLLER, Hans-Hubert VOGTS, Herbert WIMMER (all West Germany)

## OWN-GOALS

Anthony DUNNE (Republic of Ireland) vs Turkey, İSMAIL Arca (Turkey) vs Switzerland, Stefan RESHKO (USSR) vs Turkey

# FINAL TOURNAMENT

# (YUGOSLAVIA - 16-20 JUNE 1976)

## VENUES (Stadia)

BELGRADE (Stadion Crvena Zvezda), ZAGREB (Stadion Maksimir)

---

## SEMI-FINALS & THIRD PLACE MATCH

### CZECHOSLOVAKIA vs NETHERLANDS

Constant rainfall throughout the day meant that the opening semi-final in Zagreb was played in appalling conditions. The Dutch were slight favourites, although the Czechoslovaks had gone seventeen matches unbeaten since losing to England in October 1974.

Early on, Anton Ondruš tested 'Piet' Schrijvers with a stinging shot from outside the box which the keeper had to fist away, but the defender had better luck in the nineteenth minute when he opened the scoring. Zdeněk Nehoda was fouled on the left by 'Wim' Suurbier, and from Antonín Panenka's floated free-kick, Ondruš rose to head past Schrijvers who got fingertips to it but couldn't keep it out.

Soon afterwards, Marián Masný was clean through, but he overran the ball and Schrijvers was able to save at his feet; then Masný got in behind the Dutch defence and squared it across the six yard line. Rijsbergen made a tremendous block tackle to deny Nehoda, but at a cost, as he injured himself and had to be replaced by 'Wim' van Hanegem.

The Dutch began the second half on the front foot, and 'Johan' Cruijff soon spun and fired in an effort. Ivo Viktor spilled it, but he managed to grab the ball ahead of 'Johan' Neeskens. In the fifty-ninth minute, the Czechoslovaks were reduced to ten men when Jaroslav Pollák, who had been booked a few minutes earlier for not retreating at a free-kick, chopped down Neeskens on the touchline and was rightly shown the red card.

Dutch pressure eventually told when they equalised with seventeen minutes remaining through a freak own-goal from Ondruš, as he sliced an attempted clearance from substitute 'Ruud' Geels' cross high past Viktor; but only three minutes later, the Netherlands' numerical advantage was over when Neeskens crazily slid in and took Nehoda out, and he was instantly dismissed.

In the last ten minutes, the Dutch looked the likeliest to grab a winner, and 'Rob' Rensenbrink should have done better when van Hanegem set him up, but he shot straight at Viktor. The keeper pushed away another Rensenbrink effort a couple of minutes later, and an extra thirty minutes were required to decide who would go through to the Final.

At the start of extra time, the Czechoslovaks freshened things up by bringing on František Veselý for Jozef Móder. After a couple of minutes he nearly set Nehoda up, but the striker dallied too long and the chance was gone. Then, in the final minute of the first period, a mistake from Ján Pivarník allowed Geels to run in on goal – but his shot lacked enough pace to beat Viktor.

The Czechoslovaks made their final substitution at the beginning of the second period, with Ladislav Jurkemik replacing Jozef Čapkovič, and for the first few minutes they were content to soak up Dutch pressure – then, with six minutes remaining, they went ahead for the second time in controversial circumstances.

Cruijff appeared to be fouled by Panenka some thirty yards from goal, but referee Clive Thomas waved play on. The ball was swiftly played down the right wing for Veselý to run onto, and his cross was inch-perfect for Nehoda to head down past Schrijvers. The Dutch were so incensed by the decision that van Hanegem refused to move out of the centre circle to allow play to recommence, and the referee instantly showed him the red card for dissent.

With a couple of minutes left, the Czechoslovaks sealed their place in the Final when Masný and Nehoda exchanged passes at a short corner. The former played the ball back some twenty-five yards, where Karol Dobiaš slid a superb ball through for Veselý to glide past Schrijvers and slam the ball into the net. Straight from the restart the Dutch thought they'd got a goal back, but Geels was flagged offside as he shot past Viktor, and moments later the final whistle sounded.

## YUGOSLAVIA vs WEST GERMANY

The other semi-final was played out in front of a huge partisan crowd in Belgrade between the hosts and the holders. A decade earlier, the Yugoslavs had denied the West Germans a place at the 1968 Finals – the only time they'd failed to qualify for a major tournament. The West Germans had gained a modicum of revenge by winning 2-0 en route to their World Cup triumph on home soil in 1974, but that had been in a group game; this time, the prize at stake was a place in the Final.

The first real opening came for the Yugoslavs, when Slaviša Žungul cut inside Hans-Georg Schwarzenbeck and let fly from fourteen yards. 'Sepp' Maier could only parry, but Franz Beckenbauer was in the right place to pass back to the keeper, then Erich Beer was caught marginally offside as he was played through by Bernard Dietz.

A goal was looking more and more likely, and the hosts obliged in the nineteenth minute after a West German attack was snuffed out by Josip Katalinski. The ball was quickly shuttled to 'Brane' Oblak, who launched a cross towards the penalty area that was superbly controlled by Danilo Popivoda, and, under pressure from Beckenbauer, he coolly slotted past Maier.

The West German keeper was almost caught out moments later when Ivan Buljan's cross came off Schwarzenbeck's shoulder, and Maier had to tip the ball over the bar. The keeper then turned away a powerful free-kick from Katalinski as the Yugoslavs threatened a second goal, which they deservedly got after half an hour from a goalkeeping error.

Žungul fired in a cross from the right, which Maier should have easily gathered, but he uncharacteristically fumbled it and Dragan Džajić, following up, had the simple task of knocking the ball in from six yards. West Germany should have reduced the deficit a minute before half-time, when both 'Uli' Hoeneß and Beer had shots blocked, before the latter somehow ballooned the ball over the bar with the goal at his mercy.

Helmut Schön made an attacking switch at the start of the second half, replacing Dietmar Danner with Heinz Flohe, but it was Yugoslavia who created the next opportunity, which they really should have taken. Džajić was sent clear down the left and his cross was pushed out by Maier only as far as 'Jure' Jerković – who, unbelievably, screwed his shot well wide of the far post.

That miss would prove costly, as the West Germans pulled a goal back in the sixty-fourth minute when Flohe blasted a drive from twenty-five yards that deflected off Herbert Wimmer and wrong-footed Ognjen Petrović; then the Yugoslav keeper blocked an effort from Hoeneß after Katalinski had been caught dwelling on the ball.

With eleven minutes remaining, the West Germans brought on Dieter Müller for his international debut in place of Wimmer. Within a couple of minutes, the twenty-two-year-old Cologne striker sensationally levelled the match when he was left completely unmarked to head home Rainer Bonhof's corner; then the home side completely switched off, as a quickly taken free-kick from Beckenbauer found Beer in acres of space. Petrović managed to turn his piledriver round the post to keep the score level, and, like the first semi-final, the match went into extra time.

Yugoslavia had the first opportunity of the first period when they were awarded a free-kick just outside the box, and yet again it was Katalinski who sent in a blistering drive, which Maier could only fist away, but they couldn't take advantage from the rebound. Hoeneß played a superb slide rule pass through to Bonhof, whose effort was well held by Petrović.

At the start of the second period, the Yugoslavs made

their two allotted changes, with Franjo Vladić and Luka Peruzović replacing Oblak and Jovan Aćimović respectively. Vladić was involved immediately, setting up Džajić to cross for Žungul, whose angled header was brilliantly saved on the line by Maier. Flohe's left wing cross found Beer, whose well-struck shot was too close to Petrović, who punched clear.

But with five minutes remaining, the West Germans went ahead for the first time in the game. Flohe skipped past a couple of tackles on the left and sent in a low cross, which Bernd Hölzenbein played back towards the six yard line, where Müller was waiting to smash his second goal into the roof of the net. Then, in the final minute, it was all over after Bonhof's shot rebounded off the base of the post and fell nicely for Müller to stroke home and complete a dream debut.


## YUGOSLAVIA vs NETHERLANDS

After the disappointment of their semi-final loss to Czechoslovakia, the Dutch rang the changes for the third-place match. With van Hanegem and Neeskens suspended, they brought in 'Jan' Peters and 'Peter' Arntz to replace them, while Geels, who had been one of the better performers when he came on in the semi-final, started in place of Cruijff. The Yugoslavs, surprisingly after their energy-sapping and demoralising defeat to the West Germans, began with the same eleven players.

The Dutch began brightly, and they should have taken the lead in the twenty-fifth minute – Arntz played a delightful ball into the box for 'Willy' van de Kerkhof, who controlled it on his chest, only to miskick with only Petrović to beat. Only a couple of minutes later, though, Geels made no mistake as he was put through by

Rensenbrink, and he slipped the ball beneath Petrović from eight yards.

Soon afterwards, Ivan Šurjak tested Schrijvers from a distance, which the keeper held comfortably, then the Dutch doubled their lead after thirty-nine minutes. Peters clipped a pass down the right-hand side of the box and 'Willy' van de Kerkhof slid a shot between Petrović and his near post from a tight angle. However, with a couple of minutes of the half remaining, the Yugoslavs were back in the game, as Popivoda's cross broke kindly for Katalinski to slam past Schrijvers from twelve yards.

The Yugoslavs made both of their permitted substitutions at the break, with Vladić and Vahid Halilhodžić replacing Aćimović and Žungul respectively. Within seconds of the restart, Halilhodžić almost equalised with a snap shot from around the penalty spot, which Schrijvers did well to hold on to. A few minutes later, he should have done better when he rose unchallenged to meet Jerković's corner, but headed a few inches wide.

On the hour mark, the Dutch came close to restoring their two-goal advantage when Rensenbrink played in 'René' van de Kerkhof, only for his effort to smack off the angle of the post and bar with Petrović well beaten. Arntz sloppily gave away possession to Oblak, who sent Popivoda racing in on goal, but Schrijvers made a magnificent point-blank save to deny the Eintracht Braunschweig striker.

With eight minutes left, Jerković was brought down just outside the box by 'Willy' van de Kerkhof, and from the resultant free-kick, Džajić lofted a magnificent shot over the wall and beyond Schrijvers' despairing dive into the corner of the net to level the match. The

Yugoslavs were in full flow now, and they should have gone ahead in their next attack. After the ball was cleared from a Dutch corner, Popivoda ran some seventy yards before pulling the ball back across goal, where Halilhodžić incredibly slid the ball wide from a couple of yards out. In the final minute, Katalinski tried his luck from twenty-five yards, which Schrijvers superbly turned behind for a corner, and the Dutch were relieved when the final whistle sounded moments later.

Holland began extra time on the offensive, and substitute 'Kees' Kist was unlucky when he surged forward and hit a shot from twenty-two yards, which cannoned back off the crossbar; then, seconds later, 'Ruud' Krol toe-poked past the post with just Petrović to beat.

Two minutes into the second period, the Dutch regained the lead. Kist launched a speculative ball from his own half, which fell for Geels, and he held off the challenge of Katalinski to shoot past Petrović from wide on the right-hand side of the box. With time running out, Yugoslavia almost equalised again; Schrijvers came out for Džajić's free-kick, but completely missed the ball. Katalinski's header was headed off the line by 'Adri' van Kraaij, and the Dutch held out for the remaining couple of minutes to claim third place.

## FINAL

## CZECHOSLOVAKIA vs WEST GERMANY

The holders, buoyed by their magnificent semi-final comeback against Yugoslavia, were favourites to retain the trophy, even though they'd had a day less to recover than their opponents. Understandably, after the hosts' elimination, the stadium was only about half full, with the majority supporting the underdogs. This was the eighth meeting between the sides, each having won three times, with one match drawn in the head-to-head. Both sides made one alteration, with Ján Švehlík coming in for the suspended Pollák for Czechoslovakia, while West Germany's semi-final hero Dieter Müller was rewarded with a place in the starting line-up, Danner dropping out. It was also a special occasion for Franz Beckenbauer, who was making his 100th appearance – the first German player to reach that milestone.

The Czechoslovaks had most of the possession in the opening stages, and they deservedly took the lead after only eight minutes. An attack down the right appeared to be halted by the West German defence, but 'Berti' Vogts took a heavy touch, allowing Masný to play the ball across the box for Švehlík. His shot was pushed away by Maier, but Nehoda, following up, squared it back into the danger area – Ondruš missed, but Švehlík didn't, as he sidefooted in at the far post. Moments later, Hölzenbein should have equalised when he hurled himself at Bonhof's corner, but he headed well over; then Bonhof stung Viktor's palms with a piledriver from twenty yards. The Borussia Mönchengladbach midfielder had another opportunity in the seventeenth minute from a free-kick on the left-hand side of the box, and his curled effort went just wide of the far post. Hoeneß found Hölzenbein free inside the area and his shot was heading into the top corner, until Viktor reached up superbly to tip the ball over the bar.

After twenty-five minutes, the Czechoslovaks went two up when Masný's free-kick was headed out by Beckenbauer only as far as Karol Dobiaš, who controlled it and let fly with a low left foot strike which zipped past Maier into the far corner. Straight from the restart, incredibly, they could and probably should have scored a third, as Masný outpaced Vogts to reach Móder's long pass, but with only Maier to beat, his shot slipped agonisingly just wide of the post. The West Germans made the most of that let-off by pulling a goal back a couple of minutes later. Wimmer received the ball on the right, then went on a run before laying off the ball to Bonhof, whose cross found Müller in complete isolation eight yards from goal, and he volleyed spectacularly past Viktor. West Germany controlled the remainder of the half, but only created one more chance, right on half-time, when Bonhof created some space to shoot from twenty-five yards – but it was too close to Viktor.

The West Germans made a change at the break, with Flohe replacing Wimmer, but it was the Czechoslovaks who created the first opening of the second half when Flohe got in a muddle trying to clear, and the ball made its way to Švehlík, who curled a shot just past the post. Moments later, Beer played a neat one-two with Müller and bored in on goal, but Viktor was quickly off his line to block the Hertha Berlin midfielders' effort; then, at the other end, Móder won the ball from Bonhof and let fly from twenty-two yards, which Maier had to turn round the post.

Ten minutes into the half, Beer was denied once more by Viktor after he latched onto Hölzenbein's pass and spun brilliantly away from Koloman Gögh, but the keeper saved bravely at Beer's feet. An amazing passage of play should have ended with a West German equaliser, but somehow the ball stayed out. Müller's centre was fisted out by Viktor only as far as Hoeneß, whose initial shot was blocked, which fell for Beer, who was also crowded out. His effort came back off Viktor at pace and ricocheted off Hoeneß against the foot of the post, and Viktor grabbed it near the goal line.

The Czechoslovak keeper then made a stupendous save to keep Bonhof's fierce drive out after being set up by Beer. A lovely dinked cross from Masný found Nehoda, whose header bounced up off the upright with Maier well beaten. With ten minutes remaining, the Czechoslovaks brought on Jurkemik for Švehlík to shore up their defence, while the West Germans made a like-for-like switch, with Hans Bongartz replacing Beer.

The substitute was involved immediately, as he set up Beckenbauer to run into the box, where the German skipper fell over Dobiaš' sliding tackle; for a few seconds it appeared that the referee had awarded a penalty, but in the end he gave a goal kick instead. With time running out, Beckenbauer launched a cross towards the back post, which was headed behind for a corner, and from it Bonhof curled it towards the six yard area. Here, Viktor mistimed his jump, and Hölzenbein leapt behind him to back head the ball into the net for a dramatic equaliser. Yet again in an extraordinary tournament, extra time was required to determine the outcome.

In the opening minute of the first period, Bongartz was played in down the left of the box and his cross was pushed away by Viktor, but – luckily for the Czechoslovaks – there were no Germans in the vicinity to take advantage. Czechoslovakia immediately made their final substitution, with Veselý coming on for Dobiaš, then Flohe tested Viktor from fully thirty yards, which the keeper had to turn over the bar. The Czechoslovaks came close to taking the lead again near the break after Masný was baulked by Vogts, and

Maier brought off a terrific save to deny Panenka from the resultant free-kick.

Understandably, in the second period, the tempo of the match dropped a notch, with a couple of the players being treated for a bout of cramp. The nearest opportunity to a winning goal came in the last minute, when Hoeneß' cross was met with a spectacular bicycle kick from Müller, which drifted beyond the post. For the first time in a major tournament Final, the winners would be decided on a penalty shootout.

Masný stepped up to take the opening spot kick, and he confidently sent Maier the wrong way; then Bonhof took the first for the West Germans, which he fired into the corner via the inside of the post as Viktor hardly moved. The next four kicks were dispatched with ease, with Nehoda and Ondruš netting for Czechoslovakia, while Flohe and Bongartz were on target for West Germany. Jurkemik slammed the fourth Czechoslovak penalty past Maier, and then Hoeneß came forward to take the penultimate kick for West Germany, which he skied well over the bar, and left Czechoslovakia needing only to convert their final kick to win. Panenka strode forward as if he was going to blast the ball, but at the last moment, he delicately dinked the ball down the middle of the goal, and Maier – already diving to his left – had no chance. After twice previously finishing runners-up in the World Cup, the Czechoslovaks had won their first ever major international tournament.

# MATCH DETAILS

## SEMI-FINALS

16 June 1976 (20.15)    Ref: Clive THOMAS (Wales)
Stadion Maksimir, ZAGREB (Att. 17,969)

### CZECHOSLOVAKIA - NETHERLANDS
### 3:1 AET (1:0/1:1)

1:0 Ondruš (19'), 1:1 Ondruš (73' og), 2:1 Nehoda (114'), 3:1 Veselý (118')

CZE: (Coach: Václav JEŽEK)
Ivo VIKTOR, Ján PIVARNÍK, Anton ONDRUŠ (Capt.), Jozef ČAPKOVIČ (Ladislav JURKEMIK 106'), Koloman GÖGH, Jaroslav POLLÁK, Antonín PANENKA, Karol DOBIAŠ, Marián MASNÝ, Jozef MÓDER (František VESELÝ 91'), Zdeněk NEHODA

NET: (Coach: Georg KNOBEL)
Pieter SCHRIJVERS, Wilhelmus SUURBIER, Adrianus VAN KRAAIJ, Wilhelmus RIJSBERGEN (Willem VAN HANEGEM 37'), Rudolf KROL, Wilhelmus VAN DE KERKHOF, Johannes NEESKENS, Wilhelmus JANSEN, John REP (Geertruida GEELS 67'), Johannes CRUIJFF (Capt.), Robert RENSENBRINK

Red Card: Pollák 59', Neeskens 76', Van Hanegem 115'

17 June 1976 (20.15)    Ref: Alfred DELCOURT (Belgium)
Stadion Crvena Zvezda, BELGRADE (Att. 50,562)

### YUGOSLAVIA - WEST GERMANY

2:4 AET (2:0/2:2)

1:0 Popivoda (19'), 2:0 Džajić (30'), 2:1 Flohe (64'),
2:2 Müller (82'), 2:3 Müller (115'), 2:4 Müller (119')


YUG: (Coach: Ante MLADINIĆ)
Ognjen PETROVIĆ, Ivan BULJAN, Dražen
MUŽINIĆ, Branko OBLAK (Franjo VLADIĆ 106'),
Ivan ŠURJAK, Slaviša ŽUNGUL, Jurica JERKOVIĆ,
Danilo POPIVODA, Jovan AĆIMOVIĆ (Capt. (Luka
PERUZOVIĆ 106'), Josip KATALINSKI, Dragan
DŽAJIĆ

WGR: (Coach: Helmut SCHÖN)
Josef MAIER, Hans-Hubert VOGTS, Bernard
DIETZ, Hans-Georg SCHWARZENBECK, Franz
BECKENBAUER (Capt.), Rainer BONHOF, Ulrich
HOENEß, Herbert WIMMER (Dieter MÜLLER 79'),
Erich BEER, Dietmar DANNER (Heinz FLOHE 46'),
Bernd HÖLZENBEIN


## THIRD PLACE MATCH


19 June 1976 (20.15)    Ref: Walter HUNGERBÜHLER
(Switzerland)
Stadion Maksimir, ZAGREB (Att. 6,766)

YUGOSLAVIA - NETHERLANDS
2:3 AET (1:2/2:2)

0:1 Geels (27'), 0:2 W. Van de Kerkhof (39'), 1:2
Katalinski (43'), 2:2 Džajić (82'), 2:3 Geels (107')

YUG: (Coach: Ante MLADINIĆ)
Ognjen PETROVIĆ, Ivan BULJAN, Dražen MUŽINIĆ,
Branko OBLAK, Josip KATALINSKI, Ivan ŠURJAK,
Slaviša ŽUNGUL (Vahid HALILHODŽIĆ 46'), Jurica
JERKOVIĆ, Danilo POPIVODA, Jovan AĆIMOVIĆ

(Capt. (Franjo VLADIĆ 46'), Dragan DŽAJIĆ

NET: (Coach: Georg KNOBEL)
Pieter SCHRIJVERS, Wilhelmus SUURBIER, Adrianus VAN KRAAIJ, Wilhelmus JANSEN (Willem MEUTSTEGE 46'), Rudolf KROL (Capt.), Petrus ARNTZ (Cornelis KIST 70'), Wilhelmus VAN DE KERKHOF, Johannes PETERS, Reinier VAN DE KERKHOF, Geertruida GEELS, Robert RENSENBRINK

## FINAL

20 June 1976 (20.15)          Ref: Sergio GONELLA
(Italy)
Stadion Crvena Zvezda, BELGRADE (Att. 30,790)

CZECHOSLOVAKIA - WEST GERMANY
2:2 AET (2:1/2:2)

1:0 Švehlík (8'), 2:0 Dobiaš (25'), 2:1 Müller (28'), 2:2 Hölzenbein (89')

CZECHOSLOVAKIA won 5-3 on penalty kicks

1:0 Masný, 1:1 Bonhof, 2:1 Nehoda, 2:2 Flohe, 3:2 Ondruš, 3:3 Bongartz, 4:3 Jurkemik, 4:3 Hoeneß (shot over bar), 5:3 Panenka

CZE: (Coach: Václav JEŽEK)
Ivo VIKTOR, Ján PIVARNÍK, Anton ONDRUŠ (Capt.), Jozef ČAPKOVIČ, Koloman GÖGH, Karol DOBIAŠ (František VESELÝ 94'), Antonín PANENKA, Jozef MÓDER, Marián MASNÝ, Ján ŠVEHLÍK (Ladislav JURKEMIK 80'), Zdeněk NEHODA

WGR: (Coach: Helmut SCHÖN)
Josef MAIER, Hans-Hubert VOGTS, Bernard

DIETZ, Hans-Georg SCHWARZENBECK, Franz BECKENBAUER (Capt.), Rainer BONHOF, Ulrich HOENEß, Herbert WIMMER (Heinz FLOHE 46'), Dieter MÜLLER, Erich BEER (Hans BONGARTZ 80'), Bernd HÖLZENBEIN

# GOALSCORERS

## 4 GOALS

Dieter MÜLLER (West Germany)

## 2 GOALS

Geertruida GEELS (Netherlands), Dragan DŽAJIĆ (Yugoslavia)

## 1 GOAL

Karol DOBIAŠ, Zdeněk NEHODA, Anton ONDRUŠ, Ján ŠVEHLÍK, František VESELÝ (all Czechoslovakia), Wilhelmus VAN DE KERKHOF (Netherlands), Heinz FLOHE, Bernd HÖLZENBEIN (both West Germany), Josip KATALINSKI, Danilo POPIVODA (both Yugoslavia)

## OWN-GOALS

Anton ONDRUŠ (Czechoslovakia) vs Netherlands

# SQUADS

## CZECHOSLOVAKIA

### GOALKEEPERS

1 Ivo VIKTOR (21.05.1942/VTJ Dukla Praha), 22 Alexander VENCEL (08.02.1944/TJ CHZJD Slovan Bratislava)

### DEFENDERS

2 Karol DOBIAŠ (18.12.1947/TJ Spartak TAZ Trnava), 3 Jozef ČAPKOVIČ (01.11.1948/TJ CHZJD Slovan Bratislava), 4 Anton ONDRUŠ (27.03.1950/TJ CHZJD Slovan Bratislava), 5 Ján PIVARNÍK (13.11.1947/TJ CHZJD Slovan Bratislava), 6 Ladislav JURKEMIK (20.07.1953/TJ Internacionál Slovnaft Bratislava), 12 Koloman GÖGH (07.01.1948/TJ CHZJD Slovan Bratislava), 13 Jozef BARMOŠ (28.08.1954/TJ Internacionál Slovnaft Bratislava), 14 Pavol BIROŠ (01.04.1953/TJ Slavia Praha)

### MIDFIELDERS

7 Antonín PANENKA (02.12.1948/TJ ČKD Bohemians Praha), 8 Jozef MÓDER (19.09.1947/TJ VSS Lokomotíva Košice), 9 Jaroslav POLLÁK (11.07.1947/TJ Košice), 15 Dušan HERDA (15.07.1951/TJ Slavia Praha), 16 František VESELÝ (07.12.1943/TJ Slavia Praha), 17 Ján ŠVEHLÍK (17.01.1950/TJ CHZJD Slovan Bratislava), 20 František STAMBACHR (13.02.1953/VTJ Dukla Praha), 21 Přemysl BIČOVSKÝ (18.08.1950/TJ Sklo Union Teplice)

## FORWARDS

10 Marián MASNÝ (13.08.1950/TJ CHZJD Slovan Bratislava), 11 Zdeněk NEHODA (09.05.1952/ VTJ Dukla Praha), 18 Dušan GALIS (24.11.1946/ TJ Košice), 19 Ladislav PETRÁŠ (01.12.1946/TJ Internacionál Slovnaft Bratislava)

## NETHERLANDS

## GOALKEEPERS

1 Pieter SCHRIJVERS (15.12.1946/Amsterdamsche FC Ajax), 17 Jan RUITER (24.11.1946/RSC Anderlechtois (BELGIUM)), 18 Jan JONGBLOED (25.11.1940/FC Amsterdam)

## DEFENDERS

2 Wilhelmus SUURBIER (16.01.1945/Amsterdamsche FC Ajax), 3 Wilhelmus RIJSBERGEN (18.01.1952/ SC Feyenoord Rotterdam), 4 Adrianus VAN KRAAIJ (01.08.1953/PSV Eindhoven), 5 Rudolf KROL (24.03.1949/Amsterdamsche FC Ajax), 20 Willem MEUTSTEGE (28.06.1952/Sparta Rotterdam), 21 Hendricus VAN RIJNSOEVER (06.11.1952/AZ '67 Alkmaar)

## MIDFIELDERS

6 Johannes NEESKENS (15.09.1951/FC Barcelona (SPAIN)), 7 Wilhelmus JANSEN (28.10.1946/ SC Feyenoord Rotterdam), 9 Johannes CRUIJFF (25.04.1947/FC Barcelona (SPAIN)), 10 Wilhelmus VAN DE KERKHOF (16.09.1951/PSV Eindhoven), 12 Willem VAN HANEGEM (20.02.1944/SC Feyenoord Rotterdam), 14 Johannes PETERS (18.08.1954/

NEC Nijmegen), 15 Reinier VAN DE KERKHOF
(16.09.1951/PSV Eindhoven), 16 Petrus ARNTZ
(05.02.1953/Go Ahead Eagles Deventer)

## FORWARDS

8 John REP (25.11.1951/Valencia CF (SPAIN)),
11 Robert RENSENBRINK (03.07.1947/RSC
Anderlechtois (BELGIUM)), 13 Geertruida GEELS
(28.07.1948/Amsterdamsche FC Ajax), 19 Cornelis
KIST (07.08.1952/AZ '67 Alkmaar)

## WEST GERMANY

## GOALKEEPERS

1 Josef MAIER (28.02.1944/FC Bayern München),
18 Rudolf KARGUS (15.08.1952/Hamburger SV), 19
Bernd FRANKE (12.02.1948/Braunschweiger TuSV
Eintracht 1895

## DEFENDERS

2 Hans-Hubert VOGTS (30.12.1946/VfL Borussia
Mönchengladbach), 3 Bernard DIETZ (22.03.1948/
MSV Duisburg), 4 Hans-Georg SCHWARZENBECK
(03.04.1948/FC Bayern München), 5 Franz
BECKENBAUER (11.09.1945/FC Bayern München),
16 Peter NOGLY (14.01.1947/Hamburger SV), 17
Manfred KALTZ (06.01.1953/Hamburger SV), 20
Peter REICHEL (30.11.1951/Eintracht Frankfurt)

## MIDFIELDERS

7 Rainer BONHOF (29.03.1952/VfL Borussia
Mönchengladbach), 8 Ulrich HOENEß (05.01.1952/
FC Bayern München), 10 Erich BEER (09.12.1946/

Hertha Berlin SC), 13 Dietmar DANNER (29.11.1950/VfL Borussia Mönchengladbach), 14 Hans BONGARTZ (03.10.1951/FC Schalke '04 Gelsenkirchen), 15 Heinz FLOHE (28.01.1948/1. FC Köln), 21 Ulrich STIELIKE (15.11.1954/VfL Borussia Mönchengladbach), 22 Bernhard DÜRNBERGER (17.09.1953/FC Bayern München)

## FORWARDS

6 Herbert WIMMER (09.11.1944/VfL Borussia Mönchengladbach), 9 Dieter MÜLLER (01.04.1954/1. FC Köln), 11 Bernd HÖLZENBEIN (09.03.1946/ Eintracht Frankfurt), 12 Ronald WORM (07.10.1953/ MSV Duisburg)

## YUGOSLAVIA

## GOALKEEPERS

1 Ognjen PETROVIĆ (02.01.1948/FK Crvena Zvezda Beograd), 12 Enver MARIĆ (23.04.1948/FK Velež Mostar), 22 Ratko SVILAR (06.05.1950/FK Vojvodina Novi Sad)

## DEFENDERS

2 Ivan BULJAN (11.12.1949/NK Hajduk Split), 3 Džemaludin HADŽIABDIĆ (25.07.1953/FK Velež Mostar), 4 Dražen MUŽINIĆ (25.01.1953/NK Hajduk Split), 5 Josip KATALINSKI (12.05.1948/OGC de Nice (FRANCE)), 20 Luka PERUZOVIĆ (26.02.1952/NK Hajduk Split), 21 Vladislav BOGIĆEVIĆ (07.11.1950/ FK Crvena Zvezda Beograd)

## MIDFIELDERS

8 Branko OBLAK (27.05.1947/FC Schalke '04 Gelsenkirchen (WEST GERMANY)), 9 Jovan AĆIMOVIĆ (21.06.1948/FK Crvena Zvezda Beograd), 14 Edhem ŠLJIVO (16.03.1950/FK Sarajevo), 15 Franjo VLADIĆ (19.10.1951/FK Velež Mostar), 16 Momčilo VUKOTIĆ (02.06.1950/FK Partizan Beograd)

## FORWARDS

6 Ivan ŠURJAK (23.03.1953/NK Hajduk Split), 7 Danilo POPIVODA (01.05.1947/Braunschweiger TuSV Eintracht 1895 (WEST GERMANY)), 10 Jurica JERKOVIĆ (25.02.1950/NK Hajduk Split), 11 Dragan DŽAJIĆ (30.05.1946/SC de Bastia (FRANCE)), 13 Vahid HALILHODŽIĆ (15.05.1952/FK Velež Mostar), 17 Slaviša ŽUNGUL (28.07.1954/NK Hajduk Split)

# Author Profile

Richard Keir was educated at Uddingston Grammar School and is currently employed by a large tour operator based in Glasgow. His previous publication was a statistical history of the Scotland national team. He is a fan of most sports and enjoys walking and travelling. He has been interested in writing books from an early age.

**Publisher Information**

Rowanvale Books provides publishing services to independent authors, writers and poets all over the globe. We deliver a personal, honest and efficient service that allows authors to see their work published, while remaining in control of the process and retaining their creativity. By making publishing services available to authors in a cost-effective and ethical way, we at Rowanvale Books hope to ensure that the local, national and international community benefits from a steady stream of good quality literature.

For more information about us, our authors or our publications, please get in touch.

www.rowanvalebooks.com
info@rowanvalebooks.com

Printed in June 2021
by Rotomail Italia S.p.A., Vignate (MI) - Italy